Presidential Campaign Communication

Presidential Campaign Communication

The Quest for the White House

CRAIG ALLEN SMITH

polity

First published in 2010 by Polity Press

Polity Press
65 Bridge Street
Cambridge CB2 1UR, UK

Polity Press
350 Main Street
Malden, MA 02148, USA

ISBN-13: 978-0-7456-4608-4 (hardback)
ISBN-13: 978-0-7456-4609-1 (paperback)

A catalogue record for this book is available from the British Library.

Typeset in 9.5 on 12pt Utopia
by Servis Filmsetting Ltd, Stockport, Cheshire
Printed and bound in Maple Vail in the USA

The publisher has used its best endeavors to ensure that the URLs for
external websites referred to in this book are correct and active at the
time of going to press. However, the publisher has no responsibility for
the websites and can make no guarantee that a site will remain live or
that the content is or will remain appropriate.

Every effort has been made to trace all copyright holders, but if any have
been inadvertently overlooked the publisher will be pleased to include
any necessary credits in any subsequent reprint or edition.

For further information on Polity, visit our website: www.politybooks.com

The publisher would like to acknowledge permission to reproduce the
following images:

Jeffrey Markowitz/Sygma/Corbis; David Maxwell/epa/Corbis;
NBCUPHOTOBANK/Rex Features; Bettman/Corbis; Ron Sachs/Rex
Features; NBCUPHOTOBANK/Rex Features; Sipa Press/Rex Features;

Dedicated to Charles J. Stewart

His distinguished career at Purdue University exemplified K. Patricia Cross's insight that, "The task of the excellent teacher is to stimulate 'apparently ordinary' people to unusual effort. The tough problem is not in identifying winners: it is in making winners out of ordinary people."

Contents

Acknowledgements

My friends , we meet at this page at the end of a long journey. It has been a journey of research and writing, of listening and lecturing. It is a journey that began in 1950s New Jersey with the Aliens and Smiths discussing campaigns.The Bahan, Colby and Szucs families joined us in Ohio in the 1970s. Countless students – people like JoLee Credle Robinson and Mitchell McKinney at UNC, Richard Pineda, Chris Salinas, Renata Kolodjiez, and Kamau Marable at Wayne State, Amy Green and David Mirfin at NC State – joined us over the years, sharing insights and posing tough questions. Research colleagues like Kathy Kendall, Marty Medhurst, Greg Payne, Bob Denton, Rachel Holloway, Rita Kirk, Juddi Trent, Bob Friedenberg, Dianne Bystrom, and Diana Carlin make Communication conferences a continuing source of intellectual stimulation. C. H. Richards, Bernard Brock, and Ted Windt have left us their wisdom and touched all who had the privilege of discussing presidential campaigns with them.

Journeys like this require tremendous support. Andrea Drugan, Clare Ansell, Susan Beer, and the staff at Polity were helpful and supportive beyond description. Ken Zagacki is a truly supportive department head and NC State's College of Humanities and Social Sciences supported this effort with significant research assignments. I have been fortunate to work with Bill Jordan, Deanna Dannels, Bob Schrag, Joann Keyton, Kelly Albada, Lawrence Rosenfeld, Bud Goodall, Sandra Petronio, and Ed Pappas.

Books, like campaigns, are hardest on those around us. Kathy characteristically made adjustments great and small so that deadlines could be met. Stephanie and Debbie cast their first presidential ballots in 2008, asked questions the book needed to address, and let me know when my answers needed work.

The end of this journey is but the end of a page. For now the trumpet summons us to embark on a new journey. The new journey will engage and test the ideas in this book and improve presidential campaign communication in America. And so, my friends , I thank you for turning this page and I invite you to pursue these ideas with me as we look toward the 2012 campaign.

PART I

FOUNDATIONS OF CAMPAIGN STRATEGY

The closing days of a presidential campaign are exciting. They are filled with cheering crowds, rousing speeches, dire predictions, and balloons – always balloons. When the votes are cast on the first Tuesday in November the two candidates who still have a chance to become president are nearing the end of a long and grueling quest that began for them years before the election. They arrive at that moment not necessarily because history will regard them as the most able leaders of their time but because they engaged more successfully than any others in strategic presidential campaign communication.

Part I explores the foundations of campaign strategy so that Part II can examine modes of campaign communication and Part III can trace the stages of presidential campaigns. Chapter 1 considers the fundamental premises that will guide our discussion, including the central role of the Constitution in the electoral process and the inherent role of communication in campaigns. Chapter 2 introduces the campaign's puzzle: finding the words and images that appeal to the audiences capable of providing the various "victory units" that the campaign needs at different times. Chapter 3 emphasizes the importance of rules and laws to election campaigns and shows how they are crafted in language and then interpreted and applied to subsequent contests. Chapter 4 considers the interface among campaign organizations, media organizations and citizens as we all work in our own way to shape presidential elections . We conclude Part I by synthesizing what we have learned in a discussion of campaign strategy.

1 Presidential Campaigns as Communication

Shortly after the 2006 elections, Survey USA conducted a series of "Head-to-Head" presidential surveys. When they asked voters to choose between familiar Arizona Republican Senator John McCain and first-term Illinois Democratic Senator Barack Obama, the result was a 510–28 McCain victory (Survey USA 2008). Less than four years later Obama defeated McCain 364–174 to win the presidency. Clearly, many people had adjusted their attitudes on this question during the presidential campaign.

The purpose of this book is to help readers better understand and more fully appreciate the ways that the people of the United States use the process of human communication to select our leaders. Politics is one of the things about which Americans talk, around which we build relationships and into which we invest ourselves. But this is not a book solely about the 2008 presidential election, for that was simply the most recent instance of a seasonal discussion that has been enacted more or less routinely for more than two centuries. Only by understanding the regularities of the process can we appreciate the importance of innovations and thus prepare ourselves for future campaigns.

Eight Fundamental Premises

We are about to explore the subject of presidential campaigns – often understandably considered the province of political science and history – from the perspective of the field of communication. So before tackling the dynamics of presidential campaign communication we need to consider some fundamental premises that undergird our approach. One reason for the increasing interest in political communication as an interdiscipline has been the dual conviction that political analyses need to be more mindful of the role of communication and that communication studies need to be more mindful of political realities. So it is that we turn to both disciplines for insights.

Premise 1: The United States Constitution Rules

Article II Section 1 vested executive power in a president who would be elected with the vice-president and hold office for a term of four years. Only a "natural born Citizen" who has "attained to the Age of thirty five Years and been fourteen Years a Resident within the United States" could be considered for president.

The Constitution also stipulated that each state would "appoint, in such Manner as the Legislature thereof may direct, a Number of Electors, equal to the whole Number of Senators and Representatives to which the State may be entitled in the Congress" although no sitting office holder could be appointed Elector. It directed the Congress to determine the day when those Electors would "give their Votes." The Twelfth Amendment (passed in 1803 and ratified in 1804) directed that "The Electors shall meet in their respective States, and vote by Ballot for two Persons, of whom one at least shall not be an Inhabitant" of their own state. They "shall make a List of all the Persons voted for, and of the Number of Votes for each; which List they shall sign and certify." The state lists are sent to the vice-president who opens all the certificates and counts the Elector's votes in the presence of the Senate and House of Representatives.

"The Person having . . . a Majority of the whole Number of Electors appointed" becomes president. If no candidate had a majority of the Electors the House of Representatives would select the president *from the top five candidates* with each state having one vote. The person finishing second in this awkward process would be the vice-president.

For more than 200 years presidential aspirants have needed the support of a majority of the states' Electors. George Washington had that support but all the others found it splintered and contested. An increasingly complex process of seeking Electors' support evolved – a process that we now call a presidential campaign.

If campaigns are a game then the Constitution is always trump. Vice-President Al Gore received 51,003,926 votes in 2000 to Texas Governor George W. Bush's 50,460,110 and many people argued that Gore had won the election. But we have seen that the national popular vote has no role under the Constitution which discusses only the states' Electors, and Bush won those 271–266. The 2000 case was not unique. In 1888 Benjamin Harrison defeated President Grover Cleveland 233–168 while losing the popular vote 5,443,633 to 5,538,163. Twelve years earlier Rutherford B. Hayes won the presidency 185–184 while Samuel Tilden won the popular vote 4,286,808 to 4,034,142. The 1824 election was especially unusual with Andrew Jackson winning both the popular vote and the electoral vote in a four-candidate race. But without a *majority* of Electors for the contest it went to the House of Representatives and John Quincy Adams became president. A five-candidate race in 1800 produced an electoral vote tie between Thomas Jefferson and Aaron Burr and the House voted for Jefferson. In all five cases a reasonable argument could be made for declaring someone else president, but *the Constitution rules.*

Premise 2: The Constitution and Laws Are Texts

The Constitution is a text that synthesizes the positions of its authors and communicates them to us through time and space. The Constitution's textual meaning is interpreted, debated, understood, and applied to unfolding circum-stances. The same can be said for all other laws and rules that follow from it because legislative passage requires the authors to find language around which a majority can coalesce. Sometimes they phrase the law in ambiguous language to avoid splintering those whose signatures they need. When they do so, those who apply the ambiguous law must debate its meaning, scope, and proper application.

Premise 3: The Constitution used Interdependence for "Checks and Balances"

Richard E. Neustadt advised President Truman before beginning to write about the presidency, and his book *Presidential Power* (1960) was envisioned as a manual for President Kennedy. Neustadt wrote in an age when American students learned that the Constitution relied upon a "system of checks and balances" created by the "separation of powers" in which Congress makes the laws, the Executive enforces the laws and the Judiciary interprets the laws. Neustadt's pivotal contribution – our third premise – was his observation that the Constitution actually created *separated institutions sharing powers.* The difference is profound, for institutions with separated powers could each do as they pleased, but separated institutions sharing powers *need each other* to complete their tasks.

Similarly, the Constitution stipulated that states would have electors and it set the minimum requirements for the president but it left the rest of the process to the state governments. Thus the Constitution shared the power of electing presidents between the national and state governments. State and national governments are interdependent in a federal system. Over time, political parties evolved, in part, as an apparatus for facilitating state and national coordination.

To win a presidential election one needs electoral votes, popular votes, money, volunteers, press coverage, and more. We shall coin the term "victory units" to refer collectively to these varied resource prizes. In an ideal sense, every citizen aged eighteen has a vote. But not all citizens register to vote, and not all registered voters vote. Moreover, many who vote do so carelessly, while others carefully prepare and vote wisely. People have varying amounts of money to contribute and differing inclinations to donate their funds to political campaigns. But it may be less obvious that people have varying amounts of time and energy to volunteer to a campaign. In these and other cases, campaigns must find the means of winning the victory units they need.

Because these victory units are unevenly distributed throughout society we have yet another example of checks and balances. The resources candidates need to win the presidency are held by others, and those who individually hold but a small share of the resources need a willing and able candidate in whom to invest their resources. Throughout the campaign fundraisers trade words for dollars, voter registration drives strive to convince unengaged citizens to participate and organizers trade words and issue positions for volunteers. Every victory unit a candidate needs is the property of an audience.

Individuals and groups guard their victory units or resources – from money to effort to votes. Candidates must puzzle out which voters they need to reach through which media with what messages. That makes the American electorate a set of audiences. The task is to discover the audience(s) controlling the victory units and the values, arguments or symbols that they value more dearly than their victory units.

Premise 4: Interdependence Requires Cooperation, Coordination, and Coalitions

Constitutional interdependence makes coalitions a functional necessity. Lester Seligman and Cary Covington (1989) explained that candidates must build an electoral coalition to win the office, transform it into a governing coalition, then rebuild an electoral coalition for re-election and then rebuild the governing coalition.

A presidential candidate needs support from various party factions and interest groups, many of which advocate a narrow range of related policies. The candidate needs political consultants including pollsters, strategists, fundraisers and communication advisors. But once elected, the new president's coalitional needs change. The president needs far more staff and appointees than worked on the campaign and different skill sets are required for judicial and executive appointments. Suddenly the president needs a working relationship with Congress – a nasty surprise for those who, like President Harry Truman in 1948, ran against congress. As head of the executive branch of the federal government, the new president needs the Bureaucracy to help implement or execute the laws. Interest groups, the Media and the General Public remain important, but not because of their contributions or votes. Instead, their support, compliance or hostility will influence the president's effectiveness and the nation's agenda. Sub-national officials such as governors and mayors as well as foreign diplomats and leaders also become key components of the president's coalition (Seligman and Covington 1989).

Who has the resources necessary to create a winning coalition? The United States is a society of people with various qualities – age, gender, race, education, literacy, income, net worth, religiosity, military service, interest in politics, optimism, fear, health and well-being, employment security, partisanship, and more – unequally distributed across the population. Then we can recognize that individual circumstances change as people live, work, and go to school. Then, when we add in an assortment of political voices and commentators labeling those qualities and circumstances and competing for them, we begin to see political life as being akin to a game of musical chairs that brings about a different stop-action picture of the resource distribution every time a new presidential campaign begins.

Seligman and Covington (1989) discussed three kinds of coalitions. A *consensus coalition* arises from a broad range of people with similar goals and views. This is probably best understood as an ideal theoretical concept, as contemporary American society is too diverse to make this a realistic campaign strategy in the twenty-first century. Moreover, the nature of presidential campaigns requires at least one party to spend the better part of two years cultivating division. That leaves two other types of coalitions.

An *exclusive coalition* is a broad range of people held together by single identity (such as ethnicity or gender) or issue (such as gay marriage, abortion, immigration reform). Notice that each of the issues listed creates at least two coalitions. Mention "gay marriage" to a mixed audience, for example, and you are likely to find some who think it is a horrible idea, some who fervently support it, some who prefer civil unions as an alternative for gay couples and some people who think it is a minor issue unworthy of a presidential campaign. Similar partitioning occurs with the other examples. The Pro-Life exclusive coalition proved to be the rhetorical vehicle that enabled Roman Catholics and southern Baptists to set aside many of their historic religious and political differences in order to coalesce around a shared purpose. Pollsters normally refer to these sets of individuals as "issue publics" because they constitute the public that cares about this particular issue. We can also think of them as potential audiences ready to help resolve the electoral puzzle. Political parties emerged as a mechanism for a variety of exclusive coalitions to find one another for political purposes and to sustain their working relationships.

Many writers have pointed to a link between televised campaigns and the rise of the candidate-centered campaign (Lowi 1985, Trent and Friedenberg 2004). This alternative to a host of exclusive coalitions is the *conglomerate coalition* – a conglomerate is a mix of groups held together by nothing more than their support of a candidate. Today it is difficult to imagine that voters could not watch or even listen to Woodrow Wilson or Theodore Roosevelt unless they could get within earshot, but the loudspeaker was not invented until 1920. From 1928 through 1948 voters could hear the candidates on their radios, and Franklin Roosevelt mastered both radio and presidential elections (winning four terms and prompting a Constitutional Amendment precluding that possibility). From 1948 into the 1970s television covered politics, but there were only three networks with evening newscasts. The arrival of cable television in the late 1970s brought CNN, the first 24-hour news channel, and C-SPAN's unedited coverage of public affairs.

The new television networks provided many new ways for presidential candidates to cultivate conglomerate coalitions. In March of 1992, millionaire businessman H. Ross Perot told CNN's Larry King that he would run for president as an independent. Perot would eventually lead both President Bush and Bill Clinton heading into the convention period. Although Perot won no electoral votes, he finished second in Maine and Utah and won 18.9 percent of the national popular vote. His 1992 campaign illustrates the ability of a candidate to build a conglomerate coalition largely through television.

All coalitions have members with varying levels of commitment. That is to say that individuals feel or imagine the coalition to be more (or less) central to their lives. At one end of the continuum we find *core supporters* who provide unwavering support. That does not necessarily mean that they will donate money, volunteer time, or even vote with the coalition. What matters is that they identify strongly with the coalition, even if other demands draw them toward other choices from time to time. For example, many pro-environment people drive inefficient sport utility vehicles that enable them to participate in outdoor activities. The point is that core supporters in any coalition are able to reconcile just about anything.

Peripheral supporters are only marginally involved with the coalition. They may adopt a behavior without paying much attention, like the person who wears a Boston Celtics t-shirt but ignores basketball. The support of such people can be won with a bit less effort than is required to persuade others, but it must be maintained in the face of continuing challenges. These peripheral supporters

Perot on Larry King

are audiences whose support is influenced by someone's allocation of rhetorical resources. But although peripheral supporters are more easily acquired than core supporters, they are more easily lost.

Premise 5: Cooperation, Coordination, and Coalitions Require Communication

Each of us moves through the world seeking to make our sensory environment *personally coherent.* Faced with an unfamiliar or novel situation, we literally "make sense" of it. We selectively attend to the stimuli we feel most able to process, we frame those stimuli in a familiar narrative and we remember the event in a way that "works" for our needs. But if each of us sought only coherence we would have a world of hermits and, more to the point, the Constitution would not work.

We therefore also strive for social coordination and cooperation. Frequently your ability to meet your own needs can be enhanced if you can simply coordinate your timing with others. At other times you need to enlist the active assistance of other people. Both scenarios invite you to engage another person for the purpose of social coordination and interdependent need satisfaction.

All of our communication seeks to achieve a balance between the two equally important goals of personal coherence and social coordination (Pearce 1989, Smith 1990). At the same time we strive to achieve social coordination with the meaningful people and groups in our lives by adapting to what they have found to be personally coherent. When we establish communication with others we create relationships that we often strive to maintain because they are satisfying in one or more ways. Because we all have multiple needs we establish a complex of relationships – a coalition – through which various people find themselves able to satisfy a variety of needs together. One simple example is the car pool – it saves Jessica money, it gets Dagwood to work on time, it offers a support network for Maria, it enables Rocky to rationalize driving his Suburban, it provides social companionship for Jermisha and it provides a professional networking opportunity for Courtney. Political campaigns similarly fulfill a variety of needs for a variety of people.

Communication as coordination involves people learning or creating shared structures for interpreting the stimuli around them. To coordinate our interpretation of symbols we learn or create languages that range from the formal (English, French, and Farsi) through dialects to informal codes and jargon or slang. To coordinate our reasons we learn logics or rationalities that range from formal logic and the scientific method and religious belief systems to conspiracy theories. To coordinate our preferences we learn or create ideologies that range from the formal (such as capitalism and socialism) to the informal like supply side economics and liberation theology. To coordinate our attempts at need satisfaction we learn or create systems of laws ranging from formally adopted legal codes to informal norms (Smith 1990, Smith and Smith 1994). One who stumbles upon a network that seems to share an interest with them will likely join it, if only on a trial basis.

When we have a connection and a shared interest among people we have the basis for a political proto-coalition. Samuel Kernell (1993) suggested that these proto-coalitions (frequently considered political factions) arise around policy directions, political cleavages, and friendships. These proto-coalitions emerge as members of a network seek out mutual needs and complementary resources at all stages of the policy process, from enactment to implementation. While many proto-coalitions are fleeting, the important ones that endure "arise not from some fleeting issue but from kindred interest or the continuing need" (Kernell 1993, p. 14). Proto-coalitions succeed when they band together in coalitions controlling sufficient victory units to prevail.

Whatever the nature of the connections and the shared interests, there are, at all times in all political societies, three imagined fiefdoms: The Lands of Us, Them and the Silent Majority. The Land of Us is populated by all of those who *believe* they live there. J. R. R. Tolkien created Middle Earth for his readers, all of whom are bound together by their common acceptance of events, places, and people that never actually happened. Sports fans typically shout "we won!" when they have no documented connection to the city or school constituting the "we" – they simply identify with it. We are part of the fiefdom of Us because we feel or believe that we are a part of it – nothing more or less is required (Burke 1969, Turner 1982).

Similarly, we rhetorically construct our Land of Them out of those who challenge our fiefdom of Us. It is in the fiefdom of Them that all our enemies' join together in our imaginings, even if they actually despise each other. This is Burke's "division" at work (1969). Others are part of the fiefdom of Them because we believe them to be part of it – nothing more or less is required.

The Silent Majority consists of those whose views are unknown or unclear. Again, we attribute views to these people. We ordinarily tend to assume that they are open-minded or undecided or perhaps uninterested, but we rarely know that with any certainty. Elected officials know that the Silent Majority is, by definition, not rioting in the streets so they include them in their fiefdom of Us. Never was this more evident than in President Richard M. Nixon's November 3, 1969 address on the war in Vietnam. Following massive demonstrations against the war and public opinion polls showing for the first time a majority opposing the war, President Nixon noted that only a small percentage of Americans were actually demonstrating against the war and that all of the others constituted a "Great Silent Majority" tacitly supporting his leadership.

As the Nixon example suggests, the political persuader's task is to align or realign conceptions of Us, Them, and Silent Majority. Thus the persuader uses available media to connect with the desired audiences and seeks to use the rules of the campaign to help citizens fulfill their needs. The candidate speaks to them in a shared language to provide coordination of symbolic meaning, reasons with them in a shared logic to help them make sense of their world, values and prefers with them in a shared ideology to help them coordinate and prioritize their beliefs, and negotiates and applies rules with them to guide the fulfillment of their everyday needs within a set of shared rules.

The persuader exploits her image and credibility to identify with the desired audience and enhance the sense of Usness while dividing herself from the others and creating a sense of shared Themness. During most of the 1940s the United States rallied against a "Them" consisting of Germany, Italy, and Japan. But with the end of the war American foreign policy lost its focus until President Truman created the "Red Fascist" image of Communism in his address on aid to Greece and Turkey. Communists were the "Them" of the Cold War Era, at least until President Reagan's visit to Moscow in 1985. Suddenly, upon Reagan's return, Soviet leader Mikhail Gorbachev seemed to be exorcised of the demons that had plagued us. Reagan was quick to find those demons again, though, in the state-sponsored terrorism of Libyan leader Moammar Khaddafi. From that point onward, terrorists and those who seem to support them (like Saddam Hussein) have been our Them. President George W. Bush rallied Americans with a rhetoric of "Them" and presided through the execution of Saddam Hussein, the elusiveness of Osama bin Laden and a reduction of terrorist attacks – all of which eventually undermined the rhetorical force of the danger of which he warned while he develop for Americans a hopeful rhetoric of "Us." That failure opened the White House door for a 2008 candidate who could effectively speak of "Hope" and "Change."

Premise 6: *The Power of the President to Persuade Is Attained through Communication*

Our sixth premise extends Neustadt's dictum about presidential leadership – "The power of the president is the power to persuade" – to say that the power of the president is the power to persuade, and it is attained through persuasion. In the current context, there could be no election campaigns – neither legal nor mythic – without communication. As Trent and Friedenberg have written, "political election campaigns are campaigns of communication." As they explain,

> Certainly numerous forms or combinations of economic, sociological, psychological, and historical factors are crucial to or reflective of the electoral process.

However, the core of each campaign is communication. This is not to argue that a variety of economic and situational needs, power relationships, and a whole host of additional elements and demands do not affect the campaign process or outcome, but rather to say that all of these other factors become important in the electoral system principally through the offices of communication.   (Trent and Friedenberg 2004, p. 12)

Political scientists Bruce Bimber and Richard Davis elaborate the point:

To note that campaigning is a communication process seems mundane, but this fact is sometimes lost on observers, including scholars, who often think of campaigns strictly in terms of public opinion figures, models of voter behaviour, the strength of political parties and people's ideological attachments, and so on. Campaigns involve all of these things, to be sure, but *the fabric holding all of this together is communication.* For this reason, to understand who is elected and why, one must think about elections in terms of how candidates communicate and what effect that communication has and does not have on the public.   (Bimber and Davis 2003, p. 45, emphasis added)

Bimber and Davis, as well as Trent and Friedenberg, are referring, to instances such as the ways that economic factors and ideological stances can be set forth in arguments or ignored by candidates, to the ways that sociological factors can be used in selecting audiences, to the ways that public opinion can be characterized and interpreted through language, and to the ways that some historical symbols and analogies mean different things to audiences with different partisan attachments. *People do not enter a campaign until they enter the campaign conversation.* Candidates cannot express their willingness to run without communication, nor can the watchdogs rehash the candidates' qualifications without communication. Private needs and wants cannot be transformed into public issues without communication, nor can public platforms be applied to our personal circumstances without communication. Candidates cannot reach out to voters without communication nor can subsequent generations learn of their electoral past without communication. In short, presidential election campaigns constitute a recurrent set of American communication behaviors. If we are to understand them from that perspective we must grapple with basic concepts of human communication.

Premise 7: The Campaign Process Creates Discernible Communication Challenges

The seventh premise is that the core Constitutional requirements and the practical need to develop coalitions create four discernible sets of campaign challenges to be met by all aspiring candidates. Working backward from the final outcome they are:

1. *The Electoral College* votes for the president and vice-president according to the Constitution. The outcome of their respective states' presidential elections very strongly influence their votes but they are not binding.
2. *The General Election* – Fifty state presidential elections on the first Tuesday in November pit the Democratic and Republican nominees against each

other as well as any "third party" or independent candidates who qualified for each state's ballot. These elections are fifty "winner-take-all" contests for each state's allocation of electoral votes (Maine and Nebraska hold state-wide winner-take-all contests for two Electors with each congressional district holding a winner-take-all contest for its Elector).

3. *The Major Party Nominations* go to the candidates who win a majority of each party's national convention delegates. These two nominations are highly valued because the two major parties have organizations in all fifty states that advantage their nominees. The nominations become official at the national party conventions, ordinarily held in late summer.

4. *State Primaries and Caucuses* have become the mechanisms that choose the vast majority of delegates to the national party conventions. Today all of the Democratic contests and most of the Republican contests are proportional, allocating some delegates to all those candidates who received votes above a specified threshold (ordinarily 15%). Basically, winning 40 percent of the state's votes wins 40 percent of the state's delegates, but rules vary by party and by state. A few Republican contests are "winner-take-all" and therefore have a substantial mathematical impact on the delegate totals.

5. *The Invisible Primary* is the multi-year period prior to the Iowa precinct caucuses when media pundits and political insiders talk about likely candidates. This "invisible primary" is the period when aspiring candidates develop name recognition, working teams and financial support. Perhaps most importantly, after many years of looking in the mirror, a person one day sees the face of someone who needs to run for President of the United States. This period is also known as the surfacing stage.

It should be apparent that one cannot become president without votes in the electoral college, that one has relatively little chance of competing for electors without being the most popular candidate in a state, that one is unlikely to be the most popular candidate in any state without having the nomination and support of one of the two major parties, that one is unlikely to win the nomination without competing strongly in a great number of primaries and caucuses and that one is unlikely to be able to compete strongly in all those primaries without the inner confidence (some would say arrogance) to believe that he or she is the single person best able to lead the country for at least four years.

Thus a presidential election is less a game than a tournament; less a battle than a quest in which a quasi-hero faces a wide array of challenges and adversaries. The goal of anyone seeking the presidency must be to move through the levels of the campaign, much as one moves through the levels of a video game.

Premise 8: There Are Two Campaigns: The Practical and the Mythic

The eighth premise is that there are always two campaigns: a practical campaign and a mythic campaign. Political theorist Murray Edelman (1964) wrote that politics is a spectator sport. As so often happens, Edelman's thoughts were soon oversimplified. Edelman's actual argument was that politics occurs on two levels – the symbolic and the practical:

> Basic to the recognition of symbolic forms in the political process is a distinction between politics as a spectator sport and political activity as utilized by organized groups to get quite specific, tangible benefits for themselves. For most men [sic] most of the time politics is a series of pictures in the mind, placed there by television news, newspapers, magazines, and discussions. The pictures create a moving panorama taking place in a world the mass public never quite touches, yet one its members come to fear or cheer, often with passion and sometimes with action . . . .There is, on the other hand, the immediate world in which people make and do things that have directly observable consequences. (Edelman 1964, p. 4)

We have a governmental system even when nobody is watching but most of what we see as "politics" has to do with watching the "good guys" and "bad guys" duke it out in the news, talk shows, and comic satires. We argue about public affairs untroubled by our own soft grasp of the facts, and then we vote (or we not).

In Edelman's sense presidential campaigns are a quadrennial spectator sport like the Olympics. Ardent fans attend to the early trials to see who will make the "team," even as the larger, modestly informed audiences tune in to watch the big media shows leading up to Gold Medal events. But unlike Olympic Games, presidential campaigns are also constitutionally governed efforts to attain practical results. Let us take a further step toward understanding this "Two Campaigns" principle.

One campaign is the legalistic quest among candidates to become the Chief Executive of the Federal Government as provided for by the US Constitution, state laws and party rules. Hypothetically, this legal process could be carried out in secret with no change in the outcome. Indeed, people are elected auditor, assessor and dog catcher with little public drama.

The second campaign is the *story* of that election campaign disseminated for public consumption, today primarily through the process of mass communication. This campaign cannot be private, for it is a story shared among observers or spectators. It is these stories that constitute most of our shared knowledge of campaigns, shaping our literature and history and, consequently, our culture. These two campaigns unfold simultaneously and they influence one another.

Thus presidential campaigns have both practical and spectator dimensions, and we pay attention to only one of them at our own peril. The importance of the Two Campaigns was succinctly captured by consumer advocate and perennial candidate Ralph Nader who wrote that, "In essence you don't run for president directly; you ask the media to run you for president, or, if you have the money, you can pay the media for exposure" (Nader 2002, p. 55). In this sense, much of campaign communication is "hero establishing" in nature. Candidates discuss what they have done and what they will do, their opponents seek to point out and magnify tragic flaws in their character, and the press seeks to reconcile it all in stories that seem to satisfactorily connect as many dots as possible.

Both the practical campaign and the mythic campaign exist through communication. This book will therefore focus on ways that we use communication to select our presidents.

Communication and Campaigns

The remainder of this book deals with the process of electing the President of the United States as a recurrent set of communication processes. Matters of communication will be central and political; sociological and historical considerations will be treated from the vantage point of communication.

In order to have human communication of any sort, five elements must be present: humans, symbols, performance, a medium and interpretation. Communication requires humans to send and interpret the meaning of the communication. But we know that these humans can be separated by centuries or by thousands of miles; that they may be intimately acquainted or anonymous. These humans "perform" by behaving – speaking, writing, broadcasting or e-mailing – symbolically with varying degrees of skill and artistry to represent their experiences to others. Their symbolic behaviors convey words, numbers, images, pictures, emoticons and videos in a performance that is an enactment of the symbols in a transmitted message. Whether the message is written, spoken, or visual it is behaviorally composed and subject to selection and editing. The humans connect through some medium. When we whisper to an intimate the moving air is the medium; when we watch television satellite transmission or broadcast transmission is the technology for conveying film or videotape to our television set. Last, but by no means least, the human recipient of the message actively interprets the symbolic behavior received through the medium to create meaning. Hopefully, the recipient's meaning overlaps in important respects with the sender's intended meaning.

All five elements are important. Different humans choose to communicate about different things, and different humans interpret symbolic performances differently. The symbols selected and their arrangements make one message different from another. Different media not only connect different networks of people, they also convey some symbolic and performative variables differently – recall watching a music video and listening to the same song on your CD or iPod. Finally, performances of the same text differ.

It is perhaps unfortunate that, even within the field of communication, people specialize. Some people focus first on the humans, others on the words and symbols, some on the media and others on the performance. But if we are to understand presidential campaigns we are going to need to be alert to all five elements and their interactions.

Summary and Conclusion

Chapter 1 explained that our purpose is to help readers understand and appreciate the ways that Americans use communication to select our leaders. We need to understand the regularities of the process to appreciate the innovations and prepare ourselves for future campaigns. We set forth eight premises:

1. The United States Constitution rules
2. The Constitution and laws are texts
3. The Constitution used interdependence for "checks and balances"

4. Interdependence requires cooperation, coordination, and coalitions
5. Cooperation, coordination, and coalitions require communication
6. The power of the president to persuade is attained through communication
7. The campaign process creates discernible communication challenges
8. There are two campaigns: The practical pursuit of victory units leading to 270 electoral votes and the mythic stories about candidates' deeds told by observers.

Thus the Constitution created the presidency and charged the states with the responsibility for selecting person to take on the job. But the interface between the enduring Constitution and immediate circumstances creates challenges that require communication. To win the office a candidate therefore needs to solve a series of rhetorical challenges in competition with all the others seeking the office.

This book is based on the premise that we use communication in many ways to select our presidents. This chapter explained that communication requires the presence of humans, symbols, performance, a medium, and interpretation. We shall explore presidential campaigns as a series of competitive efforts to solve these rhetorical challenges by managing symbols, identities, relationships, and audiences in an ongoing struggle to win the electors and the American presidency – the right, as "Interpreter-in-Chief" (Stuckey 1991) to define reality for everyone else.

Chapter 2 will introduce the rhetorical process of deciding what to say to whom to move the campaign forward through the set of campaign challenges. Chapter 3 will elaborate the point that rules and laws are texts – the product of yesterday's rhetorical situations that constrain today's choices. Consequently, rules shape the candidate's practical campaign for victory units. We will consider how rules ordinarily constrain choices and how campaigns sometimes use them creatively for strategic advantage. Chapter 4 explores the various media or technologies of human communication that simultaneously connect some people and isolate others. We will also begin to view presidential campaigns as an interface of three unique perspectives: citizens, campaign organizations, and media organizations.

Part II of the book examine modes of communication used throughout presidential campaigns. Chapter 5 discusses the three basic acts of acclaiming, attacking and defending that give political campaigns their identifiable character. Chapter 6 is devoted to analyzing campaign speeches. Candidates give a great many speeches and new technologies provide easy access to them. But we too rarely give adequate attention to their extended arguments or the ways that they use language to solve rhetorical puzzles. Chapter 7 deals with the campaign news that we get from television, newspapers and the Internet. Campaigns consider news as "free media" as opposed to the "paid media" of campaign advertising covered in Chapter 8. Chapter 9 examines the televised presidential debates that have become a signature feature of American campaigns since 1976 and now pervade the primary campaigns. The section concludes by exploring in Chapter 10 how new media provide new challenges and opportunities for presidential campaigns.

Part III synthesizes and explores the dynamics of the four stages of presidential campaigns, with particular attention to how candidates progress from one stage to the next. Chapter 11 discusses the first stage in which each aspirant tries to produce a viable candidacy by the end of the Iowa precinct caucuses. Chapter 12 is devoted to the second stage of party primaries and caucuses in which the objective is to secure the party's nomination by accumulating a majority of its national convention delegates. Chapter 13 covers the third stage of consolidating party support. Political conventions are a part of this stage but it now begins as soon as the primary process determines the nominee. Chapter 14 covers the general election campaign in which the nominees lead their forces out of their conventions to do battle with the other party by contesting their rhetorical visions to win the state elections that decide the electoral votes.

Chapter 15 concludes the book by integrating the major themes into a discussion of presidential campaigns as two quests – the practical political quest for victory units and the mythic quest for melodrama. In short, this book is intended to help the reader become more perceptive than partisan, more insightful than ideological and more appreciative than angry. That may be a tall order so, as President Kennedy invited in his Inaugural Address, "Let us begin."

2 The Rhetorical Puzzle

Millions of people have been citizens of the United States, but only forty-four have been elected president. Chapter 1 explained how the Constitution's requirements created challenges that require communication. This is the "rhetorical puzzle" of the campaign: What should one choose to say (or not say) or do (or not do) to which other persons to garner the electoral support necessary to get to the White House? This chapter will explain rhetoric as the way we think about the continuing communication challenge to maximize both personal coherence and social coordination. It requires us to learn, or to adapt to, other peoples' languages, logics, beliefs, and preferences. To attempt to influence others with communication is to engage in persuasion. The process of persuasion is necessary and important, but particular persuaders in particular situations undertake it ethically or unethically, strategically or unwisely. So let us consider rhetoric and its strategic and ethical dimensions.

Welcome to Rhetoric

Imagine walking into a room and seeing another person. What would you say? Would you speak or wait? Would you presume fluent English? Did you consider the person's gender, race, or ethnicity, and whether they were similar to your? Did you consider the person's age before speaking? What about socio-economic status? If so, how did those factors influence your communication? All of the foregoing questions pertain to *social or cultural level* predictions about the other (Miller and Sunnafrank 1982). These predictions influence our audience expectations and the communication choices we make in the hope of being understood. The important consideration here is how many questions crossed your mind before you decided what to say.

How did your relationship influence your communication? Did you imagine a total stranger, an acquaintance, a friend or an intimate? Greetings such as "May I have a dollar?" or "Do you have a minute to talk about something important?" take on different meanings in different relationships. To the extent that you spoke to an imaginary friend, did you use a generic deferential greeting to suggest cautious propriety ("Good morning, Ma'am") or did you get right to business ("May I borrow your notes?"). If you asked these questions you have moved beyond societal and cultural level guesswork to ask personal questions about the individual. The questions in this paragraph concern *psychological* level predictions about audience expectations (Miller and Sunnafrank 1982). Again, note how many questions you asked.

If you have been playing along with the scenario in the last few paragraphs you have been engaging in rhetoric. It matters not that you have not spoken, because *rhetoric* is the process of making choices about what to say to whom, about how to say it, and when. Aristotle defined rhetoric as, "the faculty of observing in any given case the available means of persuasion" (Aristotle, Rhetoric Book 1 Part 2). In the 1950s rhetorical theorist Donald C. Bryant wrote that rhetoric is the "*rationale* of informative and suasory discourse" (1953, emphasis added). He added that rhetoric serves the function of "adjusting ideas to people and people to ideas." You make basic rhetorical choices when you decide whether to acknowledge a "hello," when you decide what language to use when addressing someone, whether to send an e-mail or make a telephone call, and how and when to ask someone for a date. In fact, those following in Aristotle's footsteps say that situations pose rhetorical challenges.

Bitzer and Rhetorical Situations

Chapter 1 explained that the campaign for president calls for candidates to move through a number of political stages, including nomination and election. They do this by engaging in a series of symbolic exchanges with people who have the resources or "victory units" they need. They use words, arguments, and images to construct convergent (and divergent) understandings with various audiences to advance through the stages toward their goal. Harold Lasswell (1948) captured the essential task of communication studies like this one with his general research question, "Who says what to whom through what channel with what effect."

Lloyd F. Bitzer's, "The Rhetorical Situation" (1968) argued that life is a succession of situations notable for their imperfections. A particular imperfection may be something dangerous or it could be something less desirable than it might be. In either case, when that imperfection also seems urgent we perceive an *exigency.* It is such exigencies – *perceived imperfections marked by urgency* – that define the practical situations that each of us faces every day.

Bitzer further suggested that some practical situations contain exigencies that can be resolved by persons, who sometimes need help. When we choose to seek help (to reduce either the imperfection or the urgency) we are attempting to enlist the assistance of an *audience.* We do so in the belief that we will be able to use words or actions to constrain the behavior of others so that *they* will positively resolve the exigency for us.

Thus *if a situation's exigency can be positively influenced by introducing communication to influence the choices made by other people, the exigency is rhetorical and the pragmatic situation is specifically a "rhetorical situation."* But realize that not all pragmatic situations are rhetorical. For example, a person can reduce the water consumption that aggravates a drought, but a person cannot make it rain by simply saying "Please rain." The key points about rhetorical situations, then, are (1) that there is a person (or persons) somewhere capable either of resolving the imperfection, reducing its urgency or, possibly, both and (2) that said person (or persons) can theoretically be constrained to do so by the rhetor's choice of words.

The people whose efforts can positively modify the exigency are Bitzer's "audience." Notice that Bitzer's audience is neither the people who hear the words nor a group of people in an auditorium or sitting by their televisions waiting to hear the words (although they might be). Bitzer's "audience" consists of those persons *actually* capable of modifying the imperfection, its urgency, or both; they are the ideal audience of the people who can truly make a difference.

The rhetorical challenge is to identify the audience whose help is needed to engage them in communication, and to use words to constrain their thoughts and actions so as to achieve a "fitting response" to the exigency. A fitting response is "terminal" when it resolves the exigency once and for all, but these are rare. More often, the fitting response is "instrumental" – it moves persuader and audience toward a redefined situation in which the possibility of a terminal response is increased. Sometimes an audience can be formally empowered to take charge of the exigency, sometimes the exigency is defined or called to the audience's attention and sometimes the urgency of the exigency is diminished or postponed.

Chapter 1 introduced the exigencies facing the campaigns that we will explore. Let us now consider the audiences that comprise the American public from which the Republican and Democratic parties develop their presidential coalitions.

The Audiences of Presidential Campaigns

Social scientists have traditionally relied upon demographic analyses to track candidates' popularity among identifiable populations. You have seen many surveys that show females preferring candidate A while males prefer candidate B, or white voters preferring candidate A by higher percentages than African-American or Latino voters. But the more we hear such reports the more likely we are to think in terms of identity politics: Candidate A is the "candidate of white females" or Candidate B is supported by "minority males." Generally speaking, demographic analyses are poorly equipped to explain *why* those persons prefer the candidates unless chromosomes determine our votes. We need to look for the reasons that people prefer candidates.

The Pew Foundation's Typology of American Voters (Kohut 2005) considers the American polity as nine audiences (or proto-coalitions) that coalesce into coalitions of Republican, Democratic, and undecided voters. The Pew types are based not on respondents' demographic characteristics but on their political beliefs and values – the thoughts, arguments and preferences they are receptive to taking in trade for their victory units they control. Once we understand how these audiences prefer, we can consider them demographically. But the important distinction is that *their demographic characteristics are secondary in importance to their reasons for preferring candidates or policies.*

The Pew studies defined groups by their beliefs and preferences and then identifies each group's age, gender, ethnic, partisanship, and other characteristics. Table 2.1 shows the proto-coalitions from the original 1987 *Times–Mirror* study and the 1995, 1999, and 2005 Pew studies. It shows a generally constant 10 percent of the American population as political bystanders who take little interest in politics and do not vote. The Republican base consisted of two to three proto-coalitions and accounted for anywhere from 21 percent of the population in 1987 to 34 percent in 1995, whereas the Democratic base consisted of three to four proto-coalitions that accounted for anywhere between a low of 35 percent of the population in 1987 to a high of 41 percent in 2005. Clearly, neither party's base accounts for a majority of the population (nor even half of the population remaining after subtracting the bystanders). But, for better or worse, the entire population does not vote in any American election.

The table shows that Enterprisers (called "staunch Conservatives" in 1999) have been the constant core of the Republican coalition. The rise of Rev. Jerry Falwell's moral majority and the religious right during the 1980s helped the moralists to attain comparable numbers within the party. Many of the intra-party struggles of the 1980s had to do with the economic agenda vs. the social agenda, such that a third proto-coalition had emerged by the 1995 study. This Libertarian proto-coalition wanted government to be involved neither in the economy nor in people's private lives.

Any campaign hoping to mobilize all three Republican factions needed the support of people who wanted government to help the economy but stay out of moral issues, those who wanted government to help keep Americans moral but stay out of economics, and those who wanted government to stay out of both business and moral questions. Ronald Reagan united all three, which was one reason he was called "The Great Communicator." But after George H. W. Bush held the coalition together in 1988, Pat Buchanan challenged him for re-nomination in 1992 and Bob Dole failed to reconstruct the coalition in 1996. Indeed, businessman Ross Perot felt the need to run, twice, as an independent candidate and Bill Clinton won both elections. Thanks to Perot, Clinton parlayed 43 percent of the 1992 vote into a 370–168 electoral vote victory and 49 percent of the 1996 vote into a 379–159 victory.

Table 2.1 also shows the evolving nature of the Democratic proto-coalitions. Especially important was the disappearance of the ageing New Dealers who had supported the policies of Franklin Roosevelt and Harry Truman. Like the Republicans, the Democratic base has proto-coalitions that are incongruent. Liberals are not easily reconciled with Conservative Democrats, nor are disadvantaged Democrats easily united with the advantaged Democrats who are mostly Liberals. But Democrats have long seen themselves as a diverse "party of the people" and may be willing to grant their candidates somewhat more rhetorical elbowroom than do their Republican counterparts.

Pew researchers developed their 2005 typology by conducting approximately 1,000 telephone interviews during December 2004 and follow-up interviews in March, 2005. Their results led them to identify three proto-coalitions on the political right that voted heavily Republican, three proto-coalitions on the political left that voted heavily Democratic and three in the political center that split. Because these proto-coalitions were the audiences facing candidates in 2008 and the foreseeable future, we need to take some time to meet them.

The Political Right

The Pew "political right" in 2005 consisted of Enterprisers, Social Conservatives and Pro-Government Conservatives. They identify predominantly, but not exclusively, with the Republican Party. The three groups on the political right accounted for 29 percent of the adult population and 34 percent of the electorate. So even if a Republican presidential candidate were to accomplish the unlikely

Table 2.1 The Evolving Nature of the Few Party Coalitions

1987 Tribe	1987 %	1996 Tribe	1995 %	1999 Tribe	1996 %	2005 Tribe	2005 % pop
REPUBLICANS	**21**	**REPUBLICANS**	**34**	**REPUBLICANS**	**30**	**REPUBLICANS**	**29**
Enterprisers	10	Enterprisers	12	Staunch Conservatives	10	Enterprisers	9
Moralists	11	Moralists	15	Populist Republicans	9	Social Conservatives	11
		Libertarians	7	Moderate Republicans*	11	Pro-Government Conservatives	9
	21		34		29		29
MIDDLE	**33**	**MIDDLE**	**20**	**MIDDLE**	**19**	**MIDDLE**	**20**
Upbeats*	9	Embittereds	6	Disaffecteds	9	Upbeats*	11
Disaffecteds	9	New Economy Independents	14	New Prosperity Independents	10	Disaffecteds	9
Followers	7						
Seculars	8						
	33		20		20		20
DEMOCRATS	**35**	**DEMOCRATS**	**36**	**DEMOCRATS**	**40**	**DEMOCRATS**	**41**
New Dealers	11	New Democrats	12	New Democrats	9	Conservative Democrats	14
60s Democrats	8	New Dealers	8	Socially Conservative Democrats	13	Liberals	17
Partisan Poor	9	Seculars	7	Liberal Democrats	9	Disadvantaged Democrats	10
Passive Poor	7	Partisan Poor	9	Partisan Poor	9		
			36		40		
Bystanders	**11**	**Bystanders**	**10**	**Bystanders**	**11**	**Bystanders**	**10**

feat of winning every one of their votes, the Democrat could in theory still win 66 percent of the vote. It is also important to understand that the "Republican" vote is not monolithic.

Enterprisers account for 9 percent of the adult population and 10 percent of registered voters. Some 81 percent identified themselves as Republican, 18 percent as Independent or "no preference," and only one percent as Democrats (98% actually reported "leaning Republican"). In 2004 96 percent of them voted, and they voted for President Bush by a margin of 93–1. The Enterprisers' reported values include patriotism and an assertive foreign policy. They are very satisfied with their financial standing and perhaps understandably pro-business and against regulation. They voice little support for government help to the poor because they believe strongly that individuals are responsible for their own well-being. They are conservative on social issues such as gay marriage, but they are not much more religious than the nation as a whole.

Enterprisers watch Fox News, followed by newspapers, radio and the internet; they are the cluster most knowledgeable about world affairs. The Pew study says of Enterprisers:

> This extremely partisan Republican group's politics are driven by a belief in the free enterprise system and social values that reflect a conservative agenda. Enterprisers are also the strongest backers of an assertive foreign policy, which includes nearly unanimous support for the war in Iraq and strong support for such anti-terrorism efforts as the Patriot Act.

Enterprisers are not demographically diverse. At least 90 percent of the respondents in this cluster were white and over thirty, at least 75 percent were married males. More than 60 percent had household incomes above $50,000, more than half own a gun and trade stocks. Half attend church weekly and almost half graduated from college. Roughly a third are small business owners and/or attend bible study or prayer group meetings.

Social Conservatives account for 11 percent of the adult population and 13 percent of registered voters. None of the Social Conservatives identified with the Democrats, while 82 percent identified with the Republicans and 18 percent reported being Independent or having "no preference" (altogether, 97% lean Republican). President Bush carried the social Conservative vote 86 percent-4 percent in 2004. Social Conservatives are defined by their conservative stands on social issues such as abortion and gay marriage. Although they are not better off financially than the national average, they are less dissatisfied with their condition than some other clusters and hence they oppose government assistance for the needy. Unlike Enterprisers, Social Conservatives have a cynical view of business and express modest support for government regulation of business and the environment. They are very worried about the impact of immigration.

Demographically, more than 90 percent of Social Conservatives are white and more than half own a gun and attend Bible study groups. A majority of respondents in this cluster are female and almost half are over the age of fifty, making them the oldest of the clusters. A great number live in the southern states and are white evangelical Protestants. Social Conservatives rely on newspapers as a major news source as well as Fox News and network news

Pro-Government Conservatives account for 9 percent of the adult population and 10 percent of registered voters. Although 86 percent "lean Republican" only 58 percent identified themselves as Republicans with 40 percent identifying themselves as Independent or "no preference" and 2 percent as Democrats. Although President Bush carried the Pro-Government Conservative voters by a margin of 61 percent–12 percent in 2004, 21 percent of them chose not to vote. Pro-Government Conservatives describe religion as "very important." They are more likely to have faced unemployment and less likely to own guns than the other groups on the Right, and few trade stocks and bonds. They rely on network television and newspapers for their news. Pro-Government Conservatives have strong religious beliefs and are financially insecure. They mistrust the marketplace and expect government to act on their behalf to provide a safety net against financial ruin and immorality.

Demographically, Pro-Government Conservatives are mostly female and young. About 60 percent have no more than a high school diploma. About half have children at home and reported household incomes less than $30,000. More respondents in this cluster live in the south than in any other region, and they also include the largest percentage of minority members of any Republican-leaning group (10% black, 12% Hispanic).

Candidates for the 2008 Republican nomination will have to work mainly with these three audiences, for they are the people most likely to have registered as Republican voters and to vote in the primaries and caucuses. President Bush was unopposed for the 2004 nomination, so the divisions among these voters were not probed. But the Pew study suggests intriguing fissures within the political right.

First, the Enterprisers are the indispensable Republican base. But they stand alone in their opposition to health care policy and to raising the minimum wage. They also are the group most opposed to environmental protection and they are the only group to view the Patriot Act as indispensable to our counterterrorism efforts. They are less supportive of the moral agenda than either of the other Republican groups. The candidate(s) who reach out to the Enterprisers during the primaries will have difficulty appealing as well to the other two-thirds of their party. Conversely, candidates who strive to appeal to Social Conservatives and Pro-Government Conservatives during the primaries will not have much to offer the Enterprisers. Secondly, stem cell research deeply divides all three Republican groups whereas all non-Republican groups support it. Ironically, this issue raised by President Bush in 2004 could prove costly for his party in 2008.

The Political Left

The Pew "political left" consisted of Liberals, Disadvantaged Democrats and Conservative Democrats accounting for 41 percent of the adult population and 44 percent of the electorate (as compared to the Right's 29% and 34%, respectively).

Liberals account for 17 percent of the general population and 19 percent of registered voters. Just under 60 percent identify with the Democrats while 40 percent are Independent or reported no preference and one percent are Republican (overall 92% lean Democratic). In 2004, John Kerry won the Liberal vote 81–2 percent. Liberals favor individual choice on the abortion question, they support Gays' rights to marry and they favor environmental protection. They are highly sympathetic to immigrants and labor unions. They oppose the Patriot Act and military force as counterterrorism measures, favoring instead diplomatic methods. Liberals are the second most likely to follow news, and they are the most likely to use the Internet to get it. The Pew report says that the Liberal group:

> Has nearly doubled in proportion since 1999. Liberal Democrats now comprise the largest share of Democrats. They are the most opposed to an assertive foreign policy, the most secular, and take the most liberal views on social issues such as homosexuality, abortion, and censorship. They differ from other Democratic groups in that they are strongly pro-environment and pro-immigration.

Demographically, more than 80 percent of the respondents in the Liberal cluster were white, and about half have graduated from college. They are the least religious group and the wealthiest group on the left. They are the second youngest and a third have not (yet) married. Liberals are the largest of the groups living in urban areas and in the western half the country. They are the least likely to own a gun or to attend Bible or prayer meetings.

Conservative Democrats account for 14 percent of the population and 15 percent of registered voters. As the name suggests, 89 percent identify with the Democrats, 11 percent are Independent or "no preference" (98% lean Democratic) and 0 percent identified with Republicans. Nevertheless, Kerry won this group by a margin of only 65 percent to 14 percent in 2004. Conservative Democrats differ from the other left groups on many social issues because of their religious and conservative views. Their belief in personal responsibility moderates their support for government assistance programs and a social safety net. They tend to oppose homosexuality and gay marriage, but not so strongly as the Republican groups. They hold mixed or moderate views on regulating the environment. Conservative Democrats' views are moderate with respect to key policy issues such as foreign policy, regulation of the environment, abortion, stem-cell research and the war in Iraq.

Demographically, Conservative Democrats are less educated and somewhat poorer than the national average. Some 85 percent describe themselves as conservative or moderate and almost half attend church and Bible or prayer groups regularly. About a third own guns. The cluster contained relatively high percentages of older females (27%) and blacks (30%). They reported the strongest allegiance to the Democratic Party and more than half consider themselves "strong" Democrats. They rely on newspapers and network television for their news.

Disadvantaged Democrats account for 10 percent of the population and 10 percent of the registered voters. About 84 percent identify with the Democrats, 16 percent are Independent or "no preference" and 0 percent Republican (99% lean Democratic). They voted for John Kerry by a margin of 82 percent to 2 percent in 2004. The disadvantaged Democrats are the most economically insecure group and the most sceptical of an individual's ability to succeed alone. They are therefore strongly anti-business, and they favor efforts to help people in need by labor unions and government programs. Minorities comprise a substantial proportion of this group. Their disapproval of George W. Bush's job performance (91%) was comparable to that of the Liberal cluster.

Demographically, disadvantaged Democrats are among the least educated groups, and they are struggling. Almost four out of five say that they "can't make ends meet." More than half the households had someone unemployed during the past year and about one in four households contained a labor union member. A third of the respondents reported household incomes less than $20,000 and two-thirds had a high-school degree at most. Six-in-ten are female, 32 percent are black and 14 percent are Hispanic; about half have children at home. About a quarter of the households have guns. Disadvantaged Democrats rely on newspapers and CNN for their news.

Our discussion of the political left illuminates some of the challenges that faced Democratic candidates in recent elections. Liberals are the largest of the nine groups but they "stand far apart from the rest of the electorate in their strong support for gay marriage, and in opposing the public display of the Ten Commandments in government buildings" (Kohut 2005). That often made it difficult for Democrats to create a majority coalition with Liberals. Moreover, Liberals are less committed to the Democratic Party (59%) than are Conservative Democrats (89%) or disadvantaged Democrats (84%). Al Gore, author of *Earth in the Balance* and producer of *An Inconvenient Truth*, spoke to the center in 2000 and lost votes to Ralph Nader's Green Party candidacy. But reclaiming those Liberal votes in 2004 cost John Kerry crucial independent votes that had previously gone to Gore and Clinton.

The Political Middle

Pew's "political middle" consisted of Upbeats, Disaffecteds, and Bystanders. Together these groups accounted for 30 percent of the adult population and 23 percent of registered voters – clearly enough to matter when they gravitate toward a candidate.

Upbeats account for 11 percent of the adult population and 13 percent of registered voters. The majority either said they were Independent or reported "no preference," while 39 percent identified with Republicans and only 5 percent with Democrats (but a total of 73% lean Republican). In 2004 President Bush won the upbeat vote 63 percent-14 percent.

The Pew report says that upbeats:

> Express positive views about the economy, government and society. Satisfied with their own financial situation and the direction the nation is heading, these voters support George W. Bush's leadership in economic matters more than on moral or foreign policy issues. Combining highly favorable views of government with equally positive views of business and the marketplace, upbeats believe that success is in people's own hands, and that businesses make a positive contribution to society. This group also has a very favorable view of immigrants.   (Kohut 2005)

A candidate seeking to appeal to upbeats should know that government, business, and immigrants are credible for them. They are moderately religious and have mixed views on foreign policy. They supported the war in Iraq and military actions against those who threaten US religions.

Demographically, most upbeats are white, married, and suburban, young and well educated. They are wealthier than most of the other groups, and are second highest in stock ownership. This group has the highest proportion of adult and white mainline Protestants, although fewer than half attend church weekly. Upbeats rely on the Internet and newspapers for their news more than most others, but they are neither more nor less politically engaged than the national average.

*Disaffected*s account for 9 percent of the adult population and 10 percent of registered voters. About two-thirds were either Independent or reported "no preference," while 30 percent identified with Republicans and only 2 percent with Democrats (60% lean Republican). Bush beat Kerry 42 percent–21 percent among the disaffecteds, but 23 percent of them did not vote. Disaffecteds are under financial strain and believe that personal success is largely beyond one's control. They oppose immigration, regulatory and environmental policies as both ineffective and threats to jobs. They are moderate supporters of government assistance programs. Because disaffecteds have little interest in current events and pay little attention to the news it may not be surprising that no single medium or network stands out as a main source of news. The Pew report says that disaffecteds:

> Are deeply cynical about government and unsatisfied with both their own economic situation and the overall state of the nation. Under heavy financial pressure personally, this group is deeply concerned about immigration and environmental policies, particularly to the extent that they affect jobs. Alienated from politics, disaffecteds have little interest in keeping up with news about politics and government, and few participated in the last election.

Demographically, disaffecteds are less educated than the national average (70% have never attended any college). More than half are males. Although they live throughout the country, more live in rural and suburban areas. Somewhat higher percentages than average report owning a gun and having someone in their house unemployed in the past year.

Bystanders account for 10 percent of the adult population and 0 percent of registered voters. They distribute evenly, with 56 percent Independent/no preference; 22 percent Republican and 22 percent Democrat (96% did not vote in 2004). They are cynical about government and uninterested in the news, and they neither follow nor participate in politics. Although they get most of their news from television, newspapers, and radio, they presumably get their news as a byproduct of seeking other content from these media. Demographically, bystanders are young and have the least education, as 24 percent have not (yet) finished high school. They are less religious than any group other than Liberals with just one-in-four attending church weekly. About half say that they cannot make ends meet and about a third own guns and attend prayer meetings. They are largely concentrated in the south and west, with relatively few in the east and midwest. One-in-five bystanders is Hispanic.

The political center holds the key to most presidential elections. Clearly, it mattered in 2004. Bush carried the upbeats 63 percent–14 percent and the disaffecteds 42 percent–21 percent while the bystanders stood by – that left Kerry with too many votes to overcome.

In summary, the 2005 Pew survey of the American electorate provides us with a set of three proto-coalitions on the political right (Enterprisers, Social Conservatives and Pro-Government Conservatives). These proto-coalitions have their differences, but they generally identify with the Republican Party. The political left also consists of three proto-coalitions (Liberals, Conservative Democrats and disadvantaged Democrats) who also have their differences but who generally identify with the Democratic Party. The political center consists of upbeats, disaffecteds, and bystanders who have their differences and identify with no political party.

Each of the nine Pew groups encompass 7–17 percent of the population and neither left nor right alone can produce a majority, so candidates need to appeal to several of them. These factional struggles are very important to both parties between elections. Immigration policy divided Enterprisers (who valued cheap labor) from Pro-Government Conservatives (who feared for their jobs) and also divided Liberals (concerned for the immigrants) from disadvantaged Democrats. How did the nomination of John McCain invite or repel upbeats and disaffecteds, or even some Conservative Democrats? Which faction would lead the 2008 Democrats – the Conservative Democrats, the disadvantaged Democrats or the Liberals? To answer those questions we need to understand how campaigns use words to help people imagine themselves into coalitions and communities.

Building Coalitions with Words

A campaign could strategize to win on the basis of exclusive coalitions. It would begin by identifying the grocery list of exclusive coalitions – identity or issue publics – that would be most likely to provide the victory units they need. Then the campaign would identify the commonalities between the candidate and each of these issue publics, Sometimes this means advocating what their audiences want, sometimes it means condemning what their audiences most fear and sometimes it means attacking someone else's record. Finally, the strategy involves combining those appeals into a montage of a message that can be repeated without contradiction, elaborating for each issue public the themes that they most want to hear. Technical innovations including Internet bookmarks, search engines, cable channels and podcasts have made it easier for us to consume viewpoints congruent with our own and to avoid viewpoints disturbing to our ears. Thus we may anticipate finding a great number of exclusive or single-issue coalitions that eventually cluster together around particular candidates.

Most notable among the critics of Bitzer's rhetorical situation was Richard Vatz (1974) who argued that rhetorical situations are themselves rhetorically constructed. After all, how do we come to regard something as "imperfect" except through persuasion? How do we come to perceive "urgency" except through persuasion? How do people come to see themselves as capable of taking effective action except through persuasion? In other words, Vatz argued that Bitzer had underestimated the role of rhetoric in the creation and development of rhetorical situations.

In a subsequent essay, Bitzer (1980) elaborated his position and responded to Vatz and his other critics. He identified four stages in the development of rhetorical situations. Stage 1 consists of the "Origin and development of constituents" of the rhetorical situation. Persuaders during this stage focus on defining the imperfection and the urgency, identifying those capable of resolving the exigency and constituting them as an accessible audience, bringing the exigency to the attention of those able to address it, and developing the arguments and appeals of persuasion. A terminal response is not possible at this point, but a fitting instrumental response leads to the second stage. In the context of campaigns, candidates select the themes that call audiences into being. "End the War!" or "Health Care for All Americans" attract motivated issue publics early in contemporary campaigns, as "Protect the Tax Cuts" and "Support Our Troops!"

Stage 2 is "Maturity" of the rhetorical situation when all of the elements ripen and come into alignment for a fitting terminal response. An important distinction here is that the presidential campaign reaches maturity on election day, but the policy issues being debated reach maturity when the legislation embodying a proposal reaches a vote in Congress. In other words, a vote for the Pro-Life candidate does not outlaw abortions, nor does a vote for the End the War candidate end the war. It is a vote to give one candidate the opportunity to work on his agenda. At this point, there really is no fitting instrumental response, because the situation cannot be improved – it can only be resolved. Anything less than a fitting terminal response leads to Stage 3.

The third stage is "Deterioration," in which a fitting terminal response is no longer possible. The audience may have lost interest or control of the exigency, time may be growing impractically short, persuaders may have been undermined and/or opposing persuaders and arguments may have complicated the situation. Fitting instrumental responses are necessary to return the situation to Stage 2 (maturity) so that it can be positively resolved. When deterioration is not satisfactorily addressed it leads to Stage 4, "disintegration" in which the persuaders, arguments, and audiences disperse into the culture (McGee 1975), awaiting new persuaders to take notice and reassemble them in a new Stage 1.

As the campaign strategists work on their puzzle they seek to constrain or influence the thoughts and feelings of the audiences in possession of the victory units they need. Bitzer (1968) wrote about the persuader's ability to constrain the audience in thought and action so that they would take the desired action. Unfortunately, many people confused Bitzer's discussion of rhetorical constraints with the situational limitations facing the persuader (these are actually among the exigency's complications). Similarly, many people erroneously discuss the audience addressed by the persuader instead of the audience capable of resolving the exigency – who might have been overlooked by the persuader.

As persuaders plan to engage their audiences they can anticipate agreeing and disagreeing about the "facts" and the "interests" in dispute. Too often we presume that people agree on both facts and perceived interests, as when we agree that a proposal would raise our taxes and that we therefore dislike it. But the other combinations deserve more consideration. The late Daniel Patrick Moynihan, a respected senator from New York, reportedly liked to say that, "You are entitled to your own opinion, but you are not entitled to your own facts" (quoted in Jackson and Jamieson, 2007, p. xii). Resolving factual disagreements can often produce agreement on interests, and resolving disagreements about interests can pave the way for agreement on facts; but differences often persist.

Disagreement about interests makes it difficult for people to stand back and objectively consider the facts. A 2004 study, for example, found that supporters of President George W. Bush and Senator John Kerry believed many different factual things to be true (Kull 2004). In our digital age this may increasingly derive from the increasing assortment of news sources from which we choose, and we rely most often on the news that reinforces our beliefs and preferences. This complicates political campaigning but, more importantly, it complicates the citizen's of job of informing ourselves and reaching wise decisions. Persuaders often choose to ignore this cohort of voters as unreachable; a decision that may make strategic sense for them, but it does little to enhance informed deliberation.

Bitzer suggests two general factors that influence anyone's potential responsiveness to an exigency: *the degree of interest at stake* and the *modification capability* (1968). A persuader trying to manipulate the symbolic environment in which the degree of interest in an exigency is considered could choose words to alter some combination of six factors. First, audiences are frequently aware of a condition but uninformed about it, and the candidate can influence them with straight facts. But a candidate telling an audience how long a war or recession might last is using a second approach, adjusting factual probability, by encouraging them to see one set of facts as more likely than another. A third approach is for the candidate to enhance or diminish the proximity of a fact or interest in place and time, as when the 2004 Bush campaign kept the specter of 9/11 in the permanent present.

A fourth approach personally involves the speaker or audience with the exigency to heighten interest in it as when Hillary Clinton talked about landing in Bosnia under heavy sniper fire. But Clinton also adjusted the magnitude of a factual condition by overstating the danger, and the remark became embarrassing. The fifth approach is to heighten the connection between the interest in the exigency and the intrinsic quality of the interest at stake. The health care issue provided all candidates with heart-rending stories that used the plight of underinsured people to establish an interest in electing them.

Bitzer also suggested that our perceived capability to modify the exigency (or to affect the audience) played an important role in rhetorical situations. One seeking to manipulate the symbolic environment in which the capability of modifying the exigency is considered could address risk, obligation, expectation, familiarity, confidence, and immediacy. He suggested that people with much to gain and little at risk are more likely to act than those with much at risk and little to gain. Moreover, the likelihood of action increases when the participants know that they are expected to act, or that they alone can resolve the exigency. Most speakers and audiences are more likely to act if prepared by experience and practice to do so, and action becomes less likely if participants believe that delay or postponement is possible. These topics provide a set of themes for persuaders to cover when addressing their audiences.

Party Coalitions

Let us return to the Pew Center's 2005 report and consider the challenges faced by candidates trying to develop coalitions for nomination during the 2005–2008 period. The Pew report is important to this discussion because it demonstrated the importance to each party of maintaining its base coalition. But the Pew report concluded that "there are now large fissures within each major party as well as differences between the two parties." They reported significant cleavages within both parties that were different from the popularly held view of monolithic Red and Blue voters (Kohut 2005).

The Pew study suggested seven issues – immigration reform, protecting the environment, raising the minimum wage, guaranteeing universal health care, stem cell research, gay marriage, and public display of the Ten Commandments – had the potential to unsettle the two-party coalitions in 2008. They were highly volatile arguments with the potential to exploit the fissures *within* each party's coalition.

As the 2008 campaign developed, all candidates talked about their plans to guarantee (or at least to enable) universal health care. Protecting the environment received considerable attention, although the record high oil prices induced Republicans to call for increased offshore drilling. Similarly, stem cell research was an occasional topic of debate, but it was not a dominant topic of division.

Virtually absent from the 2008 campaign were the issues of immigration reform, raising the minimum wage, gay marriage, and public display of the Ten Commandments. John McCain had co-sponsored the Bush plan to reform immigration policy. Emphasizing his position would likely have hurt him with conservative Republicans and he led among them (92%–5%). But surely this issue could have helped McCain with Latino voters who voted for Obama by a 67 percent–31 percent margin (CNN 2008). The Bush campaign had benefitted from the gay marriage and Ten Commandments issues because they divided Liberals from everyone else, opening non-Liberal Democrats to Republicans' other messages. By avoiding those issues the McCain campaign was left to allege that Obama had socialist tendencies (82% of Conservative Democrats still voted for him) and to appeal to religious conservatives by selecting Gov. Sarah Palin as his running mate, a choice that met mixed reviews.

Clearly the economic crisis of September 2008 overshadowed all other issues and was not anticipated by the 2005 Pew report. Nevertheless, some of Senator McCain's difficulties stemmed from his campaign's inability or reluctance to deal in rhetorically astute ways with the fissures apparent in both party coalitions during the years leading up to the campaign.

It is helpful to consider Bitzer's works on rhetorical situations as a guide to rhetorical resource management for presidential campaigns. His 1968 article introduced the concepts of exigencies, audiences, constraints, and the fitting response to which his 1980 chapter added instrumentality, stages, and therefore ongoing rhetorical efforts. As students of political campaigns, we can use his framework as a starting point since every presidential quest is a long and arduous series of rhetorical situations.

Becoming Rhetorically Sensitive to Strategies and Ethics

Earlier in this chapter we considered a series of questions you might ask about addressing an imaginary person. In a very general sense, the more of the questions that passed through your mind as you decided what to say to your imaginary person, the greater your *rhetorical sensitivity*. A rhetorically sensitive person is one who:

> (1) tries to accept role-taking as part of the human condition, (2) attempts to avoid stylized verbal behavior, (3) is characteristically willing to undergo the strain of adaptation, (4) seeks to distinguish between all information and information acceptable for communication, and (5) tries to understand that an idea can be rendered in multi-form ways.   (Hart and Burks 1972)

The more questions you asked yourself before deciding what to say, the more you attempted to understand your audience and the situation – you *targeted* your greeting to maximize the desired effects and to minimize the undesirable consequences. The fewer questions you thought to ask, the less rhetorically sensitive you were in this instance.

Subsequent research developed a scale for the measurement of rhetorical sensitivity as a personal trait and identified two types of rhetorically insensitive people. The *noble self* is less concerned with achieving coordination with others than with maintaining personal coherence. Thus these people basically speak their mind and ignore the others' perspectives ("Wow, you've gained a lot of weight!"). On the other hand *rhetorical reflectors* overemphasize the others' perspectives and subordinate their beliefs, saying whatever the audiences want to hear, whether they mean it or not ("Sure, I'll help you move into your new apartment this weekend, just give me a call"). Reflectors do this because they value social coordination over coherence (Hart, Carlson, and Eadie 1980). Both of these tendencies lead people into problems, as you might easily imagine. The *rhetorically sensitive* person, on the other hand, balances coherence and social coordination. These people search for a way to say what they want to say that is well-suited to the audience (such as "It's difficult to find time to work out much, isn't it?" or "I'd like to help you move but I'm busy that day"). Hart and his colleagues regarded rhetorical sensitivity as a personality trait, but we can improve our sensitivity by studying the rhetorical choices other people make, by thinking rhetorically and by monitoring our own behavior.

Ironically rhetoric has a public relations problem. When people dismiss politicians and their "empty rhetoric" they are implicitly saying that the person made poor rhetorical choices and adapted unsuccessfully to the audience (had the speaker adapted well the complainer would have applauded the "empty" passage). Indeed, one goal of this book is to enhance your rhetorical sensitivity so that you can better solve life's rhetorical challenges, great and small, and so that you can constructively and dispassionately assess other people's rhetorical choices. As students of political campaigns we must be able to listen to those with whom we agree and disagree and to analyze their communication choices carefully. This is how you will understand why the people with whom you disagree sometimes convince others to agree, and why the people with whom you agree sometimes lose support. It is also how you will come to learn from others and how you can help those you support to wage better campaigns.

Let's return to our example of you and the person in the room. But this time, imagine that you are a candidate for president and the other person is eligible to vote. What would you say or do to the person so that on election day the person would choose to find the time to go to the polling place and cast her or his vote for you? Now repeat that exercise for every eligible voter in the country. The noble self would probably tell each voter the same thing, the rhetorical reflector would be inclined to say whatever they thought the person wanted to hear; but the rhetorically sensitive candidate would listen and then find or create common ground to the extent possible and acknowledge that differences may remain. That is the essence of the rhetorical challenge at the heart of the presidential campaign process. Clearly, it is not an easy challenge – but that is only the beginning because there are many other candidates trying to do the same thing and trying to impede your progress with your audience.

Ethics and Political Rhetoric

Our discussion of rhetoric has thus far emphasized its strategic dimensions, but only because it would be unrealistic to overlook candidates' determination to win election. This book acknowledges that those running for president (as well as their followers) adhere to a variety of political values. Our concern is with the ethics of their political communication.

It is important to understand that one can be rhetorically strategic or careless, and that one can be ethical or unethical; these are two independent concepts. Persuaders who believe that it is clever to be unethical are not necessarily strategic or successful; they are simply dishonest. On the other hand, persuaders who decline to enhance their effectiveness are not necessarily any more ethical, they are simply less likely to succeed. *Our goal as persuaders should be to be both highly effective and highly ethical.*

Fred Antczak (1989) has suggested an approach to ethical criticism that focuses on the text as a rhetorical community. In it we can see the implied author, the implied audience and the standards of conduct the rhetor sets out for them. Antczak explains how the author (our candidate) constructs a listener through the message:

> For in the way the author acts on and moves with her readers or listeners, she calls them to function in some way she calls them to realize . . . some of their possibilities . . . possibilities for perception and response, for recognizing truth, taking positions and making judgments. She teaches her reader or listener functionally how to be one who notes and follows her argumentative moves, who is swayed by the sorts of proofs she privileges. . . . [To] engage with and in a text is, at least for that time, to become morally different.   (Antczak 1989, p. 18)

Thus a campaign e-mail that invites people to read a policy statement on the candidate's web site would be encouraging a discursive community that values detailed information about policies. But an e-mail that urges its recipients to disrupt an opponent's rally or to remove yard signs or bumper stickers encourages unethical behavior. Antczak suggested several lines of inquiry that we can use to assess the ethics of rhetorical texts in presidential campaigns. Questions to ask include:

- What are the text's key descriptive and evaluative words? How do they work together to form the lines of argument that the text values?
- What value-laden language does the text offer the audience as guidance for recognizing rhetorical situations and for perceiving alternative for attitudes and actions that they may freely choose?
- How does this language open some possibilities (and obstruct others) for sustaining or denying, extending or transforming the community created by the text and the wider world in which they operate?
- What forms and modes of reasoning are held out in the text as valid and authoritative?
- What does it acknowledge a need to defend? What counts as unanswerable, and as not worth answering (adapted from Antczak 1989, p. 19).

We can consider the ethical and strategic dimensions of campaign rhetoric by considering the sudden fame of "Joe the Plumber."

Case Study: The Rhetoric of "Joe the Plumber"

Campaigning for Ohio's crucial twenty electoral votes took Barack Obama to Holland, Ohio on October 13, 2008. Joe Wurzelbacher told Obama that he was "getting ready to buy a company that makes more than $250,000 a year" (a factual statement) and floated an interest-based question that implied disagreement: "Your new tax plan is going to tax me more, isn't it?" Obama responded to the interest disagreement with two factual statements, telling Joe that "if your revenue is above 250 that [you] would get a 50 percent tax credit for health care" while the taxes on his income below $250,000 would stay the same. Obama acknowledged that any income above $250,000 would be taxed an additional 3 percent as "it was under Bill Clinton." He added that, "the reason why we're doing that is because 95 percent of small businesses make less than 250. So what I want to do is give them a tax cut." Joe did not care for the answer. "You know, I've always wanted to ask one of these guys a question and really corner them and get them to answer a question instead of tap dancing around it, and unfortunately I asked the question, but I still got a tap dance" (Rohter and Robbins 2008).

The *New York Times* investigated the factual question and reported that he would not have to pay higher taxes under Mr. Obama's plan unless his taxable income (not gross receipts from the business) exceeded $250,000 and that he would probably be eligible for a tax cut (Rohter and Robbins 2008). Joe subsequently told ABC News that he wanted to buy the plumbing company for that amount and did not know how much profit he might make from it (Ibanga and Goldman 2008). Factually, there would be people with taxable incomes more than $250,000 who would pay higher taxes under the Obama plan but Joe was not one of them.

Two days later John McCain made Joe the Plumber a centerpiece of the third presidential debate. He avoided the factual particulars to focus on interests. Obama had told Joe that, "My attitude is that if the economy's good for folks from

Joe the Plumber

the bottom up, it's gonna be good for everybody . . . I think when you spread the wealth around, it's good for everybody (Fox News 2008). McCain charged in the debate and thereafter that Obama wanted to "spread the wealth around" and the campaign suggested that Obama supported socialism. But how much of whose wealth did Obama propose to "spread around"?

To the extent that McCain's "you" addressed only the interests of the top 5 percent of taxpayers whose taxable income exceeds $250,000 his warning was clear, accurate, and ethical. But Joe was not among them and he was more likely to get a tax cut than a tax increase. Therefore using Joe to personify the danger of higher taxes to people "like him" invited McCain's audience to draw a misleading conclusion. Furthermore, the intimations of socialism acknowledged neither that Obama's plan would adjust part of the income tax to pre-Bush levels nor that McCain himself had voted against the Bush tax cuts. Thus the Joe the Plumber discourse created a community whose taxable income was not universally above $250,000 and it encouraged them to consider themselves endangered over financial interests that were not really their own. This was a violation of Antczak's standards for ethical rhetoric. McCain could easily have made this argument by basing it on someone whose taxes really would increase – someone other than Joe the Plumber.

If McCain's Joe the Plumber rhetoric was less ethical than desirable, was it a strategic success? But McCain gained 0 projected electoral votes during the two week period when Joe became famous. In the end he lost Ohio to Obama as well as many of the states most like it: Michigan, Wisconsin, Illinois, Pennsylvania and New Jersey. But the questionably ethical discourse did succeed in making Joe the Plumber a fixture. By election day "Joe the Plumber" had 547,000 Google hits – more hits than there were votes cast for either candidate in fourteen states.

Summary and Conclusion

This chapter identified the "rhetorical puzzle" of the campaign as "What should one choose to say (or not say) or do (or not do) to which other persons to garner the electoral support necessary to get to the White House?" We turn to rhetoric – the rationale of discourse – to better adapt people and ideas to one another. These puzzles arises in episodes that Bitzer described as rhetorical situations:

- The situation is defined by its exigency – an imperfection marked by urgency.
- An audience is capable of modifying the imperfection, the urgency or both.
- The situation is rhetorical if discourse can be introduced to
  - Constrain the audience's thoughts or actions to bring about either
  - A "fitting instrumental response" that moves the situation toward maturity and away from deterioration
  - A "fitting terminal response" that finally resolves the exigency.

Thus every rhetorical situation requires the candidate to identify the person(s) capable of resolving an urgent imperfection in the campaign environment and to persuade them to act in a way that resolves that imperfection.

Although we hear a great deal about demographic audiences this chapter suggested that the Pew typology of American voters' focus on what people believe makes it a more useful framework for rhetorical audiences. Pew identified nine "audiences" in 2005:

- The Pew "political right" consists of Enterprisers, Social Conservatives, and Pro-Government Conservatives accounting for 29 percent of the adult population and 34 percent of the electorate.
- The Pew "political left" consists of Liberals, disadvantaged Democrats, and Conservative Democrats accounting for 41 percent of the adult population and 44 percent of the electorate.
- Pew's "political middle" consists of upbeats, disaffecteds, and bystanders. Together these groups accounted for 30 percent of the adult population and 23 percent of registered voters.

Campaigns construct messages for these audiences seeking to increase support and to trade words for victory units so that they can advance to the next stage of the electoral process.

- Candidates use a variety of verbal tactics to influence the thoughts and feelings of these audiences.
- They try to realign their agreements and disagreements with these audiences about facts and/or interests.

- These messages should be both strategic and ethical but are sometimes unwise and unethical.
- The parties are not in complete agreement. Each is a coalition with real divisions.
- Rhetorically sensitive candidates willing to adapt to their audiences by rendering ideas in multiple ways without pandering to the audience should have an advantage when solving rhetorical puzzles.

Because the requirements for election flow from the Constitution the essential campaign exigencies are rule based, so we turn next to election rules.

3 Rules are Rhetorical Constructions

Laws and rules define many of the fitting responses of political campaigns. The best way to learn a new game is to read the rules. Who wins the presidency? The Constitution says a majority of the electoral votes. How does one acquire a state's electoral votes? Check the state's laws. Who gets on the state's ballots? Read the state's laws. Who gets to compete for electoral votes? Read the parties' rules for nomination. How can campaign funds be raised? Read the campaign finance laws. This chapter therefore considers the laws and party rules that must be met.

Rules and the Coordination of Meaning

A prominent theoretical approach to human communication suggests that all of us strive to coordinate our meanings with others. But our meanings for the word "dog" are only coordinated at a very general level. Those experiencing only retrievers assume that any dog will fetch a ball (they may think the trick is getting a dog to *stop* retrieving). But pointer owners have watched their dogs freeze and point at the ball, whereas guard dogs protect it and some who know rottweilers or pit bulls by reputation wonder why anyone would want a dog to be running at them full speed, ball or no ball. Coordinated Management of Meaning (CMM) theorists focus on the ways that persons negotiate or coordinate their meanings, and they do this by considering the communication rules that they bring to their interactions.

CMM theory differentiates between constitutive rules and regulative rules. *Constitutive rules* define the elements of the game. To play cards, for example, we need to know whether to use jokers, whether the aces are high or low and whether we need a 52-card poker deck or a 48-card pinochle deck. To play basketball we need to know at least the height and diameter of the basket, the dimensions of the ball, and the size of the court.

Regulative rules govern the sequence of play – who does what, and in what order. Rules vary in their complexity, and people vary in their understanding of the rules. Communication difficulties generally arise when people try to coordinate their meanings using different rule sets (as when I converse as though we are friends, but you listen as if we are employer and employee), when people have different conceptions of the rules (as when a divorced person begins to date after many years of marriage), or when the rules are unknown, or crystal clear but inappropriate. Sometimes these rules need to be developed or negotiated, and other times they need to be discovered or explicated.

How can we apply our discussion of rules to election campaigns? First we citizens are not simply idle spectators or observers – *we are the participants*. If you study presidential elections assuming that citizens are mere television viewers watching a sports event or some show like "America's Favorite Chef" you are trying to coordinate meaning using the wrong rules. It is an interactive game like "American Idol" in which the viewers' votes count.

Second, ours is a diverse country of many people with honest disagreements. Each person's views have as much value as any other person's views, whether those views have been dutifully researched, carefully reasoned, or neither. Every vote counts equally and candidates are at least as likely to attempt to coordinate with the poorly informed as with the intelligentsia. To paraphrase Abraham Lincoln, "The Lord must have loved the marginally informed, he made so many of them." To put it bluntly, you are not always part of the us with whom a candidate is trying to coordinate – and that alone does not make the candidate either wrong or sleazy. After all, the candidate wants to be their president as well as yours, so you cannot reasonably expect all the attention, especially if that candidate already has your support or can never hope to win it.

Third, candidates are bound by a variety of rules – some legal, some traditional expectations – of which you are unaware. You need not acquaint yourself with all of them, but it is prudent to recognize that *sometimes* candidates' hands are tied.

In the final analysis, though, the crucial thing to remember is that the rules themselves are the results of previous rhetorical struggles. People struggled for the right to make the rules, and they decided that the best way to solve the next problem would be henceforth to require (or prohibit) certain options. Rules change because people rewrite them when they dislike how they shape the tournament.

Wise political campaigns therefore study the rules and use them to their advantage. They do this by avoiding activities that will incur punishments and by doing those things that the rules reward. Additionally, they strive to offer persuasive appeals that mesh with the intended audience's rules (or norms) to magnify the effects of their message on individual citizens, and they strive to characterize their opponents as operating in violation of the audience's norms or rules.

Herbert Simons (1970, 1982) developed the requirements-problems-strategies approach to collective rhetorics to study social movement persuasion and extended it to instances where people speak on behalf of organizations, including political campaigns. Simons wrote that such speakers face imperatives that constitute *rhetorical requirements* that must be met. Laws and party rules provide such imperatives for campaigns. Simons further observed that "conflicts among requirements create *rhetorical problems* which in turn affect decisions on *rhetorical strategy*" (1970, p. 2). He noted that

> There are inevitable tensions between goals and rules, between the moral and the political, between members' role requirements and their personal values, between the need for ideological consistency and the need to adapt to new realities, between the need for organizational cohesiveness and the need of individual members to assert their individual and group interests against the interests of other individuals and groups within the organization, and even against the interests of the organization as a whole. (1982, p. 182)

Simons was describing the candidate's rhetorical puzzle with an emphasis on the imperatives or requirements.

In the context of presidential campaigns laws and rules provide the imperative requirements that candidates must meet if they hope to succeed. But the laws of fifty states and the rules of two parties will inevitably rub against one another, and the interests of various groups will motivate them to differently interpret the applicable laws and rules resulting in problems that require strategic rhetorical decisions.

The democratic spirit frequently leads us to say, "Let's put it to a vote." But who votes, and when? How are the votes counted? Is the ballot secret? Must votes be cast for a finite number of alternatives, or will "write-in" options be permitted? How is the winner determined, and what happens if there is a tie or no winner? Clearly, *elections are rule governed.* The institutional authority that sanctions an election provides its constitutive rules. But as Kathleen E. Kendall has observed, "Campaign studies rarely focus on the rules" (2000, p. 30; Lengle and Shafer, 1976). We turn now to the study of election laws and party rules to see how they impact strategic decisions.

Governmental Election Laws

The Constitution (as amended) prescribes a presidential election every four years and constituted the electoral college. Each state constituted its own elections. But because those in power write the rules state legislators often wrote or revised election laws in ways that structurally advantaged the nominees of their major parties and disadvantaged other parties.

The multiple sets of election rules provide checks and balances in the spirit of federalism. The founders could have written constitutive rules that elected the president with a majority of the popular votes had they wished to do so. Why did they not? The Articles of Confederation had failed them by providing insufficient centralization, yet many people still feared that a central government would swallow the states and cost them their self-governance. The electoral college was a compromise that combined state level representation, popular vote, and the weighting of smaller and larger states. Most presidents have characterized themselves as "president of all the people," but that is not precisely what the founders intended. Instead, as Al Gore learned the hard way in 2000, we get the president of the majority of the electors.

The beauty of the federal system designed by the founders is that each state writes its own election rules, most of which are refined and implemented by county and local boards of elections. Paradoxically, that is one of its chief frustrations. Again we are reminded that the founders could have streamlined their electoral processes had they wanted to do so. But they sought protection of the states as well as individuals in complicated procedures that we have come to refer to collectively as "checks and balances" and federalism. Why bother to design and micromanage a state level electoral system acceptable to all states when all you really need are their results?

The founders constituted a sort of presidential poker tournament with thirteen original state game tables. Some tables were worth more than others because each state's number of electors was equal to its two senators plus its house members. But each table's players constituted the kind of poker they would play – Texas Hold-em, Five Card Stud and so on – and regulated play. The winners from the thirteen tables advance to the electoral college game with chips reflecting the importance of their respective tables. As more states joined the country they got their tables and chose their version of poker. The President of the United States is similarly the person who wins the electoral tournament of individualized state contests.

Winning the electoral tournament means winning not one election but a variety of state level contests, much as teams win athletic championships by winning the season and post-season games that take them to the title game and then the Big Game. This requires campaigns to understand a wide variety of state level laws. It should also require reporters covering the elections to understand the rules. It is hard to imagine a play-by-play announcer not knowing whether a tie game had ended or required overtime, or whether that overtime meant playing an extra period or until a "sudden-death" outcome. Yet television reporters were startled to learn late on the night of the 2000 election that Florida law required an automatic recount whenever the margin of victory was less than half of one percent. Studying rules may not be exciting but knowledge of the rules is an important resource, and ignorance of them can be problematic.

Although a thorough examination of each state's election laws is beyond the scope of this book, an Internet search engine can easily provide information on different states' election laws. Some states, however, have similar rules. All of these rules make it essential for presidential campaigns to maintain extensive legal staffs lest they miss a filing deadline, get a late start on voter registration drives, solicit or spend funds illegally or simply campaign unwisely.

Campaign Funding Laws

We cannot discuss election laws without attending to laws governing the raising and spending of campaign dollars. There is an old saying that "Money is the mother's milk of politics." It means that a campaign cannot be healthy and grow without money. But just as none of us lives by mother's milk alone, raw dollars alone do not determine the outcome of an election. Campaign funds can be raised in ways that undermine a campaign's credibility, and the dollars raised can be spent unwisely. Nevertheless, campaign funding is very important and those who have been elected frequently attempt to regulate the cash flow.

Campaign funds come from three sources: individuals, Political Action Committees (PACs), and public campaign financing. Corporations, labor unions, federal government contractors, and foreign nationals are not allowed to contribute to campaigns. Federal law limits the amount that may be contributed in a calendar year by an individual and by a PAC as indicated in Table 3.1 below.

All donors and contributions of more than $200 must be recorded and reported, and are eventually a matter of public record.

Each of us has the choice of donating one dollar of our federal income tax to the public financing program. It provides funding for eligible candidates in either or both of two phases, the primary period (prior to the roll call vote) and the

Table 3.1. Campaign Funds

	To a candidate	To a National Party Committee
Individual	$2,300	$28,500
PAC	$5,000	$15,000
National Party Committee	$5,000	No limit
State, District and Local Party Committees	$5,000 combined	No limit
PAC (multicandidate)	$5,000	$15,000
PAC (not multicandidate)	$2,300	$28,500
Authorized Campaign Committee	$2,000	No limit

Source: http://www.fec.gov/pages/brochures/contriblimits.jpg

general election; it also provides grants for conventions, but only the Republican and Democratic parties have the numbers to qualify for these grants. To qualify for public financing a candidate must raise at least $5,000 from donors in each of twenty different states. If they do that, the Presidential Election Campaign Fund will match the first $250 of each donation, but the campaign must accept a spending limit (adjusted for inflation) that was $42.05 million in 2008. The party's nominee can request a general election grant to cover all campaign expenses and agree not to seek funds from individuals, PACS or party committees. The 2008 grant amount was $84.1 million.

Let us consider two recent cases in which funding rules played an important role in presidential campaign communication decisions.

Strategic Implications: Kerry's 2004 Swift Boat Dilemma

John Kerry, John Edwards, and Howard Dean all declined public financing of their 2004 primary campaigns. Several advisors and fundraisers urged Kerry to forego the $75 million general election grant. One unnamed fundraiser told the *New York Times,* "I don't think it makes sense to stay in the system. I think you could raise $30 million a month based on current trends" (Rutenberg and Justice 2004). But the Kerry campaign took the public funding.

Kerry's acceptance address emphasized his military record. "I'm John Kerry and I'm reporting for duty" he began. He challenged his listeners to judge him by his record, saying, "I defended this country as a young man, and I will defend it as president." He invoked his military service and spoke of his comrades in arms. Kerry pointed to a gigantic flag above him and said:

> You see that flag up there. We call her Old Glory, the stars and stripes forever. I fought under that flag, as did so many of those people who were here tonight and all across the country. That flag flew from the gun turret right behind my head and it was shot through and through and tattered, but it never ceased to wave in the wind. It draped the caskets of men that I served with and friends I grew up with. For us, that flag is the most powerful symbol of who we are and what we

John Kerry from 2004; author's own image.

> believe in: our strength, our diversity, our love of country, all that makes America
> both great and good. That flag doesn't belong to any president. It doesn't belong
> to any ideology. It doesn't belong to any party. It belongs to all the American
> people. (Kerry 2004)

John Kerry's acceptance address may have done more than any other single event to bridge the Vietnam era divide between Democrats and military values and sentiments. It provided a major component of his personal record by which he asked to be judged. When the speech ended the federal spending limits took effect with Kerry leading Bush in projected electoral votes, 330–210 (Electoral-vote.com 2004).

On August 20 the Swift Boat Veterans for Truth aired a commercial that challenged Kerry's patriotism and military record. It combined portions of his 1971 testimony to Congress on behalf of Vietnam Veterans Against the War and other statements about atrocities committed by American soldiers. News reports and talk shows picked up the topic. Six days later they aired a second ad that challenged accounts of Kerry's heroism. Kerry had challenged Americans to examine his record and the Swift Boat Veterans for Truth were doing just that. The group was not a PAC but a "527" – a tax exempt group spending its money not to advocate the election of a candidate but to discuss issues, yet the potential damage to Kerry's candidacy was obvious to all.

By the time the Republican National Convention convened on August 30 Bush had pulled ahead of Kerry in projected electoral votes, 305–240. The President accepted his renomination and became subject to spending limits on September 2 – 35 days after Kerry's spending had been limited.

The spending laws created a predicament for Kerry from which he never recovered. The Swift Boat Veterans for Truth were an independent 527 group allowed to use their resources on issues, and they never said "vote for Bush" or "vote against Kerry." Moreover, federal law prohibited any communication between the independent 527 the Swift Boat Veterans for Truth and the Bush people, so the Kerry campaign could not prove a connection between the Bush campaign and the ads and the Bush people could say that they were prohibited from interfering with the group's advertising. News and talk shows drew attention to the issue even when they critiqued the ads and demonstrated their flaws. That left the Kerry people to consider spending their limited funding on ads to answer the ads. But to do so would not prolong the controversy, it would reduce the funding available for October.

Strategic Implication: Obama's 2008 Reversal on Public Financing

Barack Obama's campaign raised $750 million and shattered all records for presidential campaign fundraising. Instead of running a publicly funded $85 million general election campaign, he *raised* $460 million during that period and was able to spend it without regard to federal limits. The rhetorical problem he faced was that he had indicated that he would accept public financing and limits if his Republican opponent agreed to do so.

To understand the relationship among money, rules, and communication we must first look at the rhetorical situation from the campaign's perspective. Obama's fundraising team hoped to raise $10–15 million in January depending on their Iowa finish, but they raised $28 million with 90 percent of that total coming in donations of less than $100 (Luo 2008). Obama's representatives asked the Federal Election Commission about public financing and they spoke of using it if the Republican candidate agreed to do so. But recollections vary as to whether they "pledged" to do so or simply discussed it as a possibility. *Politico*'s Ben Smith followed this question from the beginning:

> I first pressed Obama's camp on this particular point more than a year ago, on Feb. 7, 2007, when they first floated the notion. And they deliberately preserved some wiggle room then. "We're looking to see if we can preserve the option," spokesman Bill Burton said, when asked if the campaign was committing, conditionally, to public financing, I asked Burton again today if this was a "pledge," and he repeated that it's an "option." "The only reason this is an option is because we pursued the decision from the FEC.   (Smith 2008).

MSNBC (2007) carried a brief story the next day that provided more information about the Obama campaign's proposal to the FEC. "Obama is asking whether he can take money from donors who want him to be president, then give it back later. The Federal Election Commission said Wednesday that it will look into the novel question."

But the McCain campaign felt they had a deal with Obama to finance both campaigns publicly if they were both nominated. To prove it they sent Smith a

New York Times article that characterized the plan as a "promise" twice in the first two paragraphs. But neither use of the word "promise" was a direct quotation nor did the story mention any documents. The word "promise" belonged to reporter David Kirkpatrick, and it is hard to tell whether either or both candidates "promised" or committed to a "deal" or if that was Kirkparick's original contribution. Nevertheless, the McCain camp read it as proof of an Obama commitment.

By July, McCain and Obama had secured the delegates they needed for nomination and were looking toward the financing of the general election. Because Obama had raised $390 million to McCain's $153 million (Morain 2008) public financing's spending limits would advantage McCain and disadvantage Obama. But declining public financing would create an uncomfortable issue for Obama.

Obama closed the public financing option on June 19. He argued that his emphasis on an unprecedented number of small contributions was actually a better form of public financing. "It's not an easy decision, and especially because I support a robust system of public financing of elections," he said, "But the public financing of presidential elections as it exists today is broken" (Muskal 2008). Debaters recognize this as an argument to better attain present goals through a different mechanism.

Obama also invoked memories of the Swift Boat attacks and ads critical of his pastor, Rev. Jeremiah Wright, saying that the campaign needed to be prepared to defend itself against "smear" tactics.

> John McCain's campaign and the Republican National Committee are fuelled by contributions from Washington lobbyists and special-interest PACs. And we've already seen that he's not going to stop the smears and attacks from his allies running so-called 527 groups, who will spend millions and millions of dollars in unlimited donations.   (Muskal 2008)

Thus we were to understand Obama's reversal not as a fault but as a prudent response to a broken system and past Republican treachery. Yet by suggesting it when he did – after all the talk of promises and deals – Obama's position was widely regarded as a reversal, a betrayal, or a flip-flop.

The McCain campaign quickly responded, treating Obama's reversal as evidence of a character flaw.

> "Today, Barack Obama has revealed himself to be just another typical politician who will do and say whatever is most expedient for Barack Obama," McCain's communications director, Jill Hazelbaker, said in a statement. "The true test of a candidate for president is whether he will stand on principle and keep his word to the American people. Barack Obama has failed that test today, and his reversal of his promise to participate in the public finance system undermines his call for a new type of politics.   (Muskal 2008)

McCain had long advocated public financing, and a debate over this reform was not a good topic for a candidate trailing his opponent by $237 million. But it was a godsend as a vehicle for undercutting Obama's character and his slogan of "Change You Can Believe In."

The 2008 public financing controversy illustrates how election laws shape a campaign's rhetorical resources. The laws regulate who can contribute to whom and thus influence the financial resources with which they can press their respective cases. Additionally, the candidates' ethical commitments to various funding schemes provide vehicles for them to enact their commitments to initiative (fundraising), populism (number of small donors), and free market funding and spending vs. government regulated enterprise. Interestingly, the 2008 controversy undermined Obama' character primarily among those who did not support him (if we attend to continuing fundraising and popular votes), but he gained millions more dollars, avoided spending limits, demonstrated that he knew how to play hardball politics, and positioned himself to press for campaign finance reform from the winner's perspective. McCain, on the other hand, found one of his pet projects crumbling during his own presidential contest and he found himself supporting government involvement instead of the freedom of the market.

Political Party Rules

Political parties are not governments; they are public organizations rather like clubs. Parties have rules that they enforce rather than laws enforced by the courts. Although one can officially join a party, belonging to a party is largely a state of mind and all one need do to switch parties is change one's mind. Consider the odyssey of Senator Joe Lieberman of Connecticut.

Lieberman was the 2000 Democratic vice-presidential nominee who later lost in his state's Democratic primary. He then won his Senate seat as an Independent and continued to work with the Democrats. But Lieberman supported the Iraq war and he became in 2008 a vocal and visible supporter of his old friend John McCain, the Republican nominee; McCain reportedly wanted Lieberman as his vice-presidential nominee. Lieberman's speech at the Republican convention was critical of Senator Obama and the Democrats, and he frequently appeared with McCain at campaign rallies. After the election many Democrats wanted Lieberman removed from the Senate Democratic Caucus, but President-elect Obama dissuaded them and he continues to be an Independent senator who supported the Republican nominee and works with the Democratic majority. Even at the top, it seems, party identification is a state of mind.

By winning a major party's nomination one can count on roughly a third of the votes – considerably more than any Independent can expect. This is like campus Homecoming Court elections in which the nominees from large sororities, clubs, and departments can expect more votes than the nominee of the Stamp Club. Frequently, the most interesting contests are those seeking to win the major party nominations. The reason these nominations are so important in presidential politics is that a major party nominee is assured of a place on the ballot in all 50 state ballots, thereby enabling them to compete for all the electoral votes. Despite their considerable support Ross Perot, Ralph Nader, George Wallace, and many other Independent and minor party candidates had to spend substantial effort just to get onto state ballots.

As a club or non-governmental organization each party establishes the rules for its own contests, and those of us who merely identify with them normally pay little attention to their rules. Much as the president is chosen by the electoral college, the party nominee is chosen by the delegates to the national party convention.

Each party establishes its own arbitrary number of delegates and allocates them according to their rules. In 2008 that meant a Democrat needed to win the commitments of 2,104 delegates and a Republican needed 1,230,

The Rise of Primaries

Party officials once picked their candidates in the proverbial "smoke-filled rooms." But by 1900 reformers including the Progressive Movement were urging primary elections in which citizens would narrow the field of candidates. A *primary* is an election held by one party as opposed to a *caucus* which is a meeting, not an election. Caucuses grew out of the American tradition of the town meeting. People gather together in public places or even homes to discuss their governance. When people caucus to select leaders or delegates they converse, then vote. This ordinarily takes more time than voting (although, in fairness, one probably should count the time spent waiting in line to vote). But a caucus has the inherent potential to build and enhance personal working relationships. At a caucus you can tell people that your street needs its potholes repaired and you may learn why that is a more complicated problem than you had thought. The caucus might ask you to take on a position of responsibility in the community, and you may find that the people with whom you deeply disagree are actually nice people. None of these things happen in a primary election where you vote by secret ballot and go home.

The 1912 campaign was the first in which multiple primaries were held in a presidential campaign (Kendall 2000) but they remained a secondary influence until 1960 when Senator John F. Kennedy used primaries in West Virginia and Wisconsin to derail the apparently certain nomination of Senator Hubert H. Humphrey of Minnesota.

By 1968 President Lyndon B. Johnson's Democrats were deeply divided. His support of equal rights for all Americans had alienated conservative Democrats, especially in the deep south, and Alabama Governor George C. Wallace ran as the American Independent Party candidate. Meanwhile, Johnson's pursuit of the war in Vietnam incurred opposition from the left. Senator Eugene McCarthy challenged Johnson in the New Hampshire primary and Senator Robert F. Kennedy also entered the race. With liberal and conservative Democrats abandoning him President Johnson announced on March 31 that he would neither seek nor accept his party's nomination. Robert Kennedy's victory in the California primary on June 6 propelled him into the lead for the nomination when, moments later, he was shot and killed. The resulting Democratic convention in Chicago was a fiasco. Anti-war protestors charged that the party leadership was unfairly blocking anti-war candidates to advantage Vice-President Humphrey, who received the nomination. Police dragged reporters from the hall and clashed with demonstrators in the streets, in what the Kerner Commission would later call a "police riot."

With the Democrats thus splintered, Richard Nixon won a 301–191 electoral vote majority by edging Humphrey by less than 3 percent in states with 84 electoral votes. Wallace won four states with 46 electoral votes and changed significantly the pool of voters to be divided between Nixon and Humphrey in the battleground states. Thus, despite polling only 512,000 votes more than Humphrey (0.5%), Nixon won the election. But the Democratic Party was in ruins.

The Democrats responded to the 1968 debacle by creating the McGovern–Frasier Commission to revise their nomination rules. Foremost among the reforms was the requirement that states open their nomination process to citizens. The Commission ended the winner-take-all rule in Democrats' contests for delegates. Henceforth, all candidates receiving 15 percent of a Democratic primary's votes would divide proportionately that state's convention delegates. This reduced the likelihood that any candidate could quickly win the nomination with a handful of close primary victories. The second important reform was that each state's delegation had to be representative of minority populations.

The Democrats first used their new system in 1972, nominating Senator George McGovern who knew the new rules better than anyone else. The Republican Party eventually adopted many – but not all – of the Democrats' reforms. Today it is not unusual to have differently conducted Democratic and Republican primaries on the same day or to have their primaries held on different days. Some states hold "binding primaries" that commit the delegates to vote for a particular candidate at the convention, while others elect uncommitted delegates and hold a presidential preference ballot or "beauty contest."

The most important change since 1972 is that both parties' nomination systems are handled through a system of primary elections and caucuses in which "The People" determine the delegates and thus the nominations. But one indirect result is that a run for the White House now entails a long string of costly state campaigns; hence, fundraising and political money have become increasingly important since the 1972 reforms. Every solution carries the seeds of a new problem.

One member of the McGovern–Frasier Commission was Iowa Governor Harold Hughes, and he had to meld his Party's new rules with his state's rules. Fortuitously, Iowans had been gathering together in a system of annual caucuses since before statehood. Hughes reasoned that Iowa Democrats could, every four years, pick their convention delegates along with handling their local business. Ed Muskie, Humphrey's 1968 vice-presidential candidate, quietly finished just behind "uncommitted" in 1972's Iowa presidential precinct caucuses. Who knew where that would lead? In 1976 Georgia Governor Jimmy Carter abandoned his New Hampshire campaign and flew to Iowa to campaign for the caucus vote, to the consternation of his staff. Like Muskie, Carter finished second to "uncommitted" but the press proclaimed him the winner and the myth of Iowa's importance was born.

The Primary Schedule and the Issue of Frontloading

State parties try to schedule their primary at the most strategic time. New Hampshire law requires that its primary be the first in the nation, but Iowa's precinct caucuses can be held first because they are not primaries. Conventional wisdom and popular mythology hold that Iowa and New Hampshire disproportionately influence, and perhaps even determine, the eventual nominees. Several states have therefore reasoned that they could become more influential if they, too, had earlier primaries. This has given rise to the phenomenon referred to as *frontloading* the nomination process – disproportionately scheduling too many contests early in the campaign.

Like a game, a campaign can begin with the question, "Is it better to play first or last?" It often seems advantageous to play first even though the game cannot be won with one move. But when a football team wins the coin toss it ordinarily defers the choice until the second half. The 2007 college football championship game began with Ohio State returning the opening kickoff 93 yards for a touchdown and a 7–0 lead; but the final score was Florida 41, Ohio State 14. No game is won in the first quarter, as many Iowa caucus winners can attest. Games have key turning points, many of which can be identified by the rules, and others can be inferred from the rhetorical puzzles created by the rules. That may be why home baseball teams get to bat last and walk away with the victory. In short, the desirability of playing first or last depends on the objective of the game and its timetable.

The presidential nomination game requires a candidate to amass a majority of the party's convention delegates. So the strategic question should not be "Is it better to play first?" but "When will the outcome be decided?" Delegate counts could accumulate quickly in the days of winner-take-all contests, but proportional results have slowed that process considerably. Although the decision point for nomination now occurs well in advance of the party conventions it cannot occur immediately after Iowa and New Hampshire that together distribute only about 3 percent of the total delegates. The requirement to remember is that neither party's nomination can be won or lost after Iowa and New Hampshire. The problem is that states frontloading their primaries remove themselves from the point of decision. Still the issue of frontloading persists.

As an alternative to frontloading, states seeking to enhance their influence on the selection process ought to seek likely strategic tipping points along the campaign trail and position themselves there. This is precisely what happened in 2008 as the extended contest for nomination made the late primary states of Pennsylvania, North Carolina, and Montana important – a scenario that surprised even those states.

Strategic Implications: The Myth of Hillary Clinton's Quick Nomination

Under the McGovern–Frasier rules used by the Democrats since 1972, every state's delegates are divided proportionately among all candidates receiving 15 percent of the votes cast. The first and second-place candidates often win comparable delegates and the winner rarely leaves with a huge share relative to the others. The crucial objective for a Democratic candidate is to draw 15 percent of the vote to get a seat at the table when the delegates are divided, with the stakes increasing as the number of candidates shrinks.

By late 2007 many polls showed Hillary Clinton surpassing the 50 percent support threshold among Democrats. This led to speculation that she would win lots of primaries and quickly capture the nomination. But party rules could reward her with only a proportion of the delegates in each contest. Since those polls also showed Barack Obama above the 15 percent threshold and John Edwards hovering around it, one might better have projected that Clinton would accumulate 50–60 percent of the available delegates with Edwards and Obama splitting the rest. Clearly, she would lead the others, but Democratic rules for allocating delegates could not enable her to seal quickly the nomination. Although the 28 Democratic contests scheduled through February 10 were to allocate 306 more delegates than required for the nomination, Clinton could mathematically clinch the nomination by then only if she alone cleared the 15 percent minimum in every contest. This was unlikely because 69 percent of the respondents had yet to decide upon a favorite Democrat a month before Iowa. If Clinton won 60 percent of the vote in all 28 contests with Obama and Edwards barely clearing the 15 percent hurdle she could have won as many as 60 percent of the delegates; but Clinton would have been 774 delegates short of nomination.

Would Clinton's campaign then still have the look of the formidable juggernaut portrayed by the press, or would she appear to commentators as losing ground to her opponents? Would her opponents not appear to be surprisingly resilient and popular? As rules determine the technical outcome any failure to fully understand the implications of the rules influences the news reports that affect public perceptions, campaign contributions and candidates' prospects.

Democratic Party rules always undermine their frontrunners' efforts to win quickly in a crowded field. Obama won delegates in states that Clinton never expected to need – Alaska, Idaho, Montana, Nebraska, North Dakota, Utah, and Wyoming – to supplement the proportions that he won even when she fared well.

Strategic Implications: Super Tuesday 1988

The 1988 Super Tuesday fiasco provides another illustration of the importance of timing. In the 1980s many Democrats were concerned that liberal candidates had failed to run well nationally. To draw them toward the right, they reasoned, they should route them through the southern states so that they would have to adapt to an audience of more conservative voters. They did this by establishing "Super Tuesday" with ten southern states holding their primaries on the same day. The results were not quite as anticipated, as liberals Michael Dukakis and Jesse Jackson won most of the delegates and Al Gore placed third. Gore, the southern candidate, was left to battle Dukakis and Jackson in the northeast and midwest. Meanwhile, no Democrat had to visit the south from Super Tuesday in March until the post-convention campaign in September, and the New Englander Dukakis did not exactly bet the ranch on winning Mississippi and Alabama. But what would have happened if those ten states had scheduled one primary every six days for sixty days? Then all of the candidates would have been in the south for two months or more. Instead of dealing with "southern issues" in one week's worth of television ads, they would have needed to balance continually their southern and non-southern audiences week after week. One of Michael Dukakis's lasting contributions to campaign lore was his observation that the race for the nomination is a marathon, not a sprint. Dukakis meant that candidates need to pick up the delegates they can in each contest without exhausting the resources they will need for the long haul.

Strategic Implications: Winner-Take-All

As the states hold their primaries and caucuses the parties allocate their convention delegates to the candidates according to the rules in place. The race for the nomination is *officially* over when the delegates conduct the roll call of states at the party convention. But because so many of those delegates are bound (at least for a ballot or two) by the results of their state's primary or caucus the nomination is *technically* settled whenever one candidate has won a majority of the party's convention delegates. Most likely, the race *effectively* ends when all the candidates but one end their campaigns and join in support of the survivor. The Republican Party continues to permit winner-take-all contests and they hasten the effective end of the contest for nomination.

In 1988 George H. W. Bush edged Bob Dole in the New Hampshire primary and Dole accused the Bush campaign of misrepresenting his record. Republican Super Tuesday contests included ten winner-take-all primaries that accounted for 488 delegates – far more than had been won to date. Bush won all ten states to pull ahead of Dole 488–0. The contest for the nomination was essentially over, even though an average of 93 percent of registered Republicans had chosen not to vote in those ten primaries. The lesson is that Republican candidates have crucial building blocks toward nomination.

In 2008 winner-take-all contests included California, Connecticut and Delaware. A modified approach awarded each congressional district's delegates to the district's winner and the state's at-large delegates to the statewide winner in Michigan, South Carolina, Florida, Georgia, Oklahoma, and Tennessee among the early contests.

Former New York Mayor Rudy Giuliani held commanding leads in all California, Connecticut, and Delaware in October of 2007, suggesting a 219 delegate lead over his competitors. Giuliani would be difficult to defeat with proportional wins – unless he stumbled badly before those February 5 primaries. Indeed, he first encountered difficulties in Iowa and withdrew, then withdrew from the January 8 New Hampshire primary and banked everything on Florida's January 29 winner-take-all primary. Giuliani drew only 15 percent of the Florida vote and never made it to the winner-take-all states that had looked so promising for him.

Giuliani was losing the Enterprisers to Mitt Romney while Mike Huckabee of Arkansas had support from Social Conservatives and Pro-Government Conservatives seemed to like Fred Thompson. But as these "favorites" bumped heads John McCain attracted enough votes in the winner-take-all states to win their delegates. He outdistanced his rivals by 250 delegates in these six states while averaging less than 40 percent of the vote.

Strategic Implications: The 2008 Michigan and Florida Delegations

The Democratic Party sought to referee the frontloading stampede by adopting a rule that it would decide which states would be allowed to hold their primaries

Table 3.2. Delegate Support for Republican Candidates

	McCain %	McCain Delegates	Romney Delegates	Huckabee Delegates
Michigan	30		26	4
South Carolina	33	19		5
Florida	36	57		
California	42	155		
Connecticut	52	27		
Delaware	45	18		
	Avg. 39.6	276	26	9

Source of data: CNN.com

earlier than February 5. They selected Wyoming, Nevada, and South Carolina to provide a geographic balance to Iowa and New Hampshire. But none of those are among the most populous states, and that failed to satisfy the larger states. The first problem arose when the Florida legislature voted to hold its primary on January 29 – one week ahead of the party's approved date. Florida officials were determined to challenge the Democratic Party's rule. Probably all too happy to throw some fuel on the fire, Republican House Speaker Marco Rubio said,

> We have people who get invited to a big party where they drop a balloon and people wear funny hats . . . But they don't have any role to play. At the end of the day, the truth of the matter is that the nominee of either party is going to want to make sure they have not offended the big donors and the biggest activists in the most important state in the country that is electorally available.   (Goodnough, 2007)

Should the Democratic Party punish Florida for this decision? It was, after all, Florida in which the slimmest of Republican margins made George W. Bush President. But a lack of enforcement would only add momentum to the front-loading movement that they sought to slow, and it would sorely test the support of the states that complied with the February 5 date. On the other hand, the date of the Florida state election was determined not by the Florida Democratic Party but by the state government – a Republican legislature and a Republican gover-nor. The Republicans in state government had found a way to ensnare Florida's Democrats in their own party's rules. Faced with this choice, the Democratic National Committee voted to allocate 0 convention delegates to Florida, and the candidates abandoned the state.

Undeterred by the Florida case, Michigan voted to move its primary to January 15. This not only violated the Democrats' February 5 rule, it moved Michigan ahead of New Hampshire, whose state law requires it to have the first primary. But the internal dynamics are important. Katharine Q. Seelye reported that a Michigan primary would draw two million voters and a caucus perhaps 100,000. Senator Clinton led in Michigan and wanted the primary, so her opponents did not. The John Edwards campaign was managed by former Michigan Congressman David

Bonior who had a good working relationship with labor. They reasoned that the unions' proven ability to mobilize supporters would have a greater impact on caucuses than on a primary (Seelye 2007). They mobilized enough votes in the legislature to move the primary and the Democratic Party predictably penalized Michigan. Cancelling the primary disadvantaged Clinton and slowed her march to the nomination but it did nothing for Edwards.

As Clinton and Obama struggled for delegates the Florida and Michigan questions plagued the party. Michiganders proposed a new primary for March and the national party accepted the idea – if Michigan paid for the election since they caused the problem. The primary was never held, and Obama sealed the nomination with a May 7 victory in North Carolina despite a narrow loss to Clinton in Indiana. The presidential preferences of Democrats in Michigan and Florida – two of the largest states – remained uncounted as Obama and Clinton struggled to the finish line.

Democratic Party officials met in Washington on June 1, 2008 to resolve the Michigan and Florida question before the last primaries. Senator Clinton sought to have all delegates seated with full voting powers. Her position would accomplish two instrumental goals. First, adding the 367 disputed delegates to the total would have increased the mathematical majority needed to win the nomination by 184, and at that time Obama was only 42 delegates away from victory. Much as the Edwards people had moved the Michigan primary to slow Clinton's anticipated nomination, Clinton sought to add delegates to the total to delay Obama's victory. The second objective was to emerge with a net gain of 111 disputed delegates that would reduce Obama's lead from 202 to 91 (Nicholas and Hook 2008). In short, Clinton's plan would change their standing relative to nomination from Obama -42 and Clinton -244 to Obama -226 and Clinton -317. But winning required Clinton's advocates to justify overriding her party's rule and its prior decision without any sanctions whatsoever.

The Obama campaign offered a surprising response. Instead of arguing that the Florida and Michigan delegates should not be seated or that they should be seated without votes, they agreed that all the delegates be seated but with only one-half vote each. Obama could afford to be generous because his proposal would provide Clinton with a net gain of only 55.5 and a less troubling extension of the total needed for victory. The Obama plan would put him -134 with Clinton at -281. Obama's plan recognized party rules and maintained some sanction against the states that had violated the rule. The Party adopted Obama's proposal endorsing a norm of reasoned compromise and respect for their rules.

Obama began working with Clinton to consolidate the party. In August he wrote a letter urging the Democratic Party to grant full votes to the Florida and Michigan delegates, and they did. When the roll call of states reached New York it was Senator Clinton who moved that the convention nominate Obama by acclamation, rendering the final delegate count meaningless.

The Florida and Michigan cases illustrate how rules themselves can prove to be the fitting instrumental responses to a rhetorical exigency. Florida's flaunting of the Democratic Party rules makes sense when one considers their Republican legislature. Florida *is* important, but it is rarely necessary to confront rule systems during the rule governed process. It is normally much wiser to strategically exploit the rules in force. Rather than bucking the tide, campaigns should analyze the rules to see how else they can enhance their strategic importance. Incurring punishment from the Democratic National Committee is not a fitting instrumental response – unless you are a Republican.

It can also be appropriate if you have little chance to win your primary, which is what happened in Michigan. Michigan Democrats seeking either to defeat or to slow Hillary Clinton's nomination found that violating party rules would punish the state in a way that was disproportionately hurtful to her campaign. This reduced the urgency of catching the frontrunner Clinton by taking the Michigan (as well as Florida) chips off the proverbial table.

Edwards, Clinton and Obama each in succession attempted to use the rules to advance their objectives. This is not quite to say that they "played by the rules" but more precisely that they "played the rules." The Edwards campaign violated the rule to keep Clinton from winning primary delegates that could quickly end the contest. Clinton sought to have the violations ignored to forestall Obama's victory and shrink his lead. Obama sought a compromise on the enforcement of the rules to maintain his lead and, later, to consolidate the party. It seems likely that Democrats will reconsider this rule and its enforcement before 2012.

Summary and Conclusions

This chapter began with the premise that laws and rules define many of the fitting responses of political campaigns. CMM theory showed us that humans use constitutive rules to define their activities and regulative rules to coordinate their choices within those activities. We also saw that rules and laws establish imperative requirements for campaigns that often conflict to create problems that require strategic decisions.

Governments craft election laws. We saw that:

- The Constitution determines who wins the presidency.
- State laws govern their elections and determine the electors.
- Campaign finance laws regulate who can contribute how much money to whom and how it can be spent.

We considered the some strategic implications of these laws:

- John Kerry declined to use his restricted general election funds to answer the 2004 Swift Boat attacks to save them for late advertising.
- Barack Obama declined public financing in 2008 to avoid those spending limits but had to defend against criticism for reversing his position.

Political parties establish and enforce rules for their members. We saw that:

- Both parties turned increasingly to primary elections and caucuses after 1912.
- The Democrats abolished winner-take-all delegate contests after 1968 and allocate delegates proportionately. The Republicans allow both methods.
- Each party schedules its primaries and many states seek to hold early contests even before delegate majorities can be determined.

We considered some strategic implications of these party rules, including:

- The unlikelihood of a quick Hillary Clinton nomination in 2008.
- The failure of the 1988 Super Tuesday plan to produce a more conservative Democratic nominee.
- The important of winner-take-all contests for Republican nominations.
- The intentional violation of Democratic rules in 2008 by the Republican controlled Florida legislature and Michigan Democrats seeking to slow Clinton's momentum.

Communication in the electoral arena is guided by a complex web of national, state and local laws and national and state political party rules. These laws and rules are written and rewritten by people to solve yesterday's puzzles. They are then interpreted and applied in unfolding situations. Awareness of the rules is essential for the candidates, it can help reporters tell us what is really going on, and it can help citizens to be effective participants.

Rules provide mechanisms for coordinating persuasive activities. But they are not static. Rules are embedded in language and they are interpreted both by the participants and by the authorities that enforce them. Candidates who understand this can minimize the predicaments they encounter and create positive fitting response to their rhetorical puzzles.

But the rules governing the tasks of the campaign are themselves part of the challenge. Those who help the candidate can exploit the rules as the Florida Republicans did when they managed to have their opponents' convention delegates withdrawn. They can also violate the rules to incur punishments, as Michigan Democrats did, in a way that slows an opponent's campaign for the White House. And they can use financing rules not only to generate funding but to create issues that shape the campaign.

4 Perspectives on Campaign Media

Whereas Chapter 2 discussed presidential campaign communication from the perspective of "who says what to whom" this chapter explores campaign communication from the perspectives of connections: "how 'who' connects with 'whom'." Communication cannot exist without a medium any more than it can exist without people or messages. Each medium is a delivery mechanism – a conveyor belt – that captures some stimuli and directs them toward potential recipients who unpack them. But the choice of conveyor belt has important consequences for the kinds of stimuli conveyed and for the recipients reached. We shall see how the technologies that connect some people isolate them from others. We shall also see that humans use communication technologies for a variety of purposes. Thus we shall see that people organize around their purposes and use media in sophisticated organizational ways as well as very personal ways. A surprising number of web pages and blogs devoted to creative arts display French composer Claude Debussy's observation that, "Music is in the space between the notes." Our concern in this chapter is with the space between the communicators and the technologies used to bridge those spaces.

What Does a Medium Convey?

Each communication medium has a unique capacity to transmit some stimuli while filtering out others. Marshall McLuhan wrote of the evolution of societies that, "The medium is the message" (1964, p. 1). He meant that, "the personal and social consequences" of a medium result not from the content it carries or from the uses to which it is put, but from the changes the medium produces in our ways of sensing the environment and associating with one another. Content is not unimportant – photographs transmitted electronically by American soldiers in Iraq provided the world with the disturbing images of conditions in Abu Gharib prison, for example. But McLuhan likely would have argued that the more important change was the new potential that enabled soldiers to communicate audio and visual stimuli to people outside the military chain of command. But digital technology is only one among many changes that have altered the ways that humans associate to convey stimuli.

We can easily forget that air is the basic communication medium. When we speak our vocal folds create vibrations, and we shape that moving air with our facial muscles to create sounds. We direct those sounds towards our intended listeners, hoping to vibrate their eardrums in ways that they will be able to decode. Candidates do this – a lot. But until the public address system made its appearance in the 1920 campaign they could only talk to those citizens who could get within earshot. This privileged the leather-lunged orators who could project their voice the farthest.

The invention of the microphone that brought the public address system also made radio possible. The key development was the microphone's ability to capture sounds, convert them into electrical impulses capable of transmission and then to electrically vibrate a speaker. Candidates with microphones could reach many more listeners than candidates without microphones. But microphones filter out visual stimuli and convey only audio stimuli. Sometimes the nature of the sound is more noticeable than the content of what is conveyed. This is why most of us prefer to listen to digital music and why FM stereo stations broadcast music and AM stations have become the home of news, talk and information.

Radio did little to help the 1928 Democratic nominee, New York Governor Al Smith. Already saddled with the exigency of overcoming strong opposition from those who feared electing the first Catholic president, Smith had a strong urban New York accent. Smith's manner of speaking reportedly alienated many voters in one of the first campaigns to make heavy use of radio broadcasting. Four years later many of those voters embraced Franklin D. Roosevelt – who spoke with a more patrician New York dialect. But radio obscured the fact that Roosevelt, paralyzed by polio,was ordinarily confined to a wheelchair.

Television would combine audio and visual stimuli. In 1960 many pundits said that Vice-President Richard Nixon won the first presidential debate on radio debate while viewers awarded it to Senator John F. Kennedy. They speculated that Nixon's fidgeting and five-o'clock shadow cost him the debate and the election. Appearance soon become a staple of campaigns in the television era, leading to complex pre-debate negotiations over the height of the candidates' podiums, the distance between them, stage lighting and other visual elements.

Sometimes the technical perils of electronic media have rhetorical and political consequences. In January of 2004, Howard Dean thanked his boisterous supporters for their hard work in the Iowa precinct caucuses, in which he finished only third. Dean found himself in a noisy hall and felt the need to speak loudly above the noise. But he faced a highly directional microphone that captured little of the crowd noise. So when Governor Dean expressed his determination to continue his campaign through the next several primaries and finished with a cheer, he overpowered the microphone with a sound that struck television viewers as appropriate neither to the crowd nor to his third place finish. Pundits christened Dean's performance the "I Have a Scream" speech, and the unfortunate moment dominated his coverage for the next week when he sorely needed to control the message.

For better and for worse, Dean's "scream" can be seen as opening the door for YouTube's importance in 2008. YouTube would welcome videos from anyone capable of capturing video, as well as from the campaigns themselves. Amber Lee Ettinger created a YouTube phenomenon as "Obama Girl" with her 2007 music video "I Got a Crush on Obama" (viewed more than nine million times by September 2008). Although viewed a "mere" 100,000 times Hillary Clinton also became a YouTube sensation when she seemed to choke back a tear. YouTube items like these are significant because they generate responses and parodies that stimulate an entire second tier of campaign debate; this one energized by citizens rather than by the campaigns or media organizations.

As speech, loudspeakers, radio, television and YouTube convey candidates and other people in whole or in part, print media are depersonalized. The printing press has always been crucial to the emergence of a growing sense of nationalism, which depended everywhere on the development and distribution of printed materials in vernacular language as shared texts (Anderson 1983, 1991). Thus when it came to campaigning for president, it was natural for candidates to disseminate their ideas in print.

The significant feature of the printed message is its permanence. Unlike the spoken message, the printed message can be reread it can be reread. The previous sentence was not a typographical error but an illustration of the point – the redundancy created confusion and the printed word (as opposed to speech) invited you, dear reader, to pursue closure. Consequently, printed matter is better suited than live speech to the presentation of complex campaign arguments. That is one reason why candidates' remarks so often refer audiences to their web sites.

But the permanence of the printed word means that it can haunt a candidate. The rise of journalism created a combination of forms in which a candidate's spoken words are partially captured in print and reported as part of a news story. Frequently, an opposing campaign or interest group quotes a few words from that story as part of an attack, visually displaying the name of the newspaper in their print attack. In this fashion a campaign can transform a fleeting spoken word into a potentially lethal attack by stripping it of its context, repackaging it and giving it a newfound permanence.

Additionally, print media can be mailed to people and therefore they can be more precisely targeted to the desired audience. In the early days of campaigning it was much easier to distribute printed documents than it was to transport the candidate, and once read the documents could be passed from hand to hand. Nevertheless, print media are ill equipped to convey the look and feel of the candidate in the ways that audio and visual media can.

Indeed, direct mail is perhaps the campaign medium most underestimated by non-professionals. If the key to solving a rhetorical puzzle is getting your message to the audience capable of rectifying the exigency, then getting your message to those specific people by name is ideal – and mail is a far better way to do that than either radio or television. Compared to radio and television, mass mailings are inexpensive to produce and distribute and they can be targeted to the audiences the campaign must reach. The accuracy of the targeting is probably apparent if you reflect on how rarely your reaction to a piece of direct mail is, "Why would they send this to me?" Yet we see clashing commercials as a matter of course during our favorite television programs because they cannot differentiate among those viewers who watch it.

Campaigns have long relied upon election boards for lists of registered voters. But direct mail played an important role in the rightward turn of the Republican Party in 1980. The 1978 treaties to provide Panama with control over the Canal proved to be one of the most hotly contested issues of the 1970s. Presidents Johnson, Nixon, Ford, and Carter as well as the Joint Chiefs of Staff supported the treaties, but many conservatives, including Ronald Reagan, opposed it as a "giveaway." The emerging "New Right" movement circulated petitions and sought contributions to block the treaties, and direct mail guru Richard Viguerie compiled the names. When the time came to run Ronald Reagan against President Carter in 1980, Viguerie and the New Right had a candidate, an issue, and a data bank of irate citizen activists (Smith and Smith 1994, Stewart, Smith, and Denton 2006). Pro-Life and Pro-Choice groups were similarly able to deliver mailing lists to candidates they supported, and the politicized churches of the religious right brought still more names. Today, the Omega List company (Omegalist.com) provides a large number of conservative mailing lists, including Adopt a Platoon (74,116), the American Civil Rights Union (69,553) and the Freedom Alliance (47,194).

Lawrence M. Kimmel, the CEO of Grey Direct, anticipated the changing nature of direct marketing two years before the first 2008 presidential primary. "In a world of declining TV viewership, falling newspaper circulation and waning radio and magazine effectiveness, direct mail has remained an attractive channel to deliver targeted messages," Kimmel wrote in *Advertising Age* (2006). "[M]arketers with real direct-marketing expertise have been able to expand their utilization of mail. However, this is now going to change . . . Don't get me wrong: Direct mail will be a critical communications technique for years to come, but in 2006 we will start mailing less" (Kimmel 2006).

Wait – "Direct mail will . . . start mailing less"? Kimmel explained that apparent contradiction:

> the traditional advertising business is in crisis. Consumers are rejecting intrusion advertising en mass. Over 70 percent of DVR users skip through commercials. Satellite radio has eight million customers. Over 100 million folks have signed up for the Do-Not-Call list. And spam is uniformly despised. Consumers are clearly telling us that they don't want to be subjected to irrelevant advertising messages when they're watching TV, listening to the radio, having dinner, reading their e-mails or opening their regular mail.   (2006)

Thus, "direct marketers of the world need to become more rigorous in applying our time-tested techniques to a broader array of media. And traditional marketers should be turning to direct marketers more frequently to help them navigate the path to optimal ROI and profitability" (Kimmel 2006). Because an impending 2-cent increase in postage threatened to increase mailing costs and thus undermine client profitability, professionals like Kimmel planned ways to market directly through new media. The new opportunities for direct marketing included Facebook advertising, e-mail, and postcard marketing. All of these direct marketing media would play major roles in the 2008 presidential campaigns.

This section has explored how some of the major media used for presidential campaign communication convey some stimuli and not others. Audience targeting is easier with some form of mail, complex arguments are better in print, and candidates' personal qualities are better conveyed through radio and television. Another way to look at this is to say that trying to target a complex argument to your desired audience through television will reach too many of the wrong people and none of them will be able to fully process its complexity. It is comparably difficult to convey your candidate's warmth and charm in a written policy statement. Thus the message the campaign wants to send to its intended audience is conveyed to them through the medium designed to emphasize and distribute the appropriate signals.

At What Trough Doth Thy Audience Feed?

How do we choose our communication partners? All too often we engage audiences of convenience – those in our e-mail address book, our friends and colleagues – rather than those persons actually in a position to address the exigency positively. Many students, for example, discuss a disappointing grade with a friend instead of talking to the professor who might better clarify the material or possibly rectify a grading error. We also frequently select a medium of convenience – a preferred technology rather than the best means for reaching the audience able to address our exigency in the most appropriate way. For example, most of us have instinctively telephoned to complain about a billing mistake only to find ourselves without any written evidence of the conversation or the nice employee's assurance that we should simply ignore the bill. We need to remember Bitzer's advice: handle rhetorical situations by selecting the audience capable of providing the fitting response we need. That means that one should select the audience before the medium.

We therefore turn now to two related questions. The general question concerns which people are at the receiving ends of these conveyor belts. More specifically, we want to know where those nine herds of citizens discussed in Chapter 2 graze for their political information or, even more graphically, at what information troughs they feed. For only when the campaigns understand where the audiences get their information can they put their messages before them.

Political scientist Samuel Popkin argued that voters reason, but that they are prone to following "information shortcuts" (1994). He explained it with the old joke in which a police officer finds a man who had been drinking heavily looking for his car keys not where he lost them but under a street light because "the light is better." For Popkin, most voters are on a similar "Drunkard's Search" for relevant political information, preferring to look where it is easy rather than where good information can be found.

One of the easiest places to search for political information is your mailbox. You check it daily for bills and magazines and, lo and behold, there is a direct mail card. By the time you identify it as political junk mail you have read its message. What could be easier? As you reach the door you hear the phone ringing, and you answer it. Alas, it is an automated telephone call from a campaign (a "robocall"). This message was also easy to find, but you may well hang up before hearing the point of the message. Having checked the mail and the telephone, you sit down at your computer, log on, and check your e-mail. There are two e-mails from campaigns – one telling you how urgently they need your help to catch up and the other excitedly telling you how well things are going and that therefore they need your help more than ever.

Everyone is able to get mail; the campaigns need only identify the addresses of the individuals they need to reach from an appropriate database. Almost everyone is able to receive a telephone call, but the national Do Not Call list complicated this path and calls to mobile phones are generally avoided. But who actually uses e-mail?

Jeremiah Owyang is a senior analyst at Forrester Research and the host of the "Web Strategy by Jeremiah" blog. When he asked people about e-mail, his sister in college replied, "I only use e-mail to get a hold of old people like you. Out of my hundreds of friends, only ONE does not use Facebook or MySpace." This echoes the observation of author and speaker Don Tapscott (paraphrased by Mitch Joel) that, "Young people don't use e-mail anymore. They see it as a traditional form of communication. They use it to thank their grandparents for a birthday gift (or other times when they have to speak with old people)" (Joel 2008).

A study of Internet users by the e-mail-targeting firm ExactTarget identified six types of users. *Retired* Internet users buy things online (81 percent) and 94 percent reported being influenced by direct marketing. A second group, *established professionals*, also shop online with 92 percent having made an online purchase. Women in this group are the more likely to use instant messaging, texting, and social networking to communicate with friends and family. This suggests that both the senior voters and the professionals who were connected to the Internet by 2008 should have been receptive audiences for online direct marketing campaign appeals.

The other four groups appear to be less obviously politically relevant to direct marketing by Internet. Over half of the *young homemakers* preferred direct mail and e-mail for marketing but relied on social networks and SMS during the day. Wired users prefer text messages only for urgent customer service matters. College students were concerned about spam and regarded text and social networks as off limits for marketers. Although the youngest group, teens, cannot yet vote, their use of social networking is greater than any other group and may suggest the increasing importance of that medium in the 2012 election cycle.

Television today is nearly ubiquitous. Nielsen Research reports that 98 percent of American households have had televisions since 1999 (TV Basics 2009). But the rise of cable television in the 1980s brought a huge increase in the number of channels available to viewers. Today, the proliferation of television networks available by cable and satellite has made it almost meaningless to speak of television in general. Perhaps someone out there watches all 700 channels, but most of us use our remote controls to delete the channels that do not interest us. The "favorites" button enables us to keep a few channels at our fingertips. Some people delete the shopping channels, some people leave them in and some mark them as favorites. Some people delete sports channels, some leave them in, and some make them favorites. Some people delete C-SPAN and the other news channels, some leave them in and some make one or two of them favorites. And so it goes. Thus we have a society in which 98 percent of us have televisions but few of us have the same television environment.

It is unlikely that very many people have identical bookmarks set on their Internet browsers, but at least there are software programs like Mozilla's "Foxmarks" that make the prospect possible. But how would multiple citizens today maintain identical television viewing environments? They would first have to match their choice of antenna, cable, or satellite service then (after the 2009 disappearance of analog television) they would choose between digital and high-definition, after which they would need to make a common add/delete decision for every single channel, including premium channels and pay-per-view. In short, today's neighbors no longer see the same worlds through their televisions. But it might be even more accurate, from a communication perspective, to say that today's neighbors no longer live near one another.

We should therefore think of presidential campaigns as arising in a polity populated by networks of people already connected to one another. This requires us to expand our conception of television networks from the broadcasters (the network headquarters and its affiliated stations) to include its core and peripheral audience members. For example, whereas the Fox News network reports the news, we should conceive of [the Fox News network] as the larger coalition of those who gather and report the news for Fox, those who sponsor it with commercial advertisements on Fox, those citizens who rely on Fox for their news and those who patronize their advertisers. We should conceptualize [CNN], [MSNBC], [Bloomberg], [ABC] [CBS], [NBC], [BBC], and others in the same way. Each viewer with a television remote control decides which networks to join and which to avoid. The [C-SPAN] network includes no advertisers, but its funding comes from the subscribers to cable and satellite television through the industry, and public officials are, functionally, advertised products. Word of presidential campaigns spread through these connecting networks in ways that differentially interest the people they connect.

The Media that Connect also Isolate

McLuhan considered every medium of communication to be an extension of a sense enabling us to see, hear, smell, touch, or feel something that would otherwise be beyond sensation (McLuhan 1964). Thus the printed word can convey ideas from one person to another. But the printed word also isolates people – those who cannot see, those who cannot read, and those who cannot read the particular language. To share the written word is to withdraw from those who cannot read (or who do not receive it). To instant message with your buddy list is to exclude those who are not on that list. To speak in public is to separate from those unable to attend and even from those out of earshot. So it is, to some degree, with every medium of communication.

We belong, first and foremost, to interpersonal networks. These include friendships, clubs, support groups, churches, recreational groups, professional organizations, labor unions, retirement groups, charitable and volunteer organizations, veterans' organizations, and more. When a worker decides to join a labor union and becomes a member of the International Brotherhood of Teamsters he thereby decides not to join the National Federation of Teachers or any other union. But the teamster and the teacher are fellow members of the interpersonal network known as organized labor, thereby isolating themselves from non-union workers as well as management. Similarly, joining one church separates one from all the other churches and from secularists.

Malcolm Gladwell (2000) has suggested that some people serve as connectors because they seem to know lots of people. In that sense, we need to consider "tell-a-friend" along with telephone and television when we consider communication technologies. Some of these connectors route information to the intended audiences and others influence the way it will be received. The classic work by Everett

Rogers, *The Diffusion of Innovations* (2003), explains that some people are "early adopters" of ideas and techniques on whom others depend. Others are a source of general opinion leadership (Katz, Lazersfeld, and Roper 2006) on whom we rely for their opinions about movies, music, and classes to take and even politics. More recently, researchers associated with the Roper Organization found that among every ten people there is one who influences the behavior of the other nine (Keller and Berry 2003). While interpersonal influence remains important it would be supplemented by other media.

The last half of the twentieth century saw the rise and faltering of television broadcasting as a tool of presidential campaigning. The 1948 political conventions were the first to be televised by the networks, even before great numbers of viewers had the televisions on which to watch them. From the 1950s through the 1990s the conventions were the political Olympics for the network news divisions, but the twenty-first century brought reduced coverage by the Big Three networks. Dwight Eisenhower's 1952 campaign pioneered the use of television ads, and his Democratic opponent, Adlai Stevenson, grudgingly followed suit, complaining that it made the election of a president like buying a bar of soap. From the 1960s through the 1970s candidates ran national advertising campaigns. But by the 1980s they had begun to target their ads locally lest their message reinforce what their opponents wanted their supporters to hear. By 2008 both campaigns were also running "web ads" for those who wanted to see them without buying expensive broadcast airtime.

Television remained the dominant source of campaign news for all age groups in 2008 despite a remarkable increase in Internet use. Although 72 percent reported that television was their primary source of campaign news, that figure represented a 4 percent decline from 2004 (Pew 2009). Viewers relied on cable networks (46 percent) more than the traditional networks (24 percent) or local stations (13 percent). But the Internet moved past both radio and newspapers into second place as the primary source of campaign news for all age categories (Pew 2009).

What had happened to television? First, broadcasting was replaced by "narrowcasting" as the proliferation of cable channels fragmented the viewing audience. Such channels as CNN, Fox News, MSNBC, CNBC, and C-SPAN began to provide 24/7 coverage of political news. They developed audiences who turned to them rather than to the traditional eclectic networks when they wanted political news. At the same time, the media organizations found unpleasant the cost-benefit ratio of providing large-scale coverage of conventions and campaigns for a shrinking audience. Campaigns similarly found that more narrowly targeted television messages better served their purposes, and their media buys could be somewhat less expensive if they did not buy nationally. Of course, the byproduct of these choices was to insulate voters not targeted with ads and insulate from the parties those viewers content to watch the regular network programming.

Newspapers and magazines are widely available to us, but mainly by subscription. *Advertising Age* data for 2006 indicated that the top two US magazines by circulation are *AARP: The Magazine* (23.4 million) and *Reader's Digest* (10 million) – more than the next seven magazines combined. That next tier includes five magazines that reach more than 23 million readers: *Better Homes and Gardens* (7.6 million), *Good Housekeeping* (4.7 million), *Ladies' Home Journal* (4.1 million),

Woman's Day (4 million), and *Family Circle* (3.9 million). The news magazines accounted for 9.1 million readers: *Time* was no. 7 (4 million), *Newsweek* was no. 15 (3.1 million) and *U.S. News and World Report* was no. 31 (2 million).

This means that the September 2008 *Reader's Digest* interviews with Senators McCain and Obama reached more readers than all three weekly news magazines combined. Although the news weeklies reach their readers four times a month, they mostly reach the same subscribers and each issue has a shelf-life only 25 percent as long as that of a *Reader's Digest.* Diane Salvatore's interview with Michelle and Barack Obama for the *Ladies Home Journal* reached more readers than *Time* and almost as many readers as *Newsweek* and *U.S. News* combined. More important even than the circulation, though, is the ability of these interviews to connect the campaigns with some voters in private while insulating them from those who do not subscribe to, or read, the magazine.

Our discussions of television, magazines, and direct mail have all emphasized ways of conveying political messages to targeted audiences. When the Internet began to boom in the 1990s everyone sensed that it would be important to political campaigning. The 1992 Clinton campaign was the first to use a web site to post speeches and other information, but not unlike television in 1948, there were still few users out there. The 1998 congressional elections were the watershed, and by 2000 all of the major candidates were using web sites. Bruce Bimber and Richard Davis (2003) found that decided voters visited candidate web sites in 2000 and found them very useful, but undecideds and nonvoters did not use them. Thus Andrew Chadwick (2006) notes that only 11 percent of respondents in a Pew study mentioned the Internet as a source of news for them about the 2000 campaign (compared to television 70%, newspapers 39%, radio 15% and magazines 4%). Nevertheless, the web sites provided an important means of reinforcing these voters and facilitated a turn from candidate-centered campaigns toward issues. Yet even in 2000 online campaigning basically meant candidate web pages and e-mail.

Red and Blue Media

The polarization of American public opinion has been so often asserted in recent years that the existence of a domestic "culture war" between red states and blue states is now largely assumed. The terminology stems from the broadcast networks' tradition of reporting election results by coloring the Republican states red and the Democratic states blue; when these states seemed to stay red and blue over the course of several elections they were deemed red states and blue states. But Morris Fiorina (2005) analyzed public opinion on key issues and concluded that American citizens are no more polarized than they were a generation ago. What is now highly polarized, he argued, is the gap between the political elites and the choices offered to citizens (candidates, policies, and arguments) by those positioned to offer public choices.

Fiorina attributed the polarization of political elites to the expansion of government into previously private spheres and an increase in participatory democracy. These trends combined to disproportionately involve political purists and those with the capital needed to participate heavily and frequently. But these forces typically peak during campaigning and ebb during governing.

In addition to Fiorina's explanation we should also notice that new communication technologies (including cable news networks, web sites, and blogs) have created red and blue media environments. Beginning with the move from national network radio to local radio in the late 1940s and continuing through the proliferation of cable channels, magazines, satellite and online radio, downloaded music libraries and blogs, the technological trend has been away from shared communication toward personalized communication. The consequence of this personalization on the ways that we associate has been that we no longer need subject ourselves to music, entertainment, information, viewpoints, or interpretations that bore or irritate us. Our new [networks] enable us to communicate with like-minded people and to avoid those people and ideas that cause us discomfort. The proliferation of audiences requires each source of information to be attentive to its audience's needs and interests.

This is far different from the era of the 1960s through the 1980s when American network television news provided viewers with thirty minutes of common ground. Network anchors brought us the big stories guided by the fairness doctrine (an affirmative responsibility to present all sides of controversial issues). But the end of the fairness doctrine, the proliferation of outlets and the invention of programmable remotes and Internet bookmarks enabled us to fill our lives with more of the information and viewpoints we like, and less of what we dislike.

Campaign Organizations, Media Organizations, and Citizens

Political candidates, citizens, and professional media personnel are all intertwined. Candidates approach campaign media interested in using them to reach citizens with their messages. Because advertising and travel are costly they rely heavily on "free media" by working with, and through, journalists and talk show hosts. But those media professionals have their own perspective, owing heavily to the fact that presidential campaigns provide them with a profitable business season, comparable in some ways to merchants' Christmas shopping season. Candidates provide journalists with the raw materials for news stories, political customers provide media sales forces with clients who want to produce and buy advertisements and political talk provides jokes for entertainers and willing guests for interview programs.

Meanwhile, citizens go about their everyday lives: they commute to work, spend time with their children, walk their dogs, pay bills, mow lawns, and the like. Along the road of life they graze for information where they find it. Their personal relationships provide shortcuts to political information, political humor encourages them to infer tidbits of presumed knowledge and, increasingly, new communication technologies encourage them to express their insights and frustrations with others.

The American National Election Survey provides a useful diagram of the flow of campaign messages (Figure 1 as presented by Benoit 2007). The figure shows three separate sources of political messages: "candidates," "news media," and "voters." It will probably be more useful for us to conceive of candidates as "campaigns" because messages originate from campaign workers other than the candidates. Similarly, it may be more useful for us to conceive of voters as

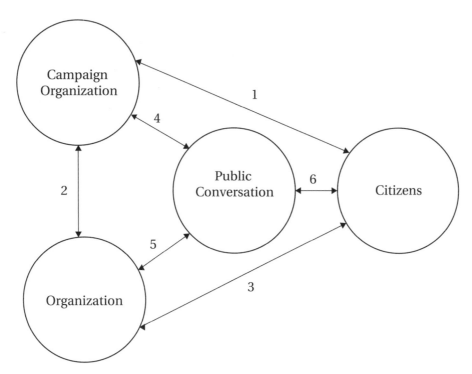

Figure 4.1 Messages in Political Campaigns
Source: Adapted from NES, 2003

"citizens" because people other than voters talk about the campaign and because people only become voters on election day.

The NES figure enables us to differentiate among six kinds of campaign messages: (1) campaign to citizen, (2) campaign to news media, (3) news media to citizen, (4) campaign to public discussion, (5) news media to public discussion, and (6) public discussion to citizen. It is tempting to observe that campaigns communicate directly with voters, indirectly with voters through the news media and very indirectly with voters through the news media and the public discussions the in turn influence. But that is a temptation to oversimplify the diagram.

To say that campaigns communicate "with" citizens is to say that they both send messages and seek them out. Campaigns survey voters, conduct focus groups, interact with citizens at campaign events and in other ways seek to discover what citizens think and feel. Similarly, campaigns do not merely talk to the news media, they read and watch them to learn how their messages are being characterized and to learn about their opponents and citizens. For their part, the news media do not merely report to the citizens, they monitor them and portray citizen opinions through public opinion reports and interviews with everyday people. In short, each of the arrows is bidirectional.

It is also crucial to understand that the campaigns and news media are organizations; or more precisely, they are clusters of people bound together in organizational communication. Every campaign, newspaper, and network has managers and workers in some kind of hierarchy, they have an organizational mission or purpose, and it is only through their communication practices that they can carry them out. When one observes a "lack of organization" they are actually identifying a degree of dysfunctional organizational communication.

On an operational level it should also be noted that presidential campaigns communicate with news media and citizens for the ultimate purpose of winning electoral college votes. It is easy to overlook the fact that commercial news organizations communicate with presidential campaigns and citizens for the ultimate purpose of building audiences and enhancing their profitability. Once we remember that, it is not difficult to view news organizations and presidential campaigns competing with one another for the hearts and minds of the citizenry. This is not to say that news organizations are concerned only with profitability. Rather, it is to say that news organizations, like the campaigns they cover, are attuned to the interests and beliefs of the citizens in their audience who can choose to get their news from other organizations.

If the campaigns and news media are all contesting to win over citizens, those citizens are not simply passive receptors. More than fifty years ago Westley and MacLean advanced an influential model of mass communication that illustrated how audience members checked information received from the mass media with other information available to them. Today, the Internet not only makes it easier for us to cross check things we learn from news organizations, it makes it easy for most people to bookmark sources of information that they find believable. Just as we download the music we want to hear instead of waiting for disc jockeys to play what we want, and just as we rent DVD and download television programs and movies instead of waiting for them to air, we can easily seek out the information we want and disregard the rest.

In short, contemporary presidential campaign communication occurs among active information seeking citizens, presidential campaigns and news organizations. All three interact among themselves and with one another. If we are to understand presidential campaigns, we must understand how campaign communication looks from each of these three perspectives.

Presidential Campaign Communication from the Campaigns' Perspective

Every presidential campaign seeks, first and foremost, to win. Every candidate has things that he or she would hope to accomplish as president, but knows that these cannot be accomplished without winning the election. Moreover, we do not legislate on the campaign trail, so the problems of climate change, immigration, and energy cannot be solved with commercials, speeches or debates. The only real question is, "Which candidate do you prefer?" But that question can be approached in several ways.

A campaign that begins by talking about issues on the minds of citizens has an advantage over a campaign that begins by talking about issues that do not interest citizens. Issue polls can help prospective candidates identify those topics. So can news coverage, because those who speak out on topics in the news can embed themselves in the story. But the early days of the campaign (the surfacing stage) make it prudent for the campaign to devote special attention to the issues that especially concern those citizens willing to contribute resources. This may be a better time to advocate capital gains tax cuts and investing in social programs than "soaking the rich" or helping illegal aliens. It is also important to build and enhance working relationships with fellow partisans across the country who can help organize the campaign at the state and local levels.

Just as campaigns are selective about choosing their issues, they also devote a great deal of attention to "framing." Robert Entman (1993) has explained that, "to frame is to select some aspects of a perceived reality and make them more salient in a communicating text" (p. 51). Health care, for example, can be framed as a social problem, as a problem for our economic competitiveness, as a problem of encroaching government or as a moral issue. Stem cell research can be framed as a moral issue, as a health care issue, or as a scientific problem. In short, every possible issue can be framed for the public in a number of different ways and each campaign must decide how it wants to frame each issue it raises.

No campaign expects to win every vote. Thus each campaign must decide which citizens it needs to engage, when, and about which issues. Ordinarily there is no compelling reason to talk with the other party's supporters or non-partisans during the party primaries; there will be time for that during the general election campaign. But the campaign does need to communicate with likely voters in the states holding upcoming primaries. Television commercials can be useful for this purpose, but they are expensive to produce and air and they reach opponents as well as supporters. For this reason more carefully targeted media are becoming important – web ads, e-mails, and podcasts as well as mailings.

Campaigns need to communicate with news organizations early and often if they are to be portrayed in news reports as serious candidates. In 1976 Georgia Governor Jimmy Carter kept surprising the press in Democratic primaries. Despite his two terms as Governor of California, Ronald Reagan was frequently labeled "an actor" and in 1988 Pat Robertson bristled at being called a "religious broadcaster." George W. Bush reportedly established good personal relations with the campaign press corps during the 2000 campaign by giving the reporters nicknames and bantering with them.

Presidential Campaign Communication from the Media Organizations' Perspective

Media organizations in the United States have traditionally disseminated two general kinds of content: entertainment and public information or news. Both have become significant for today's presidential campaigns. Dramatic programs frequently draw their inspirations for stories from contemporary issues and their treatment of those issues frames them for citizens. Jon Wiener (2007) blogged for *The Nation* that Jack Bauer and *24* provided more effective arguments for the role of torture in national security than the Bush administration. Episodes showed Bauer fighting not only international terrorists but those opposed to torture.

The late night talk show monologues rely heavily on the candidates for their jokes. They also invite them and for special appearances. Bill Clinton appeared on the Arsenio Hall show in 1992, playing the saxophone and chatting about his

Tina Fey as Sarah Palin

remark that he had tried marijuana but had not inhaled. When John McCain abruptly suspended his 2008 campaign because of the financial crisis he cancelled on David Letterman, and the host gave him a rough time for several evenings.

The Daily Show with John Stewart and *The Colbert Report* as well as *Saturday Night Live* provide extensive political satire. Stewart is particularly adept at showing video clips of candidates saying the things they later claim not to have said. Colbert's humor frequently exaggerates or extends candidates' positions to suggest their weaknesses. SNL's parodies of debates have become classics, and Tina Fey's impersonations of Republican vice-presidential nominee Sarah Palin were entertainment highlights of 2008. In all of these cases citizens acquire political information as a byproduct of entertainment.

Political talk shows like those of Rush Limbaugh, Hannity and Colmes, Keith Olberman, and Bill O'Reilly stomp roughly along a delicate tightrope between entertainment and news. Their content is entirely political but it can hardly be intended for all citizens. The stars' personal styles are more important to these programs than the content, as suggested by the tendency of audience members to tag their new information with, "So and so said." These programs owe much of their success to the proliferation of radio stations and cable networks that makes a small stable audience valuable to advertisers. When we had only the Big Three television networks a program ordinarily needed a 30 percent share of the audience to prosper, but with more than 100 channels on cable that share is much smaller.

Radio disk jockeys also play a potentially important role during campaigns. I remember local morning newscasts about the Bush–Dukakis campaign in 1988 being followed by Bobby McFerrin's catchy, "Don't Worry Be Happy" – a nice antidote to the challenger's criticism of the administration's policies.

Their chatter about Bill Clinton's sexual escapades, Janet Jackson's Super Bowl wardrobe malfunction, gas prices, and failing businesses all contribute to their audience's sense of the policy environment.

The basic unit of journalism is the story, and no regularly scheduled story is either as long or as dramatic as a presidential campaign. Nimmo and Combs (1990) suggested that continuing coverage turns the drama of news into melodrama as a single story becomes a soap opera. They maintained that our political experiences are mediated by the "melodramatic imperative" that provides the logic of television journalism. "Moral justice is at the heart of most melodrama . . . Suspense is the key . . . Anxiety reigns . . . And characters traits are clear cut: Good are good, bad are bad. Finally, happy endings are preferred but not essential . . . Tragic endings suffice" (p. 16).Whereas the dramatic imperative of a story is tension, the melodramatic imperative drives the hunger for the next chapter. If television news was melodramatic in 1990 it is no less so today.

A year before the contested 2000 election, two years before the 9/11 attacks and six years before Hurricane Katrina, Kovach and Rosenstiel's book *Warp Speed* (1999) identified five characteristics of the news that already worried them. The first was a "never-ending news cycle" in which "the press is increasingly oriented toward ferrying allegations rather than first ferreting out the truth." The second trend was that "Sources are gaining power over journalists" by dictating the terms and time frames for the use of information. Third, "There are no more Gatekeepers" because the proliferation of news outlets have varied standards. Kovach and Rosenstiel asked "What does the news organization that requires high levels of substantiation do with the reports of those with lesser levels of proof?" Fourth, they argued that "Argument is overwhelming reporting" as economics drives the need for cheap chatter to fill the time and space. Finally, a "Blockbuster Mentality" provides cheaper and easier rewards than worldwide reporting of diverse stories. As audiences fragment new organizations seek formulaic stories that reassemble, however temporarily, the old mass audience (Kovach and Rosenstiel 1999, pp. 6–7).

News organizations begin gearing up for the presidential campaign years in advance. Much advance preparation is needed before sophisticated operations can be undertaken, and each campaign year brings news innovations. For example, XM satellite radio launched POTUS '08 – a 24-hour channel devoted exclusively to the presidential campaign news – in October of 2007.

Presidential Campaign Communication from the Citizens' Perspective

We can conceive of the citizenry very generally in terms of those citizens who are interested in politics and those who are not. Whatever their political party, the interested citizens follow the news, have a degree of knowledge about and opinions on the issues of the day, and have some familiarity with the people who are considered to be potential candidates. They begin to pay attention to campaign stories a year or so before the Iowa caucuses, they may talk about who they think will eventually win the nominations, and they may contribute time and/or money to advocacy groups, parties or even exploratory campaign efforts. These citizens seek information, so they read widely, search the Internet and watch C-SPAN coverage of public affairs. These people want policies, facts and specifics; they dislike generalities and misrepresentations, and they often point them out to others.

FactCheck.org is a project devoted to "Holding Politicians Accountable." It results from many years of research by Kathleen Hall Jamieson who has long been concerned about false claims and political messages that invite false inferences. The distinction is not only important, it is in many ways the lifeblood of contemporary political rhetoric. For example, 2000 Democratic vice-presidential nominee Joseph Lieberman addressed the 2008 Republican convention to urge bipartisan support for John McCain and opposing Barack Obama for "voting to cut off funding for our American troops on the battlefield" (FactCheck.org). Listeners trusting Senator Lieberman would reasonably infer that Senator Obama had regularly voted against war funding and that this differentiated him from Senator McCain. But upon further investigation, FactCheck.org discovered that, "Obama has voted in favor of war-funding bills at least ten times since becoming a senator. The McCain camp and Republicans cite one vote Obama cast against a funding bill as justification for their claim – but that vote came after President Bush had vetoed a version of the bill that included a date for withdrawal from Iraq." In other words, Senator Obama did cast one vote against war funding but cast many more votes for funding "American troops on the battlefield" than against it. Thus FactCheck.org rated Lieberman's statement as "seriously misleading" even though it was factually correct. Because a factually correct statement that tells only part of the story can mislead us, discrepancies like this one matter. But only the most politically interested citizens are likely either to find them or to care about them.

Citizens uninterested in politics have other things to do. But they stumble upon political information as they watch Jay Leno and David Letterman or "Saturday Night Live," "The Colbert Report," and "The Daily Show with John Stewart." Their daily activities expose them to the whims of fortune – good and bad – that will prepare them to embrace or reject the political appeals that eventually come their way. Because they are not actively seeking political information they make do with the information that comes their way. The "information shortcuts" described by Samuel Popkin (1994) are especially useful for these people. If your child is having trouble in school then our schools are in trouble. If you have trouble making ends meet then taxes are too high and the economy is bad. If you are better off than you were four years ago the country is on the right track. These people thrive more on a "gut-level" connection with a candidate, such that facts and specific policies are less important than themes and images.

Most importantly, people talk to one another. Each of us has a circle of acquaintances that encompasses people of varied genders, ages, incomes, religions, ethnicities, and political interests. If you pause to reflect on it, you can probably think of those people you learn from about public affairs as well as those who turn to you for political information and guidance. These interpersonal relationships are important influences on each of us.

The Interface

Campaigns, media organizations, and citizens interact to create presidential campaign communication as we know it, and they connect with one another through various media of communication. A student of presidential campaign communication can explore the media the citizens use to acquire whatever they feel they need to cast a vote. Or one can study the media that campaigns use to reach directly the voters in their proto-coalitions or to reach them indirectly through the media organizations. Or one can study the ways that media organizations make use of presidential campaigns to fulfill the reading and viewing needs of their audience members such that they remain financially viable for their shareholders and true to their commitment to public service. The mistake most of us make is to forget that people are actively and simultaneously engaged from all three perspectives; there are no passive receptors.

John Zaller (1998) advanced an important explanation for the dynamic interaction among campaigns, news professionals, and citizens based on the adversarial posture of journalists toward politicians. He argued that journalists are a professional community comparable to doctors, architects, and professors who value their independence to create their own product.

> The kind of product they wish to create is one that requires as much personal skill and expertise as possible. The exercise of skill and expertise is not only inherently satisfying; it also leads to higher pay and higher status. Journalists have an occupational interest in a relatively activist and autonomous conception of journalism, one that offers more than stenographic transcription of what others have said and that has appeal beyond the lowest common denominator of the mass market. Journalists want to be members of a profession that adds something to the news – a profession that not only reports, but also digs, selects, frames, investigates, interprets, and regulates the flow of political communication.   (Zaller 1998)

In other words, journalists have a professional commitment to adding something of value to what has been said by the campaign organization. This cannot always be to those campaigns' advantage, because competing campaigns are unlikely to welcome the same journalistic contributions. Thus the campaigns periodically criticize the campaign reports and sometimes seek to manage it. But such criticism and management offend journalists' professional standards. Zaller notes that journalists who merely transmit politicians' statements relinquish control over the news product and lose professional standing, status, good assignments, and professional advancement. Indeed, they lose those opportunities and status because they perform only a minor function.

At issue, then, is a struggle for control of communication about the political information. As Zaller noted, journalists are professionals who want to work like other professionals – architects, doctors, lawyers, and professors – in a way that exhibits their specialized knowledge. "Journalists seek to control the content of the news and to use this control to maximize their independent and distinctive voice in the news. This occupational interest brings journalists into regular conflict with politicians, who, as noted earlier, also have a clear occupational interest in controlling the content of the news" (Zaller 1998).

Who then monitors this struggle between politicians and journalists? Zaller says it is the mass audience that serves to constrain both the politicians and the journalists and thus influences the balance of power between them. The citizenry has no permanent rational interest in having this struggle won by either the politicians or the journalists. "Their interest, rather, is in having the two groups share control, as actually occurs in practice most of the time" (Zaller 1998).

Media organizations strive to meet their own needs faced with their readings of audience interests and the available messages from the campaigns. Citizens turn to the media that suit their needs for information helpful to them as they live their lives, and glean information about the campaigns and they are variably receptive to messages from the campaigns according to their party preferences and level of political interest. The campaigns try to get their message to their citizen proto-coalitions and to maintain positive relations with media organizations. The result is a dynamic and complex struggle.

Summary and Conclusions

This chapter has emphasized the media that connect communicators and convey stimuli. We have seen that:

- Each medium has a unique capacity to transmit some stimuli and filter others.
- Each medium privileges communicators able to use it well.
- Print media invite rereading and complex arguments while audio invites simpler transient messages.

Strategically, campaigners need to discern where their intended audiences get their information. We saw that:

- Most of us turn to messages of convenience in our mailboxes, e-mail, and television commercials.
- E-mail is used for a a variety of purposes by distinguishable audiences.
- 98 percent of us have television but we create personalized television environments with our add/delete options.
- We bookmark different web sites and create personalized Internet environments.

Moreover the media that connect people isolate them from others. We saw that:

- To share the written word is to withdraw from those who cannot read (or who do not receive it).
- To instant message with your buddy list is to exclude those who are not on that list.
- To speak in public is to separate from those unable to attend and even from those out of earshot.

Thus presidential campaigns arise in pre-established networks of communication. The more political media reach networks that, like the party elites, increasingly cater to polarized red and blue audiences but many people get their information from less politically oriented sources.

We have also seen that presidential campaign communication looks different from the perspectives of campaign organizations, media organizations, and citizens.

- Campaigns want to win so that they can govern.
- Media organizations are involved in a permanent effort to serve the ongoing needs of their customers so that they can stay in business, and presidential campaigns provide one of their busy seasons.
- Citizens, busy with their daily lives, want interesting and concise information that will help them decide whether to vote and, if so, for whom.

Presidential campaign communication cannot be well understood as the linear delivery of candidates' messages to voters, either directly or indirectly through news organizations. Instead, we need to consider the three way interactions among participants.

Citizens have varied media use patterns in their lives and relatively few are inclined to change those habits radically to find the best political information, so they make use of the most helpful information that comes their way. Campaigns use a creative mix of the available media to reach the audiences they need, sending different messages through different media to reach different target audiences. Media organizations, for their part, try to use the flood of campaign messages and their audiences' need for information to expand their market share and to build a larger audience for the post-campaign use.

Synthesizing Part I

In every presidential contest the objective is to be preferred by a majority of the Electors when then they gather to record their votes. That makes the Electors the audience members capable of resolving the terminal rhetorical exigency. Sent by their states and guided by state laws, the Electors are otherwise uncommitted but ordinarily responsive to the voters in their states. Therefore the candidate's strategy resolves into a simple question: "How can I be preferred by more voters than any of my opponents in states with electoral votes sufficient to produce an electoral vote majority?" We will revise that question later. But it already implies a strategic plan.

First, recognize that state voters have track records. Utah, Nebraska, and others vote heavily Republican while DC, Massachusetts and others vote heavily Democratic such that each party's nominee can identify and count some states as "safe" and others as "hopeless." Normally, one begins to strategize by banking the electoral votes that can be won by generic Republican and Democratic nominees. The remaining states – those too close to consider safe and those that "swing" from election to election – are the "battleground states."

Second, analyze the voters in each of the battleground states. Who are these people who will decide the election? What is the relative strength of the candidates among them? Whose support must be or retained and won to carry each state?

Third, ascertain what the battleground voters you need care about. This often varies from state to state. Moreover, the voters one needs to attract may want something quite different from those one needs to retain. Issue polls, focus groups, and web postings provide useful information in this regard. Perhaps the voters one seeks want health care reform because of the "pre-existing condition" issue while those who oppose it worry about Big Government. A candidate could thread that needle by speaking out against government health care and proposing a law prohibiting insurance companies denying coverage for pre-existing conditions. If the key voters oppose restrictions on guns is it because they are hunters, drug dealers, militia groups,or people protecting their homes? Are those concerned about the role of religion in American life evangelical Christians, Jews, Muslims, or atheists? Are target voters worried about interest rates because they are too high for them to buy a home or too low to provide a return on their investments?

Fourth, transform the theoretical audience of targeted voters into an actual audience – persons able and motivated to hear what the candidate has to say. The key is to *target* the people who need to be reached and cultivate an identity for them. This process of "constituting a people" (Charland 1987) will be discussed in

Part II. It involves the creation of an identity for the particular "We the People" the campaign seeks to represent. Audience construction always entails virtual tickets of admission, like the $1,000 a plate dinner to hear the candidate or appearances before the Veterans of Foreign Wars or the NAACP Convention. Other tickets are more subtle, as when a candidate visits a barbeque restaurant unannounced or tours a plant. An easy way to get attention is to visit the state and speak. But those who show up to hear the candidate are often already supportive, and when that happens the candidate's message fails to reach the new audience. Toward the end of a campaign many pollsters and commentators focus on undecided voters, assuming that they would turn the tide; but they rarely ask how these people can be undecided so late in a polarizing campaign. Often more attention to the reactions of voters soft in their support for the candidates can prove more revealing.

Fifth, find the information trough at which the target audience feeds. Many people think that broadcast advertising reaches the broadest audience, but your ticket of admission to this commercial message is to be a devotee of the program during which it airs – and *Law and Order, Hannity and Colmes, Oprah,* and *American Idol* attract different audiences, as do the various radio station formats. Candidates post materials on their web sites which are visited disproportionately by motivated computer savvy people who often have a positive inclination toward a candidate. All campaigns need a mix of media to reach a variety of audiences, and the mix should be based on the analysis of target audiences' informational feeding habits.

Sixth, decide what to say to whom. Any person remotely worth considering as a potential president had better be exceedingly well informed on a wide variety of topics and have policy ideas on most of them (including "this needs further study"). But only a few of these will matter to the voters at the time of the campaign. Perhaps tragically, terrorism was not a concern for voters during the 2000 campaign. A search of the speeches and commercials by Al Gore and George W. Bush reveals that neither mentioned terrorism, al Qaeda or Iraq at all and Gore mentioned Osama bin Laden only once. Within a year of the election that would change markedly. But because American voters cared about domestic policy issues in 2000, that is what the candidates discussed. There was a day when candidates could say different things to different audiences or at different stages of the campaign, but technology has largely ended that practice. Today candidates need to have positions that can carry them through nomination to the general election campaign with minimal revision. Whatever the campaign decides to say should have a central, memorable theme to which the candidate always returns – like Clinton's "New Covenant" to "Put People First" or Bush's "9/11 changed everything."

Seventh, anticipate other candidates' messages and how best to counter them. Frequently, candidates will have different target audiences and their messages may seem to pass each other in the night. But sooner or later, if the race narrows, the election will come down to a pivotal group of voters and appeals to them – like Ohio in 2004. In that contest for Ohio's electoral votes, Kerry forces struggled visibly to maximize voter turnout in populous Cuyahoga County (the Cleveland area) where there were many Democratic votes to be found. But the Bush campaign won by maximizing Republican turnout in smaller, more rural, and suburban counties in central Ohio. Thus the battle for Ohio was fought not by competing for the same voters, but for different audiences in the same state.

Campaign strategy is a rhetorical macro-puzzle that needs to be solved by working backwards from the electoral college majority through voting histories to target voters, identities, media, and messages. The campaign that tackles this puzzle by starting with whatever the candidate wants to say can win only by good luck, because the likelihood of getting the appropriate messages to the voters capable of casting the crucial votes is remote, and it is difficult enough to win the White House without compounding the challenges.

Part I has considered presidential campaigns as a rhetorical puzzle grounded in the Constitution and assorted government laws and party rules. Solving the puzzles requires candidates to enlist the help of audiences with whom they connect through a mix of communication media. In Part II we will examine the modes of communication that campaign organizations, media organizations, and citizens use throughout the campaign.

PART II

MODES OF PRESIDENTIAL CAMPAIGN COMMUNICATION

If we were studying basketball we might cover the rules, objective, and strategy of the game as we did in Part I and then skip to a discussion of famous games. But it would behove us to know about the athletic acts that the players use to play the game – dribbling, passing, shooting, as well as offensive and defensive schemes. For only when we understand those component acts can we understand how they fit together in a game and the strategic wisdom of choosing one over another to accomplish the objective.

Part II therefore considers the communication processes – the modes of communication – that comprise presidential campaigns. Chapter 5 examines the basic speech acts of saying positive things about oneself, attacking the opponent, and defending against attacks. Chapter 6 considers the presidential candidates' use of extended speeches. Chapter 7 takes a closer look at the campaign journalism that provides so much of what citizens know about campaigns. Chapter 8 discusses campaign advertising and Chapter 9 looks at debates. In Chapter 10 we consider how new media provide new opportunities for creative campaigns to perform their familiar tasks.

The modes of communication discussed in Part II are the tools in the campaigns' toolbox, the colors on their palette. They use them all in a strategic mix and therefore we need to study them all lest we come to understand presidential campaigns as they would appear through a single window. Like a basketball coach or a knowledgeable fan, we need to understand campaigns' choices in the context of the options available to them.

5 Acclaiming, Attacking, and Defending

If an exigency invites a fitting rhetorical response, then similar or recurrent rhetorical exigencies should invite similar fitting responses (Bitzer 1980). Each campaign asks how previous campaigns' strategies succeeded or failed, and the pattern of responses becomes a rhetorical form. Each of these forms is a composite of speech acts and the three major speech acts in presidential campaigns are acclaims, attacks, and defenses.

The Three Speech Acts

William L. Benoit has conducted a great deal of research on political campaign communication, much of it concerning the ways that campaigns blend their communication acts to influence voter preferences. Benoit tracks how candidates use communication to acclaim, attack, and defend. An "acclaim" is any statement that stresses a candidate's own advantages or benefits, whereas an "attack" is any statement that stresses the opponent's undesirable qualities or policy missteps. It is important to note that an attack can focus on the opponent's character, on a policy or course of action, or both (Benoit 2007).

A "defense" is any statement that responds to an "attack" – whether to prevent further damage or to restore the attacked candidate's lost preferability. Sometimes candidates choose not to defend because doing so requires them to acknowledge the attack and to perpetuate the news about it. They may not defend lest they be pulled onto the attacker's issues, preferring to engage in acclaims and attacks of their own. Or a campaign may avoid defending because they do not want to seem defensive (Benoit 2007). But most attacks need to be swiftly and decisively answered. It is the interplay of acclaims, attacks, and defenses that gives political campaign communication its distinctive character.

Because an acclaim seeks to highlight a candidate's advantages or benefits it will have factual, value, and connective components. The factual component asks the audience to agree that what the candidate says about some act, deed, or trait is accurate and truthful; the value component asks them to agree that it is positive and advantageous; and the connective component asks the audience to accept the association among the fact, the value, and the candidate. A candidate who says, "As governor I reduced government spending in my state," is making a factual claim (that government spending was reduced during that administration), and implying a value claim (that reducing government spending is preferable to increasing government spending), as well as implying that the candidate is connected to those two components (that the governor wanted spending reduced and was influential in making it happen).

Acclaims invite attacks, although Benoit does not say so. Some campaigns let their opponents travel the country acclaiming, "I have a record of cutting government spending," without responding but most respond with an attack. They can attack the factual component (arguing, for example, that the state's spending actually increased or that it did not decrease until after the governor left office). They can attack the value (arguing that the reduction in spending led to a collapse of essential services, a decline in student test scores or a loss of jobs to other states and argue, instead, for investing government revenue in the state). Or they can attack the connection (arguing that state spending decreased under the governor only because the legislature defeated the governor's budget and passed their own, or that the governor took no noticeable leadership on the issue). Some attacks may try to connect an acclaimed fact to an undesirable character flaw, shifting the focus from policy to character. Each of those three lines of argument can, in turn, focus on the policy or on the character of the candidate: the policy was a bad idea, or the episode reveals that the candidate is a bad person who should not be entrusted with the presidency.

Attacks, in turn, invite defense. Factual attacks can be defended with better facts, value attacks either by bolstering the value that has been attacked or by arguing that a different value explains the original acclaim. Value attacks are particularly important because when poorly defended they transcend the episode and undermine the candidate. Attacks on connections invite defense not only of the connection, but of the campaign's characterization of the connection (e.g. "reduced spending," "led the fight to reduce spending," "went along with those who reduced spending," or "caved in to those who sought to reduce spending") and of the character traits the connection implies.

A student of campaign discourse could keep score of each campaign's acclaims, attacks, and defenses of policy and character. Benoit did so in a series of exhaustive content analytic studies (see especially 1999, 2007) that complete the columns of the table. Benoit's (2007) data confirm that challengers devote a greater proportion of their discourse to attacks in acceptance addresses, TV spots, debates, and direct mail, whereas radio spots are the only medium where incumbents attack and challengers acclaim. Challengers and incumbents devote about 70 percent of their utterances to policy and 30 percent to character, but Democrats were significantly more likely to emphasize policy and Republicans to emphasize character. Primary campaigns witnessed significantly more acclaims and character statements, while general election campaigns have seen more attacks (and debate defenses) and character statements. Winning candidates emphasized policy (70%) and acclaims (70%) in primary TV ads, acceptance speeches, and direct mail; losers disproportionately emphasized character (35%) and attacks (30%) in acceptance addresses and direct mail. Statistically, there seems to be reason to run a positive, policy oriented campaign.

Two theoretical questions, however, have yet to be explored. The first concerns the lateral progression of campaign discourse from left to right: Which acclaims draw attacks and which attacks draw defenses? Which defenses undermine which attacks, and which attacks undermine which acclaims? The second unexplored area concerns the vertical progression of the table: How do discussions (acclaims/attacks/defenses) of past deeds impact impressions of future plans and goals?

How do discussions of policy impact impressions of character, and vice versa? Interesting as Benoit's data are, they do not yet enable us to answer those questions. That requires us to study the unfolding discourse of a campaign.

The Benchmark: Richard Nixon and "Checkers" (1952)

One familiar line of attack in political campaigns is corruption. Ordinarily one candidate charges that the other pursued personal gain, meaning that the person attacked has a character problem as well as a policy problem. The person attacked can defend character charge or policy. When a candidate is attacked like this, the advisors go back to "Checkers."

When General Dwight Eisenhower chose California Senator Richard M. Nixon as his running mate in 1952 Nixon's campaign speeches attacked the Truman Administration on the issues of "Corruption, Communism and Korea" (Nixon 1962). On September 18 the *New York Post* published a story about a "Secret Nixon Fund" "devoted exclusively to the personal comfort of Senator Nixon" (Nixon 1962, p. 5). The story did not support it's claims of "secrecy" or exclusively personal use, but when hecklers began asking Nixon to explain the fund the charges gained attention. Nixon realized he had a problem when the Republican *New York Herald Tribune* gave serious attention to the allegations.

Richard Nixon faced an intricate rhetorical puzzle. He needed to clear his name but the allegations were unsupported and unclear. Moreover, *Herald Tribune*'s publication of the story signalled Republican establishment doubts about Nixon's candidacy. Eisenhower advised Nixon to go on television and detail his public life and, as Nixon was leaving for the studio, Eisenhower's top advisors recommended he end his speech by resigning from the ticket.

Richard Nixon addressed the nation on television for half an hour on September 23, 1952 (Nixon 1952). Addressing America "as a man whose honesty and integrity has been questioned" he dismissed the question of whether he had acted illegally "because it isn't a question of whether it was legal or illegal, that isn't enough. The question is, was it morally wrong?" He then defined the grounds that would constitute "immoral" conduct: personal use, secrecy, or special favors. Having set out his standards, Nixon promptly addressed them. "Not one cent" of the fund "ever went to me for my personal use. Every penny of it was used to pay for political expenses" to spare taxpayers. Moreover, "It was not a secret fund," he said, explaining that when asked about it he told the reporter, "'Well, there's no secret about it. Go out and see Dana Smith who was the administrator of the fund.' And I gave him his address." Finally, as to undue influence, he said "no contributor to this fund, no contributor to any of my campaigns, has ever received any consideration that he would not have received as an ordinary constituent. I just don't believe in that" (Nixon 1952). All three responses were offered at face value by "a man whose honesty and integrity [had] been questioned."

The next portion of the speech encouraged identification by asking viewers how they might handle the demands and financial challenges of serving as a senator. The first three options were billing his Republican political expenses to taxpayers, being "a rich man. I don't happen to be a rich man, so I couldn't use that one" and putting his wife on the payroll. The fourth alternative would be for

Nixon's 1952 TV Address

him to continue to practice law, but he expressed personal ethical reservations about this course as well. He invited viewers to judge him for themselves, noting that his opponents used some of these techniques.

Nixon then introduced an audit from an accounting firm and disclosed his financial records and housing purchases in almost painful detail. He summarized by saying "That's what we have. And that's what we owe. It isn't very much. But Pat and I have the satisfaction that every dime that we've got is honestly ours" (Nixon 1952). And then, for a parting shot at his critics, he mentioned receiving a crate at the train station.

> It was a little cocker spaniel dog in a crate that he'd sent all the way from Texas, black and white, spotted. And our little girl Tricia, the six year old, named it "Checkers." And you know, the kids, like all kids, love the dog, and I just want to say this, right now, that regardless of what they say about it, we're gonna keep it.

The puppy passage invited viewers to perceive Democrats as people who would take the little dog away from the Nixon children.

Nixon then cited the chair of the Democratic National Committee as saying that "if a man couldn't afford to be in the United States Senate, he shouldn't run for the Senate." He turned it on them by saying:

> I believe that it's fine that a man like Governor Stevenson, who inherited a fortune from his father, can run for president. But I also feel that it's essential in this country of ours that a man of modest means can also run for president, because, you

know, remember Abraham Lincoln, you remember what he said: "God must have loved the common people – he made so many of them."

Suddenly, Stevenson and the Democrats were the party of the wealthy and Nixon, Lincoln, and the Republicans are the party of the common people.

Still remaining was the matter of Nixon's status on the ticket. Nixon took ownership of the decision and steered the feedback Eisenhower wanted away from the Eisenhower team.

> But the decision, my friends, is not mine. I would do nothing that would harm the possibilities of Dwight Eisenhower to become President of the United States. And for that reason I am submitting to the Republican National Committee tonight through this television broadcast the decision which it is theirs to make. Let them decide whether my position on the ticket will help or hurt. And I am going to ask you to help them decide. Wire and write the Republican National Committee whether you think I should stay on or whether I should get off. And whatever their decision is, I will abide by it.

Nixon, not Eisenhower, had deep roots in the Republican Party. When the telegrams and calls poured in to the RNC they overwhelmingly favored keeping Nixon on the ticket. Eisenhower greeted Nixon in Wheeling, West Virginia and pronounced him "my boy." But as Garry Wills (2002) observed, there was never after Checkers any trust between them.

Richard Nixon's Checkers speech was the first use of television to respond to an attack. But what makes it so important is the mixture of sophisticated maneuvers employed in one speech. It carefully defined the charges in ways that encouraged the answers he sought to provide, it encouraged audience identification, it made Nixon's personal preferences the moral standards, it counterattacked and it empowered the audience in whose hands Nixon wanted the decision to rest.

Deflating Acclaims: Gore and the Internet (2000)

On March 9, 1999 CNN's Wolf Blitzer asked Vice-President Al Gore what distinguished him from his Democratic opponent, Bill Bradley. Asked for an acclaim, Gore said, "During my service in the United States Congress, I took the initiative in creating the Internet. I took the initiative in moving forward a whole range of initiatives that have proven to be important to our country's economic growth and environmental protection, improvements in our educational system" (Gore 1999). A careful reader would notice that Gore said "initiative" three times and "Internet" once as he tried to establish initiative as the difference. But Blitzer moved on, and articles about the interview did not mention Gore's acclaim for several days. The Daily Howler said this was because most reporters were aware of Gore's leadership in Congress, and they quoted a 1994 *Washingtonian* reporter who had written, "Internet. There's no escaping it. It seems like only yesterday that Al Gore was preaching the merits of the *I-way* to a nation that still thought the *Net* was something used only for catching butterflies."

Two days after the interview Michelle Mittelstadt's AP wire story headlined that "Republicans pounce on Gore's claim that he created the Internet." The article began, "Vice-President Al Gore's claim that he is the father of the Internet drew amused protests Thursday from congressional Republicans." In the days that followed the *Washington Times* carried reactions including "Mr. Gore recently took credit for inventing the Internet" (John McCaslin), "[Steve Forbes] joked in an interview yesterday about Vice-President Al Gore's claim of having invented the Internet" (Ralph Z. Hallow) and "Al Gore. Inventor of the Internet" (Rowan Scarbrough). In each case, critics held Gore accountable for a factual claim that he had not made, while granting Gore the value claim that the Internet was a good thing. Not so William Kristol, whose editorial in the *Weekly Standard* on March 18 said, "Mr. Gore has some explaining to do to parents. As everyone now knows, Mr. Gore invented the Internet, which means the vice-president is responsible for making hard-core pornography available to elementary schoolchildren at the local library" (DailyHowler.com 2000).

Gore never fully extricated himself from this tangle. How could he defend himself without seeming defensive and calling still more attention to the controversy? But his critics escalated it from a criticism of policy to a criticism of his character .

The Candidate's Religion

Roderick P. Hart wrote that Americans deal with the delicate question of church/state separation by expecting politicians to acknowledge the presence and power of a benevolent supreme being, without becoming formally denominational (Hart 1977, 2005). But religion is culturally important in a land settled by people seeking freedom from religious oppression, and many perceive it as a valuable window on the candidate's inner self. Thus the question, "How will your personal religious beliefs affect your presidency?" has become increasingly popular despite Article VI Section 3 of the United States Constitution, which stipulates that "no religious Test shall ever be required as a Qualification to any Office or public Trust under the United States." But the clearly unconstitutional nature of an official religious test has not prevented citizens' groups and some in the media from stirring fears and prejudices.

John F. Kennedy (1960)

Rumors that John F. Kennedy would take orders from the Vatican undermined his candidacy with key southern voters and distracted the press from his rhetorical agenda. Kennedy planned to win the 1960 Democratic nomination by defeating Minnesota Senator Hubert Humphrey in the West Virginia primary, and polls had shown that Kennedy could win as much as 70 percent of the vote there against Humphrey. But aides Ken O'Donnell and Dave Powers arrived to find a very different situation.

> "Well," Bobby [Kennedy] said to [a room of precinct workers] pleasantly, "What are our problems?" A man jumped up and shouted, "There's only one problem. He's a Catholic. That's our God-damned problem!" The room broke into an uproar with everybody yelling at us that nobody in the state would vote for a Catholic in a contested presidential primary, or even in an election for dogcatcher. We were stunned by the suddenness of the wild emotional outburst from a group of people who had been working enthusiastically for Kennedy over the past several

months and who had never shown much concern about the religious issue up to
that time.   (quoted by Friedenberg 2002, p. 48)

Kennedy could hardly afford to ignore the issue, but he needed to defuse it without making matters worse. Although Kennedy could have addressed the issue in West Virginia, he chose the Greater Houston Ministerial Association as an audience capable of positively resolving the exigency – an audience of intelligent clergy with whom he could hope to reason.

Kennedy spoke of the kind of America in which he believed. He reframed the issue by inverting the factual portion of the attack that highlighted his religion, saying "I am not the Catholic candidate for President. I am the Democratic Party's candidate for President who happens also to be a Catholic" (Kennedy 1960).

Kennedy reminded his audience that the Constitution prohibited religious tests and that our forefathers "fled here to escape religious test oaths that denied office to members of less favored churches when they fought for the Constitution, the Bill of Rights, the Virginia Statute of Religious Freedom." He underscored his point with an example particularly well suited to his audience of Texans – the Alamo – where, "side by side with Bowie and Crockett died Fuentes, and McCafferty, and Bailey, and Badillo, and Carey but no one knows whether they were Catholics or not, for there was no religious test there." In fact, Kennedy's assistant, Dave Powers, was originally asked his to find out how many Catholics had died at the Alamo. But as Powers told the story, the lack of evidence led Kennedy to recast the speech into the more powerful, "there was no religious test" at the Alamo. This passage of Senator Kennedy's speech challenged the Baptist ministers, as leaders of public opinion, either to articulate and justify a need for unconstitutional religious tests in a nation founded on freedom of religion, or to oppose such attacks on his candidacy as challenges to the rights of all.

Lest the ministers be inclined to argue for such a test, Kennedy reminded them that they themselves had been similarly attacked in the past:

> For while this year it may be a Catholic against whom the finger of suspicion is
> pointed, in other years it has been and may someday be again a Jew, or a Quaker,
> or a Unitarian, or a Baptist. It was Virginia's harassment of Baptist preachers,
> for example, that led to Jefferson's statute of religious freedom. Today, I may be
> the victim, but tomorrow it may be you until the whole fabric of our harmonious
> society is ripped apart at a time of great national peril.

Rhetorical critic Robert V. Friedenberg found that in addition to opinion polls "a wide variety of religious leaders, journalists, and political figures, as well as the behavior of the Kennedy campaign, all suggest that his speech was a success" (Friedenberg 2002, p. 64). Kennedy's Houston address had provided a fitting response that hastened the deterioration of the imperfection and its urgency.

John F. Kerry (2004)

John Kerry was another Massachusetts senator who in 2004 became, in Kennedy's words, "the Democratic Party's candidate for President who happens also to be a Catholic." But the circumstances had changed during the intervening forty-four years: Roe v Wade had legalized many abortions and Kerry personally supported Democrats' efforts to keep the abortion decision personal rather than governmental. Thus where Kennedy needed to persuade non-Catholics, Kerry needed to persuade Catholics. As Steven Waldman (2004) wrote on *Slate*, "John Forbes Kerry's Catholicism raises a different question: Will he end up taking orders from the Vatican *too little?*"

Senator Kerry's problems reached new heights in early 2004 when St. Louis Archbishop Raymond L. Burke said that he would deny Kerry communion, and several other bishops concurred (Zapor 2007). The divergence between Kerry's Catholicism and his politics was a source of disturbance; a wedge issue that the Republicans were unlikely to ignore. During the Democratic convention, for example, the Republican National Committee's Director of Catholic Outreach e-mailed his team leaders that Kerry,

> Voted at least SIX times against the ban on partial birth abortions; Voted to allow federal money to distribute morning-after abortion pills in America's schools; Voted against requiring parental notification for a minor child's abortion; Voted against the federal Defense of Marriage Act in 1996, joining only 13 other Senators; Pledged to nominate ONLY those individuals to the Supreme Court who would uphold Roe v. Wade.   (Gillespie 2004)

Kerry's puzzle was clearly unlike Kennedy's.

John Kerry needed to persuade Catholics that he was true to the religion they shared. Where Kennedy had needed to defeat the religious test issue, Kerry needed to explain his membership in two conflicting proto-coalitions. Senator Kerry might have accomplished this task with a thoughtful and reflective speech. Instead, he tried to avoid the attacks, often responding too brusquely and carelessly to questions. Where Kennedy chose his audience with care, we know not whom Kerry addressed on such occasions; where Kennedy was somber, Kerry was belligerent; where Kennedy carefully developed his argument from his audience's perspective, Kerry simply let fly. The Catholic vote accounted for 27 percent of the 2004 electorate, and this approach helped "the candidate who happened to be Catholic" lose the Catholic vote to the President (who happened *not* to be Catholic) by a margin of 52 percent to 47 percent (Stewart, Russonello, and Sternfeld 2006).

Would a careful speech on the subject have made a difference? The Catholic News Service thinks so. "On the first day of November 2007," they wrote, "John Kerry finally gave a roomful of religion reporters the speech they waited to hear from him during the 2004 presidential campaign, when he was the Democratic nominee." The article suggests that Kerry finally figured out what he might have said: "You have a position on abortion, but you don't have a policy. I have to have a policy . . . He also said he doesn't think it's a contradiction to say he is both 'pro-choice' and 'anti-abortion.' One can have a deeply held belief that all life, including of unborn infants, is sacred, he said, while also accepting that in a pluralistic society making all abortions illegal would constitute an unfair imposition of those beliefs on others" (Zapor 2007). But Kerry found the solution to this puzzle more than two years after the rhetorical situation had disintegrated.

Obama on Race and Religion (2008)

The question of the candidate's religion took an unusual turn in 2008 when critics charged that Barack Obama was unfit to be president because he was secretly Muslim and/or because he followed the teachings of Reverend Jeremiah Wright at Chicago's Trinity United Church of Christ. Each presented the candidate with a different rhetorical puzzle.

The Muslim issue surfaced in late 2006 when conservative blogger Debbie Schlussel worked from Obama's name and parentage to point out that "In Arab culture and under Islamic law, if your father is a Muslim, so are you . . . In Islamic eyes, Obama is certainly a Muslim. He may think he's a Christian, but they do not" (Schlussel 2006). She also said he had attended a Muslim school for two years. Insight.com said that the issue had been raised by the Clinton Campaign and conservative talk show hosts savored the Obama-Clinton subplot. Media Matters. com complained that Insight.com was run by "the company controlled by Rev. Sun Myung Moon that also operates the *Washington Times* and the wire service United Press International" (Media Matters 2007a). When a member of the Obama campaign called Fox's reporting "appallingly irresponsible" Fox "cited Insight as the source of the allegations" (CNN 2007).

While Fox News reported the allegations CNN sent a reporter to investigate the school in Jakarta. John Vause reported. "I've been to those madrassas in Pakistan . . . this school is nothing like that." By January 26 the mainstream media were discounting Obama's "Muslim ties" but continued the discussion. Media Matters astutely observed that correspondents discussing the charges blurred the issue of accountability:

> Anderson Cooper, David Gregory, and Soledad O'Brien have all asked Sen. Barack Obama about smears leveled against him, purportedly by his political "opponents" or "enemies." But . . . by framing their questions in terms of political "opponents," they ignored the media's role in promoting these smears, and in some cases originating them.   (Media Matters 2007b)

With mainstream media and reputable politicians distancing themselves from the charges, e-mails began spreading them. About.com noted "No proof is offered by those who make these claims – no sightings of Barack Obama attending a mosque, no pictures of him reading the Koran, praying to Mecca, or observing Islamic holidays with his family." On the other hand, they also noted that most of what we know about Obama's and his parents' religion comes from him (About. com [2008]). FactCheck.org and Snopes.com also investigated the charges and found them to be false. Snopes reported that:

> One version of the e-mail in circulation claims "We were told this was checked out on 'snopes.com'. It is factual. Check for yourself." And includes a link to this web site. It's our guess that whoever included that bit was counting on folks to not check, as our article says just the opposite: the polemic is not factual but is false.   (Snopes.com 2009)

But leaving the defense to his staff and the media fact checkers did not stop the e-mails.

Senator Obama needed personally to engage the allegations. He spoke with

George Stephanopoulos on ABC's *This Week* on September 7 and said, in part, "You're absolutely right that John McCain has not talked about my Muslim faith." When the interviewer corrected him Obama said, "Well what I'm saying is that he hasn't suggested that I'm a Muslim, and I think his campaign upper echelons have not either" (YouTube 2008). Obama's use of the phrase "my Muslim faith" invited blogs and YouTube postings that gave the controversy fresh legs for a time.

The Obama/Muslim controversy was a Rorschach test. Those wary of him or his name were prepared to believe the charges. Republicans were prepared to believe that the Clinton people had raised the issue, and Clinton supporters were prepared to see it as the work of the "vast right-wing conspiracy" that had attacked her husband. But nobody seemed to have independent evidence sufficient to convince people inclined to believe the charges. That campaign was sufficiently successful that Obama had to personally deal with it during the ABC interview, and his careless phrasing compounded the problem.

The Jeremiah Wright issue arose when Obama's web site posted a "Fight the Smears" response to the Muslim allegation on January 24, 2008, saying "Barack Obama is a committed Christian. He was sworn into the Senate on his family Bible. He has regularly attended church with his wife and daughters for years" (My.barackobama.com 2008). The defense against Islam was an acclamation of his Christianity. He was "a *committed* Christian" who "*regularly attended church.*"

What church has he been attending all those years, one might fairly ask, and to what sort of Christianity has that committed him? Their church was Chicago's Trinity Unity Church of Christ led by the Reverend Jeremiah Wright. As February saw citizens becoming more familiar with Obama's Christianity, Hannity and Colmes invited Reverend Wright to appear on their Fox TV Show.

Sean Hannity introduced Wright's church as "a separatist movement, drawing comparisons to Branch Davidians" who had been involved in a fiery altercation with federal forces in Waco, Texas. He launched directly into his concern, asking. "Now, Reverend, if every time we said black, if there was a church and those words were white, wouldn't we call that church racist?" Wright said, "No, we would call it Christianity . . . We don't have to say the word 'white.' We just have to live in white America, the United States of white America." Rev. Wright wanted to discuss the theological tradition and context of his church, but Hannity did not. Eight times Rev. Wright asked Hannity if he had read anything about liberation theology or its leading thinkers and each time Hannity avoided answering with responses such as, "I studied theology; I went to a seminary. And I studied Latin," and "You're very angry and defensive."

Alan Colmes apparently tried to help Rev. Wright by asking, "Aren't there black churches all over America that say pretty much what your church says?" and Wright agreed. The problem was that "We've been singled out ever since the audacity of hope speech, ever since the Democratic convention, ever since the book 'Audacity of Hope,' ever since journalists found out that Barack was one of our members" (Hannity and Colmes 2008).

The overall message generated by this conversation was that Rev. Wright led a separatist church focused on black values that excludes whites in a manner that seemed un-Christian to their seminary student host, who found him oddly angry and defensive. Colmes and Wright inadvertently extended that characterization to encompass most other black churches. Rather than illuminating Wright's church or teachings, the program encouraged viewers to infer that most black churches are racist and separatist. The questions grew, as did the desire to answer them.

Barack Obama dealt with the controversy in a March 18 speech at the Constitution Center in Philadelphia. His exigency was his long-term relationship with Wright's allegedly separatist ministry and, by implication, other black churches. Obama distanced himself from Wright's "incendiary language" and "views that denigrate both the greatness and the goodness of our nation, and that rightly offend white and black alike." He singled out Wright's recent remarks that "expressed a profoundly distorted view of this country – a view that sees white racism as endemic, and that elevates what is wrong with America above all that we know is right with America." He reminded his listeners that he had previously "condemned, in unequivocal terms" Wright's offending statements.

But if Obama distanced himself from Wright's ideas or values then "Why not join another church?" He explained that "the snippets" on television and YouTube were not "all that I know of the man."

> The man I met more than 20 years ago is a man who helped introduce me to my Christian faith, a man who spoke to me about our obligations to love one another, to care for the sick and lift up the poor. He is a man who served his country as a United States Marine; who has studied and lectured at some of the finest universities and seminaries in the country, and who for over 30 years has led a church that serves the community by doing God's work here on Earth – by housing the homeless, ministering to the needy, providing day care services and scholarships and prison ministries, and reaching out to those suffering from HIV/AIDS.

Obama and Wright were connected as two imperfect people bound together in an interpersonal relationship. Obama broadened his focus from Wright to Trinity to black churches in general, whose members are bound by community:

> Like other predominantly black churches across the country, Trinity embodies the black community in its entirety – the doctor and the welfare mom, the model student and the former gang-banger. Like other black churches, Trinity's services are full of raucous laughter and sometimes bawdy humor. They are full of dancing and clapping and screaming and shouting that may seem jarring to the untrained ear. The church contains in full the kindness and cruelty, the fierce intelligence and the shocking ignorance, the struggles and successes, the love and, yes, the bitterness and biases that make up the black experience in America.

It is this interface among Rev. Wright's personal contributions, the black experience, and Christian teachings that created a community for Obama. "He contains within him the contradictions – the good and the bad – of the community that he has served diligently for so many years."

Because of this interconnectedness, Obama could "no more disown him than I can disown the black community. I can no more disown him than I can disown my white grandmother – . . . These people are a part of me. And they are part of America, this country that I love."

Perhaps the most important innovation in the speech was Obama's criticism of Wright for not believing in the supremacy of the Obama campaign's central theme: Change.

> The profound mistake of Reverend Wright's sermons is not that he spoke about racism in our society. It's that he spoke as if our society was static; as if no progress had been made; as if this country – a country that has made it possible for one of his own members to run for the highest office in the land and build a coalition of white and black, Latino and Asian, rich and poor, young and old – is still irrevocably bound to a tragic past. But what we know – what we have seen – is that America can change. That is the true genius of this nation. What we have already achieved gives us hope – the audacity to hope – for what we can and must achieve tomorrow.

In this passage Obama put his campaign on the line, for he was saying that those who believe him to be a disciple of Wright's could not also believe his rhetoric of change. Those who believe in his orientation toward change, however, are given a familiar framework for differentiating his worldview from Wright's.

The key to Obama's speech was the pursuit of perfection. Speaking at the Constitution Center enabled him to discuss the Constitution. "The document . . . was eventually signed but ultimately unfinished," he said. "It was stained by this nation's original sin of slavery." A former Constitutional Law professor, Obama explained how the document enshrined an ideal and provided procedures for attaining a "More Perfect Union" and committed his campaign to that mission. Obama helped non-black listeners see how there might be anger in the black community that could seep into the remarks of black clergy, and he helped his non-white listeners know how there could be anger in the white community that could find its way into the remarks of some white clergy.

Obama's larger objective was to unify. Where his predecessors had spoken of Catholicism and his critics spoke of Islam and Afro-centric separatism, Obama transcended religious differences, saying, "what is called for is nothing more and nothing less than what all the world's great religions demand – that we do unto others as we would have them do unto us." To do so would require looking beyond race in recommending future policies. He did this by positioning white, black, and Hispanic Americans together in an imperfect world.

- This time, we want to talk about the crumbling schools that are stealing the future of black children and white children and Asian children and Hispanic children and Native American children . . .
- This time we want to talk about how the lines in the emergency room are filled with whites and blacks and Hispanics who do not have health care.
- This time, we want to talk about the fact that the real problem is not that someone who doesn't look like you might take your job; it's that the corporation you work for will ship it overseas for nothing more than a profit.
- This time, we want to talk about the men and women of every color and creed who serve together and fight together and bleed together under the same proud flag.

"This union may never be perfect," Obama concedes, "but generation after generation has shown that it can always be perfected."

Although public reaction to Obama's speech was positive the controversy continued to simmer. Then Wright told Bill Moyers that Obama had "responded as a politician" in Philadelphia. Three days later at the National Press Club Wright said "If Senator Obama did not say what he said, he would not ever get elected. Politicians say what they say and do what they do based on electability . . . " (Brune 2008). These and other statements at the amounted to a repudiation of Obama's speech, and continued to overshadow the campaign's message. On April 29 Obama held a press conference to say, "The person I saw yesterday was not the person I met twenty years ago. His comments were not only divisive and destructive, but they end up giving comfort to those that prey on hate" (Wright 2008). He had been forced by Rev. Wright and his critics to disassociate himself from a man he had said he could not disavow.

It would be difficult to argue that Obama "won" either the Muslim or the Wright issues; the first would not go away and the second caused him considerable anguish and a reversal of position. But the Wright episode created the rhetorical situation that invited the Philadelphia speech, and that almost certainly helped him to broach the topic of race in America and to use it to reach out to undecided Democrats.

Kennedy, Kerry, and Obama handled the questions about their religions in different ways. Kennedy spoke, Kerry did not; Obama spoke in one case but not the other. All three declined to be defined by their religions, Kerry perhaps to a fault. Kennedy's speech was the benchmark for this exigency for nearly fifty years, until Obama used religion as a way to discuss imperfection and the struggle toward perfection.

In the final analysis, however, persuasion depends upon one's ability to influence the audience capable of resolving the exigency. Kennedy's speech was unique because he chose to take his case not to a friendly audience or an audience of convenience but into the lions' den. There he faced Protestant clergy capable of influencing public opinion, looked them in the eye and reasoned with them.

Summary and Conclusions

This chapter has explained the sequence of acclaiming, attacking, and defending at the heart of presidential campaigns.

- An "acclaim" is any statement that stresses a candidate's own advantages or benefits.
  - An acclaim has factual, value and connective components
  - Acclaims invite attacks
- An "attack" is any statement that stresses the opponent's undesirable qualities or policy missteps.
  - An attack can counter the factual, value, and/or connective component
  - An attack can focus on policy or character
  - Attacks invite defense
- A "defense" is any statement that responds to an "attack."
  - Factual attacks can be defended with better facts

- Value attacks can be defended by bolstering the value that has been attacked or by arguing that a different value explains the original acclaim
- Connections must be defended in terms of the particular acclaim.

Benoit's research demonstrates that the overwhelming majority of campaign statements are acclaims about policy, and that losing candidates are the most likely to emphasize attacks on character. But candidates cannot run on acclaims alone – sooner or later they must engage their opponent's acclaims with an attack.

We considered several case studies of this process. They showed that:

- If Nixon had not attacked corruption the Democrats might not have charged him with corruption.
- But Nixon turned their attack upon his character into an attack on theirs while making the Republican National Committee rather than the Campaign Organization his jury.
- When Gore acclaimed that "he took initiative" in Congress to differentiate himself from Senator Bradley his critics construed it as a claim that he had invented the Internet and used it to attack his character.
- Kennedy defended against attacks on his religion by emphasizing that importance to all Americans that there are no religious tests for the presidency.
- Kerry failed to satisfactorily answer Catholic critics' attacks that his policies conflicted with his religions.
- Obama struggled with e-mail attacks on his purported Muslim background and acclaimed his devout Christianity.
- Obama's acclaimed Christianity brought his association with Rev. Wright to the fore and the attacks on Wright, and his response to them, led Obama to renounce his pastor.

The increasing attention to questions pertaining to candidates' religious beliefs suggests that there is a critical mass of citizens who feel that there ought to be some sort of religious test for political office. Although the founders explicitly rejected this value, we have amended the Constitution 27 times to address things they did not foresee or to resolve disagreements with them about slavery and suffrage. Rather than attacking candidates on unconstitutional grounds with anonymous e-mails, advocates of religious tests might seek publicly to amend Article VI of the Constitution to allow religious tests. This would be a radical change, to be sure, but it would be an honorable and Constitutional strategy. Meanwhile, candidates must be aware that the more they acclaim, the more they invite attacks.

Finally this chapter should have made it clear that acclaiming, attacking, and defending are a communication sequence – an ongoing argument. Many of us dislike the attention that attacks receive but it is unrealistic to expect campaigns to consist only of acclaims because in a competitive situation acclaims invite responses. What we can do, as we have done in this chapter, is to reconstruct the argument to better understand and critically evaluate it.

6 Campaign Speeches

The oldest of the campaign communication modes we shall consider, and one of the most familiar, is the campaign speech. Speeches provide candidates with opportunities to offer extended personal arguments. It is a speech that can provide a detailed critique of what has gone wrong and how we need to fix it. It is a speech that can set forth a vision of the kind of society we can create. It is a speech that engages listeners in a personally memorable contact with a candidate. Sadly these speeches are often reduced to sound bites and catch phrases that obscure the very features that make the speech unique. But this is not a new phenomenon. Almost any speech that is remembered today has been reduced to a sound bite. A speech needs to convey its main point in a memorable phrase, but there should be more to that point than the phrase.

Studying Campaign Speeches

The tasks of speechwriting and rhetorical analysis are not very different. The speechwriter drafts a speech and then uses rhetorical analysis to revise and polish it. A rhetorical critic examines a speech for evidence of the choices made in its preparation and considers them in comparison to the choices that might have been made, frequently drafting an alternative text to illustrate what could have been said. Rhetorical scholar and speechwriter Craig R. Smith suggested that the critic create a potential or ideal speech. "To create this ideal, the critic would need to ask many of the questions that the creator of the artifact had asked. In the case of rhetorical criticism, one needs to hypothesize which configuration of proofs – that have been predetermined by audience, speaker, and message – under what form will best solve the rhetorical problems thrown up by the situation" (Smith 1970, p. 139). Armed with this ideal the critic can consider where the delivered text succeeded and where it fell short. Understanding the rhetorical situation is one way critics and speechwriters sketch out the best potential choices.

General Considerations

We can therefore frame our consideration of campaign speeches with some basic considerations that guide speakers and students of speeches. First and foremost, the whole speech matters. Never should a serious student of speeches rely on reports about a speech. The transcript of the speech (as delivered, if that can be verified) is essential. A speaker intent on having the audience remember a single point or sentence would be unwise to speak for an hour, but many do so. Precisely because speeches allow speakers to detail their plans and programs we ought to consider them fully and thoughtfully on their own terms. The critic of campaign speeches will often want to compare reports about the speech and commentary on it with the speech, but that comes later.

Speech transcripts used to be difficult to obtain. Then C-SPAN began televising campaign speeches, early web sites of the 1990s posted speech texts and search engines helped us locate them. Today campaign speech texts and video can be easily located and downloaded through Google, Yahoo, and other search engines. Americanrhetoric.com is a particularly valuable site that maintains an extensive speech bank of historic and contemporary speeches that can be easily accessed.

The second general consideration is to hold all speakers to the same high standards whether you support them or not. Much as the sports teams we support sometimes play poorly and their opponents play well, the candidates we support do not necessarily fulfil their rhetorical potential nor do their opponents necessarily craft poor speeches. Good critics can find strengths and weaknesses in speeches without regard to their personal politics, although all speeches are not created equal.

The third consideration is that an analysis of a speech should illuminate the speech. It should explain how and why the speech worked for whom, what was notable about it, and what the reader can take from it to inform the analysis of other speeches. Thus I prefer "rhetorical analysis" to the more common term "rhetorical criticism" that seems to inspire beginners to judge something a "great" or "failed" speech more than illuminate. Too often such judgments say more about the critic than the speech and provide little of lasting value to its readers.

Analyzing Speeches

There is no single way to study a speech but we can set forth some general guidelines. The first step is to closely study the speech transcript without regard to its context. This "intrinsic analysis" of the text is important because our knowledge of the context can influence our expectations and affect our impression of the speaker's words. Read the speech as a detective would read a letter left at a crime scene. Begin with obvious questions and then look at subtleties.

What does the speech say? This calls for attention to the speaker's extended argument. You might outline the speech's points to determine what points or arguments the speech attempts to make. You can then go through your outline and note other points that were not made. For example, in 2008 both major candidates sought to "reduce our dependence on foreign oil." But when we study their speeches we find that one wanted to drill for oil in Alaska and offshore to "reduce our dependence on *foreign* oil" while his opponent wanted to develop other kinds of energy sources to "reduce our dependence on foreign *oil.*" They advanced the same claim but in substantially different ways.

Once you have the arguments down you can ask what kind of proofs the speech used to support them. Are they simply asserted at face value? Does the speech develop the arguments with human stories or narratives that foster identification between speaker and audience or with impersonal evidence and statistics? Does the support provided actually prove the argument or does it help the audience feel positively toward the speaker?

What values are used to portray good things and what values are used to portray bad or frightening things? Because many politicians frame political issues in moral terms it is helpful to look for indications of their moral philosophies. The same is true of values like "freedom" (For whom? From what? To do what?), "progress" (Along what path? Toward what goal? At what cost?) and "patriotism" (What is best for America? How does one help America?).

What is the overall tone of the speech – is it joyous, angry, worried, or hopeful? One indication of the tone is its complexity. Does the speech use language and sentence structure that is simple or complex? Short sentences are easier to deliver and more easily digested but they rarely enable the speech to fine-tune its ideas. Another indication of tone can be found in metaphors. Does the speech use the language of nature (light and dark, seasons and storms, mountains and oceans), religion, war, athletics, and the like consistently, mix them or generally avoid them?

Armed with these observations about the text the rhetorical analyst can begin to ask some speculative questions. First, what do all of these observations imply about the audience(s) that might like the speech? One could reasonably expect a speech full of military language, for example, to be better received by a veterans' organization than by pacifists, and biblical references would probably not fare well with an Islamic audience. Second, what do these observations imply about the speaker? What can you infer from them about the speaker's preferred sources of good information, grasp of history, and worldview? Do they provide clues as to which people the speaker trusts and mistrusts, or to which of the Pew types she belongs?

After studying the transcript several times to answer these questions you should listen to an audio version of the speech to see if the speaker's delivery enhanced the written text or conflicted with it. Then take the next step and watch the video to see how the setting and physical delivery enhanced the written text or conflicted with it. In this way you add one dimension at a time to your analysis of the transcript.

The second step is to consider the potential of the rhetorical situation. This "extrinsic analysis" requires research into the circumstances that brought about the speech, including the speaker's objectives and audience reactions to it. News accounts are helpful here as well as polls, articles by campaign personnel and memoirs. Blogs and editorials provide reactions to many speeches, and when they do not it may indicate that the speech went unnoticed.

The third step is to move from the descriptive to the analytical part of the critical process. This calls for you to compare the actual speech that was given to the potential speech called for by the rhetorical situation (Smith 1970). This ordinarily leads us to see some good choices that produced fitting responses and others that produced less than ideal responses. Which of these strikes you as more important? Perhaps the speech fulfilled its potential except for overly complex sentences that seem to have inflicted only minimal damage. Or maybe the speech was beautifully crafted but addressed the wrong audience. That decision is yours and you should make it carefully on the basis of your descriptive analyses.

Why did the actual speech compare as it did to the rhetorical situation's potential? When you think you have that answer you will want to read the literature about that explanation. Generic Criticism suggests that recurrent rhetorical situations such as announcement speeches should have generic features and you may find that the speech you analyzed perfectly fulfilled its generic requirements or that it failed to meet them. Narrative criticism focuses on stories and you may discover that the speech's stories were well or poorly used. Argumentative Criticism analyzes the arguments and proofs and Dramatistic Criticism explores the social dramas and motives implied by the speech. Any rhetorical criticism text can help you decide which of these and other critical approaches can best help you explain how the speech fulfilled, or failed to fulfill, its potential. It is important to remember that scholars have analyzed a great many speeches and their published works can help you to explain the speech you have chosen to study.

The remainder of this chapter will analyze several important campaign speeches that are suggestive of recurrent exigencies in presidential campaigns to illustrate what we can learn about a campaign by studying speeches and to illustrate the analytical process.

Case Studies: Creating a People with a Past and a Mission

We will consider how three kinds of speeches work to introduce a candidate, motivate disappointed party faithful to back the nominee and then coalesce the nominee's potential supporters into a People with a historic mission in opposition to the other party. We will compare two speeches that publicly announce that the candidate will run for president, two convention addresses by defeated candidates and two nomination acceptance addresses. Because we are concerned with a candidate's campaign to build a personal electoral coalition from audience value and policy preferences we need a theoretical framework that will connect our observations about audience identity.

Maurice Charland's (1987) theory of "constitutive rhetoric" seems a good fit. He described how a speaker creates an audience of subjects with an identity prior to formally persuading them. He suggested that a speaker "hails" listeners; much as a policeman says, "Hey, you there," the speaker says, "My fellow Republicans (or Democrats)" and demands individual listeners or readers to respond, "Who, me?" The speech's ideology "recruits" listeners with appeals like, "you who work two jobs to make ends meet" or "you who know that taxes are too high." Thus the speaker uses the key terms of the campaign's ideology to mark off a space for prospective followers.

Individual listeners who hear themes with which they can identify step into the nominee's space and become the nominee's People. Those inside that space share the speaker's rhetorical present. But effective constitutive rhetoric must extend that shared present backward into a shared past with a historical narrative of community that "masks or negates tensions or differences between members" (Charland 1987, p. 140). These shared historical narratives help Republicans revel in Reaganism without reflecting on his break with Nixon, Ford, and Kissinger as it enables Democrats to cherish their support for civil rights and ignore southern Democrats' historic support for segregation.

A second theoretical framework will help us understand how speakers create shared historical narratives. The earliest American rhetorical form developed in the Puritan sermon. The preacher reminded his congregation that they were a unique people, chosen by God for a mission to create His community in the wilderness. The terrible trials and tribulations they faced were explained either as Divine tests of faith or as Divine punishment for the Puritans' straying from their sacred mission. Relief from the hardships of life could be found only through renewed obedience to God – as set forth by the Puritan leaders.

When the Puritans declined the form persisted in secular form as the "jeremiad" – Americans as a chosen people with a sacred mission who construe their challenges as tests of faith for straying from their basic principles (Bercovitch 1975). Kurt Ritter (1980) found that many presidential acceptance speeches had the rhetorical characteristics of jeremiads. Instead of quoting the gospel they quoted presidents and other great Americans, each party crafting its own version of "real Americanism." Thus, the new wrinkle was that problems could be attributed to "false prophets" of the other party who had led the people astray.

The jeremiad complements constitutive rhetoric because it explains how the constituted community's problems result not from their lack of effort or intelligence but from either their insufficient belief in their shared historical narrative or the false leadership of those who misunderstand the constituting narrative. The problems can therefore only be resolved by believing ever more fervently in their unifying narrative, shared identity, and leaders and rejecting and denouncing their opponents. Yet a jeremiad can have no appeal unless there is a shared identity infused with a historical narrative inscribed with ideological principles from which people could stray and then return.

This synthesis of constitutive rhetoric and jeremiads prepares us to look at how campaign speeches call a people into being, inscribe them with an ideological historical narrative and attribute problems to a lack of faith in the historical narrative and its fundamental precepts or to the temptations of false prophets.

Announcement Addresses

The traditional announcement address exemplifies generic criticism because certain things must happen if the candidacy is to become public knowledge. This speech normally takes place at a location symbolizing an important aspect of the candidate's message. The event should be planned and staged to convey a sense of enthusiasm for the person's candidacy. The speaker needs to show how her or his life story has led to the decision to run for the presidency, establishing it as a fitting response to the nation's needs and the candidate's preparation. Let us consider how Barack Obama and John McCain handled these tasks.

Barack Obama's Announcement

Barack Obama announced his candidacy in Springfield, Illinois on February 10, 2007. He told the story of his move to Illinois to introduce his character traits. He was "without money or family connections" when "a group of churches ... offered me a job" that he accepted, "motivated then by a single, simple, powerful idea – that I might play a small part in building a better America." His work took Obama "to some of Chicago's poorest neighborhoods [where] I joined with pastors and lay-people to deal with communities that had been ravaged by plant closings."

The speech further implied that Obama learns from his experiences. In Chicago he learned that "the problems people faced weren't simply local in nature" and that "when a child turns to violence, there's a hole in his heart no government could ever fill." Although an Ivy Leaguer with a Muslim name, "It was in these neighborhoods that I received the best education I ever had, and where I learned the true meaning of my Christian faith."

The lessons Obama learned on the streets of Chicago motivated him to study law and to run for public office. "I went to law school, because I wanted to understand how the law should work for those in need." He "became a civil rights lawyer, and taught constitutional law" and eventually "came to understand that our cherished rights of liberty and equality depend on the active participation of an awakened electorate." Those ideas took him to the Illinois State Senate.

The biographical portion of Obama's address used the theme of his personal commitment to "building a better America" to give purpose and structure to his résumé. He twice aligned himself with Christianity and distanced himself from the wealthy while demonstrating his active concern for those in need.

But Democrats who take the side of the underprivileged against the wealthy are often attacked for engaging in a rhetoric of "class warfare." Obama's speech took a different approach by elaborating the theme of convergence. It was in state politics where Obama "saw all that is America converge":

> farmers and teachers, businessmen and laborers, all of them with a story to tell, all of them seeking a seat at the table, all of them clamoring to be heard. I made lasting friendships here – friends that I see in the audience today.

Indeed Obama had learned that the key to Americans converging is to be experienced in state, not national, government:

> It was here we learned to disagree without being disagreeable – that it's possible to compromise so long as you know those principles that can never be compromised; and that so long as we're willing to listen to each other, we can assume the best in people instead of the worst.

Convergence in Illinois had brought beneficial results.

> That's why we were able to reform a death penalty system that was broken. That's why we were able to give health insurance to children in need. That's why we made the tax system more fair and just for working families, and that's why we passed ethics reforms that the cynics said could never, ever be passed.

Moreover, his state level experience convinced Obama to offer hope for the nation at large:

> It was here, in Springfield, where north, south, east and west come together that I was reminded of the essential decency of the American people – where I came to believe that through this decency, we can build a more hopeful America.

And thus he concluded that he should run for president:

> And that is why, in the shadow of the Old State Capitol, where Lincoln once called on a divided house to stand together, where common hopes and common

dreams still, I stand before you today to announce my candidacy for President of the United States.

Obama's announcement speech needed to show that his life had prepared him to be a Democratic candidate for president. The speech did that by telling a linear story about the need for persons of varied interests to come together through state government to solve their common problems and create a better America. People and interests can converge in cooperative teamwork when they learn to "disagree without being disagreeable." Most importantly individuals need to enhance their cooperative abilities, as Obama did when we attended law school.

But Obama's story failed to address a key question – how he would deal with disagreeable people. Those disagreeable people are implicit in his story of national government and they lurk offstage in foreign affairs. Jimmy Carter and George W. Bush were state convergers who had met their match in Washington – how would Obama prove more successful?

John McCain's Announcement

Republican Senator John McCain told a different kind of story when he announced his candidacy in Portsmouth, New Hampshire on April 25, 2007. Implicit in McCain's story was his duty to serve his country. He announce his candidacy "grateful for the privileges this country has already given me; mindful that I must seek this responsibility for reasons greater than self-interest; and determined to use every lesson I've learned through hard experience and the history I've witnessed, every inspiration I've drawn from the patriots I've known and the faith that guides me to meet the challenges of our time, and strengthen this great and good nation upon whom all mankind depends."

McCain returned to America from his ordeal as a Vietnamese prisoner of war. "While I was away, I fell in love with my country. I learned that what's good for America, is good enough for me. I have been an imperfect servant of my country ever since, in uniform and in office, in war and peace. I have never lived a single day, in good times or in bad, that I haven't thanked God for the privilege." McCain did not say why he served, suggesting that service for him was an end in itself.

McCain's theme was divergence and he explained it in terms of international strife. "We are fighting a war in two countries, and we're in a global struggle with violent extremists who despise us, our values and modernity itself." American success would depend on our policy choices:

> If we are to succeed, we must rethink and rebuild the structure and mission of our military; the capabilities of our intelligence and law enforcement agencies; the purposes of our alliances; the reach and scope of our diplomacy; the capacity of all branches of government to defend us. We need to marshal all elements of American power: our military, economy, investment, trade and technology. We need to strengthen our alliances and build support in other nations. We must preserve our moral credibility, and remember that our security and the global progress of our ideals are inextricably linked.

Solving those problems required decisive action.

> When I'm president I'll offer common sense, conservative, and comprehensive solutions to these challenges. Congress will have other ideas, and I'll listen to them. I'll work with anyone who is serious and sincere about solving these problems. I expect us to argue over principle, but when a compromise consistent with our principles is within reach, I expect us to seize it.

McCain presented an image of himself as a leader that was supremely confident. Consider his personal acclaims in the following passage:

> We face formidable challenges, but I'm not afraid of them. *I'm prepared* for them. I'm not the youngest candidate. But *I am the most experienced. I know* how the military works, what it can do, what it can do better, and what it should not do. *I know* how Congress works, and how to make it work for the country and not just the re-election of its members. *I know* how the world works. *I know* the good and the evil in it. *I know* how to work with leaders who share our dreams of a freer, safer, and more prosperous world, and how to stand up to those who don't. *I know* how to fight and how to make peace. *I know* who I am and what I want to do.

There is no uncertainty or modesty here; some audiences like that and others wince.

Senator McCain's announcement speech tells a story of a man prepared to run for the Republican nomination. He is a determined warrior, prepared once again to serve his country. He twice disavowed personal interest, which may suggest that he had heard criticism of his personal ambition or that he felt it especially important to convince people that he did not seek personal power. McCain's story presents a man unafraid of being perceived by his adversaries as disagreeable. But McCain's speech hinted that he might be unprepared to find accommodation with those who are neither his allies nor his adversaries – those in his party who lean toward other candidates and undecided voters in the general election.

Comparison

We said that announcement speeches normally take place at a location symbolizing an important aspect of the candidate's message. Obama spoke in front of the Illinois capitol where he and Abraham Lincoln had served and McCain spoke in the state holding the first primary. Obama's site was the highly symbolic, and McCain's Portsmouth, New Hampshire announcement could have been at the Soldiers and Sailors Monument – but if he gave it there the symbolism was under utilized. The event should be planned and staged to convey a sense of enthusiasm for the person's candidacy, and both campaigns did so. The speaker needs to show how her or his life story has led to the decision to run for the presidency, establishing it as a fitting response to the nation's needs and the candidate's preparation.

Obama and McCain both used their life stories as required by the situation, but the differences between them are readily apparent. Obama told of a man running to make America a better country from the inside whereas McCain told of a man running to protect America's future in a threatening world. Obama sought to do so through domestic convergence and McCain sought to do so through international divergence. Obama spoke of cooperation and McCain implied a readiness to command.

Convention Speeches ▨▨▨▨▨▨▨▨▨▨▨▨▨▨▨▨▨▨▨▨▨▨

Party conventions consist of many speeches. They are an important part of the consolidation process because they allow many voices to be heard and applauded. Ordinarily the party wants to consolidate behind the nominee after the primaries, but sometimes a faction seeks to lay claim to the party's future direction. They provide an opportunity for us to consider factional voices within parties as vanquished candidates try to unify their party while securing their own positions. This section will consider how two speeches did so in different ways.

Jesse Jackson's Patchwork Quilt of Unity

One particularly effective unifying convention speech was Reverend Jesse Jackson address to the 1988 Democratic National Convention. The convention was held in Atlanta, and Rev. Jackson made the time and place of the meeting significant. "We've come to Atlanta, the cradle of the old south, the crucible of the new south," said Jackson. "We meet tonight at the crossroads, a point of decision" to face the question: "Shall we expand, be inclusive, find unity and power; or suffer division and impotence?" Jackson's speech makes Atlanta a metaphoric crossroads of time and culture, where the new south meets the old south. It is significant like "Jerusalem, the intersection where many trails met. A small village that became the birthplace for three great religions – Judaism, Christianity, and Islam." Historically it is at such crossroads "where different people met, different cultures, different civilizations could meet and find common ground." But where some speakers would see conflict in the Middle East crossroads Jackson saw blessings: "When people come together, flowers always flourish – the air is rich with the aroma of a new spring" (Jackson 1988).

Jackson used urban gathering places to move from Atlanta in the south to another crossroads closer to the party's base:

> Take New York, the dynamic metropolis. What makes New York so special? It's the invitation at the Statue of Liberty, "Give me your tired, your poor, your huddled masses who yearn to breathe free." Not restricted to English only. Many people, many cultures, many languages with one thing in common: They yearn to breathe free. Common ground.

Jackson then brings his audience, steeped in his theme of diverse peoples convening at crossroads, back to Atlanta.

> Tonight in Atlanta, for the first time in this century, we convene in the south; a state where Governors once stood in school house doors; where Julian Bond was denied a seat in the State Legislature because of his conscientious objection to the Vietnam War; a city that, through its five Black Universities, has graduated more black students than any city in the world. Atlanta, now a modern intersection of the new south.

But if Atlanta is the crossroads for all of these diverse people, who are the specific peoples that need to come together?

"Common ground," Jackson repeated, is "the challenge of our party tonight – left wing, right wing." One might reasonably expect a speaker with Jesse Jackson's liberal credentials to urge the party to the left, but he did not. Instead he urged them toward cooperation and mutual understanding. "Progress will not come through boundless liberalism nor static conservatism, but at the critical mass of mutual survival," he said. "It takes two wings to fly. Whether you're a hawk or a dove, you're just a bird living in the same environment, in the same world." Rev. Jackson transitions from those birds to the biblical lion and lamb who live in peace "Because neither lions nor lambs want the forest to catch on fire. Neither lions nor lambs want acid rain to fall. Neither lions nor lambs can survive nuclear war. If lions and lambs can find common ground, surely we can as well – as civilized people." He reminds his audience that "The only time that we win is when we come together."

Jackson then used the metaphor of a patchwork quilt to speak to all of the divided Democratic constituencies listening to him. "America is not a blanket woven from one thread, one color, one cloth," he began.

> When I was a child growing up in Greenville, South Carolina and grandmamma could not afford a blanket, she didn't complain and we did not freeze. Instead she took pieces of old cloth – patches, wool, silk, gabardine, crockersack – only patches, barely good enough to wipe off your shoes with. But they didn't stay that way very long. With sturdy hands and a strong cord, she sewed them together into a quilt, a thing of beauty and power and culture. Now, Democrats, we must build such a quilt.

Having presented the central metaphor of the quilt and linking it with "sturdiness," "beauty," "power" and "culture," he forthrightly addressed each group:

- Farmers, you seek fair prices and you are right – but you cannot stand alone. Your patch is not big enough.
- Workers, you fight for fair wages, you are right – but your patch labor is not big enough.
- Women, you seek comparable worth and pay equity, you are right – but your patch is not big enough.
- Women, mothers, who seek Head Start, and day care and prenatal care on the front side of life, relevant jail care and welfare on the back side of life, you are right – but your patch is not big enough.
- Students, you seek scholarships, you are right – but your patch is not big enough.
- Blacks and Hispanics, when we fight for civil rights, we are right – but our patch is not big enough.
- Gays and lesbians, when you fight against discrimination and a cure for AIDS, you are right – but your patch is not big enough.
- Conservatives and progressives, when you fight for what you believe, right wing, left wing, hawk, dove, you are right from your point of view, but your point of view is not enough.

Then Jackson stitched those patches together:

> But don't despair. Be as wise as my grandmamma. Pull the patches and the pieces together, bound by a common thread. When we form a great quilt of unity and common ground, we'll have the power to bring about health care and housing and jobs and education and hope to our Nation. We, the people, can win.

Even when Jackson's message stung his listeners it was part of a larger message of unity, cooperation, and hope that inspired his audience. Jesse Jackson's quilt metaphor was too long to be an ideal sound bite, but it is a marvellous example of a convention speaker using language to stitch together the factions of his party.

Pat Buchanan's Culture War

Pat Buchanan was a speechwriter for Presidents Nixon and Reagan and a prominent conservative voice in his own right by 1992 when he challenged President Bush for the Republican nomination. He won 38 percent of the New Hampshire vote and three million votes in primaries but not the nomination. His convention speech of August 17 sought to consolidate Republicans around President Bush's candidacy and Buchanan's ideas.

Buchanan's speech drew a stark line between his audience and the Democrats. He characterized the Democratic convention as a masquerade "where 20,000 radicals and liberals came dressed up as moderates and centrists in the greatest single exhibition of cross-dressing in American political history" (Buchanan 2008). He noted that "A militant leader of the homosexual rights movement could rise at the convention and say, 'Bill Clinton and Al Gore represent the most pro-lesbian and pro-gay ticket in history.' And so they do." The Democratic agenda did not represent Americans, in Buchanan's view, but "would impose on America" policies including "abortion on demand, homosexual rights, discrimination against religious schools, women in combat units."

For Buchanan the 1992 presidential election was not to be about disagreements but about something much deeper and more fundamental.

> My friends, this election is about more than who gets what. It is about who we are. It is about what we believe and what we stand for as Americans. There is a religious war going on in this country for the soul of America. It is a cultural war as critical to the kind of nation we shall be as the Cold War itself, for this war is for the soul of America.

It is difficult to image language more divisive than Buchanan used here. But notice that the task of consolidation requires him to help his audience minimize their sense of the gulf separating Bush and Buchanan. After all of his campaign criticism of Bush, it would have been out of character for Buchanan to heap praise on him. The alternative was to accentuate his differences with the Democrats and he had many to articulate. So when Buchanan told his people why he was supporting President Bush those reasons sounded somewhat more anti-Clinton than pro-Bush. Bush is a "patriot and war hero" while Clinton "sat up in a dormitory room in Oxford and figured out how to dodge the draft." Bush "co-authored and co-signed the policies that won the Cold War" while Bill Clinton's foreign policy experience "is pretty much confined to having had breakfast once at the International House of Pancakes."

In an important phrase Buchanan then said, "And in that struggle for the soul of America, Clinton and Clinton are on the other side, and George Bush is on our side." The sentence is clear: (1) there is a cultural war for America's soul, (2) the Clintons are in cahoots with those who threaten America, (3) it is up to "our side"

– Buchanan and his listeners – to fight them and protect America, and (4) in that context of war we need Buchanan to tell us which side the president is on – the side of Buchanan, his listeners, and America.

The contested leadership of the party is also evident as Buchanan discussed the lost primary challenge. He hailed "the 3 million Americans who voted for Pat Buchanan for president" and told them that "I do believe deep in my heart, that the right place for us to be now – in this presidential campaign – is right beside George Bush." This is the rhetoric of temporary and pragmatic consolidation. By saying "now – in this presidential campaign" he gave notice that he and his people might not be around in the future unless the party embraced their concerns.

He then lists how and why "we stand with George Bush" – freedom of choice for religious schools, "against the amoral idea that gay and lesbian couples should have the same standing in law as married" couples, right-to-life, voluntary prayer in public schools, against women in combat units, for the rights of localities to "control the raw sewage of pornography," and for "federal judges who interpret the law as written." These were not Bush's major issues, they were Buchanan's. He would stand with Bush on his own ground and establish culture war rhetoric as the agenda of the Republican Party.

Buchanan's speech sought consolidation by describing a fundamental culture war for the soul of America in which the Clinton Democrats were the enemy and his followers were America's hope. Because Bush was preferable to Clinton, Buchanan urged his followers to consolidate with him – at least for 1992 – on the rhetorical agenda that Buchanan had advocated on the campaign trail.

Comparison

Jesse Jackson and Pat Buchanan each addressed his party as a defeated candidate for nomination and each urged party unity. Jackson emphasized common ground – telling the factions of his party that "you are right but your patch is not big enough." His people had failed because of their divisions and they needed to resist the temptation of self-interest and stitch their patches together into a quilt of unity to succeed. His scriptural allusions added a tone of morality to that strategic message and enhanced his image as a voice of conscience in the party. Buchanan emphasized differences with the Clinton Democrats to warrant his endorsement of President Bush as the standard bearer for Buchanan's culture war agenda. He provided a powerful narrative for the party and put a price tag on it – share it or lose our support.

Nomination Acceptance Addresses

The nomination acceptance address is the critical juncture of every presidential campaign. Like every bridge, the acceptance speech both joins and separates two disparate phenomena. In this case, it separates and joins a race for leadership of a political party and a partisan contest for national leadership. Every nomination acceptance address is, therefore, a response to a bi-directional rhetorical situation, and each must fulfil two major functions. First, the acceptance address must unify all party factions behind the nominee. The second requirement is that

The Setting of the Obama Acceptance Speech

it must establish contrasting visions of the parties to frame the general election campaign. Theoretically, a nominee can perform both functions well, perform one well and one poorly (or not at all), or fail to perform either function.

Obama's Acceptance Spectacle

An acceptance address is an important rhetorical situation, but an historical coincidence scheduled Obama's address for the anniversary of Martin Luther King's "I Have a Dream" speech. The event was further magnified by moving it from the Convention Hall to 76,000-seat INVESCO Field at Mile High Stadium, home of the Denver Broncos football team. A set of Greek columns was built, perhaps to evoke the image of King in front of the Lincoln Memorial.

The acceptance speech normally begins with some kind of hailing of the delegates and like-minded viewers. But Obama rented a football stadium and literally invited people to step into it with him. Rather than consolidating outward from the delegates, Obama constituted them anew in a different place with the nominee, delegates, and supporters all stepping into that space together in a way that was symbolically both inclusive and egalitarian.

Convention halls are assemblies of state delegations but Obama constituted the stadium as an assembly of personal followings. He thanked key individuals and thus inscribed them as icons of party values. Hillary Clinton was the "champion for working Americans, and an inspiration to my daughters and to yours" and Bill Clinton was an advocate "who last night made the case for change as only he can make it." Ted Kennedy "embodie[d] the spirit of service" and running mate Joe Biden was "one of the finest statesmen of our time, a man at ease with everyone from world leaders to the conductors on the Amtrak train he still takes home every night" (Obama 2008b). Each acknowledgement worked like a hyperlink to the icon's convention speech supporting Obama and invited the icon's substantial public following to step into Obama's reconstituted party.

Obama introduce his historical narrative of The American Promise. "It is that promise that has always set this country apart – that through hard work and sacrifice, each of us can pursue our individual dreams but still come together as one American family, to ensure that the next generation can pursue their dreams as well." Importantly, Obama vested the continuing of the American promise not in heroic people (like McCain?) but in "ordinary men and women." This expanded his potential audience.

Ritter's (1980) study of acceptance jeremiads noted that nominees often describe their time as a crucial moment in the nation's history when the chosen people are beset by a host of afflictions. Obama did so, saying that, "We meet at one of those defining moments – a moment when our nation is at war, our economy is in turmoil, and the American promise has been threatened once more." He charged that the problem "is a direct result of a broken politics in Washington and the failed policies of George W. Bush." Essentially a "false prophet" had led Obama's people astray from their commitment to the fundamental values that protected the American Promise.

But because President Bush was not the Republican candidate in 2008, Obama's speech needed to implicate McCain in his critique. That posed a challenge because Bush and McCain had been adversaries in 2000 and McCain had branded himself a "maverick" who "reached across the aisle." Obama therefore constituted an opposition People by shifting focus from Bush to the Party that nominated him. McCain and Bush shared the GOP DNA that had caused the problems and resisted change, even as Obama embodied the change-oriented DNA of the "young man from Kenya and a young woman from Kansas."

Despite the partisan DNA McCain claimed to be a maverick Republican. So Obama praised his military service and then argued that McCain's political record was 90 percent Bush:

> But the record's clear: John McCain has voted with George Bush ninety percent of the time. Senator McCain likes to talk about judgment, but really, what does it say about your judgment when you think George Bush has been right more than ninety percent of the time? I don't know about you, but I'm not ready to take a ten percent chance on change. The truth is, on issue after issue that would make a difference in your lives – on health care and education and the economy – Senator McCain has been anything but independent.

Obama's framing of McCain's independence chose three issues on which the public largely disapproved of Bush's leadership – health care, education and the economy (even before the late September financial crisis). He then linked McCain's votes and Bush's ideas and reduced the likelihood of change under McCain to a mere 10 percent. Finally, and most importantly, the phrase "on issue after issue that would make a difference in *your lives*" (emphasis added) appropriated for the reconstituted Democrats anyone who feels that health care and education and the economy make a difference in their lives and relegates to his reconstituted Republicans those who think that other issues make a difference in their lives (implicitly evoking memories of gay marriage and flag burning).

Barack Obama's discussion of the American promise makes outstanding use of antitheses to reconstitute his followers. The following passage would not be unexpected at a Democratic convention:

> It's a promise that says we have the obligation to treat each other with dignity and respect. It's a promise that says businesses should live up to their responsibilities to create American jobs, look out for American workers, and play by the rules of the road. Ours is a promise that says government should do that which we cannot do for ourselves – protect us from harm and provide every child a decent education; keep our water clean and our toys safe; invest in new schools and new roads and new science and technology. Our government should work for us. It should help us. It should ensure opportunity for every American who's willing to work. That's the belief that I am my brother's keeper; I am my sister's keeper.

This is fairly standard rhetoric that most Democrats would applaud. But Obama did not use it, not in that form.

Where would we expect to hear the following passage – at a Democratic or Republican convention?

> It's a promise that says each of us has the freedom to make of our own lives what we will. It's a promise that says the market should reward drive and innovation and generate growth. Ours is a promise that says government cannot solve all our problems. Our government should not work against us; it should not hurt us. It should ensure opportunity for those with the most money. That's the promise of America – the idea that we are responsible for ourselves.

This second passage is unlike the first, but it articulates feelings familiar to many people.

Each of the reconstructions above could have served as the ideological statement of a presidential nomination address (admittedly for a narrow party, but they nominate candidates, too). Each passage constitutes a rhetorical space for a People and invites Americans to step into that space.

Obama's speech used both passages to reach a wide variety of Americans. After asking, "What is that promise?" he offered seven consecutive compound sentences, each of which joined ideals that are often expressed separately:

1. It's a promise that says *each of us has the freedom to make of our own lives what we will,* but that we also have the *obligation to treat each other with dignity and respect.*
2. It's a promise that says the *market should reward drive and innovation and generate growth,* but that *businesses should live up to their responsibilities* to create American jobs, look out for American workers, and play by the rules of the road.
3. Ours is a promise that says *government cannot solve all our problems,* but what *it should do is that which we cannot do for ourselves* – protect us from harm and provide every child a decent education; keep our water clean and our toys safe; invest in new schools and new roads and new science and technology.

4. Our *government should work for us, not against us.*
5. It should *help* us, *not hurt* us.
6. It should *ensure opportunity not just for those with the most money and influence*, but for *every American who's willing to work.*
7. That's the promise of America – the idea that *we are responsible for ourselves*, but that *we also rise or fall as one nation*; the fundamental belief that I am my brother's keeper; I am my sister's keeper.

   That's the promise we need to keep. That's the change we need right now. [emphases added]

Obama's address constituted space for *both, very different, constituencies* and then *married them* in his Invesco Field ceremony.

Obama used the American Promise to frame his policy agenda, and he used his policy agenda to constitute the promise. Key items included reversing the accomplishments of the false prophet: a tax code that "doesn't reward the lobbyists who wrote it, but the American workers and small businesses who deserve it." He would also "stop giving tax breaks to corporations that ship jobs overseas, and . . . start giving them to companies that create good jobs right here in America" and "cut taxes – cut taxes – for 95 percent of all working families" to protect the American Promise for future generations.

Obama also prescribed constructive actions for change: "end our dependence on oil from the Middle East," "tap our natural gas reserves, invest in clean coal technology, and find ways to safely harness nuclear power," "help our auto companies re-tool," "invest in early childhood education," and "recruit an army of new teachers, and pay them higher salaries and give them more support." The operative commands for the People are "tap," "invest," "find," "help," "build," "meet," "invest" (again), "recruit," "pay," and "support." This section advocated nine actions that most people could perform to renew their commitment to first principles and bring about the changes required to defend and protect the American Promise.

Even as Obama promised to do things for Americans he emphasized the ethic that the American Promise required of them: "Individual responsibility and mutual responsibility – that's the essence of America's promise."

> Yes, we must provide more ladders to success for young men who fall into lives of crime and despair. But we must also admit that programs alone can't replace parents; that government can't turn off the television and make a child do her homework; that fathers must take more responsibility for providing the love and guidance their children need.

It was only in closing his speech that Obama alluded to King's "I Have a Dream" speech. As King's dream was "deeply rooted in the American dream" so was Obama's American promise deeply rooted in King's dream. For it is this promise itself that constitutes Obama's core idea of America, and the fundamental key to our success.

> This country of ours has more wealth than any nation, but that's not what makes us rich. We have the most powerful military on Earth, but that's not what makes us strong. Our universities and our culture are the envy of the world, but that's not

what keeps the world coming to our shores. Instead, it is that American spirit –
that American promise – that pushes us forward even when the path is uncertain;
that binds us together in spite of our differences; that makes us fix our eye not on
what is seen, but what is unseen, that better place around the bend. That promise
is our greatest inheritance.

But if Obama's "American Promise" is reminiscent of King's "Dream" his "better
place around the bend" that "keeps the world coming to our shores" is reminiscent of Reagan's "shining city on a hill" – an image appropriated from John
Winthrop's address to the Puritans as they prepared to disembark from the
Arabella. It also draws upon Lyndon Johnson's vision of a "Great Society" and
Franklin Roosevelt's "New Deal" for the American people and the foreign policy
of the "good neighbor."

Barack Obama's nomination acceptance speech was a spectacle of immense
proportion that reconstituted his audience in the tradition of American excep-
tionalism and attributed our assorted tribulations to our eight years of following
false prophets who misunderstood the essence of America. His message was a
modern secular jeremiad ideally crafted for the rhetorical situation best suited
to jeremiads. Simply tweaking policies could solve none of the problems Obama
identified, because the underlying problem was spiritual. Only by renewing their
faith in the American Promise could ordinary Americans rediscover the spirit that
would, in yet another defining moment, enable them to come together and solve
problems by preserving the American Promise.

McCain's Call to Fight

John McCain won the 2008 Republican nomination without enthusiastic support. Social Conservatives who had backed Arkansas Governor Mike Huckabee
were displeased by his stands on abortion and stem cell research. Enterprisers
who had supported Mitt Romney of Massachusetts balked at his admitted un-
familiarity with economics. Talk show personalities such as Ann Coulter and
Rush Limbaugh made no secret of their distaste for McCain. But, like George Bush
in 1988, McCain benefited from wins in several winner-take-all primaries.

During the pre-convention period the McCain campaign managed to soothe
much of the anti-McCain talk within the party's tent with relentless anti-Obama
rhetoric. But they provided little in the way of new positive appeals for their unen-
thusiastic supporters. Their emerging strategy seemed to be one of making the
election a referendum on Obama, much as Bush in 2004 had made the election
a referendum on John Kerry whom they portrayed as unfit to command. But as
the convention approached McCain still needed to consolidate the Republican
coalition.

McCain's acceptance speech was not like Obama's. He spoke in the convention hall and affirmed tradition rather than change. He acknowledged by name
only his wife, mother, Laura Bush, and Obama. Laura Bush's husband was "The
President" and her in-laws were "the 41st President and his bride of 63 years." By
characterizing the other candidates as those "who opposed me" McCain made
himself the inspiration for their campaigns and minimized the values, policies,
and agendas they had articulated (McCain 2008).

If McCain was hesitant to name other Republicans he nevertheless referenced himself: 125 times (105 "I" and 20 "me"). McCain's self-references were roughly double Obama's 65 (56 "I" and nine "me"). McCain's address hailed citizens based on their identification with, and respect for, him.

The central theme of McCain's address emerged early as constituted his people around his personal willingness to fight. His narrative reminded us that he fought in the past:

> I've fought corruption, . . . I've fought big spenders in both parties, . . . I've fought to get million dollar checks out of our elections. I've fought lobbyists who stole from Indian tribes. I fought crooked deals in the Pentagon. I fought tobacco companies and trial lawyers, drug companies and union bosses. I fought for the right strategy and more troops in Iraq.

McCain's narrative reminded us of his current fights:

> I fight for Americans. I fight for you. I fight for Bill and Sue Nebe from Farmington Hills, Michigan. . . . I fight for Jake and Toni Wimmer of Franklin County, Pennsylvania. . . . I fight for the family of Matthew Stanley of Wolfboro, New Hampshire.

McCain's story says "I fight" or "I've fought" thirteen times, but not once does it say either "we've fought" or "we fight." The space constituted by McCain's historical narrative was not a collective history of a People but an intensely personal history. He constituted for Republicans a space in which he continues to fight alone, exhorting his listeners to join him in the future fight:

> Fight with me. Fight with me. Fight for what's right for our country. Fight for the ideals and character of a free people. Fight for our children's future. Fight for justice and opportunity for all. Stand up to defend our country from its enemies. Stand up for each other; for beautiful, blessed, bountiful America. Stand up, stand up, stand up and fight.

McCain's fighting spirit was not in doubt.

The audience might not have been surprised to hear McCain say, "Americans, traditionally, love to fight. All real Americans love the sting of battle," or "all this stuff you've heard about America not wanting to fight, wanting to stay out of the war, is a lot of horse dung." Indeed, that might have been better for the occasion because it is a collective narrative of Americans as a people. But those words come from General George S. Patton's address to the Third Army, as depicted in the opening scene of the film *Patton* (1970), further evidence of the speech's military DNA.

But General Patton was a warrior not a recruiter. As a nominee for president John McCain needed both to rally his troops and to recruit for the campaign ahead. Potential recruits could expect him to cover three issues implicit in his call to arms: Who is the enemy? How should we fight the enemy? What will victory yield?

But McCain's enemy was not clear. Four years earlier George W. Bush skilfully merged terrorists, abortionists, and others into the monstrous enemy of "Evildoers," and Ronald Reagan opposed an "evil empire," but McCain offered only an array of allusions. We would fight against "judges who legislate from the benches" and "failed school bureaucracies." We would fight "countries that don't like us very much," "al Qaeda," "Iran," and "Russia's leaders." In short, McCain's address provided a readiness to fight with less sense of an enemy than his Republican predecessors.

Nor did McCain's battle orders sound very much like fighting. They included "standing up" for values, helping unemployed find jobs, and using community colleges to train people. Time and again McCain used verbs that no thesaurus would link to "fight" – stop spending, produce, build, develop, increase the use, encourage the development – without reconciling them with his call to fight.

Despite those shortcomings McCain's address could have pictured the world that our fighting would eventually produce. Lyndon Johnson had his "Great Society" and Ronald Reagan helped us imagine a "Shining City on a Hill." McCain could have consolidated his followers and justified all that fighting with a vision of a brighter day. But the better world that a fighting McCain–Palin America would produce was not envisioned in the speech. Most of his future references were instrumental, such as "We have to catch up to history, and we have to change the way we do business in Washington." In short, the address did not offer any view of a future so different from that facing his audience as to warrant all the fighting he urged.

Comparison

Obama's acceptance speech effectively constituted his people by creating a vast new space in the stadium, using party icons as links to their supporters, and explaining the shared historical narrative of the American Promise. He used jeremiad's potential by critiquing the "false prophets" of the GOP and urging that we move forward by returning to the fundamental American promise. McCain's address ineffectively constituted his people be over-emphasizing himself and providing little in the way of a shared historical narrative beyond our willingness to fight. Moreover he ineffectively used the jeremiad's potential because the path to the future through fighting failed to explicate either the enemy or the nature of the fight.

Summary and Conclusions

A speech is the communication mode of choice when the campaign wants personally to engage an audience with an extended argument. It is not a good choice when they have very little to say or when nobody is listening to them. We have seen in this chapter that a speech is far more than a sound bite but that it should make its main point memorably. General consideration when studying speeches include:

- Studying the transcript of the whole speech
- Holding all speakers to the same high standards regardless of our political preferences
- Illuminating the speech by explaining how and why it worked for whom

Although there is no single way to study a speech there are four general stages. These include:

1. Study the transcript without regard to its context to understand its arguments and support, values, tone, and their clues about the audience and the speaker.
2. Study the rhetorical situation to understand its origins, objectives, and effects.
3. Compare the speech delivered to the speech called for by the rhetorical situation.
4. Use an analytical framework to explain the speech's success or failure.

We illustrated this process with case studies of announcement, convention, and acceptance speeches from the perspective of constitutive rhetoric that calls a people into being and jeremiads that call on those people to use their shared past to chart their future. We found that:

- The announcement speech can provide insights into the motivation for the campaign and the likelihood of its appeal. Obama told of a life devoted to making America better through convergence while McCain told of a life devoted to defending America.
- Convention addresses can suggest how the party sees itself and the campaign. Jesse Jackson warned Democratic audiences to be wary of self-interest and to unify for victory. Pat Buchanan spoke of a culture war dividing Republicans from Democrats and endorsed President Bush with that narrative.
- The nomination acceptance address is a rich source of information about the candidate, the party, and the campaign it is about to undertake. Obama used the stadium, party icons, and the American Promise to constitute his people and urged them to believe in that promise and reject the Republicans who had led them astray.

Speeches are the communication mode that give candidates the most leeway to say what they want. But for their speeches to reach America's citizens they require news coverage, and that is our next topic.

7 Campaign Journalism

Chapter 3 explained presidential campaign communication as continuing interaction among citizens, campaign organizations, and media organizations. As zoology students dissect dead things to understand living systems we deconstruct communication systems to see how they foster shared understandings. This chapter explores the role of media organizations in providing news of the campaign organizations to the citizens because contemporary presidential campaigns would not be what they are without campaign journalism.

What is "News" and What Does it "Do"?

Tribune Publishing Company President Jack Fuller defined "news" as "the report of what a news organization has recently learned about matters of some significance or interest to the specific community that the news organization serves" (Fuller 1996, p. 6). Fuller's definition provides a good starting point for our discussion.

News Attempts to Report "Reality"

Reporting is a difficult job. Let us try to understand what it is like to report the reality of a simple event. Imagine the two of us sitting at the only occupied table outside a bagel shop. You feel a bit self-conscious because you have yet to read the whole book, and I am excited to talk with a reader. Cars and people pass as we talk. You notice some of them, like the local character playing his mandolin behind me. You nod politely to express your agreement with me and to cover your distractions, and I perceive that as encouragement to bore you further still. Suddenly we hear a screech and a thump at the traffic light behind us. When the police and reporters arrive we seem to be the only two witnesses. Driver One says he was stopped at the red light but Driver Two claims he stopped abruptly during a green light. I say that we did not notice because we were deep in conversation. You are pretty sure that the first car was stopped for a while when the second car hit it, but you are not sure about the light because you were also noticing mandolin man, listening to me and monitoring your behavior to show polite interest.

What *really* happened? There was first a molecular reality in which bagels were ingested and bumpers reconfigured. But much hinges on the four social or perceptual realities which are "pictures in our heads" that we construct. How does one report this story? Does one report driver no. 1's perspective or that of driver no. 2, my uncertainty or your suspicion? Does one personalize the drivers ("105-year old driver collides with mayor's daughter") or reduce it to an impersonal statistic ("There were no fatalities in the city's 27th traffic accident today")? Actually, there were five separate realities. The reporter's job is to construct one story from those five realities.

The point is that people have different perspectives – and therefore different perceptual realities – as events unfold around them. It is short-sighted to say that language conveys reality because we have already constructed our reality when we begin to convey it. Participants, witnesses, reporters, video personnel, and editors all need language and narrative to construct the reality that each contributes to the news story they try to convey to their audience.

The Basic Unit of Journalism is the Story

The basic unit of journalism is the story and the reporter's task is to "get the story." Form matters. News consists of reports, but not all reports are news. Humans are storytellers, rhetorical theorist Walter R. Fisher (1987) argued. Because we think in narratives we find it helpful to learn through stories. Thus the history of civilization has been narrated by balladeers, epic poets, town criers, and reporters. Each sorted multiple realities to create a narrative that competed for listeners and readers in the marketplace. Some become popular, dominant narratives and others faded. History's winners enshrine and teach their narratives.

Each narrative enacts a set of values that govern its audience appeal. The listener or reader judges the story's "narrative coherence" – how well it works as a story (Fisher 1987). We expect the elements of dramatic logic: *actors* (heroes, villains, and fools), *acts* (performed by the actors), *style* (actors' expressive behaviors), *plots* (unfolding scenarios that connect the characters and events), *scene* (a setting for the drama), *motives* (aims and purposes for the actors' choice of acts) and *sanctioning agents* (an entity that justifies the events and the outcome of the drama). We expect stories to unfold in a particular sequence that conforms to dramatic logic:

> The introduction creates the tone, sketches the characters, details the setting, establishes opening events, and supplies nuances necessary for understanding the drama. The pace of the plot picks up, action rises, and opposing forces join the dramatic conflict. . . . Then something happens . . . to provoke a crisis. Action subsides . . . But there must be a final resolution in keeping with the overall rhetorical vision evoked by the drama. (Nimmo and Combs 1983, p. 15)

Reporters write the stories, editors enhance them and audiences try to understand them using the test of narrative coherence.

Thus as political scientist Thomas E. Patterson said: "The news is not a mirror held up to society. It is a selective rendition of events told in story form" (1993, p. 60). As television network reporters turned the presidential campaign events from 1988 through 2004 into stories the candidates' speaking parts – their "sound bites" – became shorter and shorter. Candidate sound bites that averaged 42 seconds in 1968 were down to 10 seconds in 1988 and 7.8 seconds in 2004 (Farnsworth and Lichter 2007). Beyond those few seconds we see the candidate's mouth moving but hear the reporter's voiceover narration. Part of the change can be attributed to the increasingly sophisticated technologies that enable the news organizations to take a stronger hand in message creation than their predecessors four decades ago. Part of it can be attributed to the professional journalist's need to add something of value to the story (Zaller 1998). And some of it is surely due to the journalists' sense of their responsibility to serve as a watchdog on the campaign.

News Updates a Continuing Melodrama

Contemporary journalism is less a barrage of one-shot stories than a progression of timely updates – what the news organization has *recently* learned. This is especially true of presidential campaign journalism that begins with speculative stories about who might run and continues through the last analysis of the election results.

Consequently, campaign coverage turns stories into melodrama – serial dramas of moral justice that nurture audience anxiety about the tensions among characters who are Good and Bad (Nimmo and Combs 1983). Since the news organization must update the melodrama, melodramatic logic demands that they allocate their resources to covering further the storylines already introduced to the audience – whether by their organization or the competition.

Like afternoon and prime-time soap operas these news melodramas "hook" their audiences into news dependence for the next installment of the drama. Campaign news can therefore be expected to consist largely of narrative reports that update the suspenseful soap opera of moral justice with whatever the news organization has been able to discern since its last report. Will the candidate withdraw from the race? Who will be picked for vice-president? Who won the debate? How will it all end? The web and mobile phones now bring us a steady diet of "breaking news" to pique our interest.

Portraying a presidential campaign as a struggle between good and evil poses risks to the news media. Neither party wants to be portrayed as evil nor does either party see itself portrayed as quite good enough. Thus a second struggle emerges between the campaign organizations and the media organizations as each accuses the media of favoring the opposition. The consequence has been increasingly negative coverage of all candidates through 2004 (Farnsworth and Lichter 2007).

In 2008 many people felt the news media favored Barack Obama over John McCain. Data on reporting after the conventions does show coverage of McCain to be 57 percent negative to only 26 percent negative toward Obama. But the majority of those McCain stories were predictably about the horse race that was going badly for him and those stories were 61 percent negative while Obama's horse race stories were about 60 percent positive. The fair question might be how the press could write 40 percent of their horse race stories to be positive for McCain and negative toward Obama. When McCain attacked Obama it resulted in 65 percent negative coverage for Obama and 65.9 percent negative coverage for McCain (Pew 2008).

The melodramatic nature of campaign news complicates the correction of factual statements. As stories help us to know they protect what we know from counterargument, even when it is wrong. Arguments invite disagreement and debate about facts but storytelling invites audiences to accept the facts for the sake of the story. Kathleen Hall Jamieson and Paul Waldman believe that stories undermine journalists' responsibility to serve as "custodians of fact" because it "becomes particularly difficult when the relevant facts are embedded in a compelling narrative" (2003, p. 23). Thus the reporter's task of helping citizens check the factual statements of politicians and others is complicated by the very nature of the "good stories" we choose to cherish.

News Covers Matters of Some Significance and/or Interest

Like teachers, journalists live with the reality that not everything of importance is interesting, and everything interesting is not necessarily important. To talk about only important things is to risk boring one's audience but to talk only of interesting things is to overlook some topics of importance. Both interest and importance are subjective judgments. A topic may be interesting *to* an audience but not important *for* them to understand, or it might be important *for* them but not interesting *to* them. The challenge is to make important topics interesting to one's audience and to find the overlooked importance of interesting topics. Thus are reporters engaged in a process of rhetorical adaptation similar to the candidates' adaptation to their potential voters.

Efforts to maximize both significance and interest while maintaining objectivity have resulted in four informational biases of American news, according to Political Scientist W. Lance Bennett (2009). The first of these is the *personalization* of information which encourages the audience to take the information personally. Stories about rising interest rates often focus on a young couple anxious to buy a home rather than on economic forces. Pulitzer Prize-winning writer Tom Hallman, Jr. (2009) advises journalists to (1) reduce the distance between the reader and the story, (2) write about people rather than things, (3) direct the emotion of the reader, (4) control the pace, (5) make small things universal by grounding them in universal themes, (6) write with a confident narrator's voice, and (7) write "strong middles and powerful endings." This becomes problematic when emotional involvement in the story displaces knowledge about the forces that created and sustain the predicament. News organizations respond energetically to personalized information, as they did with "Joe the Plumber" in 2008, often reporting stories of more interest than importance.

The second informational bias is *dramatization* of information (Bennett 2009). A new piece of information must fit into a good story to merit coverage. This is why reporters pay so much attention to the campaign "horse race" rather than to policy issues that might bore audiences. Scandals and mistakes also attract inordinate attention because they enhance conflict and drama. Press "feeding frenzies" have cultivated a climate in which honest mistakes appear never to happen (Sabato 2000).

The *fragmentation* of news into isolated stories is the third informational bias. Each story is a piece of the melodramatic jigsaw puzzle with less attention paid to the overall context and the fit among the pieces (Bennett 2009). This provides an incentive for continuing audience involvement in the campaign melodrama.

Bennett's fourth informational bias is the *authority-disorder bias* (2009).

Bennett argues that contemporary American news is preoccupied with disorder and the ability of officials to restore things to normal. The emphasis on disorder – terrorism, financial meltdowns, runaway immigration, and moral decay – foster anxiety and enhance the melodrama. But by adding the second question – whether public officials are capable of restoring order – journalists add a second storyline that focuses on actors and motivations. Rarely do reporters question whether returning to "normal" is the best path.

Bennett's informational biases are important because they suggest the kinds of stories that news organizations are most likely to pursue and report. They cannot report the stories they do not attempt to cover, and their devotion of resources to personalized, dramatic, fragmented stories of attempts to restore order can distract them from impersonal, holistic reports about the reasons for dissatisfaction and alternative paths toward the future.

The News Organization Serves its Community Audience

There are forty-five newspapers in Chicago. The *Chicago Tribune* and *Chicago Sun-Times* are the most likely to reach the national audience. The *Chicago Defender* and *Chicago Standard News* serve Chicago's African-American community, the *South Suburban Standard* serves the southside African-American community and the *Windy City Word* serves the west side African-American community. *The Eagle, El Imparcial, El Sol de Chicago, Nuevo Siglo* and the *Lawndale News* all cover news for the Latino community. The *Chicago Chinese News*, The *Chicago Jewish News*, The *India Tribune*, The *Irish American News* and The *Polish News* serve their particular communities. There are six college newspapers and twelve local and/or suburban papers. Each newspaper can be expected to report news affecting its community to its audience. Of course, Chicagoans can also subscribe to *USA Today* and The *Wall Street Journal* if they prefer news about the national and financial communities to news of Chicago.

Meanwhile, a few hundred miles northeast across Lake Michigan, readers in Antrim County, Michigan are served only by the weekly *Antrim Review*. For daily news they can subscribe to out-of county papers like the Traverse City *Record Eagle*, the *Grand Rapids Press*, The *Detroit News* or *Free Press* or the *Chicago Tribune*. But none of those newspapers is likely to feature Antrim County's business closings, school bonds, fires, or elections.

News organizations in Chicago, Antrim County, Michigan, and elsewhere make their news decisions mindful of their audience. They report stories that they expect to interest or impact their audience, not someone else's audience. When they achieve a fitting response between their stories and their audience they cultivate a loyal following. This increases the likelihood that communities around preferred storytellers, and that is where popular news anchors and columnists enter the picture.

News organizations want regular readers and viewers, partly to provide advertisers with a steady demographic target audience. None of those forty-five Chicago newspapers is likely to say, "Read each paper every 45th day." But what is good for the news organizations is not so good for the citizenry. When we become part of some organization's stable audience we lose track of their unreported stories and of our available alternatives. It is like eating all of our meals at the same restaurant or buying all of our clothes at the same store.

As today's audiences constrain and judge the struggle between politicians and reporters for control of political communication they vote for news sources by subscribing and bookmarking. "Television news" remains the main source of public information but that phrase means different things to the nine Pew groups who rely on different news outlets for their versions of the campaign story. Enterprisers are the most reliant on television, by which 46 percent of them meant Fox News. The other two Republican leaning audiences, Social Conservatives and Pro-Government Conservatives, were less likely to watch Fox than CNN or the networks. Conservative Democrats were twice as likely as Liberals to watch the networks while Liberals, young respondents, and the highly educated were the most likely to turn to the Internet rather than television news (Kohut 2005). In short, today's nine Pew groups are drinking from different streams of campaign news that enable them to construct, follow, and maintain different understandings of the campaign.

News Defined

We began this section with Fuller's definition of news which, while good, captures neither the appeal of news for those who need it nor the audience's ability to resist discordant information. Thus we can summarize our discussion with an alternative definition: News is a collaborative melodrama of contemporary events that stimulates the audience appetite and facilitates the integration of new information into their preferred narrative structure for protecting their community, knowledge, beliefs, and values.

Dynamics of Campaign Journalism

We proceed mindful of Murray Edelman's observation that politics is part spectator sport so that we can distinguish The Campaign Story that unfolds by the hour from the practical campaign for votes, delegates, and electoral votes. At about the time on-air reporters held their telephone next to their microphone to convey news of the Kennedy assassination Edelman wrote that "politics is a series of pictures in the mind, placed there by television news, newspapers, magazines, and discussions. The pictures create a moving panorama taking place in a world the mass public never quite touches, yet one its members come to fear or cheer, often with passion and sometimes with action" (Edelman 1964, p. 4). Edelman wrote when three networks competed for a national audience but news media have proliferated with all news stations and networks as well as local and national newspapers for niches of the national audience.

The twentieth century saw the rise of powerful news organizations and new media that enabled almost anyone to share narratives as blogs. Much can be said about the centralized ownership of major news organizations and about the decentralized access to blogs and primary sources in the Internet. But running through those changes is the central task of the reporter constructing and sharing a narrative of events with an audience. As we approach that process, we

John Edwards; authors' own image.

now know that audiences may be more receptive to a "good story" that builds on their beliefs and values than to a story that challenges their beliefs, values, and preferred stories.

Pack Journalism

Timothy Crouse travelled with the reporters covering the 1972 Nixon and McGovern campaigns and described his experiences in his book *The Boys on the Bus* (1972). Crouse introduced the term "Pack Journalism" to describe the kind of reporting at work when an ongoing set of personnel beset by social pressures of the workplace cover the same candidate for long periods of time.

> The pack was divided cliques – the national political reporters, who were constantly coming and going; the campaign reporters from the big prestige papers and the ones from the small papers; the wire-service men the network correspondents; and other configurations that formed according to age and old Washington friendships. The most experienced national political reporters, wire men, and big-paper reporters . . . were at the top of the pecking order. (Crouse 1972, p. 7)

But despite their social hierarchy, the members of the Pack "all fed off the same pool report, the same daily handout, the same speech" such that all of them were "isolated in the same mobile village. After a while, they began to believe the same rumors, subscribe to the same theories, and write the same stories" (Crouse 1972, p. 8).

Yet the Holy Grail of reporting is said to be The Scoop – the exclusive story. The reporter's dilemma is therefore how to get and report an exclusive story that is not repudiated for being out of step with the pack reports. Crouse found little incentive for pack reporters to report unique stories because their news organizations all received Associated Press reports. Many worried that their editors would respond to a scoop by saying, "Hey, if this is such a hot story , how come AP or the *Washington Post* doesn't have it?" (Crouse 1972, p. 10). Pack reporters therefore kept pace with the perspective of the chief AP political correspondent and others high in the pecking order to satisfy their editors' charge to report the "real story."

Without realizing it, Crouse's Pack journalists were following Fisher's second test of a good narrative – "narrative fidelity" (1987). Fisher said that we all test a story to see whether it conforms to our knowledge, beliefs, and values, or requires us to change them. Audiences prefer stories consistent with what they already know and value, are appropriate to the pending decision, promising in terms of impending effects, and consistent with what they regard as a preferred basis for conduct (Fisher 1987). Editors are similarly inclined to prefer stories that fit with traditional campaign news and with the other reports they are getting. *Newsweek*'s Karl Fleming told Crouse, "The editors don't want scoops. Their abiding interest is making sure that nobody else has got anything that they don't have, not getting something that nobody else has" (Crouse 1972, p. 10).

Framing, Agenda-Setting and Priming

Jamieson and Waldman (2003) explain that reporters view the world through "lenses" and construct news stories that are shaped by "frames." A frame defines the nature of the problem, diagnoses the problem's cause, renders moral judgments and suggests remedies for the problem (Entman 1993). Different news organizations employ reporters and editors with different lenses and they have organizational philosophies, missions, and practices that equip them with somewhat different frames.

The founders were familiar with the English model in which the Crown licensed the press to advance the royal frame, and they wanted something different. That is why the First Amendment to the Constitution sought to insure journalistic marketplace in which a variety of narrators independent of government could report and frame the news. Their idea was to provide a marketplace of narrators – the governors and the press – who would provide citizens with a variety of narrative accounts in which to believe. But the marketplace functions poorly when the narrators report as a pack or when consumers fail to window shop. Three theories suggest implications of this dysfunctional marketplace.

Agenda-setting research suggests that media coverage influences what citizens think about, but not what they think (Leighley 2004). There is considerable research supporting the thesis that more citizens pay more attention to the topics heavily covered in the news than to topics covered less. Issues and people covered in the news move up the public agenda and those covered less slide down the public agenda. During 2008, for example, $4 gas and September's economic meltdown moved the economy up the political agenda ahead of the Iraq War.

S. Robert Lichter and his colleagues identified a preoccupation with network coverage of the horse race rather than issues thus keeping the question "who will win?" higher on the agenda than questions such as "whose policies are more sound?" or "who should win?" (Farnsworth and Lichter 2007). Consider what happens when the campaign enters the awutumnal debate season. We might hope that news organizations would contrast the candidates' policies and platforms, fact check them for us, and help us understand the real meat of the campaign. But do the media increase their attention to policy issues or simply get caught up in the debate hoopla?

To explore this question I studied the Vanderbilt Archives' network newscast abstracts from week prior to the first Bush–Gore debate in 2000 through the Friday following their last debate. Every story mentioning the presidential campaign was coded for story placement (one for the lead story), for story duration in seconds and for the subject of the story. Specifically, "contest" stories discussed polls, strategies, reactions and likely outcome of the debate, "issue" stories discussed tax plans, health care, foreign policy and the like, and "mixed" stories ("Bush criticizes big government" or "Gore discusses prosperity").

The results indicated that issues lost. The networks carried thirty-seven contest stories and thirteen issue stories, devoting 125 minutes to the contest and only forty-five minutes to issues. CBS ran twenty contest stories, NBC had ten and ABC had seven but placed them more prominently in their newscasts. The point is that the network professionals got it backwards in 2000 – the debates lured the reporters away from the coverage of issues to cover strategy and horse race stories instead. The horse race perspective saw the debates as opportunities for updates. They provided stories about preparation, briefing, strategies, and possible outcomes and missed opportunities to report on policy issues like government surpluses or education. That pattern of reporting encourages a public agenda emphasizing the contest over the issues.

In 2008 the horse race accounted for 53 percent of news stories compared to the 20 percent about policy issues. The focus on the horse race increased sharply during the last three weeks (Pew 2008) even though the projected electoral votes were not changing very much (Electoral-vote.com 2008). The three weeks prior to the election might have been a time when citizens could have used non-partisan information about the issues.

Framing theory suggests that citizens will think about issues in ways consistent with their portrayal in the media (Leighley 2004). Although terrorist acts were often framed as criminal acts deserving arrest and trial, news coverage after 9/11 adopted the Bush Administration's "War on Terror" frame (Jameson and Waldman 2003).

Consider national reporting of the Iowa precinct caucuses. The national story frames Iowa as a dramatic and pivotal first battle in which it it is nearly impossible to win nomination without winning the Iowa precinct caucuses. But consider the records. Republicans did nominate their Iowa winners in 1976 (President Ford), 1996 (Robert Dole), and 2000 (George W. Bush). But they nominated Ronald Reagan who finished second to George H. W. Bush in 1980, they nominated Bush in 1988 after he finished third behind Dole and Pat Robertson, and in 2008 they nominated John McCain who finished fourth behind Mike Huckabee, Mitt

Romney, and Fred Thompson. Democrats did nominate Iowa winners in 1980 (Jimmy Carter), 1984 (Walter Mondale), 2000 (Al Gore), 2004 (John Kerry), and 2008 (Barack Obama). But 1972 nominee George McGovern finished behind "uncommitted" and Ed Muskie in Iowa and Carter also trailed "uncommitted" in 1976, and Michael Dukakis placed third in 1988 while Bill Clinton ran fourth in 1992. In short, winners of Iowa's precinct caucuses have won the Republican nomination three out of six times (50 percent) and the Democratic nomination five out of nine times (55 percent). Candidates other than the first place finishers have been nominated by their parties seven out of fifteen times (46.6 percent). The record says that winning the Iowa precinct is not an important predictor of nomination – in fact, it is worse than a flipping a coin. Yet the dominant news story consistently frames Iowa's caucuses as crucial.

The Iowa reporting problems do not end there. As we shall see in Chapter 11 each Iowa Republican caucus conducts a non-binding straw poll to see whom their attendees favor, then they select their local delegates to their county caucus. Democrats line up in presidential candidate preference groups to decide which candidate's people get county delegates, then each of those clusters picks their people. But the news organizations largely ignore that rule-governed campaigning and conduct exit polls of the attendees to project the percentage of the statewide vote each. In short, the news organizations frame Iowa's four-tiered caucus process as a one day primary. The disconnect between the news event and the actual political event is stark, but the news story can be more easily digested by people outside of Iowa even if it is largely irrelevant.

A more accurate frame for the Iowa precinct caucus story would be that it is a contest to finish among the top four, since no one has yet been nominated by either party after finishing worse than fourth in the Iowa precinct caucuses. But the dominant frame is both familiar. Audiences have heard it and when they recognize it they can integrate the new campaign into what they believe to be factual. Moreover the dominant frame is more dramatic because it invests so much more in finishing first, even though that investment is historically unjustified. A reporter telling the Top Four story risks having an editor respond (as my students sometimes have), "Why does your story differ from what everyone else is reporting?"

Priming goes further than agenda-setting or framing to suggest that voters will base their choices more heavily on issues covered by the media than on issues not covered by the media (Leighley 2004). Thus the Swift Boat Veterans' charges against John Kerry would have primed voters to consider those charges as important, but so would the efforts by some news organizations to investigate and debunk those charges.

Viewing Events through Different Windows

Often overlooked in discussions of agenda-setting, framing, and priming is the premise that each of us is influenced only by the media we follow. Surely no Chicagoan reads all forty-five of their available newspapers. One who reads only Polish may well have her agenda set, her issues framed and her vote primed by *Katolik*; but she would be as free from the influence of Chicago's *Sun-Times*,

Defender, Nuevo Siglo and *Irish American News* as the home without cable television is free from CNN, MSNBC, and Fox News. Theoretical purists may contend that the major newspapers influence the general political conversation in which our Polish reader is immersed, but at that point the general political conversation may also be affecting the news coverage in even more fundamental ways.

We can get a sense of how a campaign looks through different media lenses by comparing the networks' stories about a short-term campaign. The network newscasts cover a long stretch of primaries and caucuses all around the country after Iowa and New Hampshire and they have about twenty-four minutes of program time to cover all of the day's news. By 1996 South Carolina had become an important transitional contest between New Hampshire and the Super Tuesday primaries but it was not yet part of the Pack's campaign mythology. It was in the limelight for only a week and, with President Clinton unopposed, the Republicans had the only campaign. Kathleen E. Kendall compiled a videotape of network stories about the 1996 South Carolina Republican primary campaign that enabled us to compare the networks' individual South Carolina stories.

Viewers of ABC (13:42) and NBC (10:33) saw more coverage than viewers of CBS and CNN (6:33 and 5:18, respectively), but half of ABC's coverage came too late to help the state's voters. NBC provided most of their coverage well before the polls opened. CBS and CNN largely ignored South Carolina after their stories on the debate. Indeed, all four networks' viewers learned about the debate but only two networks reported the election's outcome.

First, the networks perceived different horse races. CNN viewers learned that Bob Dole was in front but NBC viewers heard that Steve Forbes had the most delegates and money. ABC's lead story implied that Forbes led followed by Buchanan then Dole, but they associated Dole with the key issue of the economy. CBS saw Buchanan as most likely to endure with Forbes able to continue as long as he was willing to pay the bills, but they worried about Dole's prospects if he should lose.

Second, viewers of all four networks heard a story of conflict between the new global economy and small-town textile mills. All networks framed the issue as the rational advantages of international trade against the emotional and irrational fear of unemployment. None suggested that those profiting from the new economy might also be emotionally self-interested. Nor did any report a rational case for the dispossessed – no 1990s version of Reagan's "safety net for the truly needy." Indeed, all four narratives dismissed the latter position with the label "protectionist" while providing no comparable catch phrase for the pro-trade position. This story privileged Bob Dole, Steve Forbes, and even Lamar Alexander while marginalizing Pat Buchanan as a demagogue armed with passion, a simplistic irrational solution, and a platform that was simply "parroted" by his followers.

Third, the networks imposed markedly different frames on the candidate debate. One highlighted their serious discussion of policies while the other three networks focused on their treatment of one another. ABC and NBC framed the debate as combat while CBS framed it as a mix of theatre, food fight, and playground brawl. Forums like this are important for attracting media and voter attention, for direct policy interactions, and to winnow candidacies, but they leave the participants bruised and battered, foster citizen alienation from all of the candidates, and sometimes advantage uncontested nominees such as Bill Clinton and Ross Perot. Moreover, the more of these campaign debates there are the more the voters must depend on the news media's summaries and characterizations of the debates rather than the actual debates – a dependency that significantly transforms the speech act from a candidate debate to a story of their combat.

Finally, all four networks engaged in serious omissions. ABC and NBC viewers heard about the small downs of Greer and Iva but nothing of Charleston. Viewers heard nothing of Columbia except that it held a debate and flew the Confederate flag over the capitol building. Only ABC discussed the Christian Conservatives who reportedly accounted for 40 percent of the state's Republicans. Although the economy was the central issue viewers heard only one comment from one economist. None of the networks mentioned party loyalty or organization as important in the primary campaign, minimizing Dole's most significant resource. Steve Forbes was billed as the initial frontrunner by two networks but his platform was ignored, and Lamar Alexander was simply dismissed as bankrupt in terms of both money and ideas.

This case study shows elements of pack reporting by the four networks especially with regard to their story of the rational global economy vs. the emotional fears of the old economy and their emphasis on the debate. But it also suggests that each network told its own story to a considerable extent. The core audiences of each network were told different things about South Carolina, thus contributing to different agenda-setting, framing, and priming for those three audiences. Our discussion of the 1996 South Carolina Republican primary reports should not be taken as the basis for generalizing to all campaign coverage. It was simply one week from the primary phase of one election campaign.

The Problem in the Rearview Mirror

Since most citizens get most of their information about presidential campaigns from the news, we all have a stake in their getting it right. But too often the campaigns are doing one set of things and the reporters are telling an altogether different story. The result is a misinformed citizenry.

There are a great many wise individuals in the journalistic profession who recognize the problem we have been discussing – usually after the fact. Karen Tumulty of *Time*, for example, said "there are a lot of narratives that the press bought into in this campaign . . . I think the number of times we've been wrong in this campaign is far greater than the number of times we've been right" (quoted in Hart 2008, p. 10).

Nevertheless there is little reason to think that American campaign reporters will abandon the cherished narratives any time soon. The misguided narratives provide an ongoing plot that guide reporting, enhance our appetite for information updates, increase our dependence on narrators who understand the plot, synthesize the new information with whatever we have previously taken to be factual, encourage identification or division rather than critical reflection, privilege the media organizations over the campaign organizations, and transform naive reporting into the "dramatic surprise" that improves the melodrama.

Thomas E. Patterson's landmark book *Out of Order* (1993) argued that the press in America is a miscast institution in the electoral process. "The press is in the news business not the business of politics," he wrote, "and because of this, its norms and imperatives are not those required for the effective organizations of electoral coalitions and debate." Patterson's writings argue that officials, candidates, and the media have all failed to provide the citizenry with the kind of electoral democracy they deserve.

Historian Rick Shenkman faults the people for allowing those officials, candidates, and media to fail them. Candidates may puff up their records or lie about their opponents and reporters may focus on the horse race or tell the wrong Iowa story, but Shenkman is unwilling to let the people avoid accountability as mere passive bystanders in the campaign process. He therefore holds us all accountable for the sorry state of campaign journalism:

> Just as a people get the government they deserve, they also get the media they deserve. If the public wanted a media establishment willing to take on the myths politicians peddle, we would have such a media.   (2008, p. 199)

Shenkman (2008 p. 3). argues the people are frequently "given the choice between a harsh truth and a comforting myth" and all too often embrace the comforting myth. Viewed from this perspective it is the people who encourage personalized, dramatized stories of order threatened and restored. In such a context the news organizations offering only harsh truths will struggle to find a core audience in the marketplace of news.

The path toward better campaign journalism and a better informed electorate begins with each citizen taking on more personal responsibility for their own information. This requires, first, an acceptance of the principle that citizens are information seekers not passive receptors of information. We would look with scorn on a presidential candidate who did not campaign and a newspaper that ignored a candidate's rally in their city, but an alarming number of people are comfortable saying, "I don't follow the news," or "politics doesn't interest me." More people need to begin to feel embarrassed to say such things.

The second step is for each of us to diversify and enhance our informational diet. It is naive to rely on a candidate for all of our campaign information and it is similarly naive to rely exclusively on news organizations for that information. Reporters write stories some of which are about policy issues. But responsible authorities abound in issue areas such as economics, immigration, health care, and international relations – people whose careers are devoted to studying those subjects systematically. They can be found all across the political spectrum and it is wise to sample their work; many of them are essentially apolitical. Their books, articles, and blogs are more readily available now than ever before.

The third step is to diversify our news consumption beyond network news. As Farnsworth and Lichter say of the Big Three networks, "Something is very wrong with election coverage when the one-liners are on the evening news and the serious discussions are on Leno and Letterman" (2007, p. 184). One can only object that they should have included John Stewart and Stephen Colbert. Yet the reader realizes that television news does not consist solely of the Big Three networks any more. Farnsworth and Lichter's data for 2004 indicated that Fox News was more one-sided than the Big Three networks, they just went the opposite direction. That finding appears to fall far short of Fox's goal of "fair and balanced" news.

The national television news program that stood apart from the rest in a positive sense was the PBS News Hour. Ironically, PBS does a better job of covering presidential campaigns because they employ so many fewer reporters. This enables their viewers to hear twice as many minutes from the candidates in sound bites averaging 52 seconds (compared to 7.8 on the networks). While the networks give 74 percent of their time to journalists and 12 percent to candidates, PBS gives 21 percent to candidates, 24 percent to journalists and 55 percent to others. Perhaps most importantly, PBS devoted 67 percent of their sixteen minutes a day to substantive coverage (as opposed to the horse race) while the networks were devoting 71 percent of their twelve minutes to the horse race; that breaks down to eleven minutes of substantive coverage daily on PBS as compared to five minutes on the Big Three networks.

Yet another ray of hope for consumers of television news is local television. If, as the saying goes, "All politics is local," then perhaps local television news provides the news we need. Surely those 1996 South Carolina voters were not totally dependent on the networks for their television news, and the staff permanently assigned to cover the state's issues would have had the contacts, the context and the time to cover those issues for their community. Unfortunately, Pew Center data show that viewers in the top 200 markets turned away from local news in all time slots during the 2008 election year. So if the local coverage of the presidential campaign was good, fewer people watched it. Moreover, Pew has found smaller local television news audiences every year since 2006 (Pew 2009).

Newspaper coverage of presidential elections has been better than television coverage (Farnsworth and Lichter 2007). But we must acknowledge the Pew Center for Excellence in Journalism's Annual Report on the state of American newspapers: "The newspaper industry exited a harrowing 2008 and entered 2009 in something perilously close to free fall. Perhaps some parachutes will deploy, and maybe some tree limbs will cushion the descent, but for a third consecutive year the bottom is not in sight" (Pew 2009). So even though newspapers are doing a better job of campaign journalism, they are failing. The Pew Center worries that the day is at hand when we will have a major metropolitan area without a newspaper.

That leaves the Internet as our increasingly important source of news. But David T. Z. Mindich (2005) argues that our increasing reliance on the Internet for news is not increasing our political and civic knowledge. A Pew survey in February of 2000 asked 1,078 people to name candidates running for the Republican nomination. Although 62.8 percent named George W. Bush only 25 percent could name John McCain, 16 percent could name Steve Forbes and fewer than 8 percent could name any of the other five. Part of the problem, Mindich maintains, is that people log onto the Internet for a variety of purposes and pick up their news while online. Unless they are motivated to access news they will settle for the headlines, factoids, and amusing clips that cross their paths. Moreover, his data indicated that fewer than half of respondents younger than forty-five felt the need to get the news – any news – every day. Mindich therefore worried that "getting my news from the Internet" might refer to a low news threshold. And where do we get our Internet news? Frequently from the online sites of the newspapers struggling to stay in business and from the news networks whose reporting we have found to be so often disappointing.

Summary and Conclusion

In the three-part presidential campaign consisting of campaign organizations, media organizations, and citizens, the citizens get most of their information either directly or indirectly from the media.

- We developed a definition of news as "a collaborative melodrama of contemporary events that stimulates the audience appetite and facilitates the integration of new information into their preferred narrative structure for protecting their community, knowledge, beliefs, and values."
- We saw that news consists of stories that update a larger story that is not always in tune with the campaign being enacted by the candidates.
- Even misleading narratives are embraced if they are familiar, reinforce what we believe we know about campaigns, and help us integrate new information into our existing knowledge. But for those same reasons they complicate the process of discovering and correcting factual errors, they emphasize personalities and conflict and encourage opinion rather than thought.
- News stories tend to be personalized, dramatized, fragmented, and concerned with authority and disorder. Campaigns that understand these tendencies can exploit them to their advantage.

The chapter also explained that news organizations have audiences with whom they are interdependent. This means:

- News organizations and their audiences are much like candidates and their voters.
- The campaign press is inclined to report as a pack, covering the same stories in the same way. For example, the national media coverage exaggerates the importance of the Iowa precinct caucuses.
- Within media different outlets tell somewhat different stories. For example, each television network had different subplots within their common South Carolina primary story.

Therefore, getting our news consistently from the same few sources provides us with a narrow view of the public agenda, exposes us to just a few of the many possible story frames and may prime us to vote on the basis of some considerations rather than others.

For these and other reasons many writers have echoed Patterson's charge that Americans are ill-served by the news media's heavy influence on the presidential campaign process. With newspapers falling on hard times and people getting more of their news from the Internet it is discouraging that our level of understanding is apparently decreasing. As candidates and the media struggle it is the citizenry that holds them all accountable once we hold ourselves accountable. For whether we want them to change or we want to improve the information we get through the current system we need to become active seekers of high quality information from a variety of reputable sources.

8 Advertising Candidates in the Political Market

This chapter examines the ways that campaign organizations invest their money in the production of messages for distribution through paid media for the purposes of adjusting or enhancing the refracted message provided to citizens by the free media. Historically, campaigns have paid to distribute their message in fliers and pamphlets, yard signs, and bumper stickers, newspaper ads, sound trucks, radio ads, and television spots.

There has been so much use of paid media that we can be tempted to view campaigns through the advertising window alone. But each mode is a single tool in the campaign's shed, and each is used as part of a mixture to solve the rhetorical puzzles. When free media are conveying the intended message to the target audiences it can be wasteful to advertise, but when free media fail to convey the campaign's message, or convey it the wrong audience, it is foolhardy to skimp on advertising.

The Advantages and Disadvantages of Advertising

The foremost advantage of advertising is message control. Those who produce the ad can say whatever they want. They can acclaim, attack, or defend on policy or character. Benoit's (1999) study of all presidential TV ads from 1952 to 1996 revealed that until 1996 acclaims outnumbered attacks roughly 60–40, and that policy and character attacks were roughly equal from 1958 to 1980, when policy attacks, mostly on past deeds, began to dominate. Candidates have been the source in fewer ads since 1968 as others presented more of the acclaims and attacks. The emphasis on character attacks increased during the 1990s.

The second advantage of advertising is that the producer gets to mix the message elements. Chapter 3 discussed the differential capacities of media to convey some stimuli and to background others. When Illinois Senator Paul Simon ran for the 1988 Democratic nomination the former newspaper editor made extensive use of policy position papers. When Richard Nixon's advisors discovered that citizens perceived him as awkward they created a montage of still photographs; when they found that citizens thought him distant they filmed him in small discussion groups.

The third advantage of advertising is audience targeting. Printed materials can be hung on doorknobs or mailed to lists of registered voters. Radio ads can be aired on stations whose demographic profiles approximate the profile of the campaign's target audience for the ad during the time of day that those people would be most likely to hear it. The same potential is available with cable television networks such as ESPN, BET, and Lifetime. The audiences for the non-cable networks vary more by individual program, such that spots aired on the same TV station during different programs will reach different audiences.

The main disadvantage of advertising is, of course, cost. Production costs are the first hurdle, and a campaign strapped for cash may be unable to produce the television spots they need. But once the production unit has video clips they can re-edit existing footage to create "new" spots. Once produced the ads must be aired, and air time is expensive. A campaign that invests too heavily in producing ads may find itself unable to buy enough airtime to take full advantage of their variety.

A second disadvantage of advertising is that they trigger our defense mechanisms. Most of us recognize ads, political and otherwise, and we have learned to be wary of them. We often change stations to escape commercials or use the commercials for conversation breaks from the music, news, or program content. When we do listen to commercials we often recognize that they are trying to "sell" us something and we pay cautious attention. Campaigns have tried two techniques to deal with viewer caution. One approach, more common in local than presidential races, is the TV spot that appears to be a news report. The other is the extreme attack, such as the Swift Boat Veterans for Truth attack on John Kerry, that generates free media coverage.

The third disadvantage is that advertising will always reach some counter-productive audiences. This is most likely to happen with the most expensive ads – television spots. A TV attack spot saying "Candidate B lacks the experience to lead" will reach and disturb B's supporters more than a direct mail attack or a televised acclaim like, "Candidate A is an experienced leader." This explains the emphasis on acclaims over attacks prior to 1992 as well as the outcry about "negative advertising" since then. It is negative *television* advertising that most bothers people because they see attacks not intended to reach them.

In short, the decision to advertise entails advantages and disadvantages. Each campaign considers those relative merits in terms of their campaign puzzle. Unlike candidates for the local school board or county commissioner, presidential campaigns never really have the option to avoid advertising. Instead, they try to maximize the advantages and minimize the disadvantages.

The Advertising Sequence

To the average viewer, political ads often seem to be a flood of repetitive and undifferentiated images, claims, and attacks. But advertisers long ago learned the importance of using spots to accomplish a series of instrumental goals. These phases of advertising campaigns should not be confused with the stages of presidential campaigns – a point that we will soon revisit.

In their important book *The Spot* (1992) Edwin Diamond and Stephen Bates identify four phases of political advertising campaigns: ID spots, argument spots, attacks spots and "I see an America" spots. It is important for the phases to unfold in this sequence unless the campaign's rhetorical situation justifies a different approach.

Under normal conditions the candidate must be introduced to establish the credibility necessary for advancing arguments, attacks, and a vision. The ID spots use a variety of techniques to establish what Aristotle called the candidate's *ethos* or character. They provide information to suggest the candidate's relevant expertise, they provide grounds for us to trust the candidate and they portray a variety of traits generally regarded as socially desirable that invite us to identify with the candidate.

Once the spots have introduced viewers to the candidate, a second wave of spots begins to introduce arguments. The vast majority of these arguments are acclaims that offer positive policy reasons (or sometimes character reasons such as experience) for supporting the candidate. They can range from general assertions of the campaign's slogan to specific policy proposals, and they can be single argument spots or multiple argument spots. The overall objective of the argument phase is to associate the candidate with a set of arguments that suggest what the candidate values, whose interests the candidate will represent and how the candidate would govern.

Only after the campaign has introduced the candidate and its arguments does it attack the opposition. There are three very basic reasons for this sequence. The first is that a campaign needs solid ground from which to launch an attack. The second is that, especially during the primaries, there are too many opponents to attack and an "attack first" candidate can be perceived as overly negative. The third reason for attack spots is the need to draw a clear distinction between the candidates for prospective voters. As discussed in Chapter 5, these attacks can focus on policy and/or character, and it is often wise to attack the acclaims that were put forth in the opposition's ID and argument spots. Is the opponent as expert as those ads claimed? Can the opponent really be trusted? Has the opponent always valued the interests highlighted in the argument ads? Are the policies advocated wise policies?

The closing phase of the advertising campaign airs visionary "I see an America where" ads. These spots invite viewers to visualize the country as it would be under the candidate's presidency – once all the proposed policy changes had been made and the attacked problems avoided. Foreign policy changes bring both security and peace, economic policies bring prosperity and low taxation, all children are healthy and well educated, and all of us live happily ever after – but only if the "right" candidate wins the election.

Let us return for a moment to the difference between campaign stages and advertising phases. Remember that the presidential campaign is a tournament that unfolds in four stages: surfacing, nomination, consolidation, and election. The nomination stage consists of a large number of primary and caucus campaigns in individual states, each of which requires its own four-phase advertising campaign. Running all four sets of spots in Iowa and New Hampshire does little for viewers in Nevada or South Carolina. Moreover, the general election campaign is a different contest from the primary campaigns, requiring somewhat different arguments and different attacks on a different opponent. Thus the advertising phases unfold again and again within the campaign stages.

Although good advertising campaigns use a variety of paid media, the remainder of this chapter will concentrate on television spots. Today these spots are distributed not only on paid television but on campaign web sites and YouTube. The techniques of message construction are more complex than print ads or

radio ads because television ads combine both audio and visual cues. By understanding television spots the reader will be better prepared to analyze radio, print,
and television ads and to decide which medium can most effectively convey the
key message elements to the target audience.

Types of Television Spots

Much as we can categorize ads or speeches according to whether their content
acclaims, attacks, or defends, we can categorize TV spots by their basic production techniques. Each type of spot has its own look and feel, and the advertising
teams recognize that the form is an important element of the message they hope
to convey.

Talking head ads (Devlin 1987) feature a person talking directly to the camera.
The person is most often one of the candidates, either seated at a desk or behind
a lectern. The settings are normally basic to avoid distracting from the candidate's
practiced sincerity. Richard Nixon's 1960 campaign relied heavily on talking head
spots to convey the vice-president's experience and authoritative command
of the issues. The only problem with talking head spots is that they are visually
boring, making little use of the medium's full potential to engage viewers.

Cinéma vérité ads (Devlin 1987) are actual video or film of the candidate in
action. In 1968 Nixon's campaign developed the "Man in the Arena" ads to show
Nixon interacting spontaneously with citizens about their concerns. Hand-held
video cameras have enabled producers to make these videos look even more
casual and spontaneous, but the spots into which the footage is developed are
carefully scripted and edited. This style shows the candidate interacting with
"people like us" to increase identification and to warm up candidates who are
perceived as reserved.

Documentary ads (Devlin 1987) use archival news video or other existing video
to advance a point. Faced with a growing public impression that Vice-President
George H. W. Bush was a "wimp," his campaign used film of his Second World
War heroism in a documentary spot. When his opponent, Michel Dukakis
claimed credit for cleaning up Boston Harbor, the Bush campaign aired a documentary spot showing a filthy harbor (that happened not to be Boston Harbor)
to undermine his acclaim. The persuasive power of documentary ads comes
from the "official" nature of the video that challenges the viewers to believe their
eyes.

"*Man-in-the-street*" ads (Devlin 1987) have an unfortunately sexist name, but
"people-in-the-street" sound like a mob and a "woman-in-the-street" endorsement would be ever so much worse. This type of ad shows "typical" citizens
expressing their views of the candidates and issues. The first TV spots in 1952
showed such people posing questions for General Dwight Eisenhower to answer.
Gerald Ford's 1976 campaign relied heavily on this form. Their spots mixed
people voicing support for Ford with people expressing reservations about
Jimmy Carter's candidacy. It is particularly useful when producing these spots to
find people who violate traditional stereotypes: blacks who have doubts about a
Democrat, young people who want an experienced candidate, people in veterans'
hats who worry about our engagement in foreign wars, and apparently affluent

people who want to pay their fair share of taxes to help the poor. The strategy is to momentarily disorient the viewer and open their minds to the message.

Testimonial ads (Devlin 1987) show well-known persons speaking well of the candidate or of issues closely associated with the candidate. These ads are much like the talking head except that the person is not officially part of the campaign, and they are similar to man-in-the-street ads except that the reputation and familiarity of the spokesperson provide the persuasive appeal. Testimonials have come from issue advocates, elected politicians, Hollywood stars, and musicians to name just a few occupations.

Neutral reporter ads (Jamieson 1984) are produced to look and sound like news reports. The look and feel of television newscasts have become so stylized that they are easily parodied (see for example *Saturday Night Live's* "Update" segments or the theonion.com). Campaign advertisers sometimes create such fake news spots to convey information helpful to the candidate or harmful to the opponent, hoping that the message will sink in before the viewer realizes that it is a spot. Not surprisingly, many people regard these spots as unethical and deceptive.

Concept ads are indirect spots that associate visual images or sounds in creative ways to invite viewer inferences. One famous spot from 1968 opened on a TV dial and a quiet chuckle. As the camera slowly pulled back to show the TV screen the laughter grew and grew until the man was laughing uncontrollably as the screen said "Agnew for Vice-President?" As the laughter continued (and viewers presumably looked to see what was so funny) the video changed to a slide that said, "This would be funny if it weren't so serious" (see http://www.livingroomcandidate. org/commercials/1968). The identifying characteristic of concept ads is that they do not explicitly state the acclaim, the attack, or the defense – they present and arrange the pieces and require the viewer to contribute the acclaim, the attack, or the defense.

Videostyle

If you were trying to understand the appeal of a popular song you would not study the lyrics alone (has anyone yet figured out "Louie, Louie"?). You would need a comprehensive approach that enabled you to systematically study the music, the lyrics, the performance, and so on. Television spots are also complex messages but unlike songs they have very specific rhetorical objectives to achieve in a matter of seconds. Every element of a commercial is created with care, so a comprehensive approach to political advertising is very important.

Lynda Lee Kaid developed the notion of "Videostyle" for the systematic and comprehensive analysis of political spots and she and her colleagues have used it to study a wide range of ad since 1986 (See for example Kaid and Johnston 2000). A videostyle analysis of a pool of spots considers several aspects of every commercial. Verbal content is examined to determine whether the ad is positive or negative and whether it relied on logical, emotional, or ethical (character) proofs. The coder also looks for uses of challenger and incumbent strategies in the ad. Next the coder decides whether the ad's type was predominantly an image spot (and whether it was about the candidate or the opponent), an issue spot (and which policy), or a comparative ad. Finally the coder considers nonverbal aspects of the ad. Who is the ad's narrator and what notable symbols are present in the ad? What facial expressions appear in the ad? Production choices used to create the ad are also considered. Were the camera shots close or distant, individual or group? Did the ad's production use technological distortions such as creative editing techniques, special effects visual imagery or dramatizations computer alterations or subliminal messages? (adapted from Kaid 2002).

Videostyle analysis of ads for the 2000 presidential campaign permitted Kaid to draw a number of conclusions. First the Gore campaign ran twice as many negative ads as the Bush campaign. Although both candidates emphasized policy attacks, Bush was significantly more likely than Gore to attack personal qualities. But both campaigns produced only about a quarter of their attacks, with the rest coming from their parties. Both candidates relied most heavily on logical proofs like graphs and statistics and little on character, but Gore's ads were almost twice as likely as Bush's to use emotional appeals. The vice-president's ads failed to use incumbency appeals better than the governor who used his executive experience to advantage.

Nonverbally, Bush was the featured speaker more often than Gore and he established eye contact with the camera in 26 percent of his ads. While Bush surrounded himself with people Gore surrounded himself with significant symbols. Bush was the subject of more close-ups (41–26 percent) which typically suggests warmth. Gore took advantage of more split-screen slow-motion production techniques. Both campaigns – 92 percent of the Gore ads and 83 percent of the Bush ads – used technological distortions to manipulate message variables and invite strategic impressions (Kaid 2002).

Videostyle is an important approach to understanding television campaign spots. It forces the analyst to consider a wide variety of message variables systematically and permits inferences about the large pool of spots the campaigns generate. It will be helpful to bear this approach in mind as we consider the development of campaign ads.

The Evolution of Television Advertising

The Museum of the Moving Image maintains an online display of presidential campaign TV ads called "The Living Room Candidate" at http://www.livingroomcandidate.org. This site is an invaluable resource, and the reader will want to bookmark it and watch the commercials discussed in this chapter.

The Rise of "Hard Sell"

The first use of television advertising in a presidential campaign came in 1952. When President Truman announced that he would not run, the Democrats nominated Illinois Governor Adlai Stevenson to try to hold the White House against General Dwight D. Eisenhower who had led the Allied Forces to victory in the Second World War. Eisenhower's name was a household word but Stevenson's was not. The campaign was developing as a clash between slogans: "It's time for a change" vs. "You never had it so good."

After twenty years of Roosevelt, Truman, and the Democrats, some wealthy Republicans were open to innovative campaign ideas, and they met with Rosser Reaves, master of the "hard sell" approach to early TV advertising. Reeves sent a team to interview people who had heard one of Eisenhower's speeches and reported that none remembered what he had said. He suggested running spots for three weeks, late in the campaign, to reach citizens close to their moment of decision, while limiting Democrats' time to effectively respond. His hard sell approach was to produce spots each of which would drive home an unmistakable message (Diamond and Bates 1992).

Reeves produced the famous "Eisenhower Answers America" ads (see http:// www.livingroomcandidate.org/commercials/1952). The production team went to Radio City Music Hall and recruited citizens standing in line to ask questions on camera. They filmed the candidate's answers – over and over, for Eisenhower was no actor – and edited the final spot. A woman complained about high prices and Eisenhower empathized: "Yes, my Mamie gets after me about the high cost of living. It's another reason why I say it's time for a change, time to get back to an honest dollar and an honest dollar's worth." The candidate told a man who could not afford to marry on his salary "Democrats are sinking deeper into a bottomless sea of debt and demanding more taxes to keep their confused heads above water. Let's put them on a sturdy life boat in November." The ads used the technology of television to appear to engage the candidate with everyday people articulating everyday frustrations as support for the slogan that "It's time for a change." It did not seem to matter that the candidate did not actually meet these people or that others prepared the answers.

There is little doubt that the 1952 advertising campaign helped Eisenhower in comparison to Stevenson's campaign. The Stevenson campaign reluctantly used ads. "But the Democrats back then didn't believe, deep in their hearts, in the advertising arts," wrote Diamond and Bates (1992, p. 44). "Madison Avenue was, well, so *Republican*." Stevenson was an eloquent speaker and it was those speeches that carried the burden. Unlike Eisenhower's sharply focused ads, Stevenson's ads used songs, cartoons, and parodies that fell short of inviting a serious engagement with the viewer. There were two ads featuring talking heads explaining why they would vote for him. But the candidate, who was not well known nationally, never appeared in his ads. Much of the Democrats' response amounted to warning that advertising had no place in politics, that it reduced the choice between presidential candidates to a choice between brands of soap.

Today it may be difficult for us to imagine presidential politics without advertising. But we need only turn to Great Britain where there is no paid advertising when national elections are held. In the United States paid advertising enables campaign organizations to control their message and to blanket the airwaves (if they can raise the money). Paid political advertising makes a tremendous amount of money for those who produce the ads and for the stations that sell the time. Moreover, advertising provides citizens with material for conversations that would not otherwise occur. So even if Stevenson and the Democrats had some valid concerns about political advertising, they were unlikely to get the genie of political advertising back into the magic lamp.

The first overt attack ad appeared during the 1956 rematch of President

Eisenhower and Governor Stevenson. There had been critical ads in 1952, but they were indirect attacks on the candidates. Stevenson's 1956 "How's That Again General?" ads were the first frontal assaults on an opponent. The format used footage from one of Eisenhower's 1952 spots and had the vice-presidential candidate respond as a talking head:

> ESTES KEFAUVER   This is Estes Kefauver. The General's promise to bring down prices was another broken promise. Since the Republicans took office the cost of living has reached its highest point in history. Today the consumer can buy less food, less housing, less clothing, less medical care than he could in nineteen hundred and fifty-two for the same money. The General promised a change for the better, and we got shortchanged for the worse. Think it through.   (See http://www.living roomcandidate.org/commercials/1956).

Senator Kefauver offered his viewers no data, nor did he promise that the Democrats would improve the situation. But this ad series was innovative because television viewers saw a candidate for national office personally attack the policies and veracity of his opponent, in this case the President of the United States. If the Stevenson Democrats were reluctant to use advertising to acclaim, they had fewer qualms about using it to attack their opponent's advertising acclaims.

The most important aspect of the 1960 campaign was its closeness. Vice-President Richard Nixon and Senator John F. Kennedy ran neck-and-neck from the conventions through the vote count. Polls showed Nixon leading Kennedy 47–46 percent on Labor Day and turned a 49.7–49 percent-popular vote margin into a 303–219 electoral vote victory. Clearly, the puzzle required each candidate to retain his own support and to chip supporters away from his opponent. Several ads were notable in this regard.

Nixon was generally respected but not well liked, whereas Kennedy was like-able but vulnerable to charges of inexperience. The Nixon campaign adopted the slogan, "experience counts" and acclaimed his experience standing up to Soviet Premier Nikita Khrushchev. All of the spots preserved in the Living Room Candidate exhibit show austere "talking heads" that suggest authoritative incumbency. Most ads show Nixon in a dark suit sitting stiffly on the edge of his desk, speaking sternly about issues; one features vice-presidential candidate Henry Cabot Lodge apparently giving a speech and the other is an excerpt from Eisenhower's convention address. In a spot about defense, Nixon says, "We must never let the Communists think we are weak. This is both foolish and dangerous. And so I say, let's not tear America down. Let us speak up for America" (Diamond and Bates 1992, p. 99). Notice how this passage not only conveys his view on foreign policy but also cleverly constrains the challenger's ability to critique the Eisenhower–Nixon Administration's record.

The Kennedy campaign developed two ads that met Nixon's challenge. The first allowed President Eisenhower, not Kennedy, to undermine Nixon's acclaims of experience. The ad began by reminding viewers that Republicans wanted them to value Nixon's experience then ran film from a presidential news conference:

REPORTER	I just wondered if you could give us an example of a major idea of his that you had adopted in that role, as the decider and final . . .
EISENHOWER	If you give me a week, I might think of one. I don't remember.
ANNOUNCER	At the same press conference President Eisenhower said:
EISENHOWER	No one can make a decision except me.

The ad drew its credibility from the documentary footage of the Republican president and posed less risk to Kennedy than the sort of attacks that Stevenson had used in 1956. Moreover, it engaged Nixon's major strength, experience, rather than a secondary issue.

A second important spot used visual contrasts to link the issues of personal popularity and national prestige. The video opens with documentary news film of "foreign demonstrators throwing rocks at cars, waving banners, shouting angrily" to evoke memories of a hostile reception Nixon had received in South America. Over this footage the announcer says, "Do you believe that America's world prestige is at an all-time high? Then vote for Nixon. But if you believe that America's world prestige has gone downhill in these eight Republican years," he continues as the video changes to documentary footage of Kennedy shaking hands with enthusiastic supporters, "that new leadership is needed to make America first again . . . then Vote Kennedy" (Diamond and Bates 1992, p. 103). Rather than telling viewers that American prestige has declined, the spot challenges them to provide an answer that is at odds with the visual material before their eyes.

The Arrival of "Soft Sell"

The 1952–1960 presidential campaigns represent the heyday of hard sell television spots. They told viewers what to think, and they pounded their message. But by 1964 a new approach was emerging, a "soft sell" approach associated with Tony Schwartz. Where hard sell ads told viewers what to think, soft sell concept ads used what people already thought. When people worried that hard sell ads tried to manipulate viewers, Schwartz said that his ads used "partipulation" by inviting people to participate in their own manipulation.

The most famous of Schwartz's TV spots was the 1964 "Daisy" ad for President Lyndon Johnson (see http://www.livingroomcandidate.org/commercials/1964). The ad begins with a little girl in a meadow innocently picking the petals from a daisy and counting. When she reaches nine and the petals are gone she looks upward, confused, and the shot freezes. An authoritative male counts down from ten to one as the camera zooms into the black pupil of her eye, and the screen fills with the mushroom cloud of an exploding hydrogen bomb. As the blast fades, Johnson is heard saying: "These are the stakes: To make a world in which all of God's children can live, or to go into the darkness. We must either love each other, or we must die." The ad aired once; yet it is discussed in virtually every book on campaign advertising.

A hard sell ad would have said something like, "Barry Goldwater favors the use of nuclear weapons. That kind of leadership is dangerous. It will kill innocent children." The Daisy spot did none of those things; it invited the viewer to say them. The picture of the little girl, the chirping birds, and her awkward counting ("One, two, three, four, five, seven, six, six, eight, nine, nine") plucked a universal "aw, isn't she sweet" chord, and suggested no reason for concern. The idyllic tone was abruptly broken with the frozen frame, the darkening screen, the tinny military countdown, and an unsettling reverberation that combined to pluck a different chord of imminent danger. Suddenly everything vanished in the mushroom cloud – the girl, the flower, the field, the birds, and the sense of impending danger. After the explosion the sound faded and with it any hope of saving the girl from annihilation. Over the desolation, Johnson sermonized, "These are the stakes: To make a world in which all of God's children can live, or to go into the darkness. We must either love each other, or we must die." Viewers brought to the viewing their awareness that Goldwater had spoken in favor of the use of tactical nuclear weapons and their knowledge that Johnson and Goldwater were adversaries. By tapping into the viewers' knowledge and beliefs the spot invited them to draw the desired inference.

Kathleen Hall Jamieson explained the power of the Daisy ad in an interview with David Hoffman. "The reason people read Goldwater into the 'Daisy' commercial," Jamieson said, "was because everything in that ad is speaking to their fears about nuclear weapons, and everything in the campaign was magnifying Goldwater's stands about nuclear weapons. And so you naturally invest that into an open message that invites those fears" (http://www.tonyschwartz.org/JamiesonInterview.html). Goldwater campaign aide Clifton White said he would explain to people, "No, he didn't say he was going to use an atomic bomb. He did say that one of the weapons we could use in Vietnam was a tactical nuclear weapon for defoliating forests . . . to take the leaves off, so that we could see them down there" but White's listeners would just nod and say, "Yeah, but we can't drop the bomb," as if Goldwater had actually suggested it (Diamond and Bates 1992). It is that disconnect that made the Daisy spot most powerful and the cleanest ad of the campaign according to Jamieson, because "to the extent that Goldwater is in the ad he was invested there by the audience. And the audience isn't going to indict itself for dirty campaigning." (Jamieson n.d.). The soft sell approach to political advertising was not timid.

The Man in the [Edited] Arena

The important development on the advertising front in 1968 was the Nixon campaign's *cinéma vérité* approach. Some of his advisors, including Pat Buchanan, argued that they did not have a great need to rely on advertising because Nixon was already well known. But Roger Ailes argued that no candidate would ever again be elected without a successful advertising campaign. As the campaign began to find the intersection of these two principles they sent observers to watch existing film of Nixon. Speechwriter Ray Price concluded that, "The more spontaneous he was, the better" (Diamond and Bates 1992).

Sixteen years after the "Eisenhower Answers America" spots Ailes put Nixon with a group of citizens and let them talk. These "Man in the Arena" spots allowed Nixon to be spontaneous. Yet because they were invited, recorded, and edited the final spots were hardly candid – they were tightly controlled to make the points intended by the campaign.

The Nixon campaign also produced a number of concept spots reminiscent of Schwartz's ads for Johnson in 1964 (see http://www.livingroomcandidate.org/commercials/1968). They combined montages of still images with carefully selected music – discordant, syncopated music to evoke fear and uncertainty and soft, pastoral music to reassure – create emotional associations for the viewers. Although Nixon's voice was sometimes heard over the pictures, he was no longer the 1960 talking head sitting on his desk.

Because Nixon won his campaign has received more attention, but many observers said that another week or so of campaigning would have produced a different result. Humphrey's advertising plan came together only in the last few weeks and, coupled with a Humphrey speech distancing himself from Johnson's Vietnam policy, it significantly closed Nixon's lead.

Watergate, Reforms, and Creativity

Beginning in 1972 campaign organizations hired their own media people and, by providing candidates with an independent source of influence, further undermined the role of political parties in presidential campaigns. Richard Nixon's 1972 landslide re-election defeat of George McGovern was not the result of television advertising. But the Committee to Re-Elect the President (known by the unfortunate acronym of CREEP) raised so much money that some of the excess found its way into the assortment of sordid activities known collectively as "Watergate." These included printing an unflattering letter on an opponent's stationary, breaking into and bugging Democratic National Committee Headquarters, and paying hush money to one of the burglars. When these activities came to light they led to the resignation of many high level advisors and eventually Nixon himself, but that was after the election.

In the wake of Watergate, campaign financing came under greater scrutiny, and the rate of innovation slowed. Gerald Ford's 1976 campaign made heavy use of man-in-the street ads to cultivate reservations about Jimmy Carter, but undermined confidence in his own leadership during the debates when he seemed to underestimate the Soviet Union's influence in Eastern Europe.

No candidate for president, before or since, came to a campaign as prepared for television as Ronald Reagan. But the former movie star and television host had learned as Governor of California that the free media would provide him with opportunities to convey his personality. Thus his 1980 primary spots were conservative message ads that wisely complemented his free media coverage and distributed his message in his own terms. His 1984 re-election campaign featured concept ads built around the "Morning in America" theme. They conveyed comforting emotional images of regular folks cheerfully getting to work.

More controversial was the 1984 Reagan "Bear in the Woods" concept ad that used a visual metaphor to respond to Walter Mondale's attack on his defense buildup:

NARRATOR   There is a bear in the woods. For some people, the bear is easy to see. Others don't see it at all. Some people say the bear is tame. Others say it's vicious and dangerous. Since no one can really be sure who's right, isn't it smart to be as strong as the bear? If there is a bear? (http://www.livingroomcandidate.org/commercials/1984)

The argument was how much to spend on defense *if* there was a threat. By showing us the bear the announcer's "if there is a bear [threat]" expressed a caution that viewers' eyes told them to reject. The ad created a visual "parallel" that removed doubt about the existence of the threat, thus pointing toward Reagan's plan.

The 1988 campaign saw the rise of attack advertising to new heights and demonstrated the importance of campaign management. Michael Dukakis emerged from the Democratic Convention with a lead of seventeen points over Vice-President George H. W. Bush. But a wealth of advertising talent was poorly organized and managed, and a sound advertising plan never developed. Not only did they fail to acclaim or attack effectively, they were unprepared to defend against the attacks that were sure to come from an opponent trailing so severely.

The Bush advertising team of James Baker III, Lee Atwater, and Roger Ailes was experienced and savvy. They launched three major attacks Dukakis, all of which proved damaging. Because Governor Dukakis had acclaimed "The Massachusetts Miracle" they attacked the pollution of Boston Harbor. Footage showed oil slicks, dead fish, a floating toilet seat, a radiation warning sign and more. Kathleen Hall Jamieson has written of the spot that:

> Overall, there were clear reasons to prefer Dukakis to Bush on environmental matters. . . . [the pollution-clotted Boston Harbor ad] capitalized on the fact that new information that is vivid and accessible drives out the old and the abstract. Moreover, the sludge and slime appeared where voters were already looking – between popular prime-time program.   (Jamieson 1992, pp. 105–106)

The second attack on Dukakis benefitted from the National Security Political Action Committee (NSPAC) spot about the Massachusetts prison furlough program.

MALE NARRATOR [and TEXT]	Bush and Dukakis on crime.
[TEXT Supports Death Penalty]	
MALE NARRATOR	Bush supports the death penalty for first degree murderers.
[TEXT Opposes Death Penalty]	
MALE NARRATOR	Dukakis not only opposes the death penalty . . .
[TEXT Allowed Murderers to Have Weekend Passes]	
MALE NARRATOR	. . . he allowed first degree murderers to have weekend passes from prison. One was Willie Horton . . .
[TEXT Willie Horton]	
MALE NARRATOR	. . . who murdered a boy in a robbery, stabbing him 19 times. Despite a life sentence . . .
MALE NARRATOR [and TEXT]	Horton received ten weekend passes from prison.
MALE NARRATOR	Horton fled, kidnapped a young couple, stabbing the man and repeatedly raping his girlfriend.
[TEXT Kidnapping. Stabbing. Raping.]	
MALE NARRATOR [and TEXT]	Weekend prison passes. Dukakis on crime. (http://www.livingroomcandidate.org/commercials/1988)

Why would Dukakis have "allowed first degree murderers to have weekend passes from prison"? Probably because, as governor, he was implementing the state's program begun by his predecessor, Republican Frank Sargent. Although the Massachusetts program was unusual in granting furloughs to prisoners having no possibility of parole, many states had furlough programs (Diamond and Bates 1992). The NSPAC ad invited viewers to infer that this program was a Dukakis project, which it was not. NSPAC sponsored additional ads featuring Horton's victims and Dukakis failed to respond effectively.

The Bush campaign followed NSPAC with their own ad showing prisoners passing through a revolving door. This ad neither mentioned nor pictured Horton, but viewers could hardly avoid connecting the dots.

MALE NARRATOR	As Governor Michael Dukakis vetoed mandatory sentences for drug dealers he vetoed the death penalty. His revolving-door prison policy gave weekend furloughs to first degree murderers not eligible for parole.
[TEXT 268 ESCAPED]	
MALE NARRATOR	While out, many committed other crimes like kidnapping and rape, and . . .
MALE NARRATOR [and TEXT]	Many are still at large.
MALE NARRATOR	Now Michael Dukakis says he wants to do for America what he's done for Massachusetts. America can't afford that risk. (http://www.livingroomcandidate.org/commercials/1988)

Jamieson (1992) wrote that the Bush ad played fast and loose with its words. There were not, as it claimed, "many first degree murderers not eligible for parole who kidnapped and raped while out," there was only Willie Horton. Although the ad said "*many* committed other crimes *like* kidnapping and rape" Jamieson found that a total of 67,378 Dukakis era furloughs had resulted in 275 escapes and only one instance of kidnap and rape – Willie Horton's – not "many." There are no crimes "like" kidnapping and rape, but the spot's language invited viewers to hear it as "such as kidnapping and rape" thus implying greater frequency. Once again, the Dukakis campaign failed to defend itself against the damaging inferences invited by the ad.

The third Bush attack on Dukakis showed footage of Dukakis having a grand time driving a tank. The spot portrayed Dukakis as one of "those" liberal Democrats who was soft on defense, yet it did more than that. By showing him smiling after the viewer heard the allegations it invited the inference that Dukakis was unconcerned by the charges. Moreover, the policy attacks combine with the footage of his ride to suggest that he does not take weapons systems seriously. With those inferences drawn, the spot invited the more general conclusion that Dukakis did not seem like a Commander in Chief. The Dukakis campaign responded ineffectively, including the damaging video in their own spot.

Advertising alone did not turn Dukakis's seventeen-point lead into an 8 percent 426–111 Bush landslide, but it helped. The Bush attacks combined to

Dukakis Tank

portray Dukakis as outside the mainstream, and his feeble responses left voters wondering how he would stand up for them if he could not defend himself. The attacks drew coverage in the free media – news stories, news panel shows and talk shows – that magnified their impact. This was especially important in 1988 because television sets were just being manufactured with remote control units that, for the first time, made it simple for viewers to delete channels and to surf during commercials. It was therefore easier than ever for 1988 viewers to skip these spots – unless they were dramatic enough to attract widespread coverage in the free media. Lost in the clamor, but not on viewers, were the positive Bush ads.

President Bush reached the unprecedented Gallup Poll ratings of 89 percent approval and 8 percent disapproval n the aftermath of the Persian Gulf War (Roper 2009) and many prominent Democrats chose not to challenge him. But Bush was slow to acknowledge the country's economic struggles and Pat Buchanan challenged him in the Republican primaries while a slate of lesser known Democrats criticized Bush in their primary campaigns, and Ross Perot announced his independent candidacy. Perot led both Clinton and Bush in the polls when the Democrats convened, but withdrew from the race, leaving the anti-Bush campaign to Clinton.

One Clinton ad drew on the 1984 Reagan–Bush "Morning in America" ad to press the economic critique. "It's morning in Decaturville, Tennessee," the announcer intoned over footage reminiscent of the 1984 spot, "but for 650 people who once worked here there are no jobs. The Decaturville sportswear factory closed and moved overseas . . . It didn't have to happen. As Sixty Minutes reported, the Bush Administration used your tax dollars to lure his sportswear factory to move to

El Salvador" (see http://www.livingroomcandidate.org/commercials/1992). A second Clinton attack used documentary footage of Bush's 1988 "Read my lips: No new taxes" promise from his Nomination Acceptance speech and coupled it with an announcer saying, "Then he gave us the second biggest tax increase in American history. Bush increased the gas tax by 56 percent. Can we afford four more years?" Then the spot began Clinton's acclaims: "As governor, Arkansas has the second lowest tax burden in the country. Balanced twelve budgets. You don't have to read his lips. Read his record. (See http://www.livingroomcandidate.org/commercials/1992.)

Unlike Dukakis, Bush embraced the challenge and went after Clinton's acclaims by attacking his record on taxes and budgets. Over black and white footage of a gloomy landscape a female narrator told viewers, "In his twelve years as governor Bill Clinton has doubled his state's debt, doubled government spending, and signed the largest tax increase in his state's history. Yet his state remains the 45th worst in which to work, the 45th worst for children. It has the worst environmental policy, and the FBI says Arkansas had America's biggest increase in the rate of serious crime. And now Bill Clinton wants to do for America what he's done for Arkansas. America can't take that risk" (see http://www.livingroomcandidate.org/commercials/1992).

The attacks and counterattacks over taxes culminated in a direct exchange of ads. The Bush ad "Federal Taxes" pictured workers whose taxes the ad claimed would increase under Clinton. The Clinton campaign responded with an ad that showed all four people from the Bush spot in a divided screen (making the alleged tax increases difficult to read) under a banner clearly labeling it "Bush Attack Ad." The spot's defense relied not upon Clinton or Democratic sources but upon external authorities. The Clinton spot cleverly conceded the fear invited by the Bush ad but trumped it with the *Washington Post*'s pronouncement that it was "misleading" and the *Wall Street Journal*'s finding that Clinton's plan proposed cutting taxes for people like those pictured in the Bush ad. Yet that account forces viewers to ponder the president's motivation for such an alleged deception, and the ad provides them with that motive: "George Bush has had the worst economic record of any president in fifty years. George Bush is trying to scare you about Bill Clinton."

The 1992 campaign was less nasty than 1988, but concerns remained continued about the truthfulness of campaign ads. Viewers and media organizations sought help, and so did some scholars.

The Rise of Adwatches

The advertising campaigns of 1988 and 1992 created a climate that was unhealthy for deliberation. Citizens were justifiably losing confidence in the factual information provided them by the campaigns, and many felt their emotions being preyed upon. Media organizations seeking to act responsibly devoted pages and airtime to investigating facts and allegations, but in doing so they inadvertently helped the campaigns distribute their charges and false claims.

The publication of Kathleen Hall Jamieson' *Dirty Politics* in 1992 marked a critical turning point in the country's response to campaign advertising. Her book explained that citizens behave like "pack rats," assembling information for a voting preference but forgetting where they found that information (and whether it was fresh or rancid). She explained how ads like the 1988 Bush "Revolving Door" invite false inferences from viewers, a problem that cannot be addressed by any news story that investigates only the ad's factual claims.

Jamieson also took pains to explain how the visual grammar of television was playing into the hands of those they sought to critique. Airing the spot as part of the story, even with a reporter's voiceover, gives the commercial free airtime. Jamieson provided a detailed appendix that showed television news producers how to improve their adwatches.

Jamieson recommended five principles for television adwatches: previewing, distancing, disclaiming, displacing, and recapping (1992). The newscast should *preview* the adwatch with a title or logo and a lead-in to differentiate it from a commercial break. Rather than airing the spot full screen, the producer should add *distance* between the spot and the viewer by shrinking the image, displaying it in a box or TV frame, tilting it, or a combination of all three. Freezing the spot at key points interrupts its message and provides additional critical distance for the viewers. *Disclaiming* labels the spot as an ad to distinguish it from the station's message; but it is important to use a font different in type and color from those in the ad and to have the disclaimer cut across the content to visually interfere with the viewer's processing of the spot's intended message. The heart of the critique is *displacing* which, Jamieson emphasized, must be both verbal and visual. The announcer must tell viewers what is wrong with the spot, but the visual should make those points in print over the picture of the ad. These displacements can be printed as bullet points over the ad, as scrolling text, or by crossing out or wiping out the claims. Finally, the adwatch must *recap* the ad's claim, the evaluation, and what it all means because the ad will be seen more often than its critique.

Adwatch stories, thus improved, were ready to become increasingly popular and important in 1992, or so it seemed. Instead, 1992 network adwatches decreased in number by 50 percent in 1992 (Kaid and Tedesco 1996). When the 1992 reports were not neutral 87 percent were negative, suggesting that the networks chose not to "waste time" telling viewers that they could trust information from the spots they were viewing. Two out of every three spots subjected to an adwatch in 1992 was an attack, suggesting that it was easier to get away with a dubious acclaim than an attack. But curiously 42 percent of the adwatches focused on Perot ads, 20 percent on Bush ads and only 6 percent on Clinton ads, despite the fact that the Clinton ads were full of attacks on the president's record (Kaid and Tedesco 1996).

Adwatches increased during the 1996 general election campaign, but shortcomings remained. John C. Tedesco took journalists to task for failing to turn to external, impartial authorities to critique the content of the ads. "In general, the adwatches seemed to imply that the ads were 'sketchy'," wrote Tedesco, "However the adwatch journalist's or anchor's own analyses of the spots were just as sketchy" (Tedesco 2000, p. 552). He also noted that the important visual elements of the television spots, to which television news personnel ought to be especially well attuned, were largely ignored.

Why were television stations so slow to realize the potential of adwatches? Did they not understand how to do it? Did they not want to share the spotlight wth content experts? Were television stations dependent upon advertising dollars squeamish about critiquing paid advertising too well? Did they worry that their adwatches invested them too deeply in the campaign? Did they regard these adwatches as too academic for their own target audiences?

The adwatch function slowly began to be performed by people other than television stations using the emerging web sites on the World Wide Web. Unlike the television adwatches, the web adwatches could be maintained, referenced, linked, and updated.

527s, Web Ads and the Future

The millennium brought a change in the IRS tax code and full-scale use of the Internet. In accordance with the First Amendment to the Constitution, individuals are free to give their time and money to advance their beliefs. It is Section 527 of the tax code that stipulates the circumstances under which such money is subject to campaign finance laws that regulate or tax it. But the campaign finance law had to leave some room, in accordance with the First Amendment, for individuals to make contributions not coordinated with candidates or parties. Thus the language of Section 527 that defined some political money as subject to campaign finance law necessarily left some political money exempt from campaign finance law.

A "527" group is exempt from campaign finance law if, and only if, it raises money only from individuals and if its raising and spending is not coordinated with the political parties or candidates. A group that meets those two conditions is not a Political Action Committee (PAC) because it does not meet the definition. A 527 can produce and air whatever ads its wants, and neither campaign can stop them.

In 2004 the 527s favoring John Kerry, such as MoveOn.org, were raising more money than those favoring George W. Bush. This was helpful, since Republicans had historically raised more money than Democrats. Then the 527 Swift Boat Veterans for Truth began airing their attacks on Kerry. Kerry called for Bush to denounce the ads and have them stopped, but the law prevented such coordination. Bush and John McCain instead called for an end to all 527 advertising, a solution that would have hurt Democrats more than Republicans. More importantly, ending all 527 advertising would have silenced a great number of organizations that were advertising responsibly and contributing to an enriched discussion of policy issues.

The growth of the Internet opened the door for "web ads." Campaigns had been posting their commercials on their web sites so that they could be viewed repeatedly for free in addition to their purchased distribution. But web ads were created specifically for the web site. Two of the most notable ads were produced by the 2008 McCain campaign. The "celebrity" opened with footage of crowds cheering Obama. As the female announcer said, "He's the biggest celebrity in the world," viewers saw images of Britney Spears and Paris Hilton, inviting the inference that celebrity is a dubious distinction (http://www.livingroomcandidate.org/commercials/2008).

McCain's web ad "The One" intercut footage of Obama speaking with visual text, narration, and movie footage designed to invite messianic comparisons. Evangelical viewers of the ad were surely put off by the ad's suggestion that Obama and his followers regarded him as a savior, while white viewers with any racist inclinations were invited to infer that the candidate "did not know his place." Other visitors to the McCain site could enjoy a laugh at the spot's creative use of Charlton Heston's Moses parting the Red Sea and its subtle decision to treat Obama's own humor as literal statements. When, during the second presidential debate, Senator McCain referred to Senator Obama as "that one," many Obama supporters and pundits treated it as disrespectful, but those familiar with the web ad recognized the allusion to the inside joke.

Summary and Conclusions

As television viewers most of us probably have little good to say about political campaign commercials. But this chapter has explained that campaign advertising

- Is advantageous for campaigns by allowing them to acclaim, attack, or defend as they want, to mix the message elements as they wish and to send their message to their target audiences.
- Disadvantages campaigns because of its costliness, our tendency to resist advertising, and the inevitability of sending messages to some inappropriate audiences.

Overall advertising is a costly and imperfect means of message control that is useful when candidates and issue advocates want to reach us with messages that they feel are more important than the free media coverage they receive.
    This chapter explained that:

- Advertising campaigns unfold in a planned sequence: ID spots, argument spots, attacks ads and "I see an America" spots.
- Television ads use particular techniques to make their point: the talking head, *cinéma vérité*, documentary, man-in-the street, testimonials, netutral reporter, concept ads
- Videostyle is a comprehensive approach to the study of television ads that focuses our attention on the visual and verbal elements of a pool of commercials.

The chapter also recounted the evolution of televised political ads, emphasizing:

- Rosser Reeves's "hard sell" style of the 1950s and Tony Schwartz's "soft sell" approach of the 1960s
- Roger Ailes's personalizing of Richard Nixon
- The post-Watergate turn to creative imagery and concept ads such as Reagan's "Morning in America" and "The Bear in the Woods"
- The increasing use of attacks ads such as Bush's "The Harbor"
- The rise of newspapers, television, and web site adwatches

- The growth of 527 groups like MoveOn.com and the Swift Boat Veterans for Truth who attack candidates legally independent of the campaign organizations.

We have seen that campaigns have frequently presented us with inaccurate or untruthful information, invited misleading inferences, and distracted us with production techniques. We have also seen that campaigns can use ads to defend themselves and to correct the distortions, and that media organizations have used adwatches to expose the inappropriate uses of campaign ads, although not as well or as frequently as they could have.

In the final analysis, we need to realize that we viewers enable advertising to work. The more critically we attend to the ads, the more we check their claims for ourselves and think before granting the inferences they invite from us the happier we will be with our voting decisions.

9 Televised Presidential Debates: The Rhetorical Super Bowl

Today it is nearly as difficult to imagine a presidential election without televised debates as professional football without a Super Bowl. Both were actually innovations of the 1960s that pit the survivors of a series of elimination contests against each other in spectacles made for national television, and consequently both receive overwhelming media attention. The game produces an acknowledged winner who *is* the champion whereas presidential debates have only perceived winners who do not necessarily move closer to winning election. Most importantly, the Super Bowl is a just a game with no real practical or social consequences for the nation or the world but presidential debates can have important consequences for the nation and the world.

The purpose of this chapter is to understand why televised presidential debates exist as the communication forms that they are. We will consider the reasons for having debates, their history and their effects. We will consider the extent to which they are in fact debates at all and whether that matters to us as students of presidential campaign communication. We will consider the major strategies used by candidates and some techniques that citizens can use to make these events more useful. We will also consider whether debates have had a significant impact on the outcome of presidential elections.

What is a "Debate"?

J. Jeffrey Auer (1962) called the 1960 Kennedy vs. Nixon Debates "Counterfeit Debates." He explained that, "A debate is (1) a confrontation, (2) in equal and adequate time, (3) of matched contestants, (4) on a stated proposition, (5) to gain an audience decision." Auer omitted two other characteristics of debate from his list. A sixth characteristic of a debate is that the participants define and develop the issues; it is the debaters themselves who decide how to frame the stated proposition and which issues to discuss. The seventh characteristic of a debate is that debaters do not talk to each other but to an audience (an expert judge or a public audience) that renders a judgment.

How, then, have our televised "presidential debates" fared with respect to these seven characteristics of debates? Is there a confrontation between or among candidates? Certainly. Do the candidates have "equal and adequate time" to debate the issues? Moderators devote considerable effort to monitoring the equality of time. They use complex systems of warning lights and they take valuable time to lecture candidates and audiences about time management. But what about the adequacy of the time? College debaters give ten-minute speeches to explain their policy proposals but presidential candidates typically get two minutes to explain policies that they would actually implement. This invites the repetition of brief, superficial statements rather than depth and can make it difficult for us to distinguish between a candidate who fully understands the issue and one who has simply been prepared to deliver a brief statement.

Whereas a debate provides participants with a stated proposition, a presidential debate either provides an implied proposition (Resolved: That voters should prefer candidate A) or a general topic such as foreign policy or the economy. How does one debate "the economy"? That awkward problem could be addressed if the candidates themselves were to define and develop the major themes and issues. But in almost all presidential debates they are asked to respond to questions, usually from moderators and reporters but sometimes from citizens.

In a debate, matched contestants address a judge or audience. Presidential debates match the nominees of the major parties (and any candidate with 15 percent support in the polls). They are not necessarily comparably skilled at debating but they are matched as nominees. In 2008, Moderator Jim Lehrer made a point of urging John McCain and Barak Obama to address each other rather than the audience or him, a direction at odds with basic debate protocol. More frequently, candidates have been chastised for succinctly responding to a question and then trying to make their own points, suggesting that the candidates' priorities are less important than those of the questioners. True debates seek to gain a decision from either the judge or the audience. But moderators of presidential debates scold audiences for reacting to comments, and rarely offer an opinion on the outcome. Indeed, questioners are rarely consulted as to their satisfaction with the answers to their questions. Instead, pundits, polls, and focus groups are used to interpret the outcome.

Reflecting on the 1960 debates Professor Auer concluded that, "It is unhappily necessary to conclude that 'The Great Debates' were not debates in the American tradition, and the rhetorical critic sighs for what they might have been" (Auer 1962). Today one wonders if Professor Auer may have been too gentle in his criticism, for these events have become ever less like debates and more like joint press conferences. The problem is that the opportunity so rich in potential has become something less than it could be, and few of us seem either to notice or care, because they are "good television."

Thus, when asked what I think of presidential debates, my instinctive response is, "They would be an interesting experiment." It might be useful to have the candidates bring their own rhetorical agendas to the cameras, unimpeded and unaided by the press corps. After all, one of the president's crucial tasks is to define problems, issues, and priorities for the nation – why not use the debate format to see how well they can do it? Why not let the candidates engage over a topic such as, "Taxes are unnecessarily high," and then argue about which taxes, what level is necessary, and what they would do about it?

Why Debate?

Why bother to have televised presidential debates? After all, Americans somehow managed to elect thirty-four presidents without them, as there had been no presidential debates through 1959. Many people know of the Lincoln–Douglas debates between Abraham Lincoln and Senator Stephan A. Douglas who ran against him for president in 1860, but their debates were held during their 1858 Illinois Senate race won by Douglas. Thomas Dewey and Harold Stassen held a radio debate during the 1948 Oregon Republican Primary campaign and Adlai Stevenson and Estes Kefauver debated on television during the 1952 Florida Democratic Primary, but these were a far cry from national debates between representatives of the two parties.

As described in Chapter 8, the 1950s saw the emergence of television advertising in presidential campaigns, and not everyone was happy about that. There remained a dominant strain of thought that ads were undignified, and that presidential candidates should take a higher road – speaking for themselves and avoiding jingles, cartoons, and gimmicks. Thus one argument for holding debates was to provide an alternative to the tawdry influence of advertising.

A second reason for holding televised debates was to increase interest in the campaign. Although it had been technically possible for the networks to broadcast live coast to coast for much of the 1950s, it was not until the late 1950s that it became a common practice. In 1950 only 9 percent of US households had a television, but that number increased to 64.5 percent by 1955 and 87.1 percent by 1960 (TV Basics 2009). Thus the 1960 campaign offered campaign and media organizations direct access to a vast audience of citizens that had never before been available.

This confluence of a vast audience, a new technology, and a presidential election provided the news media with an opportunity to increase citizens' understanding of the issues. This educational mission was less idealistic than it may sound to us today. There was no more forceful advocate for the educational role of broadcasting than Edward R. Murrow, the legendary CBS news correspondent. Never one to avoid controversy himself, Murrow blasted his industry's avoidance of controversial informational programs with an address to the Radio-Television News Directors Association and Foundation on October 15, 1958:

> This instrument can teach, it can illuminate; yes, and it can even inspire. But it can do so only to the extent that humans are determined to use it to those ends. Otherwise it is merely wires and lights in a box. There is a great and perhaps decisive battle to be fought against ignorance, intolerance and indifference. This weapon of television could be useful. Stonewall Jackson, who knew something about the use of weapons, is reported to have said, "When war comes, you must draw the sword and throw away the scabbard." The trouble with television is that it is rusting in the scabbard during a battle for survival.   (Murrow 1958)

Murrow argued that the networks were insulating citizens from useful information about important subjects and delivering only escapist drivel. He conceded that informational programs were unprofitable, but argued that broadcast news professionals had a civic responsibility to provide them anyway, using some mechanism. He also argued that the broadcasters were more fearful of controversy than were their viewers:

> I am entirely persuaded that the American public is more reasonable, restrained and more mature than most of our industry's program planners believe. Their fear of controversy is not warranted by the evidence. I have reason to know, as

do many of you, that when the evidence on a controversial subject is fairly and calmly presented, the public recognizes it for what it is – an effort to illuminate rather than to agitate.   (Murrow 1958)

Within two years these broadcast professionals would have in the proposed presidential debates an opportunity to provide information and contribute to controversy that was nonetheless safe and mainstream.

A fourth reason to hold a debate was each campaign's persistent need to shift votes. Candidates were travelling the country by train and plane to speak to gatherings of citizens about their visions for the future, intent on changing votes a handful at a time. Surely, they reasoned, speaking to the whole nation at once would provide a more efficient opportunity to shift many more votes. If we factor in the supreme confidence it must take to run for president, we might also expect that the candidates especially liked the way a debate would present them side by side and showcase "the other guy's" weakness.

A fifth reason to debate would be to influence news coverage of the campaign. Since the debates would be a major campaign event they would attract vast news coverage. What could the reporters cover other than the candidates remarks? Moreover, the reporters would surely cover the candidates' remarks accurately because the whole nation had listened and watched for themselves. Thus the debates offered campaign organizations a way to regain a measure of control over campaign news from the press. Chapter 7 explained that campaign news came to be dominated by horse race stories rather than issue coverage. Debates seemed to offer candidates a vehicle for turning attention from the horse race to the issues.

Although we have discussed five general reasons for holding a nationally televised debate, it has not always been prudent for a candidate to agree to debate. Advisors to a presidential candidate who want to know whether it is wise to challenge the opposition to debate can consider a checklist of questions.

- *Is there an incumbent president in the debate?* Debates tend to undermine incumbents and elevate challengers. Debates are especially enticing when an incumbent is running unless, of course, our candidate is the incumbent.
- *Is the election likely to be close?* When the campaign is close the debate – or a perceived reluctance to debate – could be the final straw.
- *Do we trail the frontrunner?* When the campaign is lopsided the frontrunner ordinarily has much to lose and little to gain from debating. But trailing candidates have little to lose, especially if two candidates can gang up on the frontrunner.
- *Is our candidate a good "debater"?* Televised political debates are not intercollegiate debates, and the requisite skills are different from the rapid fire tournament delivery. We need to study tapes of the candidates' previous political debates to see the strengths and vulnerabilities of each.
- *Are there are only two candidates?* Time is precious in a debate, and a third candidate means that our candidate gets only one-third of the time. Worse, only one candidate will get each state's electoral votes and it is difficult to tell which answers by which candidates will play well for which voters in which states.
- *Will we be able to control the important variables?* This implies that we know

what is important to us and that we can secure them during the negotiations. These can include the amount of time allowed for answers, whether there will be responses or follow-up questions, staging and lighting considerations, and the choice of format, moderator and questioners. We need to know the point at which we will decline to debate unless we control the variables we value.

- *Do we have clear strategic goals for the debate?* It is prudent to know what we hope to accomplish before we begin to speak, but this is crucial when debating on national television. Do we hope to establish our candidate or undermine our opponent? Do we want to show America that our candidate has a detailed grasp of the issues or that he is a charismatic leader?

Rarely will all of these questions point a candidate in the same direction. That is why the negotiations (the "debate about debating") often drag on so long. Now that we have had debates for nine consecutive presidential campaigns it is almost inconceivable that we will have a campaign without them. Indeed, the proliferation of debates during the primaries has made these events almost as commonplace as advertisements and speeches.

The Evolution of Presidential Debates

The incentives for holding a televised presidential debate coalesced in a 1960 television environment very different from the one we know today. The only networks were ABC, CBS, and NBC, and their network newscasts were only fifteen minutes long. Candidates were simply not seen on television nearly as much as they are today. It was in that environment that Richard Nixon and John F. Kennedy changed the way that presidential candidates engaged citizens and the media.

Despite the reasons for holding debates a legal restriction complicated matters. The "equal time provision" of the Federal Communications Act was intended to insure that all candidates for public office had equal access to the nation's airwaves. Broadcasters worried that a debate between the Republican and Democratic nominees would commit them to providing equal national time for every minor candidate for president, which they could not afford to do. In 1959 the FCC ruled in favor of a Chicago mayoral candidate (who campaigned in an Uncle Sam costume) and for a time any footage of a ribbon cutting by a public official running for re-election required equal time for all of his opponents. Congress soon amended the act to exempt news programs and documentaries from the equal time provision and thus opened the way for the 1960 televised debates as news programs (Windt 1990).

It appeared in 1960 that presidential debates would become a staple of campaign communication, but there were no debates during the next three election cycles. President Kennedy had promised to debate Barry Goldwater if they were the nominees, but Kennedy's death cancelled that arrangement. New President Lyndon Johnson was far ahead in the polls by September and saw no advantage in debating Barry Goldwater. The 1968 electorate was divided among front-runner Richard Nixon, Vice-President Hubert Humphrey, and American Independent Party candidate George Wallace. Nixon had no incentive to expose his lead to two opponents and Humphrey had no incentive to provide two candidates with a forum for attacking the Johnson-Humphrey Administration, but a debate without Wallace (who would win 13 percent of the vote and 46 electoral votes) was not plausible. The 1972 scenario resembled 1964, this time with President Nixon far ahead of Democrat George McGovern.

But after Watergate the Bicentennial year of 1976 featured a close race between President Gerald Ford and Georgia Governor Jimmy Carter. Nixon had named Congressman Ford to fill the vice-presidency when Spiro Agnew resigned over a financial scandal, and Ford became president when Nixon resigned because of the threat of impeachment over Watergate. Thus the incumbent Ford had never faced the national electorate, and his opponent merged slowly through the primaries ("Jimmy Who?" was a popular campaign button). By August both candidates had incentives to debate – President Ford trailed Carter by 33 percent, but Carter had a recognition problem. With the FCC now considering debates a bona fide news event, equal time considerations were off the table. We have had televised debates ever since.

Debate Strategies

Televised debates present campaign organizations with a rhetorical situation as discussed in Chapter 2. To achieve a fitting response candidates must proceed wisely – analyzing the situation and developing strategies. Over the years we have seen the emergence of pre-debate, debate, and post-debate strategies.

Pre-Debate Strategies

The first and most evident pre-debate strategy is to lower public expectations for the candidate's performance relative to the opponent. Like the coach who praises the winless team he is about to face, the campaign strives to minimize public expectations to avert the dreaded "upset." Campaigns know that the media will frame the candidates' abilities for the audience in the weeks prior to the debate, and they dare not find themselves in the position of making their points less impressively than expected. This is also a good time to praise the opponent's debating skills. In 2004 Republicans pointed to the extensive courtroom experience of Democratic vice-presidential nominee John Edwards.

The second pre-debate strategy is to determine your target audiences and how to reach them. The target audience for the debate may be unique. For example, if there is to be one debate on the economy and one on foreign policy the campaign may try to reach different people in each debate. They must also decide whether it is more important to energize their supporters, to win over undecided voters or to bore opposition citizens into not caring who wins.

The third pre-debate strategy is to devise and rehearse possible answers. The campaign staffs provide detailed extensive briefing books for the candidate. They decide whether it is best to respond with specifics or a general principle. Sometimes they deflect a question with a humorous remark. The least prepared debater was unquestionably Ross Perot's 1992 vice-presidential candidate, Admiral James Stockdale. Perot's campaign was based almost entirely on his own ideas and Stockdale was his close friend. But the two did not meet before the debate and Stockdale floundered. More frequently, we hear poor performances attributed to "over preparation" – candidates so heavily briefed that they try to do too much and tie themselves in rhetorical knots.

Debate Strategies

The first debate strategy is to relate answers and issues to an overall theme based on the pre-determined strategy (Trent and Friedenberg 2004). Kennedy did this in the very first debate, connecting everything to "leadership." John McCain tried to do this in 2008 with "Joe the Plumber" but his repetition of the name overshadowed the theme.

The second strategy is to cultivate an image that resonates with the target audience (Trent and Friedenberg 2004). A citizenry rocked by Vietnam, Watergate and the pardons of draft evaders and President Nixon looked for a president they could trust and Jimmy Carter used the debates to convey that image. Reagan used his 1980 debate to enact the role of a confident leader and Obama used the 2008 debates to demonstrate his grace under pressure.

The third debate strategy is to hold your opponent accountable for unpopular things. It is fairly easy for a challenger to lay anything on an incumbent president's doorstep and more difficult for an incumbent to blame a senator or governor for large-scale problems, but try they must.

Legislators are particularly vulnerable to the "flip-flop" charge that they have been on all sides of an issue. Imagine that you are a senator who wants to replace the income tax with a national sales tax. A bill comes to your committee to raise the income tax for 30 percent of taxpayers, so you vote against it. Then you vote against a bill that would cut taxes for 30 percent of taxpayers because you want to scrap the system rather than tinker with it. But your own bill dies in committee and the tax cut bill gets to the full Senate, where you vote for it because it lowers taxes for many people. You flip-flopped! Your opponent will also say that you voted against tax cuts (which you did) while ignoring the fact that you also voted for tax cuts. Once a debater gets an opponent explaining the legislative process in self-defense that candidate has great difficulty getting the focus back on his rhetorical agenda.

The fourth strategy is to avoid living up to your opponent's portrayal of you. The 1980 Carter campaign had portrayed Ronald Reagan as a rash extremist who would endanger social security and medicare and conduct a trigger-happy foreign policy. Reagan used the debate to project a calm, reasonable demeanor that undermined Carter's image of him.

The fifth strategy is the counter-punch, and it is most effective when the format calls for an answer, a response, and a rejoinder. Candidate one begins with a balanced answer like "We need to strengthen the military and to balance the budget." The second candidate invariably tries to say more about both points and runs out of time on one of them (balancing the budget). At that point the first candidate counter-punches by attacking the second's inattention to balancing the budget. In the rare cases where the second candidate does provide a balanced answer the first candidate is free either to continue with both or to pick one and ride it to the finish line.

A sixth strategy is to control the dramatistic appeal of the candidate's narrative. Kenneth Burke explained that our language choices when telling a story reflect our philosophical priorities. We can illustrate his point with a simple example of five different versions of the same incident.

Act:	Kathy walked and took her dogs.
Scene	The daffodils were blooming through the melting snow as Kathy and her dogs walked through the park.
Agent	Kathy always looked forward to being outdoors, especially with her energetic pointer and her loyal St. Bernard.
Agency	Walking two dogs can be difficult but the retractable 20-foot lead allowed one dog to roam while a leather leash kept the other nearby.
Purpose	For both humans and dogs walking is good for the cardio-vascular system and general well-being.

In the very first presidential debate John F. Kennedy emphasized leadership (purpose) while Richard Nixon debated policy mechanism (agency). We saw the opposite in 1988 when George H. W. Bush talked about "family values" (purpose) and Michael Dukakis focused on managerial competence (agency). In 2004 John Kerry and the Democrats tried to focus on President Bush (agent) while the president talked about the dangerous world we lived in (scene). Since patterns will emerge, candidates in a debate might as well tell stories in the ways that help them achieve their strategic objectives.

Burke was also interested in the words we choose to depict the story elements we emphasize. Subtle differences often matter (a Facebook friend recently got quite a reaction when she wrote "I miss sex in the city" instead of "I miss *Sex and the City*"). Candidates often depict their opponents' acts as "opposing" or "voting against," and most audiences seem to accept them as interchangeable. But one can be construed as "opposing" something by simply asking the responsible question, "How are we going to pay for it," and we have already seen that legislators frequently vote against specific bills that would achieve goals that they do not oppose. Was the agency for dealing with the 2008 financial crisis a "rescue" or a "bailout"? Should the presidential agent be a "hero" or a "servant of the people"? These are but a few examples of the ways that candidates can use language choices to shape the narrative for the target audience.

Lastly, all campaigns strategize to dominate the news bites aired after the debate and forevermore (Trent and Friedenberg 2004). These are the gems that we remember, whether they are important or not. They are ordinarily called "sound bites" because most of them have been verbal. ABC News.com provides us with a hall of fame:

"There is no Soviet domination of Eastern Europe, and there never will be under a Ford administration" (Ford in 1976)
"I am not going to exploit, for political purposes, my opponent's youth and inexperience" (Ronald Reagan age 73 in 1984)
"I served with Jack Kennedy. I knew Jack Kennedy. Jack Kennedy was a friend of mine. Senator, you're no Jack Kennedy" (Lloyd Bentsen in 1988) (ABC 2004)

Ford meant that the people of Eastern Europe were proud and determined to live again in freedom, but few people heard it that way. People stopped talking about Reagan's age and fitness for office, and we will never know exactly when his Alzheimer's began to affect his judgment. Many voters thought Bentsen's rebuke of Dan Quayle was out of line but Quayle curtailed his references to Kennedy after that. Most importantly, each of these sound bites drove everything else out of news stories about the debates and today they are about all that anyone remembers from several hours of debates.

Some of the crucial news bites have been visual. Ronald Reagan began the 1980 debate by striding across the stage and extending his hand to the shorter President Carter, upstaging the president. President Bush looked at his watch during 1992's first ever Town Hall debate, prodding many to wonder if he found his people's questions a waste of his time. In 2000 the camera caught Al Gore rolling his eyes, and in the first 2008 debate John McCain seemed to avoid looking at his opponent until the debate was over.

These images are not only conveyed through newscasts. *Saturday Night Live* in particular has developed a reputation for debate parodies. In 2008 Tina Fey's impersonation of Sarah Palin's debate style heightened audience awareness of her mannerisms (such as winks and "you betcha") and her argumentative strategies.

The point is that something will dominate the news bites, and the odds are no better than 50–50 that the audience's perception will advantage you rather than your opponent. But planning, preparation, and performance can increase the likelihood of a fitting or favorable response in the larger campaign context that actually matters.

Post-Debate Strategies

Yankee catcher Yogi Berra was not talking about presidential debates when he said, "It ain't over 'til it's over" or he would have said "The debate begins as soon as it is over." Put differently, the candidates' debate matters less than the debate about the candidates' debate.

During the closing statements everyone close to the candidate, as well as experts brought to the debate site for the occasion, converge on the "spin room." There they take questions from the reporters covering the debate. The spin room is no place for candor. Spinners hawk their wares like cable TV pitchmen. "Our candidate made his case to the American people tonight," they say, "he was very presidential." The opponent typically "kept repeating the same old buzzwords we have heard for years" and almost certainly "demonstrated that he was out of touch with the mainstream of American politics." Yada yada yada.

"Spin" has developed into a large, coordinated effort to influence the news narrative about the debate. Spinners' task is to provide journalists and thus citizens with a context for interpreting whatever happened in the debate in a positive light with regard to their goals for the debate. They can talk mainly about those goals and then say something like, "I think Americans saw that tonight." Why would strategists let reporters characterize the debate when they can provide them with quotes for their stories that have the potential to provide a more fitting response? No debate reporter can ignore the spinners because the rest of the pack covers them.

In recent years we have seen several efforts to find alternatives to spin. Professor Diana Carlin of the University of Kansas began the "Debate Watch" program as one such alternative. Since 1992, Debate Watch has helped set up hundreds of live debate viewings around the country. When the candidate debate ends, the television is turned off and a Debate watch moderator facilitates a discussion of the debate uninformed by the network commentary and spin. Carlin and her colleagues analyzed several of these discussions in *The 1992 Presidential Debates in Focus* (Carlin and McKinney 1994). Debate Watch is now formally associated with the Commission on Presidential Debates, and its web page (www.debates.org) provides information about holding Debate Watch sessions.

As another alternative to spin several networks have tried to offset the spinners with focus groups of undecided voters whose reactions are examined as seriously as an autopsy. Yet their focus on undecided voters presumes that they were the target audience, an assumption that is not always valid.

One objective of the spin period is to win the journalists' debate over gaffes and one-liners. Did President Bush look at his watch because he was bored with the debate or because he wanted to signal moderator Carole Simpson that Perot and Clinton were talking too much? Did Bentsen put Quayle in his place for comparing himself to President Kennedy or did he overstep the bounds of decorum and invite people to feel sorry for Quayle? Interestingly, the media paid more attention to Al Gore rolling his eyes and sighing than they did to the substance of the Bush comments that induced his reaction, a choice that indicates how the media focus on the debates as television, sometimes at the expense of content.

In addition to spin, a second strategy is to follow up on the debate with ads that underscore and reinforce the themes highlighted during the debate (Trent and Friedenberg 2004). Such ads provide the campaign with more message control than does spin, and they can directly target their spots and mailings to the audiences they need. This is important if the debate message is to be fully coordinated with the rest of the ongoing campaign.

A third strategy is to win the interpersonal networks' debates about the debate. This is where our personal opinion leaders come into play. In the days after a presidential debate we all talk about it. "What did you think of the debate?" we ask one another between classes, in line at the bagel shop, and on e-mail. These conversations help us to fine tune our perceptions by finding out what people we like and/or respect (as well as those we dislike and disrespect) thought of the debates.

Existing social networks are especially important in this regard as we turn to family and friends. If an older male relative says, "I'm the same age as McCain and I worry about us expecting someone our age to be at the top of his game" he has the potential to impact our thinking more deeply than would a stranger or a spinner. Similarly, males wondering whether women who had supported Hillary Clinton found Sarah Palin appealing were especially likely to attend to the views of females in their family, co-workers, and friends. In 2004 the Bush campaign developed an extensive array of existing social networks, through churches and other micro-targeted associations (Sosnick, Dowd, and Fournier 2008). When the debates came along these people could easily contact one another to talk about Bush's success and Kerry's shortcomings. The Obama campaign did this even more effectively in 2008 using social networking sites such as Facebook.

With all this spinning, advertising, and networking going on it may not be surprising that perceptions of the debate results vary until several days after the debate. As Yogi might have said, nobody noticed how bad Nixon looked until days or weeks after the debate ended. This is one reason why the length of time between debates is an important variable. Each campaign needs time to assess the results of one debate and then to plan for the next one. This is probably less a matter of new technologies assembling and distributing information than it is a reflection of citizens' need to digest the debate about the debate.

The Effects of Debates

What effects have televised presidential debates had on presidential campaign communication? There are a variety of ways to answer that question and scholars have used most of them. In this section we shall discuss briefly some of the major findings from the perspective of instrumental and terminal responses produced by televised debates.

Have Debates Produced Terminal Results?

One way to assess the overall impact of debates from 1960 to 2008 is to compare the outcome of "debate elections" to "non-debate elections." The last six incumbent presidents who ran for re-election without debating won all six elections (Nixon in 1972, Johnson in 1964, Eisenhower in 1956, Truman in 1948, and Franklin D. Roosevelt in 1944). The six incumbents who did debate won three elections (G. W. Bush in 2004, Clinton in 1996, and Reagan in 1984) and lost three (G. H. W. Bush in 1992, Carter in 1980, and Ford in 1976). Moreover, two of the three incumbents who lost debate elections had won elections in which they had debated (Carter in 1976 and G. H. W. Bush in 1988). Clearly, televised debates have not been kind to incumbent presidents.

There are two possible explanations for incumbents' difficulty in debate elections. One explanation is that the debates equalize the candidates by enlarging our impression of the challenger and diminishing the imposing symbolic stature of the president, as they become simply two men on a stage who fill the television screen. The president's authority is reduced as he answers questions designed to hold him accountable for his record. The other explanation is that we now have debates because we have become a more diverse and critical electorate. Many observers have said that Vietnam and Watergate burst Americans' idealistic conceptions of their presidents, and the prevalence of debates in contemporary campaigns may be more a symptom than a cause of our skepticism toward incumbents. In all likelihood both explanations contribute to incumbents' reduced rate of re-election.

A second way to ask the question about terminal results is to ask how often the debates have made a demonstrable difference in the outcome of an election. That is frequently they are framed for us by the media, but how can one isolate the effect of the debates when there are so many things going on in the campaigns at the same time? Two elections are widely thought to have hinged on the debates – 1960 and 1980 – so we can begin by considering those cases.

The Nixon–Kennedy Debates (1960)

Vice-President Richard M. Nixon entered the first of four debates with a non-significant 47 percent-46 percent lead in the polls over Senator John F. Kennedy. Afterward, the immediate question was not "What did these candidates have to say about the challenges facing the US?" but "Who won?" Gallup showed Kennedy winning 43 percent to 23 percent and Schwerin Research put it at 39 percent–23 percent for Kennedy; radio listeners regarded it as a tie (Windt 1990).

Once the public opinion polls showed Kennedy to have won the debate, analysts began to explain the data. Retrofitting hypotheses to data makes for poor empirical research but it is the mother's milk of media controversy. It offers the look and feel of research while providing no controlled test of the hypotheses – it is speculation that invites further speculation. This speculation fed upon itself and produced a number of urban legends or myths that frame our sense of presidential debates to this day. These are myths not because they are necessarily wrong, but because we believe in them despite a lack of evidence.

Myth 1: Kennedy won on television but Nixon won on radio. The Gallup and Schwerin data indicated that viewers rated Kennedy's performance significantly higher than Nixon's; this difference disappeared among radio listeners. But the radio Nixon did not rate better than the radio Kennedy, they tied (Windt 1990). Only one study showed Nixon outperforming Kennedy among any medium's audience: a Sindlinger study reported in *Broadcasting* magazine found that 48.7 percent of the radio listeners chose Nixon as the winner to only 21 percent for Kennedy, 30.2 percent of TV viewers picked Kennedy to 28.6 percent for Nixon. But the sample sizes were too different – 282 listeners and 2,138 viewers – to warrant comparison (Blumenthal 2007).

Myth 2: The data on television and radio audiences can be compared because they were essentially random samples of citizens. Steven Chafee explained that the televised debates were unavailable to few people in 1960. "Those who could listen to debates only on radio were . . . situated for the most part in remote rural areas, they were overwhelmingly Protestants and skeptical of Kennedy as a Roman Catholic candidate (Chafee 2000). Did Sindlinger's sample of 282 radio listeners disproportionately measure the reactions of people from remote rural areas who were skeptical of Kennedy as Chafee posits? We will never know because the data have been lost. But Chafee's informative explanation and the small sample should provide reason for caution.

Myth 3: Nixon fared worse on TV because he looked sickly and unshaved. Nixon had been hospitalized and was pale for a Californian. His make-up was substandard and his suit was not well chosen. If we were to view the debate today and then answer the question, "Which candidate looked more presidential?" an overwhelming majority of us would doubtless answer "Kennedy." But 1960 viewers were not asked that question. Indeed, Russell Baker's lead story for the *New York Times* said nothing about either candidate's appearance until very late in a long article. In short, the candidates' physical appearances did not jump out at reporters. Moreover, there is no evidence that Nixon's supporters, or even undecided citizens or Kennedy supporters for that matter, regarded his physical appearance as more important than what the candidates had to say. Finally, as communication scholar Richard Perloff wrote to the *New York Times*, "you can turn the [explanation] around by suggesting that Kennedy lost on radio because listeners were turned off by his Boston accent" (Perloff 1996).

Myth 4: The first debate was decisive in John F. Kennedy's victory over Richard M. Nixon. On Labor Day, the traditional start of the campaign in those days, Nixon led 47–46 percent in the Gallup poll, and that was where the candidates stood heading into the first debate in late September. After the first debate, Kennedy held a 49–46 percent lead that he held through the last of the four debates (Windt 1990) with the popular vote splitting 49.72 percent for Kennedy and 49.55 percent for Nixon. Surely this four-point swing must have been decisive – except that all of these polls reported differences between the candidates that were within their poll's statistical margin for error. If we imagine that the citizenry was split 48 percent for each candidate with 4 percent undecided and/or not voting, a poll estimate of 48 percent (+ or – 3 percent) would be considered accurate for numbers ranging from 45 to 51 percent – a range that perfectly encompass Nixon's scores of 47, 46, and 49.55 percent and Kennedy's scores of 46, 49, and 49.55 percent. Put differently, the change in numbers looks important because reporters covering an excruciatingly close race used a microscope to study a gross estimate. The "lead" that changed after the first debate was not statistically meaningful before the debate, so its change was not statistically meaningful either. However, Windt was on the right path when he wrote that, "The exact role and importance of the 1960 debates played in the election of John Kennedy are subject to dispute. However, the belief that without the debates Kennedy could not have won is firmly established" (1990, p. 1). The 1960 debates were decisive in the sense that everything is potentially decisive in so close a campaign.

Unfortunately, the myths about the Nixon–Kennedy debates took root and grew in part because there were no debates in 1964, 1968, or 1972. Lost in all of the preoccupation with whiskers and shifty eyes were two clear differences between the candidates' communication styles that were politically significant. The first is that Kennedy's goal was to emphasize a positive theme – leadership – while Nixon's goal was to dispel his unwelcome image as a political hatchet man (Windt 1990). "Leadership" provided Kennedy with a consistent way to address every issue and question (the country has suffered from a lack of leadership, Democrats will provide leadership) to which Nixon did not consistently respond. On the other hand, Nixon had no consistent theme uniting his positions, many of which became defensive as he attempted to differentiate himself from unwanted positions.

The second difference was that Kennedy debated from the perspective of goals and Nixon, the experienced college debater, picked away at the means of achieving them (Windt 1990). The focus on goals allowed the less experienced candidate to project a sense of stature and vision, while the focus on means invited the audience to perceive Nixon as lacking in vision and direction despite his experience.

The 1960 debates established a precedent that is now a prominent feature of presidential campaign communication. There was more to the debates than Nixon's appearance, but to this day the roles played by a positive theme and enduring goals continue to influence perceptions of candidates' presidential potential.

The First Televised Debate

The Carter–Reagan Debate (1980)

A year before the election the Roper Center's polls showed President Carter with 32 percent job performance approval and 55 percent disapproval. Then Iranian demonstrators overtook the American Embassy in Tehran and fifty-two Americans were held hostage for 444 days. Within a month Americans had rallied around the president and approved of his performance by a 54–35 percent margin despite the hostage crisis, a sour economy and Senator Ted Kennedy's challenge to the president for the Democratic nomination. The president's approval ratings stayed above his disapproval ratings until March and he held on to win the nomination from Kennedy in a convention roll call vote at a time when his disapproval ratings were twenty points higher than his approval ratings (Roper 2009).

The 1980 debate period provided the Carter campaign with a delicate opportunity. The Kennedy challenge had cost Carter support among liberal Democrats, but a debate with the conservative Reagan could remind them of their overall preference for Carter. The Carter people expected that to be easy because they regarded Reagan as simply an actor whose lack of substantive policy expertise would be revealed in a debate. The unwelcome guest at the party was Independent candidate John Anderson, a moderate Republican Congressman from Illinois who drew more support from Carter than Reagan. The president therefore declined to participate in the September 21 debate that featured Reagan and Anderson.

Carter and Reagan debated in Cleveland on October 28, 1980 – a week before the election. By then 55 percent disapproved of the president's job performance and only 31 percent approved. According to Kurt Ritter and David Henry (1992) Carter had three strategies to guide his debate performance. First, the president planned to attack Reagan without elaborating his arguments. Advisor Patrick Caddell warned against actually debating Reagan because the idea was to lay out the issues for the voters. So Carter verbally jabbed at Reagan, launching 21 attacks while answering only one of Reagan's attacks.

Carter's second strategy was to discuss a complicated list of themes and policies designed to appeal to a variety of target audiences. But Carter was so busy providing these little targeted speeches that he was judged to have evaded 42 percent of the questions while providing complete answers to only 16 percent (Ritter and Henry 1992).

The third Carter strategy was to pounce on the mistakes that they were certain Reagan would make. They were unprepared for a Reagan who did not self-destruct. As if that were not bad enough, they had Reagan speak first to put more pressure on him, but thereby also gave him the last closing statement, which Reagan used to great advantage. In short, all three strategies developed by the Carter campaign proved disastrous.

The Reagan campaign took a very different approach. Their first priority was to focus on President Carter's record. Reagan attacked sixteen times and Carter answered only once, but Reagan answered fifteen of Carter's twenty-one attacks (Ritter and Henry 1992). The second strategy was to appeal to the audience not with complex lists but by being pleasant, humorous, and "safe." Reagan was likeable, certainly in comparison to Carter, and he did not play the part that the Carter people had planned for him. Reagan's third strategy was to show compassion by relating to undecided citizens so that they might find him a safe alternative to the unpopular president. He asked them to pose for themselves the now famous question: "Are you better off today than you were four years ago?" In short, the Reagan strategy was well conceived and executed.

Polls showed that the close race between Carter and Reagan opened up to a Reagan lead in the days following the debate. Reagan carried 50.75 percent of the popular vote to Carter's 41 percent and Anderson's 6.6 percent. But more indicative of the debate's importance than this 9 percent margin was the electoral vote outcome: Reagan 489, President Carter 49 and Anderson 0. Although the debate provided the president with an opportunity to salvage the election, Caddell's strategy was seriously flawed. Then again, a president with 55 percent disapproval does not provide much for his advisors to use, and televised debates are not the best place for unpopular presidents to become popular – especially when the opponent is Ronald Reagan.

What we do not know about 1980 is the projected distribution of electoral votes prior to the Carter–Reagan debate. Perhaps the debate enabled Carter to add Maryland, West Virginia, and Rhode Island to the ticket's base of Georgia, Minnesota, and the District of Columbia – but that seems unlikely. It seems far more reasonable to grant that the 1980 debate contributed significantly to the outcome of the election. Through the first nine rounds of televised presidential debates, then, the 1980 debate stood alone as an example of the debates' ability to decide an election. Then came 2008.

The Obama–McCain Debates (2008)

Many factors contributed to Barack Obama's victory over John McCain in 2008, but we have more evidence than usual with which to assess the impact of the debates. CNN's respondents thought Obama won the debate 51–28 percent. The Quinnipiac Survey zeroed in on three swing states – Florida, Ohio, and Pennsylvania – because no candidate had won the presidency since 1960 without carrying at least two of them. Respondents in all three states said that Obama did the better job and won the debate, but at least 84 percent in each state said that the debate did not change their minds. The post-debate Obama lead increased non-significantly in Ohio (by 1 percent) and in Florida (by 2 percent) and by a more impressive 9 percent in Pennsylvania (Quinnipiac 2009), suggesting that few of these swing state voters found reason to switch to McCain.

Electoral-vote.com tracked state polls and projected electoral vote totals every day of the campaign. The graph reprinted below plots McCain's and Obama's projected electoral votes against the 270 needed for victory and shows key moments along the timeline. It shows that McCain led Obama until late May, about the time that it became clear that Obama would be the nominee. It further shows that Obama's lead had virtually disappeared by the start of the conventions, then Obama gained ground and McCain lost ground during both conventions, with the Republican Convention have the greater benefit for Obama. Again McCain recovered, edging ahead of Obama just as the Wall Street meltdown hit and hurt both candidates. But as the days passed Obama had pulled ahead going into the first debate on September 26.

Figure 9.1 shows that McCain and Obama held steady for a few days after the debate, as we would expect, but then McCain's projected electoral votes suddenly plummeted and Obama's sharply increased.

The period following the second debate shows another, less dramatic Obama increase and McCain decrease, and CNN's polls gave the second debate to Obama, 54–30 percent. The third and final debate shows yet another McCain drop and Obama gain, and again CNN's polls gave the final debate to Obama (58–31 percent). The CNN data show that Americans, by a substantial majority, perceived Obama as having handled the debate opportunities better than McCain. The Electoral-vote.com data indicate that these perceptions of their debate performances were matched by changes in the projected electoral votes. There is no reason to underestimate the impact of the financial meltdown on the election, but evidence suggests that the debates provided a public forum that magnified the disparity that had begun to develop shortly before the first debate.

What did Obama and McCain do in the debates to produce this impact? Obama seemed to concentrate on undecided voters and those who regarded him unfavorably. Like Reagan in 1980 he did so by staying calm and reasonable under attack and by treating his opponent with respectful interest. McCain talked to his base of supporters and attacked Obama, often with sarcasm. He interrupted Obama and sometimes seemed to show disdain for his opponent, like Al Gore in 2000. McCain probably solidified his base but he needed to draw people away from Obama, and this debating style had not worked well for others.

We began this section by asking if televised debates have had terminal effects.

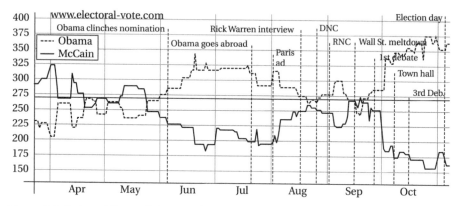

Figure 9.1 Projected Electoral Vote Totals
Source: © http://electoral-vote.com/evp2008/Pres/ec_graph-2008-all.png

We can now say that incumbent presidents have lost with much more frequency when they have debated. It also seems that televised debates have rarely decided the outcome of a presidential election but they played extremely important roles in Ronald Reagan's 1980 defeat of President Jimmy Carter and Barack Obama's 2008 defeat of John McCain.

Instrumental Effects of Televised Debates

Televised presidential debates have exhibited several instrumental effects. They have attracted audience interest and built public confidence in democracy. They have mainly reinforced audience views but have been known to shift votes (usually within the polls' statistical margin of error). Debates seem to help voters set their personal political agendas and increase their knowledge, if sometimes about matters of lesser importance. They do serve to modify candidate images but freeze general campaign attitudes at pre-debate levels (Trent and Friedenberg 2004).

Table 9.1 reveals that the large audiences attracted by televised debates have come in two distinct phases. From 1960 through 1992 fourteen of the fifteen debates attracted audiences ranging from 60–69 million viewers (the sole exception being the 80 million who watched the sole Carter–Reagan debate in 1980). But ten of the eleven presidential debates from 1996 through 2008 drew audiences ranging from only 36–56 million viewers (the exception being the 63 million who watched the second McCain–Obama debate). In other words, only one presidential debate of the last eleven ranked among the top sixteen debates in terms of viewership; this includes the extremely close elections of 2000 and 2004. Meanwhile the audience of 69.9 million for the 2008 vice-presidential debate between Sarah Palin and Joe Biden tied with the 1992 Bush–Clinton–Perot debate as the second most watched televised debate.

The reasons for the sudden and sharp decline in the audience for televised debates are unclear. Perhaps increased access to the Internet and cable news channels since the early 1990s have provided viewers with alternate sources of information about the candidates and their campaigns. Perhaps the data reflect

Table 9.1. Audiences for Presidential and Vice-Presidential Debates

Year/Candidates	Debate 1	Debate 2	Debate 3	Debate 4	VP Debate
1960 Kennedy vs. Nixon	66.4	61.9	63.7	60.4	
1976 Carter vs. Ford	69.7	63.9	62.7		43.2
1980 Carter vs. Reagan	80.6				
1984 Mondale vs. Reagan	65.1	67.3			56.7
1988 Bush vs. Dukakis	65.1	67.3			46.9
1992 Bush vs. Clinton vs. Perot	62.4	69.9	66.9		51.2
1996 Clinton vs. Dole	46.1	36.3			26.6
2000 Bush vs. Gore	46.6	37.5	37.7		28.5
2004 Bush vs. Kerry	62.4	46.7	51.1		43.5
2008 McCain vs. Obama	52.4	63.2	56.5		69.9

Source of data: Commission on Presidential Debates http://www.debates.org/pages/history.html

the number of viewers watching the debates in real time, while tens of millions of citizens recorded the debates or knew they would be able to access them on C-SPAN or YouTube. Even with the decline, an audience of 40–50 million potential voters is to be treasured and addressed with care.

Summary and Conclusions

Super Bowls and presidential debates began in the 1960s to pit the survivors of a series of elimination contests against each other in spectacles made for national television. This chapter:

- Extended Auer's definition to say that "A debate is a confrontation in equal and adequate time on a stated proposition in which matched contestants define and develop the issues by addressing an expert or popular audience to gain its decision."
- The candidate forums called "debates" are not actually debates because they feature inadequate time, no stated propositions, moderator, or panel control of issue development and a decision to be surmised by pollsters and pundits.

Obama and McCain in Debate

Debates emerged because they offered promise:

- As a dignified alternative to commercials
- As a way to increase interest in campaigns
- As a way to fulfill television's educational potential
- As a way to shift votes
- As a means of influencing campaign news coverage.

Candidates debate when it suits their strategic cost-benefit ratio to debate. Positive answers to the following questions should motivate a candidate to debate:

- Is there an incumbent president in the debate (other than me)?
- Is the election likely to be close?
- Do we trail the frontrunner?
- Is our candidate a good "debater"?
- Are there are only two candidates?
- Will we be able to control the important variables?
- Do we have clear strategic goals for the debate?

The motivation to debate influences each campaign's pre-debate negotiations, while they attend to other pre-debate strategies:

- Lower expectations for one's debate performance relative to one's opponent.
- Determine your target audiences and how to reach them with debate content.
- Devise and rehearse possible answers.

During the debate candidate strategy should focus on:

- Relating answers and issues to an overall strategic theme
- Cultivating an image that resonates with the target audiences

- Holding the opponent accountable for unpopular things
- Seeming different than the opponent's portrayal
- Counter-punching to throw the opponent off message
- Use stories with care to subtly emphasize act, scene, agent, agency, or purpose.
- Dominate the news bites

After the debate each campaign strategizes to:

- Conduct an effective spin operation to win the journalists' debate over gaffes and one-liners
- Underscore the debate themes with ads and speeches
- Win the interpersonal debate over the debates:

Clearly, debates have become one of the most strategic modes of campaign communication.
    This chapter also considered the effects of debates. We found that

- Incumbents won much more often when there were no debates.
- The evidence suggests that only the 1980 and 2008 debates clearly affected the outcome of the election. The 1960 debates may have affected the outcome but probably not in the TV vs. radio way that is part of debate mythology. The other debates did not directly influence their elections' outcome.
- Debates have attracted audiences but their audiences basically peaked in 1992.
- Debates shift only a few votes, usually within the margin of error, but those can mean important electoral votes.
- Debates also built confidence in democracy, modified candidate images, helped voters set their personal agendas and acquire knowledge. But they largely lock people in at their pre-debate level.

Debates are an inherently divisive communication form because they reduce all available positions to two sides. They are therefore ideally suited to the polarizing that is necessary during the final stage of an election campaign when each campaign seeks to cluster potential voters in every state into "us" and "them." Decided citizens can validate their candidate preference and acquire the details they need to work the water cooler at work for the next few days. Undecided voters can window shop the candidates and move closer to supporting one.
    Televised debates are a tool for informed choices but any tool can be misused. When we put too much faith in the form or the choice of format, or in the moderator or panelists to control the debate agenda, televised debates can become a crutch that we substitute for ongoing political learning and our personal responsibility to be informed.

10 Using New Media for Familiar Puzzles

The staggering impact of new communication technologies is old news. Introducing a new medium can certainly alter the way we interact to create social groups and govern ourselves in profound ways, but the truly profound changes entail more than the technology. "Mere tools aren't enough," wrote Clay Shirky (2008, p. 17), "The tools are simply a way of channeling existing motivation." The key participants in presidential campaigns (campaigners, reporters, and citizens) are motivated to build support coalitions, to tell the story of the campaign and to select a leader who helps them feel that their nightmares will end and their dreams may be fulfilled. When these key participants discover ways to use a new medium to channel their political motivations they change the process of campaign communication.

All media were once new media. Each was adopted through the general "Diffusion of Innovations" process described by Everett M. Rogers (2003). It begins with "Knowledge": we learn of the innovation but know nothing about it and have little incentive to learn. During the "Persuasion" stage we gain interest and seek information about the innovation's potential. In the "Decision" stage we consider advantages and disadvantages of the innovation and decide to adopt or reject it. In "Implementation" we use it and seek additional information. Finally, we decide during the "confirmation" stage whether to continue using the innovation or to abandon it.

The novelty of any new medium invites early adopters to experiment with it. Baby boomers experienced their first political conventions on radio. By 1960 the Big Three networks televised debates, conventions, and more. By the end of the decade most could digest campaigns in living color. The 1970s brought cable television with the first all-news television network (CNN) and a network that aired candidate speeches and rallies uninterrupted (C-SPAN). To accommodate the explosion of channels they bought videocassette recorders and televisions with remote controls. By the 1990s fax machines and e-mail facilitated person-to-person contact and the new World Wide Web popularized candidate web sites and search engines. The first decade of the Twenty-first century has witnessed the rise of blogs, social networking, YouTube, and more. Each new technology changed presidential communication because of its very newness. A technology is a tool, and the people who first figured out how best to use the newly available tool to solve their campaign communication puzzles advantaged their campaigns.

This chapter will explore the uses of the newest communication media in presidential campaigns with particular emphasis on the 2008 presidential campaign. We undertake this task fully aware that readers in just a few years will find this discussion outdated, perhaps even amusing. But that is actually the point of the chapter: today's emerging technologies are tomorrow's antiques. Anyone intent on becoming a professional campaign consultant would be better off learning how to think creatively about using an unfamiliar tool to solve a familiar problem than mastering Twitter or some other current tool that will become tomorrow's eight-track player.

Information Ages in American Politics

Bruce Bimber (2003) explained that the United States has gone through four information revolutions, which means that we have conducted presidential campaigns in five different information ages. The first age, from the nation's founding in 1789 until 1820, was characterized by local information and little attention to the sharing of information between communities or across the nation. This lack of national information inhibited both the citizens' ability to hold elected officials accountable for their policies and the development of political identities. That changed with the first information revolution (1820–1840) when the Federal Government built 13,000 new post offices and made mail an important communication technology. During the same period newspapers evolved from little merchant bulletins to "penny press" newspapers that cost less and sought a wider readership. They began covering politics and controversies to attract readers. These changes in communication technology meshed with the rise of Jacksonian Democracy, and as people began voting for the presidential electors new political parties arose – the Whigs and the Democrats – who used the mail and the newspapers to communicate with citizens. Anti-slavery groups began using the new media to mobilize during the 1830s. America's second information age – based on the wide distribution of printed letters and newspapers among literate citizens with white males over twenty-one participating more broadly in elections than ever before – endured through the Civil War and lasted until about 1880.

The second information revolution (1880–1920) was a byproduct of America's industrialization, as organizational thinking fostered specialization (Bimber 2003). Individuals found themselves connected to one another differently, through economic relationships, and those with shared interests began using their resources to speak directly to government and to demand accountability. Organizations such as the American Medical Association (AMA) began to lobby government, and political parties lost some of their influence. In this era of pluralism political parties became coalitions of interest groups. But if industrialization encouraged professionals and management to organize and lobby around their economic roles it also encouraged laborers to organize into unions of the skilled (like the American Federation of Labor) and the unskilled (like the Congress of Industrial Organizations). As the AMA lobbied, so did labor, farmers, and others. America's third information age emphasized access to inside information and access to insiders. Pluralism and elites emerged with leaders often acting as brokers of competing interests. Presidential coalitions were assembled by cobbling together leaders of various interests who could deliver their rank and file voters to the candidate (Kernell 1993 called this "institutionalized pluralism").

Barely had the second information revolution settled down when the third began. Radio emerged during the 1920s and was a political force by the 1930s, and television followed in the 1950s. The new broadcast media did not replace pluralist communication, but they altered it significantly. By introducing one-to-many communication on a national scale these electronic media personalized the relationships between presidents and their citizens. People who listened to Franklin Roosevelt's "Fireside Chats" and war addresses on the radio "knew" their president in a way that their ancestors had never known Washington, Jefferson, Lincoln, or Wilson. Theodore Lowi wrote that this had given rise to a "plebiscitary presidency" (1985) in which individuals gradually bypassed the parties and even the leaders of interest groups, and citizens began to focus on the personal qualities of their presidents. As Lowi described it a generation ago:

> The plebiscitary presidency is a personal presidency and that fact can already be seen in the campaign. The personality of the president – perhaps we should call it the personhood of the presidency, regardless of the character of the incumbent – is a combination of Jesus Christ and the Statue of Liberty: Bring *me* your burdens. Bring *me* your hopes and fears. Bring *me* your search for salvation. (1985, p. 115)

He further observed that "what is required for good television is the same as what is required for a good plebiscitary presidency" (Lowi 1985, p. 114).

Samuel Kernel (1993) described this as a shift from institutionalized pluralism to "individualized pluralism" in which presidents appealed directly to citizens without the middlemen. Radio advertising began the change in 1928 and television accelerated and magnified it with advertising and Nixon's "Checkers" speech in 1952 and the first televised debates in 1960. Notably, Nixon spoke to the nation's viewers and asked them to write to the Republican National Committee instead of meeting with the RNC behind closed doors, and the debates took the candidates and their issues directly to voters. Thus presidential campaigns became more candidate- than party-centered in this fourth information age.

By 1980, C-SPAN and CNN were providing members of congress with airtime that they leveraged into increased personal stature that soon brought an end to the seniority system of congressional leadership. By the turn of the century, Fox News, CNBC, and MSNBC were providing more 24-hour news, and it could truthfully be said that citizens had more direct access to more information via television than had ever been available before. But, as Lowi had warned, the personal presidency was an illusion. Even as citizens felt closer to their televised presidents than to their congressional representatives, those presidents remained less accountable constitutionally and mathematically to individual voters than were their senators or members of congress.

Even as the broadcast media provided citizens with greater access to political news, the pluralist interest groups frequently won policy battles against majority opinion. Bimber (2003) attributes this to the interest groups' better resources for monitoring and reporting government choices and actions – they are more interested, better organized, and better funded. This was important because broadcasting is expensive and the available airwaves are not infinite, partly because of regulatory standards. Fox changed the network landscape overnight by outbidding the Big Three networks for NFL football telecasts, a move that induced many stations to switch their affiliation to the fledgling Fox network or lose Sunday football; they then promoted their programs during the games and quickly became a viable network. But Fox was able to do this only because they had the resources to land the football contract.

The fourth information revolution began with the rise of the Internet in the 1990s. The keys to appreciating the Internet's impact are its low cost, low regulation, and high speed. The Internet provides political organizations with low-cost and high-speed means of acquiring political information as well as low-cost and high-speed means for distributing information. It provides low-cost and high-speed means for individual citizens to communicate directly with one another, even as it provides low-cost and high-speed means for media organizations to share their reports. Moreover, the Internet provides citizens, campaign organizations, and media organizations with low-cost and high-speed means for archiving and retrieving all kinds of information (Bimber 2003). Whereas the pluralist form of political communication in existence since the second information revolution has been based on bureaucratic interest group organizations, the low -ost high-speed information exchanges made possible by the Internet create the possibility for "post-bureaucratic pluralism" – clusters of competing interests without formal organizations, memberships, leaders, and lobbyists. Theoretically, interested parties could mobilize a massive outpouring of support (or opposition) through the Internet, achieve a result, and then totally disband.

Our overview of Bimber's four information revolutions should help us to realize that major changes in communication technologies have occurred before and they will come again. It also shows that the changes in our society and politics occurred because of the interaction between social changes and technological changes. People had changing communication needs when new tools for communicating came on the scene, and when those tools proved useful for fulfilling those needs the society evolved into new patterns of communication. In the midst of a communication revolution it can be difficult to see outside the proverbial box. That is why most new media are initially used to convey the content of old media. Newspapers have web sites, television aired old movies and radio programs, radio stations played recorded music, and Guttenberg printed the Bible (McLuhan 1964). Nevertheless, some changes are becoming clear.

Presidential Campaigns of the Fifth Information Age

It is one thing to trace the invention of new communication technologies and quite another to trace their use in presidential campaign communication, and our concern is with the latter. One way to trace that use is to peruse the compendiums of research conducted on presidential campaign communication following each campaign. Two regular and important sources have been the special issues on the presidential campaigns edited by J. Gregory Payne for *American Behavioral Scientist* (ABS) since 1989 and a series of books edited by Robert E. Denton, Jr. since 1993. Since the 1988 ABS issue did not discuss any new media we can consider the 1992–2008 editions for evolving scholarly attention to new media in presidential campaigns.

The New Media of 1992

The transient nature of "new" media and the danger of being left behind become quickly evident when reviewing the ABS issue on the 1992 Bush–Clinton–Perot race. Dee Dee Myers of the Clinton communication staff described a "dramatic change in the strategy of political communication . . . made possible by technological changes almost unimaginable a generation ago" (1993, p. 181). The dramatic changes to which she referred were 24-hour cable news, computer modems, faxes, e-mail, interactive satellites, and online news services. Bob Dole (1993) commented about citizens' ability to call in to live programs and their representatives. Even if the Bush campaign used the new technologies, they did so less notably and creatively than did the Clinton campaign.

The Clinton campaign's "war room" developed a five-point strategy that used new technologies to better accomplish fundamental tasks (Myers 1993). First, they used faxes and e-mail to respond rapidly to developing acclaims and attacks. Second, they used satellite feeds and faxes to get their messages about particular issues to news outlets in eighteen targeted states whose news streams reached Clinton's targeted voters. Third, they used satellite, telephone, and computers "to put the candidate in more than one place at one time" (Myers 1993, p. 182).

Fourth, Clinton took advantage of the voracious appetites of cable television's long format daily programs hosted by the likes of CNN's Larry King, ABC's Ted Koppel, MTV's Tabitha Soren, as well as Arsenio Hall and Don Imus – to acquaint the media audience with the candidate. This was a particularly useful new vehicle for challengers who lacked the incumbent's direct access to the press. Clinton and Perot both relied heavily on these "soft" interview programs, with Perot even announcing his candidacy on Larry King's show. The net result of this change was a challenge to the traditional campaign journalists' control of the flow of campaign information and a consequent turn from policy questions toward the kind of personal celebrity information elicited by entertainment hosts (Diamond, McKay, and Silverman 1993).

They went beyond this to create "electronic town hall" meetings in which candidate interactions with citizens provided the substance. This was an update of the advertising techniques Roger Ailes had developed for Nixon in 1968, but instead of editing the interactions into a few commercials the meetings were broadcast at much lower cost. Clinton and Perot both used these meetings extensively, and they served both to increase citizens' sense of involvement and to reduce the role of reporters who have an annoying tendency to ask hard questions. But Nimmo (1994) worried that Americans would soon tire of the lengthy programs, and reminded us of Machiavelli's warning that politicians dare not bore the citizenry.

Fifth, Clinton used new technologies to connect surrogate speakers with specialized audiences around the country. For example, Boston Mayor Ray Flynn was popular with union audiences, with whom he could be connected via computer and satellite feeds. C-SPAN televised a wide variety of campaign events unfiltered and in their entirety, and astute politicians such as California conservative Robert Dornan (R-CA), used the Congressional camera to add to the campaign discourse (Muir 1994).

"New media" in 1992 meant cable programs, fax machines, and e-mail, and the Clinton campaign used them to better target their messages to their audiences and to accelerate their responses to developing rhetorical situations. Myers (1993) noted in passing that the electronic bulletin board Compuserve was a useful place to find complete texts of campaign speeches, but web pages and search engines were not yet available. Thus in 1992 the new technologies of communication provided campaigns with new ways to get their messages directly to audiences, often by sidestepping the traditional media organizations.

The New Media of 1996

The 1996 election was the first presidential contest conducted with the World Wide Web. Whillock (1997) argued that the important point about the web was its audience. Web users consisted of 70 percent registered voters, and they were upscale opinion leaders sought after by the campaigns. This population also included young people, largely disinterested in politics, who did not follow traditional news outlets. They were high consumers of all media and wanted their political information unfiltered. Moreover, journalists, strategists, and academics quickly began using the web as a resource. However, only 6.4 percent of American households had an Internet user in 1996 (Whillock 1997).

But unlike other media that targeted passive receivers, web sites were constructed for people actively seeking and requesting information on particular subjects (Whillock 1998). It is those users' purposes – not the sender's purpose – that determines how it will be used, and two of the users' requirements are accessibility and speed. The Clinton campaign targeted their web site for journalists and browsers, while the Dole campaign built a site to serve as a regular resource for their supporters (Whillock 1998).

Swanson (1997) described continuing public dissatisfaction with traditional campaign news, which continued to become more interpretive, sensational, and reporter-centered (candidate sound bites had shrunk to seven seconds) even as citizens wanted complete, unfiltered, and issue-oriented news. But he saw the contributions of new media to better campaign news as still far in the future. One important innovation in 1996 was the new hyperlink technology. The web site PoliticsNow used it to link candidate statements during the presidential debates to relevant factual materials elsewhere on the web. This introduced a new level of accountability for candidates' statements the accuracy of which could be checked as never before (Jacques and Ratzan 1997).

If the web was not yet improving campaign news, it was beginning to change campaign organizing. Kern (1997) saw in the 1996 campaign the potential for developing "cyberprecincts" by using candidate web sites rather than telephones and mail to create social bonds. The 1996 web sites were rudimentary, but they provided important gathering places for supporters where they could read news of the campaign and full-text speeches previously posted on Compuserve.

The New Media of 2000

The number of citizens accessing the Internet for political information increased from 4 percent in 1996 to 48 percent in 2000 (Whillock and Whillock 2002). When that many Americans make that much use of anything, money cannot be far away. Indeed, Democrat Bill Bradley became the first candidate to raise a million dollars on the Internet. John McCain soon became the first to raise a million dollars on the Internet in twenty-four hours by targeting younger supporters and new donors. Still, Internet fundraising accounted for only 5 percent of the 2000 total, partly because many people worried about using credit cards online (Whillock and Whillock 2002).

The New Media of 2004

Andrew Chadwick called the 2004 campaign "the first real Internet election in the United States" (2006, p. 162) because of the way strategist Joe Trippi merged virtual online communities with real world communities on behalf of Democratic candidate Howard Dean.

> During the winter of 2003, Dean's staff negotiated with Scott Heiferman, the owner of an obscure website called Meetup.com. The purpose of Meetup was very simple. Rather than using the web to bring people together in virtual communities, the plan was to get them to meet in physical places, like bars, coffee chops and restaurants. Individuals could register their names and locations on the site and establish local Meetup groups based on their interests . . . .By the end of the year the Dean group on Meetup had 140,000 members, there were 800 meetings scheduled for the month of December and around 2,000 comments a day were being posted to the official Dean blog.   (Chadwick 2006, pp. 162–163)

Dean's web site allowed supporters to upload information about their Dean events, and mapping technology allowed visitors to see how to get to the events (Wiese and Gronbeck 2005).

The success of the Dean meetups led Trippi to boast, "We have an army of almost 600,000 fired-up supporters, not just a bunch of chicken-dinner donors, but activists, believers, people who have never been politically involved before and who are now living and breathing this campaign" (quoted in Chadwick 2006, p. 162).The increased use of the Internet led to expanded databases that facilitated enhanced e-mail activity (Wiese and Gronbeck 2005).

Kerry's campaign used e-mail appeals more extensively than the Bush campaign, but the Bush campaign constructed more careful arguments and sought a wider variety of citizen responses. They also added a mechanism enabling recipients to forward their message to five more people, thus expanding their reach in ways that Kerry's campaign did not (Williams and Trammell 2005).

The Bush and Kerry web sites were heavy on attacks – 80 percent of their press releases contained attacks, with Kerry's 84 percent significantly higher than Bush's 78 percent. Most of these attacks were not made by the candidates themselves; 32 percent of the Bush site's statements containing attacks were posted from other sources, whereas Kerry's site used statements by candidates (Souley and Wicks 2005).

By 2004 citizens could watch video, including campaign commercials, on the campaign web sites. Kaid and Postelnicu (2005) compared the effects of experiencing the same Bush and Kerry spots on television and the Internet (providing links and fact checks to maximize the experience). They found that viewing the television version (not, as expected, the web version), reduced their undergraduates' political cynicism, that web viewers felt they learned more, and that neither group trusted their political knowledge. The television viewing resulted in a negative shift in attitudes toward Bush while the web viewing resulted in a positive shift in attitudes toward Kerry.

Several of the 2004 web sites allowed visitors to co-create messages. Wiese and Gronbeck (2005) reported that the Dean site invited visitors to upload pictures of their pets wearing Dean paraphernalia and the Kerry–Edwards campaign encouraged supporters to build their own sites and link them to the campaign's site.

Blogs were the hot new tool of the 2004 campaign, but their impact was unclear. Lawson-Borders and Kirk (2005) estimated that 2 percent of adult web users provided political news to 13 percent through some 4.3 million sites in 2004. They described these stories as rattling around in the echo chamber of the blogosphere until they were picked up, magnified, and given stature by traditional news media. For a story in the blogosphere to emerge it therefore must create a major rattle, and journalists tracked the ranking of stories on such sites as Technorati, Daypop, and Feedster. Thus to blog is to write for "hits" and sharing. This led to a style of writing characterized by emotive language designed to connect with readers and provoke responses, and those who engage and respond stay longer in the site's world than do those who do not respond. Blogging therefore engages people in a community, providing a motivational resource for organizing that the Howard Dean campaign used to early advantage (Lawson-Borders and Kirk 2005).

News blogs were generally hailed as a way for people to access a wider variety of news and information. But Robert MacDougall (2005) offered a complex and compelling argument that the opposite trend was more likely. The ease of access and entry to blogs, the bloggers' personal control over the topics they choose to address and the tendency to engage like-minded people in exchanges about political news fosters relatively exclusive sets of blogging communities.

The New Media of 2008

The most important development of 2008 was mobility. The increased penetration of 3G network devices, iPhones, and Blackberries meant that the Internet had gone mobile. People of all political persuasions could not only call one another anywhere, any time, but they could check blogs, campaign web sites, and social networks at will. Among the newly emergent forms of content used for political information in 2008 were YouTube and the social networking sites, Facebook, and MySpace.

Back in 1992, Dee Dee Myers had seen citizens reading full texts of candidate speeches on Compuserve and Bob Dole had liked C-SPAN's televising of unfiltered video. Sixteen years later, YouTube was Compuserve and C-SPAN on steroids. There was no need to watch live speeches, 24-hour news, or even C-SPAN replays. It was all on YouTube with the click of a mouse. Obama's acceptance address at

Mile High Stadium got 1.5 million hits, his "Yes We Can" speech had 2.5 million hits, his Iowa speech three million, and his victory address five million, for a total of 12 million viewings of Obama's major speeches (Gronbeck 2009).

Was YouTube filling citizens' hunger for solid information about the real issues facing the country, free from journalists' intrusion and editorial filtering? Would YouTube be the tool that would elevate presidential campaign communication from self-serving platitudes and speculative reports to the higher standards of the citizenry? Maybe. The 12 million hits for Obama's four major speeches was only five million fewer than Will.i.am's video based on the "Yes We Can" speech. Obama's four speeches almost tied Obama Girl's original video, but the total hits for all of her candidate videos put her ahead 27–12 million (Gronbeck 2009). People were not necessarily selecting YouTube videos for their substantive contributions.

Gronbeck maintained that two YouTube items seriously undermined Hillary Clinton's presidential bid. The first was the "Vote Different" spot based on the famous 1984 commercial introducing the Apple computer. The video showed demoralized people in a bleak environment listening to Hillary address them from a large screen like Big Brother until a woman in a colorful outfit emblazoned with an Obama logo throws a hammer that breaks the screen. The closing slide says "On January 14th, the Democratic primary will begin. And you'll see why 2008 won't be like '1984'." For Gronbeck (2009) the spot "articulated some of the first doubts about her suitability for office," and it also defined January as the beginning rather than the end of the Democratic primary and challenged viewers to listen critically to her message. In the second case, YouTube lit up with parodies after Hillary Clinton aired a television ad asking who we wanted to answer the White House phone for a 3 a.m. crisis. It was an unsettling question, partly because nobody wants a 3 a.m. crisis and partly because the ad implied that Clinton expected crises. How does one engage and refute the ad? Indeed, was the ad a Clinton acclaim or an attack on Obama? YouTube privileges creativity, and in this case creative parody and humor diffused the impact of Clinton's ad.

Facebook and MySpace brought social networking into presidential campaigning in 2008, facilitating the creation of virtual communities based on shared interests. The Obama campaign excelled at this. The new software provided powerful new ways to build electoral coalitions by connecting strangers around shared interests and a candidate. They provided citizens with the potential for a much deeper sense of personal connection to one another and to the candidate, much as Franklin Roosevelt's Fireside Chats personalized the president for the public. When the candidate scheduled an appearance, his "friends" got the word, and those in the know shared the word with friends who could get tickets by adding their e-mail address to the database. The database was useful for unprecedented fundraising and for highly effective get out the vote efforts.

StumbleUpon and Digg provided new and efficient ways to save and share information from the web for future use. Editorials and other items could be collected, filed, and sent to associates' iPhones and Blackberries. Gronbeck (2009) discuss the "information-based social networking" that formed around such content rather than shared feelings toward the candidate. There is no question that the new software of 2008 enabled individuals to link into the campaigns and to become part of the candidate's community. But that could happen only because these technologies enabled individuals to deconstruct the campaign and to integrate the pieces of it into their lives in ways that worked for them.

Then came Twitter – everything you want to know in 140 characters. Campaigns used it; so did we. Great for sharing reactions and links. It was easy to scoff at Twitter because of its brevity. "What can one say in 140 characters?" many of us sniffed. One could offer "Mission Accomplished" (20 characters, G. W. Bush), "We have nothing to fear but fear itself" (39, FDR 1933), "I only regret that I have but one life to give for my country" (61, Nathan Hale), or "Ask not what your country can do for you, ask what you can do for your country" (78, Kennedy 1961). We have long distilled extended, thoughtful messages down to pithy little sound bites and Twitter encouraged us to share them.

Nimmo (1994) noted the 1992 new media's ability to provide longer messages and warned that people would tire of them, and Twitter now provided an alternative. Twitter proved a valuable resource in the hands of serious professionals. Gronbeck (2009) wrote of Twitter, "Here was open-source politics at its best: information streams, contributed to by multiple individuals and authorities, maintaining interactive discussions and even group decision making in virtual spaces." Ironically, Gronbeck's praise was too long to Tweet.

The New Media of 2012

Clearly, it would be foolhardy to speculate in 2009 about the nature of the new media that will influence the 2012 presidential campaign. But it would be even more foolhardy for campaigns, media organizations, and citizens to prepare for 2012 as if there were going to be no new media after those we saw in 2008. One change we shall surely see is an increase in the number of people using Facebook, MySpace, Twitter, Digg, SumbleUpon, and YouTube, much as we saw an increase in the number of cable subscribers, web users, and bloggers. More importantly, those increases will alter the user demographics in ways that are already dramatic. As the campaign brought social networking sites to the attention of people over the age of thirty-five, the largest increase in Facebook users from October 2007 to August 2008 – 173 percent – was among 35–54 year olds, and that pace increased to 276 percent through January of 2009. Moreover, the number of Facebook users over 55 increased 194 percent during the same period, such that the core 18–24 year-old segment now accounts for only 40 percent of all users, down from 53.8 percent six months before (Corbett 2009). The social networks of Facebook 2009 already differ from Facebook 2008, three years before the Iowa precinct caucuses.

Whatever new media emerge for 2012, the key questions will center on the uses campaign organizations, media organizations, and citizens choose to make of them. For emerging communication technologies provide presidential campaigns with new tools to perform the essential functions of campaign communication, but they have yet to alter those function. The minor league baseball manager in the movie "Bull Durham" ranted at his players, "Baseball is a simple game. You throw the ball. You hit the ball. You catch the ball"; radio, television, cable, MLB.com, metal bats, and steroids have not changed those tasks. Likewise, cable television, the Internet, blogs, social networking, YouTube, and Twitter

Obama's Facebook Page

have not changed the essential tasks of campaigning – they have changed how we do them.

Two directions have been constants in the development of new communication media – speed and personalization. E-mail reduced the time required to send written correspondence and mobile phones reduce the time we need to wait for personal voice contact. Radio and television news updated events faster than newspapers, then cable news channels and Internet headline services provided even faster updates. Magazines such as *Time, Newsweek,* the *New Republic,* and the *Atlantic* rely heavily on their Web sites and blogs, often to the extent that one wonders which is their primary product. Could there be a down-side to getting our news ever more quickly? While it is difficult to find an advantage to slow transmission, the acceleration of the news and information cycle can encourage quick reporting with inadequate reflection and assessment. This is not inherent in the technology, but it is a risk invited by new media that challenge reporters and bloggers to share as fast as they dare.

New media have become increasingly personal since the 1920s. The term "broadcasting" developed because messages were transmitted to massive audiences. Three national radio networks fed programming to local AM affiliates until the late 1940s when locally programmed stations began relying on local advertising revenue, and the expansion of FM broadcasting in the 1970s gave rise to "narrowcasting" to particularized audiences. Three television networks followed the same path for many years until UHF stations and cable networks in the late 1970s and additional networks (Fox, CW) emerged to narrowcast television. The videocassette recorder in the 1980s spawned the recording, rental, and sales industry that liberated people from the shackles of the TV schedule, and DVDs and Blu-Ray as well as Fancast and Hulu provided additional ways for people to make their own viewing choices.

This personalization that we all enjoy so much comes at a political cost, however. Unlike Presidents Roosevelt or Eisenhower, Presidents Bush and Obama cannot command the attention of their nation all at once. When President Johnson asked for the airwaves to talk to the nation about trouble in the Dominican Republic, all three networks delayed their programming and everyone saw the president – no comedy channel, no home shopping networks, no music videos, no rebroadcasts of 100 worst sports plays, and no DVDs to play. This trend toward personalization invites us to avoid everything that does not interest us, or perhaps more accurately, the sheer volume of available information and the trend toward personalization require us to filter out everything that does not interest us. Each of us develops a personal set of bookmarks through which we get our news of the country and the world. As we avoid discrepant information we learn different facts than our neighbors, and we move toward life in separate worlds. It is little wonder that we have difficulty understanding and tolerating one another. Perhaps somewhere in the future the medium will make the same core information available to all in a way that all will value and use, but that sounds oddly like Guttenberg's use of movable type to print the Bible in 1455.

The Obama Campaign's Use of New Media

As the 2008 campaign unfolded it became evident that the Obama organization was using new media in innovative ways. It quickly became the textbook case of fifth information age presidential campaigns and, this being a textbook on presidential campaign communication, it deserves our scrutiny. Let us proceed with two premises in mind. The first is that any future campaign that fails to match the Obama campaign's 2008 efforts is probably doomed to fail. The second premise is that any future campaign that merely matches Obama's 2008 campaign will be left in the cyberdust.

The first thing to note is that the Obama campaign planned from the beginning to use new media as an integral part of their campaign. Barack Obama contacted Marc Andreessen, one of the founders of Netscape and a Facebook board member, to get his ideas on the potential for online campaigning eleven months before the Iowa caucuses (Carr 2008). The campaign built their operation to scale and expanded as the campaign progressed (Lutz 2009) using a crawl, walk, run, fly pattern. "Crawling" established an online presence with a web site and monitored its conversations. In time, the operation begins to "Walk," enriching their content with podcasts, video, games, and widgets. Increased involvement with the site enabled them to "run" with it by engaging influential online voices, blogging for additional outreach, adding advertising and sponsorship and developing allies. Ultimately, the online operation took flight, embracing the sense of community through social networks, blogger tours, advocacy, contests, and mobile access (Lutz 2009).

Second, the Obama campaign recognized the importance of the mobile net. Howard Rheingold wrote that "Next comes the mobile net. Between 2000 and 2010, the social networking of mobile communications will join with the information-processing power of networked-PCs. Critical mass will emerge some time after 2003, when more mobile devices than PCs will be connected to the Internet" (2002, p. xiv). The campaign grasped Rheingold's thesis that an increasing number of people carrying mobile devices can be mobilized into "smart mobs" who are "able to act in concert even of they don't know each other" (2002, p. xii) and they eventually had ten times as many people working the online campaign as McCain (Lutz 2009). When they used the mobile network rather than paid workers to organize they saved money, and then when they raised substantial amounts of money online their balance sheet came out well ahead of their competitors'.

The third consideration was to use different social media to interact with different voter segments (Shah 2008a). Harfoush (2008) advises those using social media spaces to ask themselves four questions. First the campaign needs to ask why it is entering this particular social space. They also need to know specifically how their presence in that space will improve their brand, product, or reputation. Yet because the space belongs to others, they need to ask what value they will be adding. Finally, they should ask if their presence in the space is a good fit.

The Obama campaign used a variety of social networking sites to reach citizens segmented in a variety of ways. Facebook and MySpace enabled them to interact with citizens 18–25 while Eons.com ("The community for BOOMers") initiated interaction with their parents' peers (Shah 2008a). Obama profiles also invited interaction with African Americans on Black Planet, with Latinos on MiGente and with "Gays, Lesbians, and Everyone Else" on GLEE (Shah 2008a). Obama also used LinkedIn to interact with professional groups (Shah 2008a).

The difference in social networking statistics for 2008 are staggering. The day before the election, Obama had 380 percent the number of friends as McCain on both Facebook and MySpace, 403 percent the number of YouTube subscribers, and 905 percent the number of YouTube viewings (Owyang 2008). People spent 14 million hours on 50 million viewings of 1,800 Obama related YouTube videos (Blue State Digital 2008).

The fourth consideration for online campaigning is to use the tools with which people are familiar to reach them where they are (Lutz 2009). It is most important to ensure that people can find your content with simple and intuitive URLs. Widgets make it easy for a site's visitors to copy code to display logos, encourage donations, and even to find voting locations (Shah 2008b). It is also helpful to note that 90 percent of Americans are within three feet of their cell phones 24/7 (Lutz 2009). This makes texting, e-mail, and Twitter especially useful.

Fifth, content must be customized (Shah 2008b). Each network has its own etiquette that the campaign must learn and follow (Harfoush 2008). It is imperative that the campaign's online personnel listen to the voices on the network and interact with them in an authentic way (Harfoush 2008).

Sixth, the campaign laddered support opportunities through tiers of engagement (Lutz 2009). The web site My.Barackobama.com provided opportunities for visitors to participate at any of three levels of involvement – personal, social, and advocate. The personal level invited people to join a listserv, create a profile, donate to the campaign, comment and/or become a friend on one of the social networks. These opportunities enabled the campaign to gather thirteen million e-mail addresses compared to Kerry's three million in 2004. Moreover, the Blue State Digital company's online tools enabled them to get three million people to donate 6.5 million times online, for a total of more than $500 million, with an average donation of $80 (Blue State Digital 2008).

The social level invited people to post pictures and videos, write a blog post and to join a group. A page on Flickr.com enabled visitors to share pictures of rallies, supporters and events. The blog postings created a significant presence. From the start of the party conventions through the end of August, for example, blog postings mentioned Obama 500 million times as compared to 150 million mentions of McCain (Lardinois 2008). For fundraising, they were the first political campaign to use Blue State Digital's "Grassroots Match" program to connect new donors with their matching donors, enabling them to reinforce their commitment to the campaign (Blue State Digital 2008).

The advocate level invited people to recruit donors, host an event, or create a new Obama group. The bold step here was for the campaign to relinquish control and embrace the co-creation of the campaign's message by empowering their online advocates to serve as "brand ambassadors" (Harfoush 2008). The web site empowered these super users by proving source material in a download section for user-generated content (Lutz 2009, Shah 2008a). Obama's supporters used Blue State Digital online tools to create more than two million user profiles, to write more than 400,000 blog entries, and to post information about more than 200,000 events for others to attend (Blue State Digital 2008). All of this resulted in a "many media, one story" model in which the general Obama story allowed participants to co-create stories of hope and change. The core story was constantly refreshed by these additions and the process both embodied and enhanced the co-creators' excitement (Montoni 2009). Volunteers created about 35,000 Obama for America groups using the online tools (Blue State Digital 2008).

The seventh consideration was to use available analytics to improve engagement (Lutz 2009). They assessed the value of their downloads by measuring the number of installations, active users and uninstalls (Harfoush 2008). Viraltracker.com tracks viral videos, webisodes, movie trailers, and other messages and analyzes the extent to which they reach their intended audiences. The campaign constructed multiple versions of all e-mails and tracked their effectiveness to see which approach worked best for them (Lutz 2009).

The eighth principle was to organize online for offline action (Harfoush 2008). The Obama campaign organized precinct captains during key primaries using Central Desktop and Basecamp software programs to create an organizers' wiki. Wiki technology was created in 1995 and became widely known when Wikipedia took off during 2001. It provides a user-editable web site so that a group of people working on a shared task can write collaboratively without a webmaster. In practice, this means that the most active users have the most impact on the product rather than trying to insure that all participants have equal input (Shirky 2008). The Obama campaign's wiki enabled precinct captains to quickly share the information they had found helpful and to revise other captains' contributions in light of their local experiences. That enabled them to develop the largest organization of precinct captains in California since Bobby Kennedy in 1968, and it also proved important in Texas, which held a primary and caucuses on the same day (Catone 2008).

The campaign used a variety of new media to Get Out the Vote (GOTV), mobilizing support with mobile devices (Lutz 2009). Supporters made more than three million online telephone calls during the last four days of the campaign (Blue

State Digital 2008). Blackberries and other mobile web devices helped organize a volunteer operation that knocked on one million Pennsylvania doors the weekend before the election (Harfoush 2008). By election day Obama had 118,107 Twitter followers to McCain's 4,942. Indeed, Obama picked up 2,865 new Twitterers – 58 percent of McCain's total for the entire campaign – during the 24-hours prior to election day (Lardinois 2008). In the final 24 hours Obama picked up an additional 10,000 MySpace friends to McCain's 964 (Lardinois 2008).

In short, the Obama campaign built an extensive network with great care and heavily staffed their operation. They had a plan for using social networking that provided varied levels of participation for people as they used familiar media. They used it to organize, they used it to raise money, they used it to get their message to target audiences and they used it to get people to the polls; in other words, they used all of these new media to do the same things that campaigns have always done. They simply did it faster, better, and cheaper.

But what if they had not? What if John McCain had dominated Facebook, MySpace, BlackPlanet, MiGante, GLEE, Twitter, and YouTube and had used Basecamp to organize his workers and Viraltrack to monitor his presence on the web – would McCain therefore have won the election? Valeria Montoni (2009) wrote, "It's not about the medium, it's about the product [candidate]." Ultimately, "Relevance is the metric of success," says Montoni suggesting that campaigns "Match resources with opportunities at a profit by identifying, influencing and satisfying customer demand." In the final analysis, Obama seems to have better identified, more effectively influenced, and more nearly satisfied customer/voter demand than McCain, and the media new to presidential campaigning in 2008 were tools that helped him do so. The campaign of 2012 will provide new tools for Republicans, Democrats, and others to identify, influence, and satisfy the demands of those voters.

Summary and Conclusions

There is no question that new communication media provide new tools for presidential campaign communication. But new tools provide new, different and sometimes better ways to perform old functions to the campaigns who figure out how best to use them. This chapter explained that

- All media were once new media, adopted through the diffusion of innovations process of knowledge, persuasion, decision, implementation, and confirmation.
- It may not be long until YouTube and Twitter seem as novel as video cassettes and CDs.

We saw that the United States has progressed through four prior information ages into today's fifth age.

1. 1989–1820 local information with little sharing.
2. 1820–1880 the expanded postal system enabled information sharing and the rise of the penny press. Jacksonian Democracy led to new political parties and mobilization.

3. 1880–1930 industrialization fostered specialized economic identities and lobbying. Parties became pluralist coalitions of interest groups.
4. 1930–1990 electronic media personalized the presidency and made electoral coalitions more candidate- than party-centered. Presidential campaigns were largely television events via news, commercials, conventions, and debates.
5. 1990– the Internet began to provide high-speed and low-cost means of information exchange enabled people to organize without formal organizations.

Within the fifth age we saw the impact of new media in each election.

- The 1992 Clinton campaign took advantage of computer modems, fax machines, e-mail, satellites, and online news. All campaigns relied heavily on the cable channels' long format talk shows.
- The 1996 presidential campaign was the first to use web sites and to treat their users as a target audience.
- In 2000 citizens relied more heavily on the Internet for information and candidates began to raise money through the web.
- 2004 became the first "Internet election" because of three developments. The first was the Howard Dean campaign's merging online communities with real world communities through Meetup.com. The second was the rise of blogging as an important information source. The third was the initial opportunity for citizens to co-create messages with the campaign.
- The 2008 campaign was the first to take advantage of mobility and the "smart mobs," Facebook, MySpace, YouTube, and Internet fundraising as never seen before.
- The landscape for 2012 is already changing with older users finding Facebook and reducing the 18–24 year-olds' segment by 13 percent in just months. The role of new media in 2012 will depend both on the emerging new media and the ways that campaigns and citizens imagine to use them.

Because the 2008 Obama campaign used the available new media so extensively and creatively we examine it and found eight lessons. We learned that an effective new media campaign circa 2012 should, at the very least:

1. Plan from the beginning to use the new media as integral parts of the campaign,
2. Recognize the importance of the mobile net rather than stationary computers.
3. Use different social media to interact with different voter segments.
4. Use the tools with which people are familiar to reach them where they are.
5. Customize content for each network after listening to, and interacting with, its members.
6. Establish tiers of engagement that provide a ladder of engagement rather than the traditional support vs. non-support.
7. Use analytics to measure success and improve engagement.
8. Organize online for offline action.

However, we warned that following these eight steps cannot assure victory because:

- Any campaign that fails to match the 2008 Obama's effort is probably doomed to fail.
- Any campaign that merely matches Obama's 2008 campaign will be left behind by new technologies and new uses.
- Paraphrasing one new media professional, "Ultimately, it's not about the medium, it's about the candidate."

The Internet enabled the Obama campaign to raise an unprecedented amount of money in 2008 but it did not make fundraising obsolete. Smart mobs and wikis improved campaign organization and GOTV efforts but it did not make them unnecessary.

In short, this chapter has explained that there will always be emerging communication technologies that we call "new media." The important and interesting questions are how we use the new media to better communicate about presidential campaigns and how those new uses invite us to rethink our uses of the old media.

Synthesizing Part II

Part I concluded that the Constitution and party rules create a political exigency and that those rules combine with the dispersal of power throughout a pluralistic society, a federal system of government, and a variety of communication media to present aspiring presidents with a rhetorical puzzle. We summarized each candidate's strategy at that point in the question: "How can I be preferred by more voters than any of my opponents in states with electoral votes sufficient to produce an electoral vote majority?" and we discussed strategic implications.

Part II has covered the speech acts of acclaiming, attacking, and defending as we experience them in speeches, news, ads, debates, and new media. Although we discussed them separately it is their interdependence that is important.

First, acclaiming, attacking, and defending are parts of an argumentative chain. Had John Kerry not emphasized his military service, heroism, and patriotism in 2004 he might not have raised the ire of the Swift Boat Veterans. At the very least it was Kerry who made their attacks pertinent to his candidacy. Had Bill Clinton not emphasized everyone's personal moral responsibility the media might have been less interested in the tabloid story of his alleged affair.

Second, free media and paid media are two sides of the same coin. Advertising costs money but wooing the media has its costs as well. It is rarely worth free coverage to abandon one's rhetorical agenda.

Third, debates have rarely been decisive but they have been unfriendly to incumbents. News of the debates is often processed as horse race coverage of strategy and points instead of the policy discussions we might expect. They heighten the campaign drama but in so doing tend to lock voters into their pre-debate preferences.

Fourth, social networking has been used to attract crowds for speeches that in turn enhance the database. Conversations on these sites suggest themes that can be used in speeches and ads. Web sites carry ads for those who frequent them thus minimizing the risks of televising them to supporters of the opponent. Wikis and mobile smart mobs have enhanced campaign organization.

Fifth, citizens are increasingly taking personal control of which candidates they engage, what news and information they acquire and which people they discuss it with. That makes it increasingly difficult for media organizations and campaign organizations to control the flow of information. But it also means that as a pluralistic society we are decentralizing into smaller and smaller clusters of people who know only what we care to know about the topics we wish to know about from the sources we feel like checking. That does not enhance a nation's prospects for democratic self-governance.

We began this portion of the book by suggesting that the study of presidential campaign communication, like the study of a competitive sport like basketball, requires an understanding of the objective, rules, and strategy (Part I) and the basic acts and moves that the competitors use (Part II) within those rules to achieve their objectives. Now that we understand the acts and moves of campaigning we can refine our strategic questions to ask:

- How should I use speeches, news coverage, ads, debates, and new media
- To engage campaign organizations, media organizations, and citizens
- In the chain of acclaiming, attacking, and defending
- To be preferred by more voters than any of my opponents on election day
- In states with electoral votes sufficient to produce an electoral vote majority?"

It is now time to see how these questions fit together to create the dynamic process of presidential campaigns. That awaits us in Part III.

PART III

STAGES OF THE CAMPAIGN FOR THE WHITE HOUSE

We concluded Part II by saying that every presidential campaign boils down to the question "How should I use speeches, news coverage, ads, debates, and new media to engage campaign organizations, media organizations and citizens in the chain of acclaiming, attacking and defending to be preferred by more voters than any of my opponents on election day in states with electoral votes sufficient to produce an electoral vote majority?" Part III will show how the answers to these questions unfold in four stages, each with its own communication dynamics and ways to gauge progress.

Part III will walk us through a presidential election tournament consisting of four stages or rounds. During the first round some people try to "surface" by establishing their viability – their right to be considered serious candidates. The second round sees the viable candidates competing for commitments from a majority of the party's national convention delegates until one has a majority. Because the divisions fostered by that competition require healing, the nominees need to "consolidate" by unifying those they defeated and their supporters during the third stage. The nominees then lead their supporters into the fourth round by publicly contesting their visions in fifty-one elections (the states and DC) to determine who wins 270 electoral votes and the presidency.

Each chapter in Part III explores one stage's complex of puzzles and choices to explain the stage's communication dynamics and explain how we can track the candidates' progress.

11 The Surfacing Stage

The selection of leaders is a continuous process. Much as transitions in a monarchy are hailed with cries of "The King is dead, long live the King," C-SPAN airs "Road to the White House" every Sunday evening because the next campaign begins as soon as the last campaign is over.

This chapter explores the rhetorical challenges facing those who aspire to be considered presidential candidates and the strategic choices available to them. Different challenges face these "challengers" than incumbent presidents but we will see that aspiring candidates can adopt an incumbent style of campaigning irrespective their actual political status. We will also see that aspiring candidates' progress can tracked in national opinion polls, fundraising, and press attention.

Surfacing Defined

Judith S. Trent (1978) introduced the surfacing stage to the campaign communication literature when she wrote that "'surfacing' begins with candidates' initial efforts to create a presidential interest and image for themselves in the public imagination, and extends through a variety of public rhetorical transactions" (p. 282). The terminal rhetorical exigency in the surfacing stage is to produce a viable candidacy able to compete effectively in the Stage 2 contests for convention delegates.

Surfacing begins with the sense that running for president might not be a silly idea. It develops as the candidate shares that idea with family and friends, donors, volunteers, the media, pollsters, and party activists.

Surfacing culminates in the Iowa precinct caucuses when the first votes of the presidential campaign are cast, tallied, and reported. The Iowa caucuses are widely covered and provide an index of the candidates' relative surfacing. Aspiring candidates spend absurd resources in Iowa during this period. But because Iowans are simply selecting their precinct delegates to their county caucuses these much ballyhooed contests do not determine any convention delegates. It is therefore prudent to differentiate them from the subsequent contests that actually select convention delegates.

Failure to emerge as viable in Stage 1 need not preclude a candidate from appearing on primary ballots, but it badly damages any chance of actually winning the presidency. All of us – not just the aspiring candidates – shape the surfacing stage. When it plays out well we enter Stage 2 with a number of promising candidates for president in both parties, when it plays out badly we wonder where the good candidates went.

Communication Dynamics in the Surfacing Stage

Potential candidates interact with various audiences to attain several responses that lead instrumentally toward viability and passage to Stage 2. Notable participants in the surfacing stage are potential candidates, political activists, political donors, reporters, and elite commentators. Most ordinary citizens are disinterested or only passively interested, waiting for others to tell them who their choices will be. Those players who are interested this early are motivated; they are not passive receptors who simply react to candidates. They engage in rhetorical transactions – that is, they say things to each other such that the candidates get what they need from the audience to become viable (victory units) and the audiences get what they need from the candidates.

Crossing the Psychological Threshold

The first challenge is *crossing the psychological threshold* necessary to imagine being the president of the United States and leader of the free world, and willing to incur the risks required to run for that office. We too often underestimate this hurdle, which is an important element of heroic tales (Campbell 1949, 1968). New York Governor Mario Cuomo and General Colin Powell, for example, were two highly regarded public figures who refused the call to adventure and thereby disappointed many people. Countless other people heard the call, accepted it, and excited few voters by doing so.

Thus, the first rhetorical question one can ask is how the potential candidates' interactions with family and friends, reporters, activists, donors, and potential voters can help them cross this threshold of self-persuasion. Statements of the presidents are dutifully preserved in both the *Weekly Compilation of Presidential Documents* and in the *Public Papers of the Presidents*, but pre-presidential statements prior to the Internet were not well preserved.

The second communication challenge of the surfacing stage is for candidates to cultivate a public impression of *"fitness for the office."* It is one thing to believe that you can be president, but it is something else to strive actively to convince influential others. Among other things we expect our president, in the model of George Washington, to be one of the people yet somewhat above the people – a difficult balance to achieve. The candidate must seem knowledgeable but not pedantic, personable but not too ordinary, serious but not grim, a strong leader without being condescending, and so forth.

Establishing fitness for office takes surfacing candidates into the dreaded Land of Press Coverage, where they must cope early with the elite commentators referred to by Mark Halperin and John F. Harris (2006) as "The Gang of 500." These formidable guardians of viability are the "columnists, consultants, reporters, and staff hands who know one another and lunch together and serve as a sort of Federal Reserve Bank of conventional Wisdom" (p. 24). They play a critical role because they "believe it is crucial, before real votes get cast, that someone – specifically *500 someones* – probe deeply and pass judgment on a candidate's intellectual timbre, applicable ambitions, philosophical journey, and telling life choices" (p. 24). They interview and write profile articles about the potential candidates, creating what has been termed the "Profile Primary." These interviews ordinarily include questions such as, "What books have you read lately?" and "How often do you attend your chosen house of worship?" But they also focus on signs of discomfort, family disagreement, and anything else that may be construed as indicative of presidential fitness. These profiles acquire importance because they are read by the potential political donors, political activists, and reporters as well as the other potential candidates and the public. They therefore play a significant formative role in building, or undermining, various publics' impressions of the surfacing candidates.

James David Barber (1985) wrote that we can predict presidential performance if we understand how the candidate's character, worldview, and style developed in childhood, adolescence, and early adult success. His book, *The Presidential Character*, became popular in many circles when he seemed to predict President Richard Nixon's demise. Unfortunately, there was something else at work. Barber based his assessments of presidents' early lives on biographies written after their character traits had become recognized, not before. Thus, this approach served more to show that the biographers had found anecdotes that fit the known adults and omitted those that did not.

In the same vein, it is important to note that the interviews and investigations by the Gang of 500 occur after the person has begun to surface as a candidate. In 1979 Massachusetts Senator Ted Kennedy announced that he would challenge President Jimmy Carter for the Democratic nomination. Interviewing Kennedy for CBS Roger Mudd asked "Why do you want to be president?" The senator offered a lengthy, unfocused answer. Because he had no clear, concise, and coherent answer to the question, word spread that "he could not answer the question," and his campaign began to flounder. Since that interview, answers to such questions are carefully prepared with an eye to their acceptability.

Bruce Buchanan (1978) discussed the psychological pressures imposed by the "presidential experience" upon any occupant of the Oval Office. As a policy advocate the president is subject to frustration and dissonance, as a national symbol the president comes to expect deference, and thus experiences dissonance and, as a mediator and crisis manager, a president experiences stress. The campaign provides many opportunities for candidates to demonstrate that they have the psychological strength to handle these psychological pressures, and the media keep a watchful eye on their behavior.

Curiously, the president heads the executive branch of the federal government but runs as an individual (eventually with a vice-presidential candidate). Parliamentary systems enable the party out of power to prepare a shadow government known to citizens. But American voters have no idea who their potential presidents will choose as their secretaries of state or defense, attorney general, and so forth. These actual pragmatics of governance could help voters decide which potential presidency to prefer, but we defer them until after the election.

Nevertheless, the third communication challenge of the surfacing stage is to *assemble a professional campaign staff.* Every campaign needs a campaign manager, political strategist, fundraiser, a pollster, a communication director, a speechwriter, a legal advisor, policy advisors, advance staff, an advertising director, and more. But such staffers normally work for money, a crucial resource. So

Table 11.1. Top 10 Zip Codes for 2004 Political Donations

2004 Rank	Zip Code	Location	Political Donations (in dollars)
1	10021	Manhattan, NY	10,352,170
2	10022	Manhattan, NY	4,671,503
3	10028	New York, NY	3,652,567
4	90210	Beverly Hills, CA	3,625,627
5	20007	Washington, DC	3,408,448
6	10023	New York, NY	3,309,560
7	10128	New York, NY	3,120,984
8	10024	New York, NY	3,111,580
9	20008	Washington, DC	3,090,262
10	22101	Maclean, VA	3,029,589

Source: CampaignMoney.com http://www.campaignmoney.com/zip_codes_2004. asp

indirectly the candidate must find the set of rhetorical appeals that induce citizens with money to contribute it (to hire staff) and people with time to contribute it (as volunteers). Time, money, and people can all be squandered, and so can arguments and other rhetorical appeals.

The fourth communication challenge is therefore crucial: candidates must *mobilize and manage resources* during the surfacing stage. By campaign resources we mean time, money, people, and arguments. Importantly, our conception of mobilizing includes resource management, so that it includes investments in further resource mobilization as well as wise expenditures. Time is important because primaries, caucuses, and the general election are held on specified dates, and campaigns routinely use countdown metaphors to speak of being "three weeks out" from an election. The later the start, the less time one has. This is one of the reasons why a politician out of office can have a campaign advantage over one in office. Bob Dole resigned from the Senate to campaign for the presidency in 1996. Another way to maximize time is to recruit volunteers or hire staff, but it takes time to screen people, and it costs money to hire them.

Some political activists have financial resources that they can contribute to potential candidates' campaigns. Some less politically active people have money that they might be willing to contribute if they should come to care about a candidate. It is not unreasonable for people preparing to donate a great deal of money to prefer to give it to someone who seems to see the world as they do. Nor is it unreasonable for those donors to expect a certain amount of access – a relationship – in recognition of their generosity.

The traditional fundraising model is to appeal to the big donors early in the surfacing stage, and most donations to both parties come from just a few zip codes (see Table 11.1). In 2004 six of the ten largest donating zip codes were in New York City, three were in the Washington, DC area, and the other was Beverly Hills 90210. This pattern hardly suggests a random sample of policy interests. "Tax the Rich" is rarely a good place to begin courting those big donors. This fact goes a long way toward explaining how several campaigns can advance fairly similar programs, policies, and goals from the outset.

Asking for money is always a tricky communication act. Jill Barad (2003) advises candidates to begin by asking how much the race will cost and whether it can be raised. The campaign develops a complete budget projection, organizes a finance committee, develops a succinct fundraising "pitch," and a list of prospects who can reasonably be expected to give money. The campaign must then rate the prospects with respect to how much each can be expected to give at what point during the campaign, and to whose approach they will be most welcoming.

When meeting with a prospective donor, Cathy Allen (2003) suggests establishing "a quick, comfortable rapport" that is most easily achieved when they already know the solicitor. The candidate or solicitor should then move quickly to explain why the candidate is running for office, identify shared interests, and suggest why the prospect should find the campaign "an exciting choice." She says it is usually helpful, at that point, to share an insider's view of what is going on in the campaign (recent polls, news, or endorsements) that will help the prospect feel part of the campaign. She regards it as crucial to ask for a specific amount of money and then stop talking – "even if the pause is seemingly forever, and you find the silence unbearable . . . let your prospect break the silence." You can then explain your need for the money and cultivate a sense of urgency, but do not negotiate. Finally, "get the check." Be sure to thank all donors, and to add them to your call back list because they have already established their willingness to donate to the campaign.

Howard Dean challenged the traditional approach to fundraising in 2003 by using the Internet and populist appeals for small contributions from people dissatisfied with the usual dominance of the system by "special interests." Dean accumulated a huge war chest and became the surfacing frontrunner – heavily supported by people disenchanted with elections. But when the Dean campaign needed that money to air ads in states with primaries, they discovered that they had spent it far too early in states such as Texas for no obvious reason. Thus, they had mobilized resources but poorly managed them. In 2008 Barack Obama used the Dean model with even greater success, raising unprecedented campaign contributions from small donors.

Fifth, each campaign must *establish goals, programs, and issues* during the surfacing stage. Domestically and internationally, the United States has an almost unlimited number of *potential* goals, programs, and issues. From among them, each candidate must choose some that will be priority issues, and they must resonate with audiences.

Political activists, for example, have priorities. They are politically involved because they want some things to happen and they want to prevent other things from happening. Some want to stop abortions and others want to protect "a woman's right to choose." Some want to limit access to firearms and others want to preserve the Second Amendment's guarantees of the right to bear arms. Some want to stop the influx of immigrants and others want more protections for immigrants. Their issues are theoretically unlimited. The point is that these activists begin to look for promising potential candidates shortly after the last election.

They study politicians' past records, build bridges to those who seem to value similar objectives, and they provide support.

There is an old saying that war is always the issue in American politics, but if there is no war then the bad economy is the issue, and if the economy is doing well then the issue will be something else. This is a rhetorical determination for the candidate – what are the important issues, and for whom are they important? Senator John Kerry surfaced in 2004 largely on the theme that war in Iraq had been pursued prematurely instead of as a last resort. But once nominated Kerry struggled to convince voters that – once in Iraq – his war policies would be significantly different from those of President Bush. Republican strategists gleefully characterized Kerry's position as a "flip-flop."

Eventually, each potential candidate must undertake the sixth communication challenge of the surfacing stage and *initiate the ritual* by announcing the candidacy. Normally, candidates do this with a public speech in a symbolic location. In 2008, Barack Obama announced his candidacy in Springfield, Illinois where he and Abraham Lincoln had served as state legislators. Former North Carolina senator and vice-presidential nominee John Edwards announced his candidacy in New Orleans 9th Ward, the site of some of the worst devastation by Hurricane Katrina. Hillary Clinton, on the other hand, announced her candidacy on her web site. Like independent Ross Perot in 1992, Republican Fred Thompson in 2008 chose to announce his candidacy on a television interview program. These announcements typically discuss the candidate's reason for running and the key goals or themes of the campaign.

Why do candidates often wait so long to announce their candidacy? One explanation occurs quickly to anyone who has ever been to the end of a diving board: until you actually take the plunge you can back away and reconsider your options. But a more important technical reason is that the official announcement makes the candidate subject to a wide variety of rules, regulations, and mandatory procedures. These include spending limits that can be deferred by delaying the announcement.

During the surfacing stage the *emerging candidates and media get acquainted* and this is the seventh communication challenge, for a candidate unknown to the media is hardly a viable candidate. Typically the media refer to primary candidates collectively with disparaging terms like "the seven dwarfs" even though they are ordinarily experienced United States senators, governors, and the like. By definition this lack of stature is forgotten by stage three and the nominees are deemed worthy of the historic role they would take on. Political reporters have their antennae out for good stories. Politicians who provide the media with dull stories attract little attention and fall by the wayside. But candidates capable of generating interesting stories help the media do their work. Jesse Jackson and Al Sharpton drew attention as potential presidential candidates by becoming fixtures in the news. Neither had held an elected office (often seen as a qualification for the presidency), but they were prominent in the news whenever controversies arose.

The surfacing stage provides candidate rhetoric that generates journalistic coverage, and these converge to *shape citizen expectations and anoint front-runners*, the eighth communication challenge. As much as two years before the first contests, voters are forming impressions of the potential candidates, what issues could prove important and who might be their next president.

The default voter expectation of a challenger is, "This person has no chance." But, as the media and candidates play out the surfacing stage, one or two candidates in each party are deemed "frontrunners" by the media. Hillary Rodham Clinton was the Democratic frontrunner during the surfacing stage of the 2008 campaign as Howard Dean had been their frontrunner in 2004, but neither won the nomination. The Republican frontrunner as late as October 2007 was former New York Mayor Rudy Giuliani, whose campaign would fail miserably. Thus it is not always good to be *the* frontrunner in the surfacing stage (unless you are the incumbent), but it is important to be *one* of the frontrunners. Why is that?

Few people realize how many candidates run in the early primary contests because they cannot all be covered by the media. For example, in 2000 there were fifty Democrats and forty Republicans on the New Hampshire ballot. Few of us knew about them because only a handful received any real news coverage. The journalistic community faces a real problem. If every news organization could afford to assign reporters to cover all ninety of those candidates, and if they subsequently carried all of those ninety reports (a) there would be no other news covered and (b) we would be deluged with even more campaign trivia at great expense to their companies. The news organizations therefore make necessary calculations, assigning reporters to cover the "significant" candidates, and only those deemed frontrunners get coverage.

But how do they determine which candidates are significant? Frequently by relying on Washington insiders and influential party members for judgments of who stands a chance to win the nomination (this is the Gang of 500 at work). This creates an important, potentially vicious, cycle in which a candidate who might conceivably win the nomination *if* covered by the media is denied that coverage because he or she is judged not to have a real chance to win. Did this happen to Larry Agran in 1992? The Davis, California Mayor moved ahead of California Governor Jerry Brown in the polls, but not in the estimation of the party insiders. The press relied on their sources – the national party insiders who regarded Brown as the more serious candidate – when they decided how to allocate their resources. Without meaningful news coverage Agran dropped out of the race and Brown challenged Bill Clinton all the way to the New York primary (Meyrowitz 1992). We will never know if Agran rather than Brown might have challenged Clinton if he had received the media attention that went to Brown. But the case illustrates how important it is for surfacing candidates to convince the media decision makers that theirs is a candidacy that simply must be covered.

During the surfacing period the aspiring candidates begin to take on the identities of "establishment candidates" and "insurgents." Establishment candidates draw on themes of personal experience and their ability to work well with those people presidents need to succeed. They can call for change, but they do so emphasizing their personal ability to effectively govern effectively. This typically entails a return to principles, goals, or methods spurned in recent years by the incumbent. Endorsements by established groups are sought after and valued.

Insurgent candidates, on the other hand, treat their lack of experience as a credential. Jimmy Carter in 1976 and Ronald Reagan in 1980 ran against Washington,

Wall Street and the "insiders" whose cooperation the establishment candidate values. Grassroots organizing and fundraising often characterize the insurgent campaign, with many such candidates refusing contributions from established organizations and lobbyists.

In short, the goal of the surfacing stage is viability. Key audiences include influential party, media and other people who can grant (or deny) the campaign credibility, people with time and/or money to contribute, and political activists who shape the agenda. So in many respects the campaign will want to emphasize the issues and goals of the audiences capable of delivering what they need to become viable.

But a major surfacing pitfall is the temptation to say whatever an audience demands to hear in exchange for their commitment. This can myopically align the candidate with key surfacing audiences in ways that jeopardize the campaign's ability to persuade the audiences they will need in the later stages of the campaign.

Incumbent and Challenger Stances

Every candidate surfaces sometime. But an incumbent president seeking re-election has already surfaced. The incumbent's challenge is to discourage potential rivals for that party's nomination. George Wallace, Eugene McCarthy, and Robert Kennedy all challenged President Lyndon B. Johnson in 1968, contributing not only to his withdrawal from the race but to Hubert Humphrey's loss as well. Gerald R. Ford might have avoided a challenge by Ronald Reagan if he had made his intent to run in 1976 known earlier (Trent 1978). In 1980 Senator Ted Kennedy challenged President Carter and paved the way for Ronald Reagan's victory, and in 1992 Pat Buchanan challenged President George H. W. Bush and opened the way for his loss. Conversely, President Bill Clinton used the Republican takeover of Congress in 1994 to discourage a variety of rivals. President George W. Bush's war on terror discouraged Republicans such as Pat Buchanan whose 2004 book *Where the Right Went Wrong* sharply criticized the Administration, from running.

It is aspiring challengers for the presidency who urgently need to surface. The 2008 presidential contest was only the second in fourteen elections without a Nixon, Bush, Clinton, or Dole on the ballot. In an era when so many familiar names have run for president it may be difficult to remember that "any of us can grow up to be president," but the larger point is that the Bushes, Clintons, and Doles surfaced while most of the rest of us did not.

Because every campaign begins with surfacing and because an incumbent president need not surface, it is fair to say that every presidential election is defined by incumbency. Is a sitting president trying to retain the office? If so, the "Interpreter in Chief" (Stuckey 1991) begins with a considerable list of rhetorical resources unavailable to anyone else. These advantages include the symbolic resources of the office, a record of performance and the media attention assigned to the office. It also includes incentives for members of the president's party to overlook their differences in order to retain the White House. Challengers to the president, regardless of their party, have their own set of rhetorical opportunities and problems defined by their lack of incumbency, but these are raw materials that must be crafted if they are to become successful challenges.

When there is no incumbent president running there is nevertheless an effort by the president's party to retain the White House. Sometimes the vice-president runs as a sort of quasi-incumbent to continue the team's administration. These cases suggest the possibility that there are incumbent resources available to non-incumbent candidates who can claim and use them. Thus, almost any candidate can adopt an incumbent stance or a challenger stance, even if that requires a reversal of actual roles.

This may be easier to understand if you think of a video basketball game where it matters whether you play as the powerful Boston Celtics or the lowly Memphis Grizzlies. In such games each team has assigned strengths and vulnerabilities, and one need not be a fan of a team or from its geographic home to recognize the strategic advantage of adopting a team's identity. We can think of these campaign stances, then, as game players or "avatars" – player roles or identities that one takes on for purposes of the game. Just as chess players must choose whether to play as white (and play first) or black, each campaign must decide whether to run as incumbent or challenger.

Trent and Friedenberg (2004) observed that a challenger could run an incumbent style campaign and that nothing prohibits an incumbent from running like a challenger. In practice, most candidates employ a combination of challenger and incumbent moves to position themselves relative to their opponent. We should therefore think of these styles not as a dichotomy but as a set of archetypes or pure forms that can help us to understand the moves available to the candidates.

The Incumbent Style

Incumbents use several symbolic strategies. They can use the *trappings of the office* like the presidential seal and Air Force One and the *charisma of the office* that is generated whenever the president comes to town. They also have the *legitimacy of the office* that gives their words and actions a force unavailable to the others, as well as a presumption of *competency* that can, of course, be squandered. Incumbents also have several pragmatic strategies available to them. Because anything the president does is news, the incumbent has the power to create *pseudo-events* – events that occur only to be reported, like meeting the spelling bee winner in the Rose Garden. The incumbent can *appoint people to jobs and committees* and *create special task forces* as well as *appropriate funds and grants*. The incumbent is in a unique position to *meet or consult with world leaders* and to secure *endorsements from other domestic leaders*, many of whom join others as *surrogates on the campaign trail*. The incumbent is in a unique position to *manipulate important domestic issues* in ways that favor re-election and to *interpret or intensify foreign policy problems into international crises* (or to minimize them, as the case may be). All the while the incumbent can *emphasize accomplishments* while *cultivating an image of being above the political trenches* (Trent and Friedenberg 2004).

Although Trent and Friedenberg delineated the challenger and incumbent styles of campaigning and wrote about stages, they did not attempt to deal with the interface of campaign style and evolving campaign stages. The difference is particularly important to the incumbent president who, obviously, need not surface and who normally need not worry very much about winning the nomination through contested primaries. In short, the challenger and incumbent face different rhetorical choices as they move through the rhetorical stages. During the surfacing stage the president has little need to establish name recognition and can therefore concentrate on fundraising and pre-empting challenges from within his own party, while the challengers must start from scratch. A president who can do that can cruise to nomination and use the advantages of his office to solidify his standing while the challengers contest for delegates.

Because incumbents and challengers face different rhetorical tasks they must ask different strategic questions. Their answers to these questions shape their campaign and, in the give and take of political rhetoric, create and preclude opportunities for their adversaries. Let us consider the strategic questions facing incumbents and challengers.

1. Is the Nation Doing So Well or So Badly?

Incumbents justify their re-election in either of two general ways. The first is that the nation is doing so well that voters cannot risk changing leaders. The disadvantage of this strategy is that voters may decide that a peaceful and prosperous world offers a low-risk opportunity for experimentation with a new leader.

The second approach is to argue that despite the incumbent's efforts the nation faces terrible problems that cannot be entrusted to others. This requires careful use of alarmist rhetoric to heighten the voters' sense of imminent danger and to underscore their need for their incumbent president in such troubled times. The danger is that voters will blame the incumbent for the state of the country, or find him incapable of dealing with its problems. But an incumbent who can raise the stakes may nurture the feeling that the times require an experienced president.

2. How Will the Incumbent Divide His People?

The second and more agonizing choice facing any incumbent president must surely be how to divide the country during the campaign. For it is inevitable that the "president of all the people" must, as a candidate, take stands against some of those people, their interests, and their ideas. Although criticized and even attacked during the first term, the campaign makes it increasingly necessary for the incumbent to counterattack – but against which people, and how vehemently?

There are two broad strategies available to incumbent presidents when they must divide their nation. The first is to mobilize support outward from the center by uniting moderates and marginalizing extremists. The advantage of this "expanding island" strategy is that the president can lead and campaign from a broad base of support while leaving to the opposition a disparate set of critics who dislike each other even more than they dislike the incumbent. The disadvantage of this approach is that politically moderate voters cannot be relied upon to turn out on election day.

The second strategy is to polarize the nation around an issue on which the incumbent president has overwhelming majority support. The advantage of this strategy is that the incumbent works from an intense base of support toward the undecided voters. The disadvantage is that it risks complicating leadership during the second term when those supporters' incentives to follow the incumbent have begun to fragment.

Each incumbent campaign's success will be shaped by its answer to these two guiding questions – how is the nation doing and how will the incumbent divide the people – and by their rhetorical ingenuity in implementing their answers. But their success will also be affected by the challenging campaign's choices, because challenger campaigns face guiding questions of their own.

The Challenger Style

Without the incumbent's resources, challengers must play a different game. But the challenger stance provides its own strategic resources. Whereas incumbents emphasize their accomplishments, challengers *attack the incumbent's record*. Because the challengers must provide reasons for change, they *take the offensive position on issues*, and *call for change*. This ordinarily commits challengers to being *optimistic about the future*, for fear about the future can lead people to play it safe and stay with the incumbent. Challengers calling for a change in leadership will almost always be characterized as radical by supporters of the incumbent, so they must strive at least to *appear to represent the philosophical center or mainstream*. Finally, because of the general respect for the office of the incumbent, challengers should ordinarily *delegate the most personal or harsh attacks* to others on their team (Trent and Friedenberg 2004).

A consideration of past campaigns suggests that challengers need to consider two questions that will define their campaigns. Should they plan to co-opt or vanquish their partisan adversaries? Should they seek a quick victory or prolong the primaries to foreground their critique of the incumbent?

1. Co-opt or Vanquish Partisan Adversaries?
The central question facing challengers is whether they are engaged in a team contest against the incumbent or a free-for-all to win the nomination. The metaphor of a political campaign as war invites us to think of destroying or eliminating opponents. But with an incumbent president to beat, primary adversaries can rarely afford to vanquish one another – their partisan adversaries are the very people they will need to enlarge their coalition and challenge for victory.

In the coalitional struggle the elimination of issues, interests, or candidates from the major party encourages the rise of additional parties that pose the real electoral problems. George W. Bush was elected president in 2000 because Al Gore, the author of *Earth in the Balance* and subsequent Academy Award winner for "An Inconvenient Truth," was unable to persuade one-half of one percent of Green Party voters in Florida to prefer him to Ralph Nader. Gore lost Florida by 537 votes, while Nader took 97,488 (he also lost New Hampshire by 7,211 with Nader winning 22,198 – a win in either state would have given Gore an electoral college majority). So concerned was Al Gore with taking the political center from Bush that he alienated potential environmental supporters on his left who could reasonably have been expected to work and vote for him, rather than Ralph Nader.

2. Quick Resolution or Prolonged Critique of the Incumbent?

Each challenger campaign must decide whether its ultimate interests will be best served by a blitzkrieg of the early contests or by a marathon. This entails more careful analysis than simply whether their campaign is leading or trailing. First, rules matter. Democratic Party rules stipulate that states must distribute delegates proportionally among all those candidates receiving at least 15 percent of the primary vote. Republican Party rules have been friendlier to winner-take-all contests that enable a challenger to lock up the nomination. The Republican challenger seeking a marathon or the Democrat seeking a quick win in a crowded field is bucking the odds. This decision impacts planning.

It normally costs more to extend the primary campaign than to win quickly, but extending the campaign also increases the challengers' opportunities for reaching new volunteers and new donors. Because all challengers are contesting the incumbent they can all be viewed as working for their Party. The real issue thus becomes resource management: will an extended challenge deplete the key resources of money, people, time and arguments and lead to the deterioration of their rhetorical situation, or will it be an investment that develops resources for the Party's challenge to the incumbent that are instrumental in subsequent stages?

The third and related consideration is control of the media agenda. Presidents always get media attention, and challengers must wrestle for coverage of their critique of his performance. The best way to do that is to create a continuing melo-drama for the press, and campaigns provide predictable melodrama that is much easier to cover than are wars or scandals (Nimmo and Combs 1983). Presidential challengers who can extend their primary campaigns can crowd the incumbent from the headlines, reducing the rhetorical advantage of incumbency.

As the challengers decide whether to vanquish or co-opt one another in a sprint or a marathon, they influence their own campaigns and their chance of defeating the incumbent. The give and take of the surfacing stages attracts and alienates supporters and refines the arguments. In 2008, Hillary Clinton and Barack Obama waged a primary battle that lasted months longer than anyone expected. Although each would have liked to win sooner, the prolonged cam-paign touring road show that packed arenas in state after state enabled them to pound away at Bush and McCain. The challenging party frequently emerges from prolonged primary campaigns with an intriguing blend of policies, values, and supporters as well as a candidate shaped by the instrumental demands of the strategic process.

Keeping Score in the Surfacing Stage

The surfacing score lasts about two years. How can we "keep score" of the emerging candidates' progress with votes all so far down the road? Candidates, reporters, activists, and citizens deserve some means of tracking the race if only to understand the nature of their emerging choices. There are three important indices of the candidates' emerging viability that can be helpful if read carefully: national opinion polls, fundraising, and press coverage.

National Opinion Polls

National opinion polls provide one indicator of surfacing. We will suggest avoiding such polls in the later stages, but they give a rough measure of how the candidates are surfacing with the public. For example a Fox News poll conducted October 9–10, 2007 (retrieved October 12, 2007 from http://www.pollingreport.com) showed Rudy Giuliani at 29 percent, Fred Thompson at 16 percent, John McCain at 12 percent, Mitt Romney at 11 percent, and Mike Huckabee at 5 percent – any of which could be construed as viable on the basis of being among the top five aspirants. On the other hand, Sam Brownback, Ron Paul, and Tom Tancredo each had 2 percent, and Duncan Hunter had one percent support (since the survey had a statistical margin of error of plus or minus 5 percent these data offered little solace to the latter four).

The Fox poll found Hillary Clinton supported by 44 percent of Democrats, Barack Obama by 17 percent, Al Gore by 10 percent, and John Edwards by 9 percent; but Bill Richardson had only 3 percent support, Dennis Kucinich 2 percent, Chris Dodd and Joe Biden had one percent each and Mike Gravel had less than one percent support. Clinton, Obama, Edwards, and the non-candidate Gore (four days before he won the Nobel Peace Prize) seemed to be establishing their viability while Richardson, Kucinich, Dodd, Biden, and Gravel had yet to register with the public.

National opinion polls abound and some are better than others. One thing these polls test is the pollster's awareness of potential candidates. When, for example, did pollsters begin to include Barack Obama's name in the list of names they presented to respondents? And when did they finally decide to believe Al Gore's statements that he would not be a candidate in 2008? A second variable tested is name recognition, and without name recognition a citizen cannot volunteer, contribute, or vote for the candidate.

Surfacing candidates campaign among donors in New York, Washington, and California as well as Iowa and New Hampshire, while these polls model the national electorate. The disconnect should be readily apparent. Yet we need not ignore such polls during the surfacing stage if we can remember that they provide only one measure of viability – essentially image recognition – and that they tell us little about the candidates' prospects in any particular state contest.

Fundraising

A second widely reported measure of viability is *fundraising*. Candidates report their collections quarterly, so news reports tend to report quarterly success. CNN reported that Hillary Clinton had raised $90 million to Barack Obama's $80 million through the third quarter of 2007. Among Republicans, Mitt Romney had raised $63 million, Rudy Giuliani $47 million, John McCain $32 million, and Fred Thompson raised $13 million (retrieved from http://www.cnn.com/ELECTION/2008/money). Reports of overall funds raised frequently get lost in

Table 11.2. Google News "Last Month" Hits for Candidates

DEMOCRATS	10/17/07	REPUBLICANS	10/17/07
Hillary Clinton	37,985	Rudy Giuliani	24,172
Barack Obama	27,988	John McCain	18,595
John Edwards	22,829	Mitt Romney	17,393
Joe Biden	9,206	Fred Thompson	14,366
Chris Dodd	9,190	Ron Paul	9,228
Bill Richardson	3,779	Mike Huckabee	4,179
Dennis Kucinich	2,315	Duncan Hunter	2,642
Mike Gravel	1,163	Tom Tancredo	1,570

Source: original data

the journalistic shuffle, partly because they are in practice offset by expenditures (the CNN site also reports cash on hand). A related indicator of viability is the number of donors supporting each candidate, as this measures the number of persons feeling strongly enough about the candidate to contribute money.

Media Mentions

What happens if we simply search Google News for the candidates' names to see how many stories mentioned them? On October 17, 2007 such a search produced the date in Table 11.2. This crude exercise suggested that Democrats Clinton, Obama, and Edwards and Republicans Giuliani, McCain, and Romney had generated considerable news coverage while Democrats Biden, Dodd, Richardson, Kucinich, and Gravel and Republicans Paul, Huckabee, Hunter, and Tancredo had not.

As we consider the *Google News* hits we should realize that press coverage is correlated with public support. Although press coverage does not cause public support, name recognition is a crucial threshold. News assignment editors decide how to use their reporting staff and budget to cover the important candidates. In their shoes, would you cover the non-candidate Thompson or the three campaigns of Brownback, Paul, and Tancredo? (Here's a hint: 16 percent of your audience has an interest in Thompson while only 6 percent has an interest in the other three combined who would require triple the resources.) The point is that press coverage contributes to public support and public support contributes to press coverage.

The Iowa Precinct Caucuses: The Transition to Stage 2

A worrisome shadow looms over the shoulders of Stage 1 candidates. Again and again they are forced to ask themselves whether it is worth continuing to push toward Stage 2 and to risk possible embarrassment and annihilation. Maybe "now" is not the time to wage the campaign. Maybe it would be more prudent to work toward the election of a candidate with similar positions, values, inclinations, or simply better prospects for victory. Maybe they should just fold the campaign tent with dignity and go back to real life. "What?" asks the inner voice, "after coming this far?" Anyone who has played video games into the wee hours of the morning has tasted this feeling – "I know I should call it a night, but I'm so close to getting through to the next level." Ultimately it is the candidate's decision, and the core puzzle is internal. When the words "Game Over" flash before the candidate's eyes, will the candidate press "off" or "play"? For those who press "play" the rhetorical challenges of Stage 2 await. This is the surfacing stage at work: each candidate must "make the cut" to become a viable contender.

Understanding Iowa's Caucus Process

The surfacing stage culminates in the Iowa precinct caucuses that are the bridge from Stage 1 to Stage 2. Like all bridges, they both connect and divide. They are the first events that even indirectly affect the accumulation of delegates but none are actually at stake in the Iowa precinct caucuses because they are simply the first step in a four-tiered process.

The basic process is not complicated. It begins when the precinct caucuses elect local delegates to the party's county conventions. The county conventions then meet and elect their delegates to the congressional district conventions. The congressional district conventions elect their delegates to the Iowa state party convention. Then, and only then, do the Iowa state party conventions elect their delegates to the party's national nominating convention. But now let us see how the process plays out in practice using the 2008 Democratic Party caucuses.

The Democrats' 2008 precinct caucuses were held on January 3 and Barack Obama won 37 percent of the total delegates available to county conventions, compared to 30 percent for John Edwards and Hillary Clinton's 29 percent. By the time the Democrats' county conventions were held on March 15 John Edwards, Bill Richardson, Joe Biden, and Chris Dodd had all quit the race, so precinct delegates pledged to them could switch candidates, and Clinton and Obama worked hard to woo them. When the county votes were taken, the Obama forces had pulled further ahead, capturing 52 percent of the total delegates to Clinton's 32 percent with 15 percent sticking with Edwards even though he had withdrawn. At the April 26 district conventions, Obama extended his lead over Clinton to 55–31 percent with 13 percent clinging to Edwards. Ten days later, on May 6, Obama won the North Carolina primary and clinched the nomination by winning enough pledged delegates for the nomination. Five weeks later Iowa's Democratic Party convened to decide how they would cast their convention votes.

Republicans, Democrats, and the media hold three distinct events in Iowa. Iowans have been caucusing since before statehood. Both parties simply grafted the delegate selection process onto the caucus process during the 1970s. Republicans conduct a "preference poll" early in their meetings, with attendees marking ballots that are collected, tallied, and reported. They then elect their delegates to the country conventions; but Republicans do not know which presidential candidates those delegates prefer unless someone at the caucus moves to have them state their preference. This is not illogical or conspiratorial;

Republicans simply prefer to emphasize local governance over the presidential preference process.

The Iowa Democrats do it differently. They physically organize attendees into "candidate preference groups" and count people to determine which groups surpass the party's 15 percent viability threshold. They then physically regroup and vote. It is these presidential candidate preference groups that get the county delegates, and the winning groups then decide which people will represent them at the county meeting.

The key to campaigning in Iowa's precinct caucuses is grassroots organizing in each precinct. As many critics contend, the caucuses are more time-consuming than simple voting because citizens must attend a meeting in their precinct and participate for an hour or more. Because each precinct reports its tally, each candidate needs to get people to turn out in each precinct. In the 1980s this advantaged candidates with religious ties who sued the "church bus" strategy to advantage. Both liberal Democrat Jesse Jackson in 1984 and conservative Republican Pat Robertson in 1988 scored better than expected because every precinct has churches, most churches have buses and this network facilitated turnout. In 1988 Democrat Richard Gephardt drew on the labor union network, and in 2004 John Kerry relied on veterans' organizations. People with strong ties to the state party organization also have an advantage when it comes to mobilizing supporters for the precinct caucuses. Commercials, debates, and candidate visits can increase interest and may influence citizens' candidate preferences, but they have yet to be shown to mobilize turnout as effectively as organizational networks. The exception may be candidate visits that energize their local support teams.

Unfortunately, the national media tend to report something quite different. That is not to say that they get the numbers wrong, but they tell a story that has little to do with the parties' electoral caucuses. This should not be surprising since national reporters see the Iowa precinct caucuses as a pit stop on the road to the White House. But for Iowans and their local journalists the caucuses are an enduring part of their local governmental process. If you recall election coverage from almost any television network, you can envision a graphic that shows the name of the state, the names of the major candidates, the number of votes each received, and the percentage of the vote received. At some point the anchor importantly intones (often with a only a small percentage of the votes in) "Based on our exit polls and projections we are declaring Senator Blowhard the winner." But what does it mean to "win" the precinct caucuses?

Finishing among the top four in the Iowa precinct caucuses is a validation of viability. These eight candidates have "surfaced" and move on to Stage 2. In 2008 Democrats Obama, Edwards, and Clinton bunched closely and Bill Richardson finished fourth, while Mike Huckabee led the Republicans, followed by Mitt Romney with Fred Thompson, and John McCain tied for third. This is no small feat, as the other candidates can attest.

But the national media typically compound the confusion they created with their reporting by attributing to the Iowa "winners" a momentum that is expected to carry them to wins in New Hampshire and elsewhere. They begin speculating as to when the frontrunner will clinch the nomination (can one win a marathon at the two-mile turn?), and when others should abandon the race. They too often overlook the fact that some six to eight candidates fared well in Iowa because they had, to various degrees, satisfied the tasks of the surfacing stage *in Iowa.*

There is little question that candidates spend more time and money campaigning in Iowa than warranted by any objective criterion. But the caucuses take the campaigns out of prospective donors' boardrooms and into voters' elementary schools and restaurants. Advertising is less important in Iowa than having the support of people who know people in every precinct of every county. Support often flows to the candidates who use populist "Anti-Wall Street" and "anti-Washington" rhetoric, such as Mike Huckabee, Barack Obama, and John Edwards in 2008, John Kerry and John Edwards in 2004, George W. Bush in 2000, Pat Robertson, Pat Buchanan, Dick Gephardt, and Paul Simon in 1988. This makes Iowa's precincts a useful and important counter to the money chase. Former New York Mayor Rudy Giuliani accumulated more money than any of the Republican candidates by the end of the 2008 surfacing stage, for example, but he skipped Iowa. Former Arkansas Governor Mike Huckabee won Iowa while trailing most others in contributions. Both Giuliani and Huckabee had surfaced, but in different ways.

Thus Iowans caucus and the national pundits gaze into their crystal balls and tell us who has survived and who is headed for intensive care. But when the results are in and the campaign staffs hurry out of Fleur Drive toward the Des Moines airport for their redeye flights to New Hampshire, they know that, despite the subzero temperatures, it is time either to begin harvesting delegates or to make other career plans. For the passing of the initial threshold of viability is the death of the private citizen aspiring to be president and the birth of legitimate candidates for nomination.

Summary and Conclusions

This chapter introduced surfacing as the first stage in the continuous process of selecting a president.

- The surfacing stage begins as soon as the votes have been counted.
- "Surfacing begins with candidates' initial efforts to create a presidential interest and image for themselves in the public imagination, and extends through a variety of public rhetorical transactions" (Trent 1978, p. 282) and culminates in the Iowa precinct caucuses.
- The terminal exigency is to emerge as a viable candidate able to compete in Stage 2; non-viable candidates can continue to campaign but with little hope for victory.

The communication dynamics of the surfacing stage include

- Crossing the psychological threshold necessary to run
- Cultivating an impression of fitness for the office
- Assembling a first-rate campaign staff
- Mobilizing and managing resources
- Establishing goals, programs, and issues

- Initiating the political ritual
- Getting acquainted with the media
- Shaping citizen expectations and anointing front-runners

Incumbents and challengers approach the surfacing stage differently.

- Incumbents have many advantages:
  - Their resources include the trappings, charisma, and legitimacy of the office, a presumption of some competency, the power to create pseudo-events, the right to appoint people to jobs and committees, to create special task forces and to appropriate funds and grants, to meet or consult with world leaders and to secure endorsements from domestic leaders who can be surrogates on the campaign trail. The incumbent can manipulate domestic issues and interpret or intensify foreign policy while emphasizing accomplishments and cultivating an image of being above the political trenches (Trent and Friedenberg 2004).
  - But incumbents must decide whether to seek support because the nation is doing so well or so badly and they must decide how to divide their people into "us" and "them."
  - Strategically incumbents must decide between mobilizing outward from the center or polarizing the nation.
- Challengers' resources are precarious:
  - Challengers must attack the incumbent's record by taking the offensive position on issues and calling for change but they must appear to represent the philosophical center, be optimistic about the future, and delegate the most personal or harsh attacks.
  - Each challenger must decide whether to co-opt or vanquish the other challengers and whether to prepare for a quick victory or a prolonged primary critique of the incumbent.

We can track aspiring candidates' surfacing in three ways:

- National opinion polls track name recognition and general favorable/unfavorable perceptions.
- Fundraising reports track how many donors feel strongly enough about each candidate to invest in them while also providing a sense of the war chest that each campaign is developing for Stage 2.
- Google News hits provide an indication of the candidates' relative success in attracting news coverage.

Finally, we will focus on the top four candidates in each party's Iowa precinct caucuses because first place finishers have been nominated about half the time and nobody has been nominated after finishing worse than fourth. Those eight candidates move on to Stage 2.

12 The Nomination Stage

Chapter 11 explained how four (or fewer) viable candidates surfaced and this chapter will examine the rule-governed contests for party leadership. We will see how parties use convention delegates to choose their nominees and why they moved toward primary elections and caucuses to win those delegates, how party rules affect strategic choices and why national polls and fundraising become poor indicators of candidate progress.

Nomination Requires Convention Delegates

The ultimate exigency of Stage 2 is to win a majority on the roll call vote at the national party convention. Because those votes can only be cast by the set of official convention delegates they are the only audience capable of resolving that exigency. Therefore every candidate tries to (1) get supporters seated as delegates, (2), win the support of uncommitted delegates, and (3) discourage contenders for those delegates.

The Old Way: Party Bosses

For most of our history, influential political leaders controlled blocs of delegates and the parties nominated their candidates in convention without benefit of popular input (Kendall 2000). But the reform spirit of the progressive movement at the beginning of the twentieth century began to open the political process with measures that expanded suffrage, elected senators, and taxed income. The first presidential primaries were held in 1912, and they slowly began to cut into the party bosses' influence over the roll calls. But primaries were not a major factor. The 1920 Republican field was so divided that after nine ballots party leaders met in the original "smoke-filled room" at Chicago's Blackstone Hotel and settled on Ohio's Warren G. Harding who won nomination on the tenth ballot.

Primaries Begin to Matter

Not until the 1960s did primaries come of age. John F. Kennedy challenged front-runner Hubert Humphrey of Minnesota in the Wisconsin and New Hampshire primaries. Humphrey ran a traditional, unexciting primary campaign and relied on his support among party leaders. But Kennedy's campaign was a whirlwind of youthful glamor, excitement, and dynamism that drew large crowds. Kennedy tied Humphrey in Wisconsin and beat him in West Virginia to take the delegate lead. When former President Harry Truman questioned Kennedy's readiness for the presidency, Kennedy pointed to the fact that only he had faced voters in every Democratic primary. He went on to withstand a convention challenge from Senate Majority Leader Lyndon Johnson of Texas to win the nomination and the presidency.

Kennedy's narrow victory over Vice-President Nixon left the Republican Party divided. The moderate/liberal Republicanism of the eastern states had long controlled the party to the consternation of the western conservatives. Nixon had held the two factions together and without him the contest was wide open. Supporters of 1960 vice-presidential nominee Henry Cabot Lodge won the New Hampshire, Massachusetts, and New Jersey primaries for him but he declined to run. New York Governor Nelson Rockefeller, the liberal candidate, won primaries in West Virginia and Oregon against conservative Arizona Senator Barry Goldwater who won in Texas, Indiana, and Illinois, while Pennsylvania voted for their own governor, William Scranton. Goldwater effectively clinched the nomination by beating Rockefeller 51–49 percent in the California primary. But, as we shall see in the next chapter, the party never consolidated and President Johnson won a landslide victory over Goldwater.

By February of 1968 President Johnson's public approval had dropped to 41 percent with 47 percent disapproval (Roper 2008). Nevertheless, his nomination seemed likely because Alabama Governor George C. Wallace led conservative Democrats opposed to Johnson's civil rights policies out of the Democratic Party and into his American Independent Party. Then little-known Minnesota Senator Eugene McCarthy mobilized college students opposed to the Vietnam war to finish within seven points of the president in the New Hampshire primary. Johnson's approval dropped suddenly to 36 percent and within days, New York Senator Robert Kennedy announced his candidacy. On March 31, 1968 Johnson announced that he would neither seek nor accept the Democratic nomination. Vice-President Humphrey announced his candidacy but avoided the primaries where Kennedy and McCarthy battled it out. Kennedy seemed to clinch the 1968 Democratic nomination by winning the California Primary, only to be shot and killed moments after giving his victory speech. The resulting 1968 Democratic Convention in Chicago was a nightmare of protests, violent police overreaction, and partisan discord. Vice-President Hubert Humphrey won the roll call after avoiding the primaries. This angered many supporters of those who had participated in the primary process, and alienated them from the party.

Primaries Decide the Nomination

To avoid a repetition of this problem, the Democrats created the McGovern–Frasier Commission to propose reforms that would take effect for 1972. Those reforms required primaries and caucuses and the proportional distribution of delegates to all who won 15 percent or more of the votes in the primaries. Republicans basically followed suit and primaries have driven the nomination process since 1972.

Today primaries and caucuses determine the delegates and how they will vote well before the convention roll call. Each party has its own rules for allocating convention delegate seats to the state parties and officials. These party rules also govern how the delegates will be selected as well as whether the selected delegates will be "pledged" to a candidate or free to change their minds at the convention. Therefore, Republicans travel from state to state talking to citizens who can participate in GOP rule-governed contests for Republican delegate commitments while Democratic candidates travel from state to state campaigning among citizens eligible to participate in the DNC governed contests for commitments from Democratic delegates.

A nomination is decided when one candidate has binding commitments from a majority of the party's delegates. This is obviously easiest when only one candidate surfaces and most difficult when several candidates make it all the way to the roll call vote. This means that a campaign must strive simultaneously to win efficiently as many delegates as possible and to deny delegates and resources to the other contenders. With the change in stages, scorekeeping changes as well.

But the Democrats were not finished tweaking the primary process. By 1984 southern Democrats had become concerned about the party's inability to attract moderate and conservative voters. Virginia Governor Chuck Robb reasoned that this could be addressed by having the southern states' primaries on the same day – a "Super Tuesday." The rationale was that no candidate could be nominated without winning on Super Tuesday, and that this would require all of them to address southern concerns. But Super Tuesday 1984 provided a three-way split among three liberals – Rev. Jesse Jackson, Massachusetts Governor Michael Dukakis, and Tennessee Senator Al Gore – because Robb's plan overlooked several factors. First it overlooked the proportional distribution of delegates that meant that no candidate could win all of a state's delegates. The plan also failed to consider the fact that the citizens who voted in early Democratic primaries were historically the activists – liberal Democrats – no matter who ran. Third, by scheduling all of the southern states to vote on the same day in March they had played their entire hand too early, and the nomination process played out in the northern and midwestern states suited to traditional liberal Democratic themes even as the less active, more conservative citizens became interested in the campaign.

Nevertheless, the grouping of primaries into Super Tuesdays and even Mega-Tuesdays continues. Such groupings have enormous communication implications for no candidate can personally campaign as they do in Iowa and New Hampshire in several states at once. Instead they must rely on paid media, and media buys are expensive. This increases the pressure to raise money and undermines the ability of second-tier candidates to remain active, which in turn reduces voters' alternatives.

As primaries have grown in importance since 1912 we have seen a massive increase in public involvement in the nomination process. From the perspective of democratic political theory this surely is a good thing. Yet this gain has come with two costs. The first is that the primary process has created an incredibly expensive gateway to nomination that few people dare attempt to cross. The second is that today's campaigns frequently invite us to "shortlist" potential nominees as employers screen job applications. This encourages citizens to find simple reasons to eliminate potential presidents from consideration and we often do this for reasons that we later regret. Sometimes we eliminate them because of a silly remark or a position that has little to do with presidential responsibilities. Sometimes we eliminate them on the basis of personal failings simply alleged through attacks and scandal mongering. These choices were once made behind closed doors by people able to judge the aspirants' fitness without the sordid allegations and denials that have become all too familiar. Yet that is the nomination system we now have and it is up to us to use it wisely. With this background in mind, let us consider the communication dynamics of the nomination stage.

Communication Dynamics of the Nomination Stage

During the nomination stage campaigns use speeches, ads, debates, and new media to influence news coverage and voters to support them in their primaries and caucuses. But because they now need not merely to establish their viability but to secure a roll call majority we see a very different set of communication dynamics.

Voters Act on Candidacies in Their States

The most important new dynamic of Stage 2 is that citizens act upon candidacies. Stage 1 saw political insiders, donors, and the media interacting with potential candidates and they remain important. But real live voters step up in Stage 2. Notice that we said "voters act upon candidacies" rather than "voters react to candidates." It is important that we not think of active candidates and passive voters because it is in the nomination stage that the voters take charge of the process. It is here – state-by-state, person-by-person – that citizens become voters. They do this as the candidates try to figure out what to say and do and as the media pundits try to analyze how and why they are voting as they are.

The portal for entry to Stage 2 is the New Hampshire primary. Talk-show hosts and other cranky Americans tend to whine about New Hampshire having the first primary, so let us see why they have it. From 1831–1912 New Hampshire used a caucus system to pick their convention delegates. Their legislature instituted a presidential primary in 1913 (adjusted in 1915) to be held on the traditional town meeting day, the second Tuesday in March. The primary was second on the 1916 primary calendar and first in 1920 and thereafter. In 1977 the state legislature amended the law setting the date for New Hampshire's presidential primary to hold it, "On the second Tuesday of March, *immediately preceding the date on which any other state shall hold a similar election, which ever is earlier*" (Gregg 1997 emphasis added). Thus they have the legal claim to the first primary. Any state could have written its primary's scheduling into law but only New Hampshire thought to do so. Ironically, it means that New Hampshire will never get to vote when a delegate majority is at stake.

Because New Hampshire is geographically small and theirs is the only election held on that day, voters and candidates meet personally, often several times. We have effectively delegated to our neighbors in Iowa and New Hampshire the role of taking the personal measure of the candidates. Sometimes these voters smell a phoney. Sometimes they find that the candidate cannot explain positions or programs. Sometimes a lack of rhetorical sensitivity becomes all too evident.

Perhaps other states could shoulder this responsibility just as well or better than the people of Iowa and New Hampshire. But the culture of flinty "Live Free or Die" New Hampshire voters seems to prepare them particularly well for their task. Certainly the geography and population dispersal in New York, California, and Texas would make personal campaigns less practical in those states.

The clustering of primaries later in the calendar with multiple states holding their primaries on the same day dilutes the effect of each one. It also requires the campaigns to turn to mediated messages rather than personal contact. As the campaign progresses the candidates must speak, advertise, and debate in very different states. Yet they must continually focus on the states whose contests come up next on the schedule, and voters are not randomly distributed across the states.

Accumulate Delegates and Generate Momentum

The campaign must *accumulate more delegates than its competitors and build momentum*. Presidential nominations have always been about delegate counts. Each state party has rules that decide how its delegates will be distributed, so candidates and journalists need to understand the rules to understand what is actually at stake. Finishing first is nice, and so is winning a larger percentage of the vote than somebody else, but only delegates matter.

But reporters do not all report the delegate counts. Timothy Noah (2008) captured this journalistic phenomenon when he discussed the contest between the "Momentucrats" and the "Arithmecrats." Momentucrats are the reporters who focus on the primaries as contests for popular votes, proclaim the popular vote leader the winner, count the number of states won and suggest that this pattern is important for momentum. Arithmecrats count the delegates won and look at the delegate count in relation to nomination (Noah 2008). We should all be Arithmecrats.

Hillary Clinton followed her 2008 New Hampshire victory with "wins" in Michigan, Nevada, and Florida. But the DNC had stripped Michigan of all delegates for moved its primary, so Clinton won no delegates. Because the Nevada caucuses distribute twenty-five delegates on the basis of districts Clinton's statewide 51–45 percent margin produced another Momentucrat victory; but Obama won the Arithmecratic victory with fourteen delegates to her eleven (CNN.com 1/22/08). Then Hillary won Florida, which had also been stripped of its delegates for moving its primary. In short, Clinton had three Momentucrat victories but Obama had the only Arthmecrat win and beat Clinton in those three contests for delegates, 14–11 – and the roll call counts delegates.

Momentucrat reports of three Clinton wins sent voters a very different message than Arithmecrat reports of two ties, one Obama win and an Obama lead of 14–11. They are not equally accurate and citizens who learn only the Momentucrat story are misinformed about the progress of the campaign for nomination.

The problem with such reporting is that it cultivates the impression that the "momentum" of the campaign was with Clinton when Obama was actually the candidate making measurable progress toward nomination. Strumpf (2002) wrote that any effects of momentum are considered by the campaign in light of their *prospects for future success*. Moreover, Holbrook's measure of momentum was neither news reports nor wins but a change in the candidate's standings in the opinion polls, and those polls during the nomination stage should be the state polls in the states about to hold their primaries. In other words, one should not conclude who had the momentum after those three state contests without assessing the candidates' prospects with South Carolina voters – where Obama would win 55 percent of the popular vote and the delegate contest, 25–12. Similarly, Republican Mike Huckabee took strategic advantage of Momentucrat eulogies for his campaign to skip Florida and campaign across the south and win both the delegate and popular vote contests in Alabama, Arkansas, Georgia, Tennessee, and the West Virginia convention.

There is, of course, a reasonable middle ground regarding delegates and momentum. That is track delegates as the direct measure of progress toward the terminal goal of the nomination stage and to track other measures as they contribute to potential delegate success under the rules to be used in the state about to hold primaries. Reporters would then be reporting meaningful "winners" and they would have even more "breaking news" to report. Meanwhile, we can perhaps better sort the helpful news from the misleading news.

Citizens Learn about Candidates, Issues, and Plans

The nomination stage provides citizens with an increasing amount of information about the candidates and their activities, sometimes more than we want. We can get a sense of the change in news coverage by revisiting Chapter 11's table of Google news hits. Placing first in the Iowa precinct caucuses clearly won press attention for Mike Huckabee whose Google hits increased by a factor of fifteen over the earlier period. Mitt Romney and Barack Obama saw their hits increase about five-fold, while John McCain's increased by 4.5 and the number nearly tripled for Clinton and Ron Paul. But the quantity of information is evident in the fact that hits roughly doubled for John Edwards, Bill Richardson, Dennis Kucinich, Giuliani, and Duncan Hunter (none of whom came close to challenging anywhere). As the primaries and caucuses took shape during January, news stories increased and the bulk of coverage went to those who had surfaced in Iowa.

This deluge of news can be a mixed blessing for candidates. They intend for new information to clarify their images and positions in ways that we will like. But as their hazy images clarify we are also likely to find things we dislike, such that we drop them from our shortlist of possible candidates. "He said what about the war?" "She voted for that program?" "He wants to do what?" Never mind – There are plenty of other candidates.

Voters Adjust their Beliefs and Feelings and Get Involved

Also during Stage 2 *voters adjust their beliefs and feelings* based on campaigns, personal conversations, results from prior states, and news coverage. Among these the most important and most often overlooked factor is our personal conversations. It is in our chats with friends, co-workers, family, barbers, bartenders, and others that we sort out what we think. For example, for years, people asked one

Table 12.1. Google News "Last Month" Hits for Candidates

DEMOCRAT	10/17/07	02/07/07		REPUBLICANS	10/17/07	02/07/07	
Hillary Clinton	37,985	101,602	2.67	Rudy Giuliani	24,172	41,802	1.73
Barack Obama	27,988	135,536	4.84	John McCain	18,595	84,134	4.52
John Edwards	22,829	50,180	2.19	Mitt Romney	17,393	88,278	5.07
Joe Biden	9,206	3,130	0.33	Fred Thompson	14,366	17,097	1.19
Chris Dodd	9,190	2,638	0.28	Ron Paul	9,228	26,299	2.85
Bill Richardson	3,779	9,156	2.42	Mike Huckabee	4,179	63,926	15.29
Dennis Kucinich	2,315	6,293	2.71	Duncan Hunter	2,642	4,720	1.78
Mike Gravel	1,163	1,149	0.98	Tom Tancredo	1,570	1,286	0.82

Source: original data

another, "What do you think of Hillary?" (whose last name was never required). The resulting conversations drew together all manner of themes including health care, a female president, and her husband's presidency (for better and worse). It is through these conversations that we make public issues personal and personal preferences public. When Stage 2 comes to our state it spurs these conversations in ways that profoundly influence – whether we eventually vote in our state's primary or not.

Stage 2 *involves citizens in the campaign* as each campaign recruits volunteers, voters, and donors. Although we normally think of campaigns working to move undecided voters toward support, they also strive to activate those already passively supportive. For example, most campaigns conduct voter registration and get out the vote (GOTV) drives that move citizens up the ladder of political activism. This helps to register and turn out more of the "right kind" of voters likely to vote for the "right" candidate. But it also helps the campaign in another way: people who work actively and publicly for a campaign are less likely to defect to another candidate.

Candidates Establish "Promise Webs"

The complexities of Stage 2 create an environment in which a successful *campaign must establish "promise webs."* Everyone talks about politicians promising things, and they often do so in a way that implies "empty promises" or insincerity. But surely a person asking us to support his or her campaign to become our president must assure us of *something,* be it an issue of value, policy, or character. Moreover, the concerns of all those audiences all across the country suggest that one promise might not suffice. Sooner or later, promises or assurances proliferate. I am suggesting here that those multiple promises form a web, and that a campaign will crash in Stage 2 unless the campaign's promise web makes sense to their voters.

A successful promise web can be simple or complex. Ronald Reagan's 1980 promise web remains a classic. Candidate Reagan promised three things: he would drastically reduce the federal deficit, he would increase the military and he would cut federal taxes. His Democratic opponents fumed that Reagan could not possibly do all three things at once. Increasing the military and cutting taxes would balloon the deficit, they said, or increasing the military and cutting the deficit would require a massive tax increase, or cutting the deficit and taxes would require military cuts. Reagan's response gave his promise web its strength: "I used to think that way, too, until I learned better. Of course we can do it. We're Americans." In other words, Reagan's promise web made sense for voters not because of economic theory but because he articulated their shared faith in Americans as an exceptional people. (Postscript: President Reagan did cut taxes and enlarge our military and was re-elected decisively in 1984. By the end of his second term the deficit had more than tripled.)

Bill Clinton was the master of the complex promise web. He campaigned in 1992 for a "new covenant" of "more freedom for all and more responsibility from all." Candidate Clinton seemed to have a five-point plan for everything, and his plans were intertwined. One part of that web was particularly important – the link between welfare reform and health care. Clinton argued that many people stayed on public assistance because it provided them with health care that they could not otherwise afford and which they would lose under most welfare reform proposals. Therefore, a national health care plan was an essential step toward ending "welfare as we knew it." But opposition to President Clinton's comprehensive health care plan proved too strong, and when welfare was reformed it left many people without coverage of any kind – in part because the promise web from the campaign was seldom heard again *as a web*. This is one of the dangers of a complex web, even in the hands of so skilful a persuader as Bill Clinton.

A campaign that cannot weave its promises into a resilient web will likely have rhetorical difficulties during Stage 2. Early in Stage 2 a loose web may simply confuse voters. But as the campaign progresses, opposing candidates and a critical press will tug at the loose threads and work to unravel the web. Occasionally one of those opponents will find it useful to use one of those threads. In the autumn of 1987 the University of North Carolina at Chapel Hill invited all candidates from both parties to discuss their plans for education. Al Gore used that occasion to say that he hoped to be known as "The Education President," but that was not to be. Although George H. W. Bush did not attend the event, he later adopted Gore's mantle and began referring to himself as "The Education President." When the web is woven tightly enough, others cannot so readily borrow its threads.

Candidates Try to Balance Predictability and Suspense by Beating Expectations

The Stage 2 media drama is interesting in its own right. To sustain their interest (and ours) the tournament needs to *balance predictability and suspense*. Sports networks report the results of games but spice them up for us with rankings, power ratings, and predictions. They do all of this because they need dramatic tensions and upsets to make the athletic seasons interesting. There can be no "upsets" without a prediction. The simplest formula for excitement in Stage 2 is to presume that the results of State 1's primary are a valid predictor of results in State 2's primary (and so on). Then we get, "Iowa Winner Beaten in New Hampshire!" or "South Carolina Loser Wins California!" as though these states' voters were all cut from the same fabric. Remember that these campaigns are coordinated nationally, but they are individual contests rhetorically adjusted to each state's voters, and Americans are not randomly distributed throughout our states.

This drama is "the expectations game" in which a candidate's performance is measured against "expectations." You have probably heard coaches play the expectations game by trying to lower expectations for their performance and raise expectations for their opponents. ("Yes, we are undefeated and they are winless, but they that just gives them more incentive to beat us if we don't play our best.") Campaigns similarly downplay their preparation and effort so that they can proclaim surprise by the voters' degree of support. This also helps them shake off disappointingly close results. But the reporters are always around to hold their feet to the proverbial fire. Thus we get election stories like, "Although Jones won with 53 percent of the vote she was expected to do much better here in the state where she once lived." We may also learn something like, "Most important was the showing of Zilch who surprised everyone by winning 10 percent of the vote to finish an impressive fifth place." What really happened? If it was a Republican "winner-take-all" contest then Jones's 53 percent took all of the delegates. If not, it was a proportional contest requiring 15 percent of the vote to qualify for a share of the delegates, so Jones won at least half of the delegates and Zilch won none. Either way, Zilch's "impressive" victory won no delegates. But the expectations story begins a temporary storyline that plays over the next week until Zilch does "surprisingly" poorly in the next state.

The 2008 New Hampshire primary will be remembered for Hillary Clinton's victory in the face of polls that predicted her losing to Barack Obama by as much as 14 percent. Mickey Kaus suggested five explanations for the surprise. One was the "Bradley effect" – the hypothesis that some white citizens are more likely to say that they will vote for a black candidate than they are to vote for one. There are several reasons to doubt the current power of the Bradley effect, but the more general point is important: "saying" and "voting" are two very distinct behaviors. The second is that "ganging up on the girl" hurt the male candidates in New Hampshire. The third is that Clinton's emotional moment the last day was magnified in importance because voters process news so quickly now that the "Iowa momentum" faded quickly. The fourth is that voters heard from the press that an Obama win would seal the nomination and some voted to keep the process going. The fifth is that the independent voters who voted for McCain were the ones who would have voted for Obama if they had voted in the Democratic primary (Kaus 2008). Each of these factors probably played some role in the outcome.

Induce Candidates to Withdraw

Ultimately the key to winning a majority of the party's delegates is to winnow the field by *inducing opponents to withdraw from the race*. Incumbent presidents ordinarily secure their party's field in the year prior to the primaries, and primary challenges weakened the re-election efforts of Lyndon Johnson, Jimmy Carter, and George H. W. Bush (Johnson decided not to run).

The nomination is technically decided when a candidate wins a majority of the committed delegates but it is effectively over when all candidates but one give up the race. In that sense the nomination stage is a war of attrition – a struggle to survive and advance. Fei Shen (2008) found that the duration of a candidacy depended upon three factors: the candidate's standing in the polls, presence in traditional news media, and fundraising performance. Prior campaign media presence correlated highly with poll standing and media standing during the primaries and less strongly with fundraising performance. During the primary campaign poll standing and media presence were more highly correlated than fundraising and media presence. News coverage was most strongly correlated with campaign duration, followed by poll standing; fundraising was negatively correlated with duration (perhaps because failing campaigns were spending cash on hand). In short, a campaign that fails to perform in the polls will lose news coverage and face elimination.

The national media pressure for candidates to abandon their campaigns is an important part of the Stage 2 melodrama. National reporters seem to be on a morbid death watch, ready to pull the proverbial plug on every struggling campaign as quickly as possible. Perhaps this is because they began covering the surfacing process so early, or perhaps it is because the dramatic logic of the campaign story invites closure. There is little sign of anything ideological in this tendency as they do it to candidates across the political landscape. But supporters of the candidates being urged to quit the race nevertheless sense a bias against their candidate. Indeed, the reporters do often resemble a pack of wolves stalking the herd to isolate the vulnerable, surround them, and finish them off.

The audience of donors who provide the resources essential to continue the campaign should not be underestimated. Donors and volunteers disappointed in the results, campaign strategy, or anything else may simply stop contributing to the campaign. When they do so, the campaign will eventually shrivel and die on the vine. In 1988, for example, George H. W. Bush and Bob Dole headed into ten southern "Super Tuesday" primaries virtually tied in the Republican delegate race. Overall, 93 percent of those states' registered Republicans chose not to vote, and Bush defeated Dole in all ten states with relatively modest margins of victory. But because all ten of those states held "winner-take-all" primaries, Bush won 488 delegates and Dole won none. Although Bush remained far short of a majority of the delegates Dole's fundraising stream stopped and his campaign was dead in the water. Bush was nominated and won the presidency (Dole would be nominated in 1996 and lose to Clinton's re-election campaign). But in 1988 Dole did not so much lose as run out of gas.

When facing elimination candidate's family and close advisors are likely to influence the decision. Sometimes they decide that the race is no longer worth the effort. Key advisors may quit the campaign to devote more of their time to more promising state or Senate campaigns. Other times they refinance property or take out personal loans to sustain the campaign. Factors of commitment, cohesiveness within the core campaign organization as well as the candidate's personal orientation toward setbacks all influence the decision.

Withdrawing from the campaign creates an embarrassing rhetorical problem. After all, every candidate devoted considerable time and energy to the task of convincing campaign workers, donors, and voters that he or she was the best person to take on the job of president. So how does the candidate reconcile the campaign rhetoric with defeat? Perhaps someday a candidate will withdraw saying, "I guess I was wrong, I'm not really fit to be president," or "The voters have spoken and they are unbelievably stupid," but probably not.

Many candidates engage in "strategic retreat." They do this by emphasizing their purpose in running (personal ambition rarely seems to have motivated them). They often discuss their desire to involve some set of people in politics or to raise some issue in the public consciousness. They can then say that their campaign has in fact accomplished this goal, and that the campaign therefore succeeded. The purpose is more important than the candidate and, because of the campaign, the purpose will endure, and the candidate will work toward it in other ways.

During my 2004 field research in Iowa I attended a Des Moines rally for Rep. Richard Gephardt on the eve of the 2004 Iowa caucuses. Aware of the polls, Gephardt prepared his supporters for his withdrawal. "This campaign is not about me," he said, "I don't need to be president . . . in any way." Instead, his campaign was about making America a better place for working people like his father who had driven a milk truck. His speech was followed by the usual pep talks about getting out the vote, but most of those attending the rally filed glumly out of the ballroom, realizing that their work was near its end.

Sometimes defeated candidates try to block the frontrunner by supporting another candidate, either by name or by describing an ideal candidate. They may do this simply because they want to, or because the candidates have reached some sort of "understanding." When Rudy Giuliani withdrew in 2008 he quickly endorsed his friend John McCain. But when John Edwards withdrew he instead secured pledges from Clinton and Obama that they would make poverty an important issue in their campaigns. Although one obvious way to reach such an understanding is for the two candidates to agree on the vice-presidential nomination that is a very delicate card to play. Not only is it important to the country but, strategically, it can be used only once. Likely nominees are prudent to reserve this option until much later. More manageable are understandings about the prospective nominee's willingness to entertain goals, initiatives, or principles important to the withdrawing candidate.

Summary

In the old days, delegates often arrived at the nominating conventions uncertain of the outcome. This was the case because there were fewer primaries and even those primaries were often advisory – they did not clearly bind delegates' votes. But with the reforms that opened the nomination process our primaries now determine the delegate votes in advance of the conventions. Thus Stage 2 no longer need end with the convention roll call of states when the nomination becomes official. Once the delegates are secure, or when all but one candidate has withdrawn from the race, one candidate is acknowledged as the nominee and begins to act like one. When that happens, it is time to begin consolidating support in Stage 3.

Strategizing for Stage 2

The central challenge in Stage 2 is to win a majority of a party's convention delegates before running out of time or money. Therefore the secondary challenge is to shrink the candidate pool so that the delegates available in each contest are divided among fewer and fewer contenders. Remember always that Stage 2 is a tournament – and the only way to win a tournament is to survive and keep playing.

But the campaign is unlike a tournament that assigns opponents. Instead, the campaigns decide which state primaries and caucuses to enter based on considerations that include the number of delegates at stake, indications of likely voter support in that state, the competitiveness of the opposition, the availability of campaign funds to wage a serious effort and the pressure of other state campaigns during the same time frame. Put differently, the campaign asks, "How much do we stand to win, and how costly will that win prove to be?"

Let us consider some hypothetical campaign decisions. Imagine an early state primary that provides a key opportunity to affirm or to risk one's viability. There are ordinarily about eight major candidates working hard for votes. A candidate who makes little effort there can expect to win little more than 1/8 of the votes (usually less than that) – and that means an eighth place finish (imagine the headlines!) and no delegates (because 1/8 is 12.5 percent and less than the 15 percent minimum required for a proportional share of the delegates). But later, as the primaries drone on and the field dwindles to, say, three candidates, the same candidate might expect to attract 25–30 percent of the votes simply through name recognition with no real campaign (especially if the other two are also busy contesting other states).

It is therefore important for the campaign to map out an overall strategy for winning the necessary convention delegates. In doing so it is worth remembering the mantra of 1988 Democratic nominee Michael Dukakis: the race is a marathon, not a sprint. The Democrats' delegate majority can no longer be won quickly in a crowded field because of proportional allocation, so the key is to win a decent share of the delegates at stake as efficiently as possible and then move on to the next contest with plenty of resources. Occasionally it may be helpful to invest in a dramatic victory to help fundraising, but a good fundraising team can get support for a campaign that is simply on track and competitive.

A helpful indicator of Stage 2 progress can be obtained by calculating each campaign's resources expended per delegate won. Let us imagine, for example, that in a proportional contest Aaron won twelve delegates, Benitez ten, and Conrad ten – Aaron won, right? Sort of; but in the marathon race for a majority of the thousands of national delegates a lead of two is inconsequential. We need to consider the relative costs of those delegates to the campaigns. If Aaron spent $6 million, Benitez $4 million, and Conrad only $2 million we find that each delegate cost the Aaron campaign $500,000 and the Benitez campaign spent $400,000 per delegate, but the Conrad campaign walked away with one delegate for every $200,000 they spent in the state. If their campaign coffers were at all comparable before this primary, the Conrad campaign will be in the best shape in subsequent contests and well positioned to pick up those two delegates – and more.

What if the votes in our hypothetical example happened to be cast in one of the Republicans' winner-take-all primaries? In such cases only the front runner wins, so Aaron would get all thirty-two of the delegates and the per-delegate rate drops to $187,500 each. Meanwhile, Benitez spent four million and Conrad two million for no delegates at all. At some point Benitez, Conrad or both would have been wise to stop spending in this state to save their money for states in which they could expect more return on their investment. This is what we mean by "win efficiently and move on."

But move on to which contests? The wise campaign devises a strategy that has the potential to yield an appropriate number of delegates by winning the votes of people likely to support them. Sometimes they make curious choices. In 2004 North Carolina Senator John Edwards surprised many people by finishing second to John Kerry in Iowa, ahead of the early surfacing front runner, former Vermont Governor Howard Dean. Seeking to build on his Iowa showing Edwards turned his attention to New Hampshire. The southern senator's opponents in New Hampshire included Kerry (Massachusetts), Dean (Vermont), and Senator Joe Lieberman (Connecticut), as well as General Wesley Clark who had skipped Iowa to concentrate on New Hampshire. Edwards drew 12 percent of the votes to receive no delegates and finish fourth, a finish that cost him resources and took some of the luster from his Iowa finish.

Shortly thereafter, Edwards began to emphasize the importance of Americans talking about race, saying "We need to talk about race everywhere." Yet Edwards chose not to visit Detroit to campaign among its African-American voters in the days leading up to the 2004 Michigan primary. Edwards subsequently drew 13 percent of the Michigan vote – 2,166 votes short of the 15 percent threshold. When all of the delegates (including those not determined by the primary) were distributed, Michigan's delegate count was Kerry 91, Dean 24, and Edwards 6. Would a major rally and a policy address about race with its attendant news coverage have made the difference? We will never know. But Edwards had lost ground to both Kerry and Dean. In these two cases Edwards waged a futile campaign in New Hampshire and failed to campaign in a promising Michigan area at a crucial time, and he fell short of the 15 percent threshold in both cases. The point is that it matters a great deal when and where a candidate chooses to invest resources.

Keeping Score in the Nomination Stage

Once the nomination stage begins we need new ways of tracking progress toward the new objective. National opinion polls, fundraising, media mentions, and one's Iowa finish are no longer the best measures.

The Delegate Count

The crucial new scoreboard that arises in Stage 2 is the Arithmecrat's delegate count. CNN's excellent primary sites for 2004 and 2008 remain available for reference. Their delegate scorecard made the precise number of delegates won in every state as well as the total easily accessible to anyone. As the Obama–Clinton race progressed many sites began tracking the delegate count and this will surely become a staple of primary coverage in 2012. Many of these sites also provided a bar graph to display the number of delegates awarded in relation to the number required for nomination. Anyone seriously interested in the nomination contest should bookmark a page like this during the primaries.

Cash on Hand

Because candidates are now actively spending money their fundraising is less important than their cash on hand. The Center for Responsive Politics maintains a web site (opensecrets.org) that tracks the candidates' cash on hand as well as donations. Fundraising is always important, but the 2004 Dean campaign squandered its fundraising advantage by spending needlessly far in advance of states' primaries and they ran out of money when they need it most.

State Polls and Media

Because actual votes are being cast in state primaries the national polls become distractions and state level polls matter in Stage 2. Tracking recent state level polls can help us understand the candidates' prospects by state even though rule differences make it difficult to predict delegate strength.

Similarly, we can better appreciate the rhetorical climate of a state primary campaign by following state and local newspapers and television coverage. This is not to say that your own local media are your best source. But all significant local newspapers and television news operations now maintain web pages that you can easily access. Local reporters have the professional contacts and an awareness of the complexity of the state's issues that can elude national reporters visiting the state. It is unnecessary and unwise to expect national reporters to have a deep appreciation of state and local politics and issues in all fifty states. National reporters are barnstormers who follow the campaign into a strange land they do not know, whereas local reporters know the voters and the issues that divide them. Search engines such as Google can help you locate similar sites for the other states as their campaigns develop.

Summary and Conclusions

This chapter has examined the second stage of presidential campaigns, the contest for the party nomination. We saw that nomination requires a majority on the party's convention roll call vote such that every candidate seeks to:

- Get supporters seated as delegates
- Win the support of uncommitted delegates and
- Discourage contenders for those delegates.

Delegate commitments are won through a series of primary elections and caucuses held in accordance with party rules.

- Delegates were once controlled by party bosses.
- Primaries began to emerge in 1912, became increasingly important during the 1960s and have determined delegate selection since 1972.
- All Democratic delegates are distributed proportionately among the candidates winning at least 15 percent of the votes in each state.
- Republican rules vary by state and include proportional allocation, winner-take-all contests and winner-take-all by districts.
- Some delegate commitments are binding and others are not, depending upon the rules.

The nomination stage has its own communication dynamics. We saw in this chapter that they include:

- Citizens become voters and act directly upon candidacies
- Candidates accumulate delegates and generate momentum by achieving instrumental success
- Citizens learn about candidates, issues, and plans

- Citizens adjust their beliefs and feelings about the candidates and get involved in the campaign
- Campaign organizations construct promise webs from their commitments. These can be simple like Reagan's or complex like Clinton's, but they must rhetorically connect the campaign's individual commitments.
- Candidates try to balance predictability and suspense by beating expectations. This feeds the news melodrama that keeps interest alive.
- Candidates and the media induce struggling candidates to withdraw from the campaign. Funding is the ultimate lifeline, but because they are spending cash on hand this decision is more often based on performance in the primaries as covered in the media and polls.

The nomination contest is officially decided when a majority is achieved on the convention roll call, and we saw that this requires a candidate to survive several instrumental exigencies:

- The campaign must perform well enough in polls and primaries to satisfy media expectations and secure continuing news coverage.
- The candidate must fare well enough in state contests to accumulate convention delegates at a competitive rate.
- The campaign must win those delegates while effectively managing its resources, either winning them inexpensively or stimulating fundraising with its success.

Candidate progress in the nomination stage can best be tracked by following:

- The candidates' delegate counts
- The campaigns' cash on hand rather than their fundraising
- State level (rather than national) polls and state and local news media from states about to hold primaries and caucuses.

The nomination contest divides the party. When candidates for nomination attack one another they alienate many of those in the party whose support will be essential to their general election campaign. Thus, as soon as the nomination is assured, the nominee must begin to consolidate support, and that is Stage 3.

13 The Consolidation Stage

We saw individual political warlords arise and build personal armies in Stage 1 and then contest against each other in an elimination match for leadership of their tribe in Stage 2. But before the winners can fight for control of the kingdom they need to bring together all of the warlords and warriors they defeated. This is the consolidation stage that receives less attention than the primaries.

This chapter will discuss the objectives of consolidation, and consider the communication dynamics peculiar to this stage. We will pay particular attention to the conflicting needs of campaign and media organizations that cause them to perceive and value conventions differently. We will also consider how to track the nominee's progress in unifying their supporters.

The Challenge of Consolidating

When the nominee was unknown until the actual convention roll call the consolidation stage might last only 24 hours – from the decisive ballot to the nominee's acceptance speech. As primaries influenced the roll call consolidation was thought of as the "convention stage" because the convention clarified the nomination, unified the party, and adjourned to begin the general election campaign (Trent and Friedenberg 2004).

But, as primaries increasingly determined the delegate counts and decided the parties' nominations well in advance of the conventions, the rhetorical functions once performed by conventions became immediately necessary. National conventions remain an important part of Stage 3 but they are no longer all of it. In the fifth information age of the mobile Internet and 24-hour news no nominee can wait for a Woodstock gathering of harmony, peace, and love. Today the crucial work of consolidation can neither wait months for the convention nor can it be accomplished in the mere four days of togetherness.

The consolidation stage begins for each party as soon as its nomination contest ends and extends through the nominee's acceptance address that concludes the convention. This means that one party will begin to consolidate while the other is still settling its nomination. This is important to remember when studying their communication because they are not yet campaigning against one another – that will happen in Stage 4.

The ultimate exigency of Stage 3 is to produce a unified and enthusiastic following for the nominee. This requires the nominee to retain the support of those responsible for winning the nomination while finding ways to overcome the reservations of partisan holdouts and finding ways to appeal to those who still oppose the nominee as leader of their party.

The challenge of political consolidation in campaigns is therefore to overcome two sets of tensions. The first tension is a struggle to satisfy a wide variety of voters' personal demands, many of which are in conflict. The number of candidates and campaigns proliferated during Stage 1 as many people try to address this tension. During Stage 2 most of those campaigns won adherents but nevertheless fell short of nomination. The problem is that those campaigns raised awareness, increased divisions, and heightened expectations of success – all of which were crushed by the nominee.

The second tension occurs as incongruent campaigns conflict in the campaigns over the "right," or "best," or "true" way to interpret the world. The rhetorical challenge is to maximize the common ground and to minimize the divisions without sacrificing the beliefs that people value most.

This process results in pluralistic political parties comprised of a wide array of overlapping voter communities that inevitably conflict. As we saw in Chapter 2, the Republican Coalition is comprised of Enterprisers, Social Conservatives and Pro-Government Conservatives and the Democratic coalition is comprised of Liberals, Conservative Democrats and Disadvantaged Democrats (Kohut 2005). The Republican nominee must find ways to draw Enterprisers, Social Conservatives and Pro-Government Conservatives together just as the Democratic nominee must find ways to draw Liberals, Conservative Democrats, and Disadvantaged Democrats together. The struggles of politics are found in the interplay of these communities, in the movement of individuals among these communities as they adjust their views, and in the ability of political leaders to mobilize coalitions that produce a shared if temporary reality for them.

Candidate preference surveys frequently ask respondents whether "this candidate represents people like me." But which people are "like me" and how do we recognize them? Demographic data can tell us about the characteristics that individuals have in common but they can tell us neither whether they think they have that trait in common nor whether they believe it to be an important source of commonality. When we want to study people coming together into a community, or dividing into factions, we need to study their communication. Mathematicians teach us that $A+B=C$ but in communication we study how $U+I=US$.

Communication Dynamics of the Consolidation Stage

With the primary contests for delegates over, the nominees turn their attention to different audiences and different puzzles. The kind of person inclined to hold a grudge will have particular difficulty working through these dynamics because they involve, for the first time, spending the most time and effort on those who are not inclined to be supportive.

Consolidation Involves Six Audiences

The general rhetorical configuration facing every presumptive nominee can be characterized as having six audiences. First, there are the activated supporters. Second, there are the activated partisan opponents (who may or may not be consolidated among themselves). Third, there are the partisans yet to become interested or activated. Fourth, there are supporters of the other party and its nominee. Fifth, there are the undecided, independent, and cross-pressured citizens. Sixth, and finally, there are reporters, pundits, and bloggers in the various media. Pre-convention consolidation is not the time to worry about audiences four and five – the supporters of the other party or the independent voters. Nor is it an important time to worry about those who have already climbed aboard the campaign bandwagon. Three audiences are crucial to pre-convention consolidation: activated partisan opponents, uninvolved partisans, and the media. Each audience plays a separate role.

Partisan opponents have found reason actively to oppose the nominee during the primaries, and their concerns must be assuaged. One way to cope with this is to select their preferred candidate for the vice-presidential nomination. In 2004 John Kerry used this approach, naming John Edwards as his running mate with the hope that this would help him win southern states; a choice that proved a dismal failure. When policies alienate partisans the nominee can try to adapt or restate those policies so that they are less divisive, but this can render the campaign vulnerable to charges of contradicting itself or "flip-flopping." In any case, the important rhetorical tactic is to calm this audience rather than to further arouse them, because people have difficulty warming to their adversaries when their adrenaline is pumping.

Uninvolved partisans pose a different problem. The campaign must answer the question, "Why have they yet to become involved?" It may be that they are habitual late deciders, that their issues have yet to be addressed, that they have reservations about the candidate or that they find the campaign news boring. These people need to be excited, for if they are allowed to coast along as apathetic partisans they may choose not to vote.

Thus the campaign engaged in pre-convention consolidation must simultaneously calm the activated and activate the calm. This is the task of rhetoric, a task once described by Kenneth Burke as sharpening the pointless and dulling the too sharply pointed. If one is to do this, one needs to harness all the rhetorical sensitivity one can muster. As discussed in Chapter 2, a noble self will barge ahead and tell the partisan activists why they are misguided and a rhetorical reflector will tell them what they want to hear, thus creating an array of contradictions.

The rhetorically sensitive campaign is attentive to these multiple audiences and considers their messages accordingly. In July of 2008 the McCain campaign ran a spot showing Paris Hilton and Britney Spears to imply that Barack Obama was merely a popular celebrity, unprepared for the presidency. McCain supporters loved it, but the spot attracted controversy. Some said it was in poor taste. Then we learned that Ms. Hilton's parents had each contributed the legal maximum to McCain's campaign. Then, to top it off, Paris released her own "energy plan" spot responding to "the wrinkled white haired guy." The whole episode did little to consolidate McCain's support and may even have hurt his efforts because it played to the wrong audience.

In another rhetorically careless statement, John Kerry famously said of an 87 billion dollar war appropriation, "I actually voted for it before I voted against it." No amount of clarification could repair the damage. Had Senator Kerry said, "I voted for it when it would have been paid for by ending the tax cuts for the super rich, and voted against it only when it was paired with those tax cuts" his opponents would have had more difficulty using it to divide his potential supporters.

When candidates speak to us they seem almost universally to say, "I'm for this" or "I'm against that." Such statements readily fuel identification and division. "I am pro-life" identifies with people who oppose abortion and divides the candidate from those who support a woman's right to choose; whereas "I am pro-choice" does just the opposite. How can a candidate find a rhetorically sensitive middle ground? If we look back at the speeches that Theodore Sorensen wrote for President Kennedy, we find that he frequently used a stylistic device to do just this. Sorensen and Kennedy used a double negative construction to fend off positions they did not want to take. So, for example, Kennedy said in his inaugural address, "Let us never negotiate out of fear, but let us never fear to negotiate." In doing so, Kennedy created a rhetorical space for the pursuit of negotiations conducted in the strategic national interest. Similarly, a candidate might say something like, "Let us never allow late term abortions, but let us never allow government to make personal moral choices during the first trimester of pregnancy" – an alternative way of saying, "I support Roe v. Wade."

Media personnel constitute a third important audience during the pre-convention consolidation stage. The proliferation of new media including blogs, podcasts, YouTube, and the 24-hour news cycle (including online news updates, cable news channels, and talk radio programs) work against consolidation. Once upon a time this was the dull season of the campaign. But cable news channels and talk shows cannot allow stories to die because campaign news is the staple of their diet in presidential election years.

What would happen to the campaign news story from the end of the nomination stage (roughly April) until the conventions (roughly August) if these media personnel just left them alone or reported consolidation? Reports of conflict and tension would diminish, followed by a reduction in voters' need for news updates, which could lead to a decline in ratings and readership. But that is not the campaign environment in which we live. We see a candidate speak to an audience. Cable news channels often carry it live and headline services report it. It is posted on YouTube and bloggers comment on it. "The Daily Show" and "The Colbert Report" parody it. Rush Limbaugh, Keith Olberman, and Bill O'Reilly rant about it. The cable shows ask David Gergen, Ann Coulter, and others what they think. Charlie Rose, George Stephanopoulos, Bob Schieffer, and Tom Brokaw convene thoughtful people. Chat rooms gather and convey comments from people of highly variable insight. Reporters in the field ask the candidate if he really meant what he said and other reporters ask the opponent for reactions. Then one of the candidates says something else and the cycle starts again. While the candidates are trying to consolidate support the media coverage is fostering dissension or, as they would prefer to call it, "critical reflection."

Nominees Redefine "We" and "They"

Kenneth Burke profoundly influenced the ways that communication scholars think about human communication. One of Burke's important contributions concerned identification and division. Burke wrote that an important reason people communicate is to discover the degree to which we are made of the same substance. Two absolutely identical people would be theoretically "consubstantial" yet even identical twins have unique experiences. Thus we continually engage in "identification" of our similarities and "division" when we discover differences.

Identification and division are head and tail of the same coin – they are natural communication processes, and neither is inherently better or worse than the other. Indeed, Burke argued that every act of identification necessarily results in division and that every act of division necessarily results in identification. We might think of identification as the centripetal force drawing persons together toward a sense of "usness" and division as the centrifugal force driving us apart into "thems." The trick is to be able to read the people's communication behavior to learn which persons are moving together (and why) and which persons are moving apart (and why).

During Stages 1 and 2 the campaign organizations set themselves against the other candidates within their party. "We" supported our candidate against "them" who would take our party in the wrong direction. But in the consolidation stage "we" are the party and "they" are the other party and their nominee who would take the country in the wrong direction. To consolidate the nominee must carefully expand the "us" implied in speeches and ads to include audience preferences, values, and policies that previously belonged to assorted partisan "them" without betraying those responsible for winning the nomination.

When we hear one of our own needs or feelings voiced by another person we experience a momentary sense of recognition, unity, or "usness" – a sense of Burke's "consubstantiality." Anthropologist Victor Turner (1982) discussed a similar moment as "communitas" and rhetorical critic Ernest G. Bormann and his colleagues (1985; Bormann, Cragan, and Shields 2001) have written extensively about the process of "symbolic convergence." The initial feeling of usness or communitas is spontaneous. It occurs when persons, "obtain a flash of lucid mutual understanding . . . when they feel that all problems, not just their problems, could be resolved, whether emotional or cognitive, if only the group (which is felt in the first person) as 'essentially us' could sustain itself" (Turner, 1982, p. 48). This momentary flash of recognition is crucial to the understanding of human behavior because it is the flashpoint at which "you" and "I" become "us." Social psychologist Robert Freed Bales (1970), for example, found that members of small groups reacted both cognitively and emotionally when they perceived others to be enacting, or "dramatizing," portions of their own life stories.

This feeling of communitas or convergence can occur when we read a poem or hear a song that speaks to our life experiences, and it can happen when an orator depicts life as we have been personally experiencing it. When a speaker articulates our personal fantasies, our symbolic worlds converge. Bormann (1972, 1977) said that the fantasy theme "chains out" with each new person embracing the theme and adding to as they become a community with a shared "rhetorical vision." The community is bound together by (1) the vision and themes that the share and (2) the process of co-creating the vision.

The paradox of shared visions is that "we" cannot share our visions with "them." To co-create a shared vision "we" burrow further into our common text (actually, this book). I isolated myself from family, students, and colleagues to write it and you withdraw from your social world to read it. It is impossible to converge with another without simultaneously diverging from some others. Thus, moments of communitas, identification, and convergence are also moments of disunity, polarization, and divergence from other persons who do not share the moment and were not part of the process of creating it. Every shared vision eventually produces a "them." George Orwell illustrated this point memorably in *Animal Farm* with a utopian state based on a commandment that "All animals are equal" that was eventually revised by the corrupt pigs to say "but some animals are more equal than others."

Political party platforms illustrate how a party creates a unifying coalitional text. The party's Platform Committee members receive policy suggestions from members of the party. The committee members then debate, amend, revise, and vote on each proposal as a potential "plank" of the platform. Each platform is therefore a text that sets forth certain needs, reasons, and preferences as official party doctrine more important to the party than other needs, reasons or preferences. Moreover, the platform embodies the effort of partisans to adopt some people's language and other people's reasons to justify some other people's preferences. When well drafted, the party platform provides a shared foundation for all its candidates than any of the party's narrower constituencies alone could produce.

Convergence is the dynamic that drives the consolidation process, but as Burke wrote, every act of convergence with audience A necessarily causes divergence from audience Z (and vice versa). Consolidating nominees seek to develop a vision that can be widely shared by a coalition of communities to invite convergence. Bill Clinton and Al Gore published their 1992 vision in a book titled *Putting People First* and they used that theme to consolidate Democrats and Independents. In 2004 President Bush relied heavily on the widely shared belief that "9/11 changed everything" to deflect criticism and to defend his record.

Such moments are crucial because they entail more than argument over a policy. They are arguments that can involve audiences in governing or insulate governing from people, depending whether they consolidate around a vision they plan to implement or one that distracts voters from their policy agenda. A candidate who can maximize the involvement of defeated candidates and their supporters in the construction of a platform can enhance their sense of "usness" and help consolidation.

Nominees Engage in Fence Mending

The second communication dynamic of Stage 3 is the nominees' attention to interpersonal fence-mending after the fractious delegate selection struggles. The nature of the acclaim/attack/defense chain required all of the candidates for nomination to say things that rankled their opponents. We saw that many policy differences can be resolved through the platform process but attacks on character are likely to prove more vexing. The news media's campaign melodrama that heightened and personalized differences between the candidates with Stage 2 stories about their attacks complicate the fence mending process.

The presumptive nominee must find a way to reach out to defeated opponents, but unity depends upon those opponents rallying around the nominee. Fence mending calls for the kind of constitutive rhetoric we discussed in Chapter 6. The nominee need to engage target audiences personally to create a shared present and then develop a shared narrative history and identity that implies a coordinated effort toward a shared future (Charland 1987).

To begin reconstituting their people, Barack Obama and Hillary Clinton held a June 2008 joint appearance in the aptly named town of Unity, New Hampshire. The victorious Obama sat on a stool with his shirtsleeves rolled up and led the applause as Clinton spoke. "Unity is not only a beautiful place, it's a wonderful feeling, isn't it?" said the former candidate. "I know what we start here in this field of unity will end on the steps of the Capitol when Barack Obama takes the oath of office." Obama merged the old rivals into a new "us": "For sixteen months, *Senator Clinton and I* have shared the stage as rivals," he said. "But today, I couldn't be happier and more honored that *we're* sharing it as allies in the effort to bring this country a new and better day." He encouraged his supporters to help retire her campaign debts and she encouraged her supporters to join her and Obama in a single campaign for change. "If you like the direction the country is going, then vote for Senator McCain, but if you think we need a new course, a new agenda, vote for Barack Obama" (Zeleny 2008).

When efforts like this go well, the defeated candidate's supporters often join the effort. But they have to go very well, because the donors and key strategists had been highly motivated to oppose the now presumptive nominee. Some supporters will remain on the sidelines, but activists can become problematic as when Clinton backers James McConaha and Valery Mitchell agreed to lead Democrats for McCain (*LA Times* 2008).

Republicans had the opposite consolidation problem. Because their rules provided for several winner-take-all victories John McCain won quickly, clinching the nomination on March 4. But he was the clear frontrunner, beginning to consolidate conservatives, some of whom worked in front of microphones, who opposed him when he addressed the Conservative Political Action Committee on February 7. McCain acknowledged his responsibility to unite the party, but his language initially underscored the division among McCain, conservatives, and the Republican Party: "*I* am acutely aware that *I* cannot succeed in that endeavor, nor can *our party* prevail over the challenge we will face from either Senator Clinton or Senator Obama, without the support of dedicated *conservatives*, whose convictions, creativity and energy have been indispensible to the success *our party* has had over the last quarter century" (McCain 2008). As he proceeded to discuss their disagreements he used the words "I" nine times, "you" six times and "us" only once.

McCain then sought to establish himself as a lifelong "mainstream conservative" by acclaiming "I believe today, as I believed twenty-five years ago, in small government; fiscal discipline; low taxes; a strong defense, judges who enforce, and not make, our laws; the social values that are the true source of our strength; and, generally, the steadfast defense of our rights to life, liberty, and the pursuit of happiness, which I have defended my entire career as God-given to the born and unborn." But if he was a lifelong mainstream conservative, why was he divided from his audience? He referred to his reputation as a maverick which partially answered the question. His listeners were not mavericks but Conservatives, and it was the unpredictability of McCain's conservatism that worried them.

McCain made some progress with CPAC conservatives by personally addressing them, but this early consolidation speech fell short of its potential. He could not afford to skip the conference even though he was not yet the nominee, but surely many in his audience harbored hope that someone else might yet prevail. If he was going to present himself as a lifelong mainstream conservative then he should have spoken of "we conservatives" rather than "you and I." Like Buchanan in 1988 and Clinton in Unity he emphasized the evils of the opposition but that often sounds better coming from the runner-up than the nominee. The nominee should be able to offer listeners a basis for consolidation that is positive and shared, not negative and divisive.

Perhaps McCain would have benefited from a longer nomination contest. The potential benefit of a longer primary contest is that candidates and their supporters can work out some of their differences, finding common ground and mutual respect. When the contest ends too quickly the problems are left for the consolidation stage. This may have been one of McCain's rhetorical problems, In an essay posted on Politico.com, Historian Allan J. Lichtman wrote that:

> McCain is not a phony or apostate conservative. Rather, he is the heir to contradictions that have now splintered the once vibrant conservative movement beyond easy repair. McCain's backing for nation building in Iraq – arguably the largest federal social engineering project in US history – the Bush tax cuts and a robust national bureaucracy for homeland security undercuts his rhetorical support for limited government, fiscal responsibility and states' rights. . . . McCain is straining to appease a conservative movement that is too fragmented to be appeased. Like Humpty Dumpty after the fall, all the GOP's horses and all the GOP's men cannot put together again business and Social Conservatives, big- and small-government conservatives, tax-cutters and deficit hawks, and foreign adventurers and advocates of the humble foreign policy that Bush proposed in his 2000 campaign but quickly abandoned.   (Lichtman 2008)

In other words, the three Pew groups of the Republican coalition were fragmenting in 2008 and neither McCain nor any other Republican could find the rhetorical appeals to unite them, but McCain found sufficient delegates to clinch the Republican nomination, and then had to consolidate them. We will never know what would have transpired if McCain had staked out a more moderate position and provided CPAC with reasons to follow him and his supporters toward the political center.

Divide the Opposition

A third communication dynamic of Stage 3 is the effort to divide the other party. Knowing that it is crucial for the other campaign to consolidate it is in your interest to make their consolidation as difficult as possible. President Bush's 2004 campaign was very innovative in this regard. The Bush campaign began running attack ads as soon as Kerry clinched the Democratic nomination. They also began to push immigration reform initiatives to make it difficult for Kerry to unite his union supporters (who feared for their jobs) and liberals (sympathetic to the immigrants' plight). The president would have difficulty unifying his own supporters on immigration reform but he had their nomination and the 2004 trump card of "standing up to terrorists." The key for Bush was to complicate Stage 3 for Democrats so that he could appeal to them in Stage 4.

Nominees Interpret "The American Dream"

A key to consolidating supporters of each party during Stage 3 is an effort to reaffirm the American dream. Basically, all Americans believe in "the American dream," we simply disagree about what it is. Walter R. Fisher suggested that there are two components to the American dream. The "moralistic" dimension concerns the principles and ideals for which we stand, whereas the "materialistic" dimension is the rags-to-riches story of progress. Fisher described the 1972 presidential campaign as one in which Democrat George McGovern preached to the country about our ideals and the importance of living up to them while President Nixon provided a materialistic narrative that provided a context for the ways that Americans were living their lives (Fisher 1973).

The party conventions have become an important theatrical stage from which the parties enact their versions of the American dream. Smith and Nimmo (1991) analyzed conventions as grand opera with individuals coming forth to represent or recite motifs that would be expanded into arias or recitatives in their speeches. We now see speeches in which speaker after speaker tells an "American story." We see documentaries of the American experience. We see musical performances and thematic evenings. These are then ultimately woven together into the nominee's acceptance address. Each acceptance address seeks to capture the essential meaning of America – what we have been at our best and what we can be in the future.

It is interesting to track each party's acceptance addresses for their consistencies and changes, as well as to contrast the competing dreams in a particular election. Normally the dreams discussed are sufficiently ambiguous that audiences can fill in their own specifics. This enables the candidate to foster identification within the party while polarizing it from the other party's dream or vision. This makes convention speeches a poor moment for the discussion of policy specifics and a better place to call for general directions like tax reform, national security, and health care for all.

Occasionally we hear about an American nightmare that we must strive to avoid. This is where the use of the "American jeremiad" discussed in Chapter 6 can be used to consolidate and to divide one party from the other. Recall that the jeremiad argues that the audience is a unique people endowed with a sacred mission, whose trials and tribulations are explained either as tests of their faith in their core principles or as punishment for straying from their sacred mission. Jeremiads can therefore consolidate support by emphasizing potential supporters' shared narrative and core principles and challenging them to recommit to those principles as set forth by the nominee.

The national conventions' roll call of states legitimizes the nominees. Although some partisans may harbor doubts the nominee is their only chance for the White

House for four years. The parties also legitimize their nominees by having as many notable partisans as possible address the convention, signalling their unity and support for the nominee.

Campaigns Enhance their Infrastructure

The political convention component of Stage 3 provides invaluable opportunities for personal networking. Like other professional conventions most of the important business at a political convention takes place in the restaurants, hotel lobbies, hospitality suites, meetings, and bars rather than on the convention floor. Many delegates are simply too busy to attend all of the floor sessions. It is in these informal sessions that party faithful meet their counterparts from other states, talk to national personnel who can help them do their jobs and sign on to help the presidential campaign in their state.

Recall that groups are held together not only by their shared visions but also by the process of co-creating them with communication. Conventions provide opportunities for such communication for those who attend. They provide important interpersonal contacts that are different from the national televisual experience. Internet communication is increasingly supplementing these personal contacts, but we saw how internet contact let to Meetup.com because face-to-face interaction is important in its own right. Social networking through Facebook and My Space came into their own as tools for consolidation in 2008. But it is almost impossible to conceive of political parties as functioning organizations in a complex society without these extended opportunities for face-to-face contact. This is an important element of consolidation, because policy and value differences can often by overcome, or compounded, by personal communication.

Parties and Networks Shape Conventions as Party Meetings or Television Spectacles

Only newspapers covered political conventions for well over a century. By 1928 radio was sufficiently established to permit live broadcasting of conventions and they became a staple of the election spectacle. Conventions were first televised in 1948, and the few viewers able to watch saw Strom Thurmond lead southern delegates out of the Democratic Convention to protest a proposed civil rights platform plank. This was live television drama, and when the parties realized that they had a huge potential audience via this new medium they staged longer celebrations with more signs and balloons for the cameras; color television eventually meant even more balloons.

Television thrives on dramatic audio-visual moments and conventions have the potential to provide them. But there is an important inverse relationship between consolidating (the essence of Stage 3) and the drama that television magnifies. A party that consolidates effectively provides a dull convention for television, and dramatic conventions undermine the consolidation that is the central purpose of conventions. Media organizations and campaign organizations seem not to understand this about one another's tasks, with consequences that are unfortunate for the rest of us.

The two most dramatic conventions were the 1964 Republican convention and the 1968 Democratic convention. Goldwater – a staunch conservative whose theme was "A choice, not an echo" was not overly interested in consolidating with the Rockefeller liberals, and Rockefeller had little use for Goldwater's backers. Some of those concerned about the narrowness of the Goldwater campaign introduced a motion for the Republicans to condemn extremism in America, including the Ku Klux Klan and the John Birch Society. Rockefeller took the podium to speak in favor of the motion and he was thunderously booed by those in attendance, many of whom sympathized with the Birchers if not the KKK. Even today, the video is chilling. The Governor of New York is prevented from speaking by members of his own party because he wanted to condemn extremists, and the audience of delegates acts as a Greek Chorus seeming to demonstrate that his party was indeed rife with extremists. It was dramatic television that left the Republicans badly divided as they entered the campaign against Johnson.

The 1968 Democrats were divided among supporters of the Johnson–Humphrey administration, opponents of federal integration efforts who supported George Wallace, and opponents of the Vietnam War who had supported Eugene McCarthy, George McGovern, and the late Robert Kennedy. There were large scale anti-war protests in the streets of Chicago, and television cameras cut back and forth between the convention floor and the demonstrations, providing television viewers with a story unseen by the delegates. Chicago Mayor Daley had Connecticut Senator Abraham Ribicoff removed from the hall for criticizing the city's handling of the demonstrations. Again, television maximized the drama and severely undermined consolidation.

It should come as little surprise, then, that by the 1970s the parties had begun to script their conventions to minimize conflict. Party platform debates previously held at the convention during prime time were conducted by commissions away from the cameras. Where nominations had been decided with multiple ballots they were now decided by primaries and caucuses that allocated delegates ahead of time. By the 1990s even the suspense over the vice-presidential nominee's identity was over, as it was announced ahead of time.

Critics of the conventions, mostly in the television industry, called them nothing more than infomercials. They are basically correct – as far as television is concerned. Both parties put on a prime-time television show and minimized conflict. Why should they do otherwise? Their objective during Stage 3 is to consolidate their people, not to divide them. Nor is it their objective to fill the networks' summer viewing schedules. The conventions are an important – actually, the only – opportunity for viewers to put names and faces together with ideas and arguments. But the benefits of reaching citizens in that way are lost if viewers see only a food fight among delegates.

A network's decision about convention coverage has important implications. C-SPAN provides gavel-to-gavel coverage of the podium. This allows us to have a historical record of every speech and presentation in its entirety. It has always been C-SPAN's policy to decide what events are worth broadcasting and then to broadcast them in their entirety. They care what is important, not what is "interesting." The three traditional commercial networks – ABC, CBS, and NBC – make their money from the advertising they sell for entertainment programs, and conventions are both expensive to produce and low return for them. Thus they have devoted fewer and fewer hours of their prime time programming to the conventions. Much of their coverage consists of their anchors and correspondents reporting on the convention, with frequent cutaways from the podium. Thus C-SPAN lets the parties speak to America without selectivity or interpretation while the commercial networks maximize selectivity and interpretation.

In between those extremes are Public Broadcasting and the cable news channels (Fox, MSNBC, and CNN). By devoting more hours to the conventions they are able to provide more coverage of the speeches while also providing interpretation. But because these networks aim their telecasts at consistent year-round news audiences, their coverage and analyses may be seen to have more predictable or characteristic styles of reporting. Fox News is regarded by many television viewers to be the most angry and most conservative, CNN to be the most "politically correct" and PBS the most dispassionate and informative – but these are loose characterizations and should not be taken too seriously.

What convention coverage, then, should one watch? Ideally, each of us should strive for a mix of coverage of both conventions. We can all benefit from watching the important officials of both parties talk to each other and to us. Nobody who watches all of both conventions with any level of serious open-mindedness can truly say, "These people are all alike." Somewhere along the line each of us will probably find ourselves identifying with the arguments, values, experiences, and personalities of one party more than the other (which is not to say that we will not feel at all conflicted). Moreover, we can benefit from watching the extended discourse on C-SPAN rather than brief excerpts on the news. But we also need some analytical context for the claims and support, because it is not safe to take all politicians' arguments at face value. Similarly, it is as unwise to rely on the same analysts all of the time as it is to rely on the same politicians all of the time. A healthy convention diet is well-balanced.

Transitioning to Stage 4: The Acceptance Speeches

Although televised conventions provide an opportunity to reach a large audience, it does so at a price. Television seeks the very sort of dramatic conflict that consolidation seeks to resolve. As television has conveyed those conflicts, the parties have responded by scripting conventions and keeping their conflict management off camera. It is important to remember that conventions serve functions for those who attend that differ from those of us who watch on television.

The critics' carping about conventions notwithstanding, there are four nights of televised partisan in-gathering, couched in many more hours of speculative punditry. Party members use speeches of varied lengths and quality as well as videos and entertainment pieces to extol their core virtues and to revile those of the opposing parties. Many of these seem silly: Which party gets the cool actors? Who gets the most notable singers? Is the social diversity on stage or in the audience? But for four days, everything is a communication act designed to identify with some and to divide the party from the others.

The final night of the convention is the nominee's acceptance address. It needs to provide maximum identification of the candidate with the intended

Reagan's Acceptance Speech

supporters and maximum division from the other party. It must also so energize those who hear it that they cannot wait to share their party, issues, and candidate with the folks back home.

Consolidating by Focusing the Party

Senator Barry Goldwater of Arizona won the 1964 Republican nomination against a variety of liberal and moderate opponents. The eastern or liberal wing of the party had controlled the nomination process for decades, and there was widespread concern that Goldwater represented only a minority of Republicans. So intense was the division within the party that Pennsylvania Governor Bill Scranton led a last-ditch effort to wrest the nomination from Goldwater. Just before the convention Goldwater received a letter from Scranton that asked, "will the convention choose the candidate overwhelmingly favored by the Republican voters, or will it choose you?" The letter went on to say, among other things:

> You have too often casually prescribed nuclear war as a solution to a troubled world. You have too often allowed the radical extremists to use you. You have too often stood for irresponsibility in the serious question of racial holocaust. You have too often read Taft and Eisenhower and Lincoln out of the Republican Party.   (Scranton, quoted in Friedenberg 2002, p. 89)

Scranton closed by writing that, "In short, Goldwaterism has come to stand for a whole crazy quilt collection of absurd and dangerous positions that would be soundly repudiated by the American people in November" (Scranton, quoted in

Friedenberg 2002, p. 89). One can only wonder how Scranton expected Goldwater to react to the letter, but it clearly conveys the need for consolidation.

What can one do with such a rhetorical situation? How might Goldwater have constrained the thoughts and feelings of liberal Republicans so angry and fearful of his candidacy? Goldwater advisor Stephen Shadegg would later write that it was a time to have the prominent liberals such as George Romney, Nelson Rockefeller, Bill Scranton, Jacob Javits, Kenneth Keating, Mark Hatfield, and John Lindsay "invited to the platform. Such an invitation, couched in the proper language, would have been most difficult for a Republican to reject" (quoted in Friedenberg 2002, p. 98). But he did not do so.

Alternatively, Goldwater might have found a way to include in his speech praise for the contributions of such liberal Republicans, but he did not. He might have included some of their issues in his message to broaden the scope of his message, but he did not. Instead, Barry Goldwater presented a straightforward statement of his conservative philosophy before concluding with the line for which he is remembered:

> Anyone who joins us in all sincerity we welcome. Those, those who do not care for our cause, we don't expect to enter our ranks in any case. And let our Republicanism so focused and so dedicated not be made fuzzy and futile by unthinking and stupid labels. I would remind you that extremism in the defense of liberty is no vice. And let me remind you also that moderation in the pursuit of justice is no virtue.   (Goldwater 1964)

Goldwater's supporters roared with delight, while the liberal Republicans regarded it as frightening.

Goldwater's address consolidated his support by focusing and purifying it. It did not consolidate the Republican Party because it did not try to do so. It is clear from the nominee's own words that he sought to "focus" and "dedicate" those who agreed with him and to dismiss those who did not. As Scranton's letter had predicted, Goldwater was repudiated at the polls, garnering only 38 percent of the popular vote and losing to President Johnson 486–52. But his campaign marked the beginning of the end of liberal Republicanism and opened the door for conservative Democrats in the deep south, angered initially by the Kennedy–Johnson efforts on behalf of racial equality, to turn to the Republican Party.

Consolidating with New Beginnings

When their 1968 convention convened in Chicago, Hubert Humphrey had the support of the majority of the Democratic delegates but those who backed McCarthy, Kennedy, and McGovern to oppose the Vietnam war sought to block his nomination. Demonstrators streamed in to protest, the police steeled themselves to preserve order and violence erupted in the streets of Chicago in what the Kerner Commission would characterize as a police riot. Of course, any attempt by Humphrey to bridge the divide with the anti-war liberals would further alienate those inclined to follow Wallace or Republican Richard Nixon.

Humphrey accepted the Democratic nomination on August 29, 1968 in a speech very different from Goldwater's to the Republicans four years earlier. He moved quickly to address the divisions in reflection rather than anger:

> one cannot help but reflect the deep sadness that we feel over the troubles and the violence which have erupted regrettably and tragically in the streets of this great city, and for the personal injuries which have occurred. Surely we have learned the lesson that violence breeds more violence and that it cannot be condoned – whatever the source. (Humphrey 1968)

Having found a lesson in the violence, Humphrey found inspiration in prayer:

> I know that every delegate to this Convention shares tonight my sorrow and my distress for these incidents. And may we, for just one moment, in sober reflection, in serious purpose, may we just quietly and silently – each in our own way – pray for our country. And may we just share for a moment a few of those immortal words of the prayer of St. Francis of Assisi – words which I think may help heal the wounds and lift our hearts. Listen to this immortal saint: "Where there is hatred, let me sow love; where there is injury, pardon; where there is doubt, faith; where there is despair, hope; where there is darkness, light." (Humphrey 1968)

Having sanctified the lesson, Humphrey noted that America has faced and grown from comparable crises throughout our shared past:

> This is not the first time that our nation has faced a challenge to its life and its purpose. Each time that we have faced these challenges, we have emerged with new greatness and with new strength. We must make this moment of crisis a moment of creation. As it has been said: "In the worst of times, a great people must do the best of things." (Humphrey 1968)

At a time when media observers and many in politics were characterizing the upheaval as the beginning of the end of Democratic coalition, Humphrey recast it as an opportunity for a new beginning.

> We stand at such a moment now – in the affairs of this nation. Because, my fellow Americans, something new, something different has happened. It is the end of an era and is the beginning of a new day. (Humphrey 1968)

Calls for change may be terminal crises for some, but for Humphrey such calls for change pose no threat to Democrats.

> It is the special genius of the Democratic Party that it welcomes change, not as an enemy but as an ally . . . not as a force to be suppressed, but as an instrument of progress to be encouraged . . . Had we papered over differences with empty platitudes instead of frank, hard debate, we would deserve the contempt of our fellow citizens and the condemnation of history. (Humphrey 1968)

He invoked Democratic Presidents Franklin D. Roosevelt, Harry Truman, John Kennedy, and even the unpopular Johnson as well as Robert Kennedy and former nominee Adlai Stevenson and "his friends" Eugene McCarthy and George McGovern, and explicitly asked for their help. Humphrey then argued for closure:

> Democracy affords debate, discussion and dissent. But it also requires decision. And we have decided, here, not by edict but by vote – not by force but by ballot. Majority rule *has* prevailed, while minority rights *are* preserved. There is always the temptation to leave the scene of battle in anger and despair, but those who

know the true meaning of democracy accept the decision of today, but never relinquish their right to change it tomorrow.   (Humphrey 1968)

He went on to use the remainder of his speech to speak of his commitment to "the necessity for peace in Vietnam and in the world," "the necessity for peace in our cities and in our nation" and "the paramount necessity for unity in our country" (Humphrey 1968).

Although Richard Nixon won the 1968 election with a decisive 301–191 electoral vote margin, Humphrey had closed the popular vote gap to less than one percent. After the McCarthy and Kennedy challenges to Johnson's war in Vietnam, Wallace's challenge to Johnson's civil rights program, the murders of Martin Luther King, Jr. and Robert Kennedy and the Democratic convention debacle, Humphrey lost by only 512,000 out of seventy million votes. Moreover it was not, in the end, the anti-war liberals who cost Humphrey the election, but the nine million who voted for Wallace and gave him forty-six electoral votes.

Summary and Conclusions

Winning a party's presidential nomination is an extremely difficult feat and the Nomination Stage battles leave wounds that the nominees must heal if they hope to win. We saw in this chapter that each party's consolidation stage begins as soon as its nominee has been decided and extends through the nominee's acceptance address, meaning that each party can be working through the challenges of different stages for a time. We saw that:

- The ultimate exigency of Stage 3 is to produce a unified and enthusiastic following for the nominee.
- To do so the nominee must maximize the common ground and minimize the divisions among potential supporters without losing the support of those responsible for winning the nomination.
- Republican nominees must find ways to draw Enterprisers, Social Conservatives and Pro-Government Conservatives together and Democratic nominees must find ways to draw Liberals, Conservative Democrats and Disadvantaged Democrats together.

The nature of the consolidation stage creates peculiar communication dynamics. We saw that these dynamics include:

- Nominees' communication with six audiences to consolidate support: activated supporters, activated partisan opponents, partisans yet to be activated, supporters of the other party and its nominee, undecided/independent/cross-pressured voters and reporters/pundits/bloggers. Each of these audiences requires different messages.
- Nominees redefine "we" and "they" so that their new "us" includes supporters of their primary opponents whose shortcomings now pale in comparison to the opposition party.
- Nominees engage in fence mending by appearing with their defeated opponents and by speaking to critical audiences. But only the wary supporters can enact the consolidation.

- Nominees do what they can to divide the opposition, or at least complicate their consolidation.
- Nominees interpret the moralistic and materialistic dimensions of the "American dream" for their followers.
- Campaigns enhance their infrastructure by meeting face to face in convention to network and develop working relationships for future campaigns.
- Both parties engage in a struggle with the television networks over coverage of the campaign. The networks provide more hours of coverage for conventions they expect to feature conflict while the parties do their best to reduce conflict and want coverage for conventions that showcase their unity.

Acceptance addresses are the transition from Stage 3 to 4. We saw that Barry Goldwater consolidated his support by purifying his coalition of non-believers. We also saw that Hubert Humphrey consolidated support by speaking of a historic moment of common crisis in which Democrats understood how to use change as an instrument of progress. Thus the acceptance address is both the culmination of the consolidation stage and the opening salvo in Stage 4 – the election stage.

14 The Election Stage

It is in Stage 4 that the presidential nominees finally lead their forces out of their conventions to do battle with the other party. The terminal exigency of Stage 4 is to win more votes than the opposition in state contests sufficient to win at least 270 electoral votes. Although voters might reasonably expect a campaign to answer the question, "How would you govern us?" the pragmatists running the campaigns realize that they must win before they can govern. That realization motivates them to maximize contrasts, even over relatively minor points, to polarize the electorate into two camps.

Normally the campaign has a nominee with a vision and lots of supporters. But sometimes the nominee has a vision and relatively few supporters (Barry Goldwater in 1964 and George McGovern in 1972) or lots of supporters without a crystal vision (Bob Dole in 1996 and John Kerry in 2004). In any case, the regular season is over and the playoffs have begun. The campaigns crank up their familiar rituals. Bumper stickers and yard signs multiply. Radio and television ads engage one another. The candidates hit the campaign trail, speaking regularly and emphatically. And the campaigns and media begin to debate about debates. The communication dynamics of Stage 4 are underway.

The Communication Dynamics of the Election Stage

It is especially tempting in Stage 4 to discuss advertising campaigns, debates, news coverage, speaking at rallies, and new media. But, as we discussed in Part II, it is the coordinated mix of those communication modes by the campaigns to implement their strategy that is most important. We will therefore examine the larger dynamics of this stage that result from all of those modes.

The Focus on Battleground States

By the beginning of Stage 4 both campaigns have a good grasp of the electoral landscape. They know which states they have no chance to win and which states they cannot lose. Their attention therefore shifts to the states that will decide the electoral vote outcome – the battleground states.

The battleground strategy emerged in 1992, when Republicans had won five of six presidential elections and there was much talk of a "Republican lock" on the electoral college. Clinton strategist James Carville decided to pick that lock by abandoning the old strategy of campaigning everywhere. The Clinton campaign spent 90 percent of their resources in five crucial "battleground" states, carried four of them and won the election with 43 percent of the popular vote.

Republicans adopted the strategy and recent campaigns have focused on battle-ground states to the general exclusion of others.

The major challenge in Stage 4 is to keep one's core electoral votes safe while adding the battleground states necessary to win. The first step toward solving this puzzle is to analyze the states' voting histories and current electoral strength.

Table 14.1 shows five states' presidential votes since 1988. When that pattern holds a Republican will trail the Democrat in electoral votes, 31–14. But Republicans have been 12–0 in Alabama and Utah but 1–5 in New York, so why should they spend one dollar in any of those states? Notice that Arkansas and Ohio offer 26 electoral votes between them and Republican victories there would vault them ahead of the Democrats, 40–31. That makes Arkansas and Ohio the keys to victory – the "battleground states." Although Republicans are only 4–2 in Arkansas they lost there only when Bill Clinton and Ross Perot (both with local ties) were on the ballot. The Ohio results are 3–3.

Thus the strategy should be to (1) spend almost nothing in Alabama, New York, or Utah, (2) spend as little as necessary in Arkansas to keep it leaning Republican and (3) pour the rest of those resources into the most volatile and valuable state: Ohio.

When the table is complete for all fifty states we can sort it by times won (high to low) then by party average (high to low). The top row would then be the state won six times with the highest average percentage of the vote and the bottom row would be the electoral votes never won. The next step is to add the electoral votes from the top row down, highlighting the state that puts the candidate over 270.

Even a strong campaign must sometimes choose between losing a state from the base and pursuing a battleground state. When things are going well a campaign may challenge the opponent's safe states, if only to frighten them into redirecting their resources away from the battlegrounds.

Having partitioned the nation into safe and battleground states, the second rhetorical task is to influence the swing voters necessary to win the battleground states without losing one's core vote. We are too often inclined to presume that those swing voters are undecided, but only polling and focus groups can ascertain why voters change their behavior from year to year. Some of these people could be committed to single issues (such as abortion, social security, or the environment), they may vote for whichever candidate they believe comes closest to their views on that one issue (or they could stay home). But one can also win by inducing the opponents' soft supporters not to vote.

For a candidate seeking to win an electoral college majority, the wisdom of battleground strategy is undeniable. But there is an implicit cost to the nation: the battleground strategy insulates most of our citizens from the debate over the future of our country. I was able to observe this disparity personally during the 2000 presidential campaign. At that time I was working in Detroit, Michigan (a highly competitive battleground state), and spending most weekends at our family home in North Carolina (a safe Bush state). Detroit television stations aired wall-to-wall presidential commercials, but there were hardly any presidential commercials broadcast in North Carolina. Candidates Bush and Gore came to Detroit (Gore visited our campus twice) but neither candidate campaigned in North Carolina. ABC's "Good Morning America" broadcast live from our campus

Table 14.1. Republican Success Since 1988

State	2008	2004	2000	1996	1992	1988	Repub. Avg.	Range	Won	2008 EVs
Alabama	61	62.46	56.47	50.12	47.65	59.17	55.17	15	6	9
Arkansas	59	54.31	51.31	36.80	35.48	56.37	46.85	24	4	6
New York	36	40.08	35.23	30.61	33.88	51.62	38.28	21	1	31
Ohio	47	50.81	49.97	41.02	38.35	55.0	47.03	17	3	20
Utah	63	71.54	66.83	54.37	43.36	66.22	60.46	28	6	5

in Detroit on election morning while North Carolinians watched. In 2004 our Ohio relatives got the messages while Michiganders and North Carolinians watched. The point is that voters in battleground states receive disproportionate candidate communication while voters in "safe" states get little direct communication with candidates. Thus the strategists' rhetorical choice to communicate directly with voters in battleground states is essentially a decision to disengage from voters in the other states, leaving their political learning to the media. This hardly invigorates our national conversation about the direction of the country.

Fortunately, the battleground states vary somewhat from election to election. Although voting histories matter, so do individual candidates, current issues, and other variables. California has recently been a safe Democratic state, but not when Californians Richard Nixon and Ronald Reagan were the Republican nominees. Population changes, such as the increasing number of Latino voters in many states, are making some states more competitive and others less so.

Is there a way out of the battleground problem? Many have suggested that eliminating the electoral college would solve the problem by basing the contest on the national popular vote. But in all likelihood this would simply change the battleground approach because there will always be safe states and tightly contested states and a tipping point where the electoral vote majority is at stake. In any case, the battleground strategy provides the state audiences. The next dynamic relates to the campaign's message.

Rhetorical Agendas and Branding

Stage 4 kicks off when the nominee's acceptance speech introduces the rhetorical agenda. Crucially, the rhetorical agenda is not necessarily the party's policy agenda; the policy agenda is what they plan to do once in office, whereas the rhetorical agenda is what they plan to argue (and how). My father grew up in Millersburg, Pennsylvania on the banks of the Susquehanna River. He used to recall how rocks would be arranged across the river every year to raise the water level enough for the car ferry to continue its run from Millersburg to the other side of the river. My dad would shake of his head and recall that since he was a boy some candidate would always promise to build a bridge, but when he died at age eighty-five there was still no bridge. The bridge was on the rhetorical agenda, but the ferry was on the policy agenda, and anyone building such a bridge would need a new rhetorical agenda for Millersburg audiences.

Like the Millersburg bridge, some policy agendas maintain their rhetorical potency through political inaction. You can probably associate the following rhetorical agenda items with the political parties that have voiced them for many years.

1. "We will fight to protect your social security from their cuts."
2. "We will fight to cut your taxes; they want to take your money."
3. "We have the strongest military in the world and cannot allow ourselves to be pushed around."

4. "As the most powerful nation in the world we have a responsibility to act as a Good Neighbor and build friendships."

Statements 1 (Democrats) and 2 (Republicans) encourage mistrust and even fear of the other party and position the speaker as a sort of firewall between the dangerous opposition and the vulnerable voters. Statements 3 (Republicans) and 4 (Democrats) have been popular in campaigns, but when it comes time to govern, presidents often combine them, as in President Kennedy's famous inaugural pledge, "we will never negotiate out of fear, but we should never fear to negotiate." Stage 4 is not about governing but about contesting visions, and to do that candidates simplify and sharpen differences.

A party's rhetorical agenda should at least allude to who is going to do what, where it will be done, why, when and how. Consider a hypothetical campaign vision called, "Traditional Values in a Global Economy." Whose traditional values are we talking about and whose global economy (the disposed textile workers or the multi-national corporations)? What are we going to do – export those traditional values to China and India or adopt their traditional values? Will this be done in Washington or the states, in our churches or in our individual hearts? Why will this be done, to become better or to return to our roots or to boost our economic standing? Will this be done immediately during the winner's first 100 days, during the presidential term or over the long haul? And finally, how will it be accomplished – with legislative programs, with public–private partnerships or through individual reflection? Of course, details invite scrutiny and attack from the opposition and from the media, but ambiguity invites not only scrutiny but misrepresentation ("My opponent plans to . . . ").

A party that stumbles upon a rhetorical agenda that works would be foolish not to use it again. As they return to the same themes in campaign after campaign they develop shorthand ways of expressing their arguments in phrases and slogans. Rhetorical theorist Michael C. McGee (1980) termed these ideographs – phrases that express an ideological stance or argument in a few words. The power of ideographs is to be found in their simple and abstract rendition of some very complicated and concrete value and policy problems. It is much easier to rally around "balanced budgets" or "health care for all" or "lower taxes" than it is to figure out how to balance the budget or how to provide health care or how to lower taxes without undermining important functions and services. Similarly, it is easier to display bumper stickers that say "Support Our Troops" or "End the War" than it is to determine the best way to support those serving in our military or the best way to end the war.

As parties return to the same ideographs in campaign after campaign they develop rhetorical or symbolic capital. There is an important policy difference between advocating abortions and thinking that the decision about abortion should be personal rather than governmental. Thus the ideograph "A woman's right to choose" has greater rhetorical capital than does "I am pro-abortion" or "I am anti-life." Sharon Jarvis (2005) has shown how political parties establish brand identities for themselves, much as do products, by establishing enduring identities.

Thus the rhetorical agenda set forth in each party's vision will be heavily influenced by the brand identity the party has developed and adapted to the current exigency. Much of each vision will therefore seem familiar to voters. But there are new applications and specifics to be learned.

Contrasting Brands and Visions to Polarize the Electorate

During the election stage the campaigns bombard us with speeches, debates, commercials, and mailings, the media feed us news reports, jokes, and polls and our friends and co-workers engage us in conversations and arguments. There is a certain amount of unpleasantness to it all, and as we wish for the downpour of political messages to stop we can easily lose sight of the larger rhetorical purpose of these messages. While we would all like to see a presidential campaign unite us behind the next president the fact is that there are at least two starkly divided camps that want that to happen.

Stage 4 presidential campaign communication must polarize rather than unify voters. The point of all the messages is to contrast the brands or visions in a way that compels voters to choose sides. That is why campaigns get "nasty" at this point. Both campaigns look for the issues, arguments, symbols, and words that will put the final squeeze on those voters who have managed, until Stage 4, to remain aloof.

Stage 4 is less a search for common ground than it is a search for the phrases that divide the country into a majority supporting one candidate and a minority who do not. Thus it is mainly polarization – identification by division. But with two major parties doing this, each normally offers a different frame – one may use national security and the other economics, or one may use policies and the other character. Candidates attack their opponents from their frame, minimizing similarities and exaggerating contrasts.

Stage 4 polarizes the nation into two or more imagined communities. Each develops a shared vision complete with preferred language, values, slogans, and people as well as devil terms. But supporters are not necessarily voters and voters are not necessarily supporters. Moreover, the more polarized the nation becomes during Stage 4 the more difficult it will be for the eventual winner to be truly accepted as the President of *All* the People. Yet a candidate cannot hope to win a majority of the electors without differentiating "us" from "them."

Challenger and Incumbent Moves

Each candidate made an important choice during the initial or surfacing stage. By deciding to run as incumbent or challenger each staked out some rhetorical resources and relinquished others. By Stage 4 that choice has become extremely important. Nominees use incumbent and rhetorical styles differently to contest their respective claims to the White House, as the 2000 campaign shows.

Vice-President Gore was well positioned to exploit the advantages of an incumbent style, but he either relinquished, or executed poorly, most of the strategies available to him. Apparently unable to differentiate between the popular *policies* of the Clinton–Gore administration and disapproval of Clinton's *personal* character, Gore distanced himself from their eight-year policy record. Instead of campaigning on their Administration's accomplishments he minimized them and called for change. Rather than emphasizing their progress since the last Bush administration Gore critiqued the status quo and promised to fight for change. By relinquishing the rhetoric of incumbency Gore did something that Bush could not do for himself – he created a rhetorical contest between two challengers for the post-Clinton presidency (Smith and Mansharamani 2002).

Bush then executed the challenger strategies at least as well as Gore. Read the mood of the country as satisfied with the general direction of policies Bush charged that Clinton and Gore had been ineffective leaders. Gore described a nation fraught with problems and promised to fight against the system (of which he was vice-president). Gore proposed costly plans and pledged specifics while Bush stressed civility, cooperation, implementation of existing policies, and tax cuts premised on Clinton–Gore's sound economy.

Bush even took advantage of Gore's abandoned incumbency to run on his own limited executive record. It was Bush who sought the endorsement of government and military officials and backed the "don't ask, don't tell" policy on gays in the military. When Gore donned casual clothing to soften his image, Bush looked all the more presidential in his suit. When the second debate turned to foreign policy Bush endorsed most administration policies while Gore suggested alterations. The study of the Bush–Gore campaign identified three dimensions of the challenger and incumbent roles that refined the rhetorical themes used in political campaigns: are insider–outsider, continuity–change, and same vs. new persona (Smith and Mansharamani 2002).

The *insider–outsider dimension* of the challenger/incumbent typology locates the candidate in the political universe. In its simplest form the incumbent works in the White House and the challenger works elsewhere. "Give 'em Hell" President Harry S. Truman won in 1948 by running as the challenger to the Republican Congress's Washington establishment. This "challenger president" script would later guide several other incumbents. One can be a *positional leader* or not – as when Ross Perot mounted his first presidential campaign without a party or legitimate political office. The "positional insider" stance – identifiable in the campaigns of Michael Dukakis and Bob Dole – is "I can do this job because I have credentials, experience and access that will benefit those who support me." The positional outsider – Jesse Ventura, Ross Perot, and Jimmy Carter – says, "I can do this job because I have no political/governmental credentials, I am not part of the problems that face us, and I have spent my working life understanding the real world and ordinary Americans."

The *geographic insider* is a creature of Washington (or city hall or the state capitol, as the case may be). The geographic component of the insider–outsider dimension relates to the campaign's decision to situate itself. At one end of the continuum is Richard Neustadt's (1960) emphasis of the importance of Washingtonians to presidential success – a position that is today reflected in the equation of being "inside the Beltway" with being in the loop. The beltway stance implies that the barbarians are at the gates, anxious to destroy all that they are accomplishing. At the other end of that continuum is what Charles U. Larson (2001) terms the "wisdom of the rustic" – the claim to wisdom by those like Will Rogers, Harry Truman, and Lamar Alexander because of their distance from decision making. This rusticity often carries the presumption of purity as well as wisdom, and has often been offered as an antidote to the "mess in Washington."

In short, an insider could claim positional experience and familiarity with the geographic power center (whether accurate or not) whereas an outsider would identify a source of expertise apparently unrelated to the office sought and a geographic identity outside the beltway. Bush continually emphasized Texas to distance himself from Washington and his executive experience. For his part, Gore minimized his positional importance and aligned himself with neither Washington nor the hinterland, but engaged in a populist fighting record that served neither purpose well.

The *continuity–change dimension* of the challenger/incumbent typology concerns the candidate's policy rhetoric. The first dimension is the actual set of *policy* proposals embedded in the candidate's agenda and the party's platform – putting more teachers in the schools and more policemen on the street, restoring pride in the military, cutting taxes, and so forth.

The second component of the continuity–change dimension is the candidate's overarching style of *discourse* as a candidate of continuity or change – a style that may or may not match the policy proposals. A discourse of change can urge us forward toward a utopian age or back toward a golden age, but it is unwilling to settle for things as they are. A discourse of continuity urges patience, incrementalism and the risks of change. It mixes ideology and power – liberals may like change but not if it puts their policies at risk and conservatives may oppose change but not their own initiatives. Ronald Reagan was an activist conservative whereas Democrats' defense of Great Society programs illustrates retentive liberalism.

In short, a candidate of continuity would reiterate its goals and urge incremental pursuit of its agenda, whereas a candidate of change would articulate new goals and set forth a new agenda. Between the two archetypes fall candidates who cloak a lengthy list of policy initiatives in a rhetoric of continuity and those who urge major change without articulating the policies that would produce that change. Gore urged change rather than continuity despite widespread support for the administration's policies. Bush aligned himself with the administration's general conduct of foreign policy, supported (perhaps reluctantly) existing gun control and abortion laws and pursued a course of incremental change. The differences between Gore and Bush in terms of continuity–change were minimal, with Gore seeming to be the candidate with grander goals and aspirations.

The *same persona–new persona* dimension draws our attention to the face and character of the administration. A positional incumbent can suggest that the next term will be similar to or different from the first term, and a challenger can suggest a new style or more of the same style. In 1988 George Bush was able to cultivate the impression that he would be the extension of the Reagan–Bush administration, partly with the help of Reagan speechwriter Peggy Noonan. Similarly, Lyndon Johnson's 1964 landslide election was attributable in part to the Kennedy holdovers and his "Let Us Continue" theme.

Normally, we would expect a challenger to critique the incumbent's persona and to call for a new style of leadership. For example, the Carter campaign described the Nixon–Ford administration as dishonest and pledged never to lie, the Reagan campaign characterized President Carter as overwhelmed by the demands of the office and pledged to take charge, and the Clinton campaign depicted Reagan's heir, Bush, as being afraid to change in a changing world. Embedded in these depictions is the incumbent's willingness and ability to use wisely the resources of the office for the good of the country. In 2000 Bush pressed for a persona change – from incivility to cooperation and from "making change our friend" to "compassionate conservatism." Gore's persona was unpredictable. Would he be another Clinton, a casual everyman, a tax and spend liberal, a rude know-it-all, or some combination of them all? Bush presented a steady persona that contrasted with Clinton while Gore's effort to avoid Clinton's reputation presented too many faces.

Situationally, the election of 2000 was Gore's to lose – and lose it he did. He lost it by relinquishing the positional insider, continuity, and consistent persona advantages of the incumbent. By doing so Gore made it a race between two challengers, and Bush was better able than Gore to present a case for change. More than that, Gore allowed Bush to claim elements of incumbency – a sound economy that permitted tax cuts, enforcement of existing laws and implementation of existing policies, and a consistent personae. By election day, many voters were able to prefer Bush to preside over an era of presumed peace, prosperity, and incremental change. Only then were ballots counted.

Political Learning

It is helpful for Stage 4 to stimulate political learning about the election, candidates, and issues. Notice that I said "political learning," not "education." Presidential rhetoric scholar Theodore O. Windt liked to say that anyone who depends on politicians for education is either naive or stupid. Especially in the heat of presidential campaigns, political candidates and their advocates teach with an agenda – winning the election and gaining (or retaining) power. It is uncertain whether those who rely exclusively on talk shows or journalists are substantially better off than those who rely only on politicians.

Stage 4 stimulates *selective* learning. Because the national agenda is to decide between the contested visions, we seek out, process, and retain information that we find useful and we simultaneously avoid, process, and forget information that we find unhelpful. Early mass communication research found that audience members paid selective attention to messages that addressed their personal needs, that they selectively perceived messages so that they fit comfortably with their existing beliefs, and that they selectively retained messages that reinforced their needs and beliefs. The proliferation of cable channels and web sites has increased our opportunities for selectivity.

Our ability to bookmark web sites and to save a list of our favorite television channels (while deleting the others) has made it easy for us to keep up with news that reinforces our beliefs and preferences, lest we encounter information that makes us uncomfortable. Unfortunately, it is increasingly difficult for us to be truly well informed by maintaining a healthy diet of discrepant information. In the old days (before CNN, Fox, and the rest) ABC, CNS, and NBC had to provide news that satisfied the informational needs of fewer, larger, and hence more diverse audiences. Today's political learning encourages polarization between the visions rather than broad understanding of the overarching considerations or underlying facts. A 2004 study found that Bush and Kerry supporters believed substantially different facts to be true (Kull 2004). But this is the world in which we live.

Once one has "facts," what does one do with them? Professional reporters are trained to see those facts through a narrative lens that embeds them in stories. In practice, that means superimposing a narrative form on those facts. There must be characters, plots, settings, conflicts, and resolutions. But the increasing speed of communication in the twenty-first century has increased the demand for non-resolution resolutions – news reports that there are no new developments . . . yet, but stay tuned. Such reports heighten the drama of news, but they inhibit our ability to analyze longer term trends carefully.

During the question-and-answer period following a 2007 address at Wake Forest University, CBS Chief Political Correspondent Bob Schieffer responded to a question about media bias. Schieffer said that his fifty years of experience in journalism had convinced him that there might be a handful of reporters who followed their political predispositions, but that the overwhelming majority of professional journalists were committed to getting the story. As many social scientists are reluctant to see that "value-free" research is itself a value perspective, journalists as distinguished as Bob Schieffer are often slow to recognize the bias of the story framework itself.

What the news media choose to cover and how they cover it is an important contributor to what we learn about the contested visions. As each of us seeks to reach a voting decision we look for help in understanding the candidates' respective visions and the important implications for our lives. But the news media's "horse race" coverage provides us with more help understanding who is likely to win than in understanding what they plan to do. This should not be surprising because that is the more dramatic story. It is interesting, but it is not really important to our voting needs.

Nevertheless, every presidential candidate needs favorable news coverage as a part of the overall strategic effort. Interviews, photo opportunities, and coverage of campaign appearances are called "free media" to differentiate them from advertising that depletes the money on hand, but free media events are not so free. They normally involve meeting the needs of the reporters or interviewers, and those rarely square with those of the campaign.

Entertainment media are becoming an increasingly important source of political learning. This includes the political jokes in the monologues of Jay Leno and David Letterman as well as their guests, and others appearing on outlets like MTV and the Comedy Channel. But the half-hour length and the popularity of "The Daily Show with John Stewart" and "The Colbert Report" have made them real factors in political learning. Stewart's 2004 political episodes became a DVD set and Stephen Colbert's book was a bestseller during the 2008 campaign. Interestingly and importantly, both shows are popular among viewers under 30 – the age group least likely to read a newspaper or watch the news.

Interpersonal learning in political campaigns must not be overlooked. As we always have, Americans talk with our friends and neighbors about the presidential campaigns. We ask our friends if they saw Colbert last night and they tell us

Leno's joke. We e-mail them Letterman's Top 10 reasons why somebody should be elected president and they e-mail us a cartoon or a campaign web site. A friend gives us a campaign button to wear and we start talking about the best way to deal with health care in this country.

Citizens became increasingly facile with the Internet between 1996 and 2008 and used it in a variety of ways discussed in Chapter 10. Citizens navigated the web to find the information they wanted rather than passively accepting the information disseminated to them by campaigns and interest groups. Social networking promoted acquaintance and the sharing of interest groups, web sites and videos. The rise of YouTube made personal videos available to massive numbers of people in a participatory fashion reminiscent of Bormann's theory that communities emerge from the process of co-creating a rhetorical vision.

Each of us actively learns from the various messages available to us – and discussed in Part 2 of this book – as we see fit. We seem increasingly likely to rely on those who are likely to think as we do, and less likely to seek out discrepant information and opinion. Internet bookmarks and our television remote controls help us reinforce our beliefs and avoid challenge. That is unfortunate, because we deprive ourselves of useful opportunities to check our "facts" and to consider seriously and dispassionately the contrasting visions.

Getting Out the Vote (GOTV)

The goal of GOTV is to have more of your supporters actually vote in contests where 40 percent or more of registered voters typically stay home. Put differently, because forty of every hundred registered voters do not vote a candidate who wins thirty-one votes from every hundred registered voters will win with 51.66 percent of the votes cast. Thus no candidate needs to persuade everyone to vote. In fact, no candidate even needs to persuade half of everyone to vote. The people who believe that their votes do not count outnumber those who vote for the winner. Viewed from this perspective, every election is ultimately about voter turnout.

The central puzzle of voter turnout is which voters will turn out. I might lead you in the polls 52 percent to 47 percent but even if the polls are accurate you will beat me 28.2–26 percent if 60 percent of your people vote and half of mine vote. The closer the election, the more turnout matters. And, as Al Gore learned in 2000, a vote for a third-party candidate like Ralph Nader equals a vote not cast.

Early studies of American voters discovered that the best predictor of consistent voting was a sense of civic responsibility. Essentially, people who felt that they had a duty to vote would vote even when they were ambivalent about the candidates, whereas strong supporters would stay home if they lacked that sense of duty to vote. Although that picture has changed somewhat over the years, it nevertheless means that the campaign that is content to leave supporters alone on election day increases its risk of losing.

Turning out the vote has long been an important part of electioneering. Bars in many states close on election day because political bosses once bought drinks to get votes for their people. Today, getting out the vote (GOTV) has become highly systematic and both 2004 campaigns invested heavily in GOTV efforts.

Because repeated and swift communication with one's own people is crucial to

GOTV efforts the Internet is extremely important in this phase. Voter registration lists provide telephone and door-to-door canvassers with records that enable them to encourage voters, and then to check on them. Local organizations provide transportation as needed. The Democrats had a good GOTV system in 2004 that made use of the Internet and phone banks to get voters to the polls. But the Republicans had a much better system.

The 2004 Republican voter turnout system tapped into pre-existing groups. Instead of relying on automated telephone calls from phone banks, they used personal contacts from friends and neighbors. Throughout the campaign they built their contact networks through churches, clubs, and other pre-existing relational groups. When it came time to urge turnout, their phone calls and e-mails came from meaningful others (Sosnick, Dowd, and Fournier 2006). This proved especially helpful in turning out voters in rural areas of Ohio, and that downstate vote was enough to overcome the Democratic margin in the Cleveland area.

But as impressive as the Republican GOTV effort was in 2004 we saw in Chapter 10 how the 2008 Democrats used new media to develop an even more effective system. With mobile phones functioning as computers the volunteers knocking on doors could access their database from the field, access maps and global positioning, tweet one another, and more. But unlike labor organizations and other continuing groups that turned out the vote en masse in past elections the smart mobs of 2008 are prone to quick dissolution. They will be more difficult to reassemble for the 2010 midterm elections and 2012.

Counting and Reporting Votes

Voters cast votes in their precincts and they are counted and reported by the precinct workers to the County Board of Elections, and on to the state. Those results are legal and binding. Each party therefore monitors polling places to insure that unregistered voters do not vote in violation of election laws and that people do not vote twice. The losing candidate can ask for a recount, and the laws governing this process vary.

While the votes are being cast, survey firms conduct exit polls. Pollsters ask people in specially selected pivotal precincts how and why they voted as they did. The results of these exit polls are used to decide whether the vote is running as expected or not. As soon as the pollsters confirm that exit polls show that the actual votes are being cast in accordance with the expectations of their previous polls, they are able to project the final vote percentage and the winner of the electoral votes. That is why some states can be projected almost as soon as the polling places close.

Election night therefore yields two sets of results – the actual vote and the projected vote. People anxious to know the outcome prefer the fast projections while those who like the tension of a cliff-hanger hate to have their excitement spoiled by projections or simply like to get it right wait for the vote count. Either way, it is the actual votes rather than the networks' exit poll projections that decide the real outcome.

What happens when the results of eastern states are known in western states where the polls are still open? That has been a subject of considerable controversy for many years. Some argue that it matters very little; that voters are already standing in line or do not care about other states. But many people fear that knowledge of those early eastern projections depresses voter turnout. When and if that happens, it is most likely to hurt partisans of the disappointed presidential candidate who are running for less visible offices lower down the ballot – candidates for judgeships, clerks of court, and the like. Networks have been encouraged to exercise restraint, beginning their coverage in each region only as their polls close. But they are free from regulation of their content and there is intense competition among news organizations to get the story first, so problems in this area persist. Of course, western voters who really care can use the Internet to get those results before voting.

Legitimating the Victor

When do we know the winner of the presidential election: when the networks declare the winner, when the loser concedes, or when the winner declares victory? Hopefully you recognize a trick question and know the winner is known when the actual votes are certified and the electoral votes are cast. Why, then, is there so much attention to the other three declarations?

The network declarations of the winner have taken on symbolic importance largely because they constitute a non-governmental voice. Even the US Supreme Court, when compelled to rule on the 2000 Florida vote, was rebuked by many as a "Republican" court of political appointees. Say what one will about biased news, the news media are less partisan than any campaign organization.

The challenge is to ensure that the person elected president is accepted as the legitimate leader by the nation. This is not automatic. A game of chess ends when the winner declares checkmate. A game of Scrabble ends when one player goes out or neither can play, but it is the score that decides the game. State elections are certified by each state's secretary of state and the electoral college determines the president. Yet losing candidates congratulate the winners and then give concession speeches.

Paul Corcoran (1995) observed that it is the gracious loser who legitimizes the winner with the concession speech. The loser need not concede for the opponent to become president, nor would a concession invalidate the action of the electoral college. The concession speech is a courtesy; more of a courtesy to the Nation than to the winner.

A standard concession speech congratulates the winner on a good campaign (no matter how nasty it was), thanks supporters for their hard work (no matter how many mistakes were made) and concludes that the voters have spoken. It affirms the democratic process for all, proclaiming that the country envisioned by the founders works as ideas and candidates were tested, and the will of the people prevailed.

Many concessions accomplish a dual purpose through strategic retreat. They emphasize how far they advanced, perhaps beating all reasonable expectations. They may claim that they will continue to work for the values and goals for which they campaigned in some new, possibly even more useful, way than by being president.

In 2000, Al Gore used a version of strategic retreat to have the electoral process run its course. In order for the founders' intent to be realized and for the will of the people to be heard, the votes in Florida would need to be carefully counted (and recounted), for too abrupt an end to the process would betray those sacred ideals. Ultimately, Gore conceded not to President-elect Bush but to the United States Supreme Court.

The winner of the election, no matter how narrow, finds a way to declare a mandate. A mandate is, strictly speaking, a rhetorical fiction. The winner will typically say something like, "The voters have spoken: They want a secure America with low taxes." But in actuality, voters said nothing of the sort. Each voter simply checked one person's name on a ballot in private and we have no valid or reliable way to know how or why they voted as they did; all the rest is rhetorical construction. Perhaps they simply disliked the loser's neckties. But once elected the winner can hardly say, "I don't know why you elected me. But thanks anyway." It is by claiming a mandate that the winner lays claim to the platform, policies, and values of the campaign and to the will of the people and makes them the basis for governing.

More than anything else, the president-elect must claim victory in a way that facilitates governing. This is the beginning of the transition to the presidency, and regardless of the electoral vote tally 40 percent or more of the electorate voted for someone else. Addressing their fears and concerns must be considered more important than rewarding supporters if the country is to emerge from the country as a unified nation.

Summary

Every presidential campaign strategizes to win 270 or more electoral votes. They essentially set aside the states they cannot win and cannot lose and zero in on the battleground states that will determine the outcome. They develop a rhetorical agenda (not necessarily the same as their policy agenda) and provides them with unique brand identity. They then use all modes of communication to polarize the electorate around the two brands, searching for the words and images that will tip the battleground voters their way on election day. Candidates play out the incumbent or challenger styles they chose early in the campaign using the resources available to them and taking advantage of their opponent's strategic choices. Citizens learn about politically relevant personalities and issues from all sources but what they learn is not always as important as it is interesting. Each campaign establishes an extensive and sophisticated GOTV operation. Citizens vote and their votes are tallied and reported as well as exit polls in key precincts that enable networks to project the states' outcomes before all the votes are in. The winning candidate is legitimized by the results, the non-partisan announcements from the news media and by the concession of the losing candidate. The president-elect's victory speech finds in the results a national mandate for governing the country.

Tracking Progress in Stage 4

News stories about the likely outcome of the election have long been a staple of election coverage. These are widely referred to, derisively, as "horse race" stories because they concentrate on who is ahead or behind, and by how much. Some horse race stories come from media soothsayers who gaze into their crystal balls to tell us that one candidate has peaked and that another has yet to hit his stride. But most horse race stories rely on public opinion polls to tell us that someone is ahead 45 percent to 43 percent with 12 percent of the voters still undecided. Rarely do these stories properly tell us that the poll has a statistical margin for error (often +/- 3%) such that a more accurate account would be that some leads 42–48 percent to the other candidate's 40–46 percent, meaning that the candidates are about even in terms of national popular support.

After all of our attention to the electoral college and battleground states it should be apparent that national opinion polls measure nothing relevant to the outcome of the presidential elections. They measure what we might call "Gore votes" – the national popular votes that do not count under the constitution. Yet media organizations do a remarkably elaborate job of reporting these distracting data.

If we want to know who is leading in Stage 4 we need to know who is leading the state contests for electoral votes. Such data are readily available to all of us today, but they remained grossly under-utilized by the campaign press until October of 2008. Four of the best sites for tracking Stage 4 are:

- The electoral vote predictor at Electoral-vote.com (http://electoral-vote.com) hosted by VotefromAbroad.org.
- Pollster.com (http://www.pollster.com) hosted by YouGov/Polimetrix, Inc.
- FiveThirtyEight.com (http://www.fivethirtyeight.com)
- The Rasmussen Reports' "Electoral College Balance of Power Summary" (http://www.rasmussenreports.com/public_content/politics/election_20082/2008_presidential_election/election_2008_electoral_college_update) hosted by Rasmussen reports.

Each of these sites tracks state polls from a variety of polling firms and uses them to track electoral vote progress.

Electoral-vote.com's map colored states red for Republican, blue for Democrat and white for tied; states were dark when the lead was beyond the poll's statistical margin for error, light when the lead was within that margin and the state was merely outlined when the lead was slim. Rolling one's mouse over a state pulled up the poll numbers as well as the state's presidential percentages in 1992, 1996, 2000, and 2004. A banner showed the overall tally (on August 17, 2008 it was "Obama 275, McCain 250, Ties 13"). Clicking "Electoral College graph" took the viewer to a line graph of daily projections, demarcated by campaign events.

Pollster.com also use a map to display its aggregated state poll results but they reported only five categories: "strong," "leaning," Republican, Democratic and "tossup" states. Rolling the mouse over a state revealed the recent poll margin but no archival data. Pollster.com's expanded tossup category reflected their caution, since taking a state out of the "tossup" category meant granting that state's electoral votes to a candidate. Therefore, their overview provided a more cautious projection than Electoral-vote.com (Republican 169, Democrat 264 and Tossup 105 on August 18, 2008). Even more cautious was the Rasmussen Reports' "Balance of Power" site. It displayed a table that granted candidates only "safe"

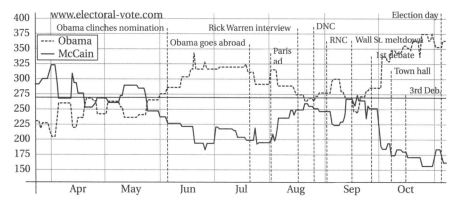

Figure 14.1 Electoral Votes
Source: © http://electoral-vote.com/evp2008/Pres/ec_graph-2008.html

or "likely" state – "leaners" joined the "tossup" states. Thus Obama's lead shrank to 210–165 in their summary.

Although we can infer the battlegrounds from the Pollster.com map we cannot get the historical background. But the Rasmussen Reports' tabular format also enables us to track the battleground states in their historic context. Table 14.2 shows the states in the three middle columns that were shaping up as the 2008 battlegrounds. The Rasmussen data show that three Republican states (Colorado, Iowa, and New Mexico) and all of the tossup states (Nevada, Ohio, and Virginia) have recently voted Republican leaning Democratic, while no Democratic state leaned Republican.

The McCain campaign faced more challenges at the beginning of the 2008 election stage because he needed to gain 106 electoral votes before Obama could win 61. Therefore the McCain campaign needed to reach further across the Rasmussen table, striving both to bring tossups and leaners back into the Republican fold and to undermine Obama's appeal in the normally Republican states. Thus McCain needed to be concerned about at least twelve battleground states, as opposed to Obama's nine states.

By the morning of election day, the picture had come into focus: Obama could win the presidency by winning every state where polls showed him ahead of McCain by 5 percent or more; McCain would only win if he won all the states where he led and those where he trailed by up to 6 percent. When the votes were counted the Democratic leaners had all gone for Obama – Oregon by 16 percent, Iowa 9 percent, Michigan 17 percent, and New Hampshire 10 percent, – as had all of the tossup states (New Mexico 15 percent, Colorado 9 percent and Nevada 13 percent, and Virginia 6 percent). The Republican leaners split with Florida (2 percent) and Ohio (5 percent) going for Obama and Montana (2 percent), North Dakota (9 percent), and Missouri (0.14 percent) voting for McCain.

One of the promises of the fifth information age was that we would all be better informed. Too often we have in practice been better misinformed because we have fallen victim to a kind of Gresham's law of information, in which the cheaper drives the dearer from the marketplace. But when it comes to tracking the progress of presidential campaigns, we can bookmark www.electoral-vote.

Table 14.2 State-by-State Balance of Power

Safe GOP (42)	Likely GOP (123)	Leans GOP (62)	Tossup (38)	Leans Dem (63)	Likely Dem (56)	Safe Dem (154)
AL (9)	AK (3w)	FL (27)	NV (5)	CO (9)	DE (3)	CA (55)
ID (4)	AR (6)	MO (11)	OH (20)	IA (7)	MN (10)	CT (7)
KS (6)	AZ (10)	MT (3)	VA (13)	MI (17)	NJ (15)	DC (3)
KY (8)	GA (15)	NC (15)		NH (4)	OR (7)	HI (4)
OK (7)	IN (11)	ND (3)		NM (5)	WI (10)	IL (21)
UT (5)	LA (9)	SD (3)		PA (21)	WA (11)	MD (10)
WY (3)	MS (6)					MA (12)
	NE (5)					ME (4)
	SC (8)					NY (31)
	TN (11)					RI (4)
	TX (34)					VT (3)
	WV (5)					

www.rasmussenreports.com

Source: Rasmussenreports.com (retrieved 8/17/08)

com, ww.Pollster.com and www.rasmussenreports.com and get this information for ourselves. But these accounts of the progress of the horse race merely reveal the changing contours of the Stage 4 rhetorical situation in which the candidates must identify and engage audiences.

Summary and Conclusion

Stage 4 is the election contest for at least 270 electoral votes. All modes of communication are heavily used by the campaign organizations, media organizations, and citizens to produce several communication dynamics:

- The opposing nominees focus their attention on the battleground states that will decide the election.
- The opposing nominees develop unique brand identities for their rhetorical agendas.
- The campaigns contrast their brands and visions to polarize the electorate, compelling wavering citizens to take sides.
- The nominees play out the final weeks of the campaign using the resources of the incumbent and challenger styles they staked out early in the campaign.
- Citizens selectively learn about politically relevant personalities and issues from news, speeches, ads, debates, new media, and personal contacts.
- The campaign organizations establish sophisticated Get Out the Vote (GOTV) operations to maximize voter turnout among their supporters.
- Citizens vote. Votes and exit polls are tallied and reported and we receive two sets of date – vote projections based on exit polls and the official vote counts.

- When the winner of the election is announced the loser's congratulatory telephone call and concession speech help legitimize the democratic process and the president-elect. The victor's speech finds in the results a mandate for leadership and governance.

The only good way to track progress during the election stage is the projected electoral vote count derived from state level polls. Electoral-vote.com, 538.com and several other web sites began reporting these counts in 2008 and we can expect to see them even more widely reported in the future. The familiar aggregate national polls (e.g. Obama 47 percent, McCain 45 percent) are meaningless and misleading because they project a national popular vote that is not relevant to a presidential election and from which electoral votes cannot be inferred.

With the election results official, the presidential campaign is over. Someone who felt the call to run has surfaced, won the nomination and consolidated support, and taken a rhetorical agenda to the people in a way that polarized the electorate into a winning majority and some others. Champagne corks pop, and hugs and congratulations abound. But now there is a country to govern and a people to reunite. And somewhere out there, among the disappointed and defeated, several people wonder if perhaps they should run for president.

Synthesizing Part III

Part III has considered how presidential campaign communication evolves through the four stages. Surfacing is the first stage in the continuous process of selecting a president. It begins, as soon as the votes have been counted, with initial efforts to create a presidential interest and image for a candidacy in the public imagination, and it culminates in the Iowa precinct caucuses. The terminal exigency is to emerge as a viable candidate able to compete in Stage 2. The communication dynamics of the surfacing stage include crossing the psychological threshold necessary to run, cultivating an impression of fitness for the office, assembling a first-rate campaign staff, mobilizing and managing resources, establishing goals, programs, and issues, initiating the political ritual, getting acquainted with the media, shaping citizen expectations, and anointing front-runners. Incumbents and challengers approach the surfacing stage differently. Incumbent advantages include the trappings, charisma, and legitimacy of their office, a presumption of some competency, the power to create pseudo-events, the right to appoint people to jobs and committees, to create special task forces and to appropriate funds and grants, to meet or consult with world leaders, and to secure endorsements from domestic leaders who can be surrogates on the campaign trail. The incumbent can manipulate domestic issues and interpret or intensify foreign policy while emphasizing accomplishments and cultivating an image of being above the political trenches. Challengers must attack the incumbent's record by taking the offensive position on issues and calling for change but they must appear to represent the philosophical center, be optimistic about the future, and delegate the most personal or harsh attacks. We track aspiring candidates' surfacing in national opinion polls, fundraising reports, Google News hits and, most importantly, the top four candidates in each party's Iowa precinct caucuses.

The candidates who surfaced engage in the nomination stage that requires a delegate majority on the party's convention roll call vote. Every candidate therefore seeks to get supporters seated as delegates, win the support of uncommitted delegates, and discourage contenders for those delegates. Delegate commitments are now won through a series of primary elections and caucuses held in accordance with party rules. All Democratic delegates are distributed proportionately among the candidates winning at least 15 percent of the votes in each state. Republican rules vary by state and include proportional allocation, winner-take-all contests, and winner-take-all by districts. Some delegate commitments are binding and others are not, depending upon the rules. The communication dynamics of the nomination stage include citizens becoming voters and acting directly upon candidacies, candidates accumulating delegates and generating momentum by achieving instrumental success, citizens learning about candidates, issues and plans, citizens adjusting their beliefs and feelings about the candidates and getting involved in the campaign, campaign organizations constructing promise webs from their commitments, candidates trying to balance predictability and suspense by beating expectations, and candidates and the media inducing struggling candidates to withdraw from the campaign. Candidate progress in the nomination stage can best be tracked by following the candidates' delegate counts, their cash on hand and state level polls and state and local news media from states about to hold primaries and caucuses.

The nomination contest divides the party, so each party's consolidation stage begins as soon as its nominee has been decided and it extends through the nominee's acceptance address. The ultimate exigency of Stage 3 is to produce a unified and enthusiastic following for the nominee. To do so the nominee must maximize the common ground and minimize the divisions among potential supporters without losing the support of those responsible for winning the nomination. That requires a Republican nominee to unify Enterprisers, Social Conservatives and Pro-Government Conservatives and a Democratic nominee to unify Liberals, Conservative Democrats and Disadvantaged Democrats. The communication dynamics of the consolidation stage include nominees' communicating with activated supporters, activated partisan opponents, partisans yet to be activated, supporters of the other party and its nominee, undecided/independent/cross-pressured voters and reporters/pundits/bloggers; nominees redefining "we" and "they" so that their new "us" includes supporters of their primary opponents, nominees engaging in fence-mending by appearing with their defeated opponents and speaking to critical audiences, nominees trying to divide their opposition, nominees interpreting the moralistic and materialistic dimensions of the "American dream" for their followers, campaigns enhancing their infrastructure by meeting face-to-face in convention to network and develop working relationships for future campaigns and both parties struggling with the television networks over coverage of the campaign. The acceptance address is both the culmination of the consolidation stage and the opening salvo in Stage 4 – the election stage.

Stage 4 is the election contest for at least 270 electoral votes. All modes of communication are heavily used by the campaign organizations, media organizations, and citizens to produce several communication dynamics including nominees focusing on the battleground states, nominees developing unique brand identities for their rhetorical agendas, campaigns contrasting their brands and visions to polarize the electorate, nominees using the resources of the incumbent and challenger styles they staked out early in the campaign, citizens selectively learning about politically relevant personalities and issues from news, speeches, ads, debates, new media and personal contacts, campaign organizations establishing sophisticated GOTV operations to maximize voter turnout among their supporters, votes being cast, tallied and reported, the winner of the election announced and the loser's telephone call and concession speech help legitimize the democratic process and the president-elect. The victor's speech finds in the results a mandate for leadership and governance. The only valid way to track progress during the election stage is the projected electoral vote count derived from state level polls.

With the election results official the presidential campaign is over; someone, somewhere, will be inclined to surface.

Conclusion: Quest for the White House

Candidates for prime minister "stand" for election, but presidential candidates "run," "battle," and "fight." American presidential campaigns have become contemporary quests. The constitutional, regulatory, and party-based rules have created an extraordinary web of impediments that function to keep people from being elected president. Yet incredibly difficult as it is to be elected president, the system also guarantees that someone will win. Presidential campaigns have become quests because in addition to selecting a leader they provide the stuff of which legends and myths are made. They have acquired the mythic qualities traditionally reserved for the adventures of Jason and his Argonauts, Sir Galahad, and Don Quixote.

The Nature of Quests

A quest begins when a normal, humble person is called upon to undertake a bold mission. This hero assembles a team of helpers and acquires a wise advisor. A long and difficult journey ensues during which the hero's team engages assorted interesting and quirky peoples to solve problems or challenges, each of which leads to another challenge in another place inhabited by another quirky folk. There are dangerous monsters to confront and defeat, temptations to resist, and deadly opposites to navigate or manage. There is often a journey to the underworld to consult with those who have gone before them (Booker 2004). They receive assistance from a variety of helpers along the way and, after winning their trials and defeating their enemies, they return home stronger and wiser because of the journey, and ready to share that knowledge and skill with his people (Booker 2004, Campbell 1949, 1968). There follows an even greater battle or final ordeal to prove the new hero's worthiness to achieve the goal which eventually turns out to be "the succession to, or establishing of a kingdom" (Booker 2004, pp. 82–83).

To frame a presidential campaigns as a "quest" is to draw from our storehouse of cultural knowledge about human quests to illuminate campaigns. It emphasizes the complicated journeys of seemingly ordinary persons who become heroic as they seek to save their people and their way of life. It also draws our attention to the ways that storytellers have told quest stories to mythologize heroes' accomplishments to legitimize their power and authority in societies.

The stories spun about campaigns by journalists and historians have woven mythic tales of campaign quests through which candidates, subsequent generations of historians and journalists and, of course, citizens understand, interpret, and assess presidential campaigns. To view presidential campaigns as a quest for the White House is to see the series of rule-governed contests as part of the hero-establishing narrative. If we believe that the United States is the world's super power then anyone who would be our president must demonstrate some of the qualities of a super hero, and the form of the quest makes that possible.

Every four years several people sense the call to step forward in difficult times. Some have life experiences that provide the raw ingredients for heroic narratives. Warriors (McCain, Bush, Eisenhower, MacArthur, Grant, and Washington) have experience in warfare and often with command. Icons (Hillary Clinton, Giuliani, Forbes, the younger Kennedys, and Jackson) are shown as personifying values or accomplishments important to substantial portions of the citizenry. Spellbinders (Obama, Bill Clinton, Reagan, Kennedy, and Franklin Roosevelt) use the power of public eloquence to excite people with their adjustment of ideas to people and people to ideas. Some likely leaders decline the call and many others toil for years on the legislative assembly line, struggling mightily to spin their laudable efforts into duly heroic accomplishments. Their challenges are much more arduous.

Those who cross the psychological threshold make it clear in their announce-ment speeches that they are ordinary people who have been told they have some skill or gift that suits them for the quest that their people require someone to undertake. Fortunately, the humble hero is befriended by a savvy political wizard and Companions who include the campaign strategists, pollsters, fundraisers, speechwriters, media experts, and others who broaden the candidate into a cam-paign organization by possessing the "knowledge and/or magical powers [to] assist the Hero and but for whom he would never succeed" (Stelzner 1971).

The hero meets the Gang of 500 and answers their questions of worthiness. He may visit the underworld and meet with former presidents or nominees. The team ventures into the ten zip codes of donor land for the gold to fund their quest. The brave knights of old were likely those accompanied by balladeers who sang songs of their bravery; no balladeers, no stories of bravery. Since the penny press, reporters have been the campaign's balladeers but YouTube simplifies that task. All too soon they find themselves shaking hands in Iowa's maize where they promise to make automobiles run on ethanol made from Iowa's corn. Some aspiring heroes fail there and go home, while others soldier onward to meet the next set of challenges.

Six to eight heroic teams emerge from Iowa and begin to battle each other in states far and wide. But every battle requires them to influence the guardians of the delegates with words, symbols, or images rather than brute force. They attack not with broadswords but with broadsides – pamphlets and commercials. They defend themselves not with a suit of chain mail but with e-mail. They joust not on horseback but in debates. In each land they must wield the weapons of language to win the hearts and minds of the natives, to parry the thrusts of their enemies and to protect themselves from the ever watchful eye of the pundits. They come to many bridges guarded by clever trolls. They answer these trolls' questions with care, for unwise answers send them hurtling into the abyss and even wise answers may come back to haunt them.

The viable candidates who survive the early skirmishes then prepare for the arduous Super Tuesday. They battle one another on the same day in lands as diverse and far-flung as Alabama, Alaska, Arizona, Arkansas, California, Colorado, Connecticut, Delaware, Georgia, Idaho, Illinois, Kansas, Massachusetts,

Minnesota, Missouri, Montana, New Jersey, New Mexico, New York, North Dakota, Oklahoma, Tennessee, Utah, and West Virginia. Because they must fight their adversaries in many lands on the same day they must fight them in ways that attract new followers to their quest. No longer can they prevail with hand-to-hand combat in individual states. They must unleash the terrible twins – television and target mailings. The twins can be very effective, but they devour resources and their sibling rivalry is fearsome.

As the quest proceeds in this succession of far-flung contests, results are kept by the tribal elders and reported to the people in the battle stories of the balladeers, who are of two types. Momentucrats count victories (regardless of tribal rules) and invite their audiences to believe that today's winners will win tomorrow's battle, irrespective of the adversaries, the resources, the battlefield or the stakes. Arithmecrats tabulate the spoils of yesterday's victory according to tribal rules and treat tomorrow's battle as a new challenge. Those who outlast their tribal adversaries or win a majority of tribal delegates are poised to become the tribe's nominee. If the balladeers perceive the ingredients for a narrative of heroic victory they can sing a song that encourages the perception of public support.

Like an Old Testament prophet, the nominee has been positioned by the journey to address the "chosen people" and remind them of their essential mission and values. An important element of the quest is the way that the it brings out the best in the hero or heroine. A quest is more than a trial to see who will lead, it is preparation to lead. But the quest for the White House has evolved rather differently. A president governs by leading an executive team but wins the presidency by seeming to stand alone. A president governs as the representative of all the people but wins the presidency by dividing those people. A president deliberates, negotiates, and persuades, but wins the presidency by speaking, debating, and advertising. There are few professions where we recruit and screen our prospective leaders on the basis of communication practices so far removed from those they will need to perform well in their jobs. But the quest story reconciles those contradictions for us by obscuring them.

The hero must then consolidate the tribal factions by healing wounds, making peace and assuring them that they are truly one tribe. The hero addresses the great gathering of the tribe and from its podium speaks simultaneously to all the people through the great magic box to demonstrate a fitness to lead and outline a vision for a shared future.

The two tribes' nominees prepare for the final ordeal in the battleground states. Suddenly, the ancient trolls reappear to guard all the bridges that must be crossed. Each troll poses more tricky questions mindful of the nominees' previous words. Each nominee manages his terrible twins (television and targeting) to do battle with their twins. The nominees engage in a series of jousting spectacles or debates before all the people and the pundits.

Finally, the nominees prepare for the great day of election by developing a vast personal organization of ground troops to mobilize citizens and turn them into voters. Each must win victories in states with enough electoral votes to surpass the 270 required for victory.

In this kind of a quest the candidate must survive and advance. How many losses can a presidential candidate suffer and yet advance? That depends – on the candidate's fortitude (or stubbornness), financial viability, and other factors. Some candidates demonstrate their heroism with overwhelming victories, others with their persistence and others by coming back from defeats.

There is always, however, one person in the land who cannot embark on a quest for the White House – the incumbent president. This is important politically because sixteen of the twenty presidential campaigns from 1932–2008 began with an incumbent president eligible for election (Truman in 1952 and Johnson in 1968 withdrew early). No journalist or historian could credibly portray any of those presidents as undertaking a quest for the position they already held. But they all had speechwriting staffs, press offices, and White House and campaign press to tell their stories.

Presidential re-election campaigns encourage two kinds of tales. As peculiar as it may sound, the incumbent is probably best served when the campaign story takes the form of comedy, in the Shakespearean sense. When this happens the terrible problems raised by the courageous challengers on their quests become part of the president's comedic tale. Mismanagement and corruption become a comedy of errors that could not possibly happen to an experienced president. Disaffected, alienated, and betrayed presidential supporters find themselves to be simply star-crossed lovers at a midsummer night's convention who kiss, make up and laugh at their silliness as they go to the polls. The president's comedic storytellers try to identify every challenging tempest and relegate it to a teapot. This narrative approach makes it increasingly difficult for the challengers to impress people with their quest. We can see this form in reporting of the re-election campaigns of 1956, 1976, 1984, and 1996 when Eisenhower, Reagan, and Clinton managed to keep Adlai Stevenson, Walter Mondale, and Bob Dole from establishing their campaigns as credible quests. But Gerald Ford's bicentennial "I'm feeling good about America" campaign failed to stop Jimmy Carter's populist quest for change in 1976.

When the challengers' quest for the White House is taken seriously the president has a political problem beyond the reach of comedic form. The alternative is to tell the story of "overcoming the monster" (Booker 2004). This story tells of people in good times whose life, liberty, and pursuit of happiness are threatened by a monster running amok. The monster has been either dormant or at least benign until selfish, unthinking, or careless people loosed it upon the land. It becomes increasingly apparent that those people want to exploit the monster's destructive potential and ride it into power. But fortunately the people have a heroic leader in their president. He bravely rallies the nation, engages the monster and its attending hordes, and defeats them in a defining contest to restore peace and prosperity to the land. In 1964 President Johnson sought to unite the people against the monster of a conservatism associated with white supremacy and the first use of nuclear weapons. In 1972 President Nixon led the "great silent majority" of Americans against the monster of a liberalism associated with a lack of patriotism and patience that caused disruptions of law and order. By 2004 President Bush had been leading the fight against the monster of terror for three years, but the campaign expanded the fight to include those whom he warned undermined national resolve by proposing that we consider other ways of fighting the monster.

There is a political significance embedded in the rhetorical potential of the quest, comedic and monster campaign stories. Campaigns demand a massive amount of stories – the candidates need to "get out the word," a growing number of media outlets have space and air to fill, and citizens need information at many moments. Stories are most easily generated and absorbed when they fit into an overall pattern, like the continuing melodrama. The quest provides just such a frame for covering challengers from surfacing through election day, just as the monster story provides a compelling storyline for covering the president. Taken together, these stories foster conflict and polarization. One who sees the state of the union as "out of joint" and wants someone heroic to succeed in the quest for the White House must have great difficulty turning to news from a source that sees that quest as releasing a dangerous monster that threatens the good people protected by the president, and vice versa. Yet inevitably the news outlet with the storyline that alienates us has the better topics and facts than news outlet with the storyline we prefer.

Conclusion

Presidential campaign communication continues to evolve. Sixty years ago there were no television ads, no debates, no all-news radio stations or cable channels, no extensive mailing lists, no e-mail, no web sites, no social networking, and no Twitter; nor were people aged 18–20 and many African-Americans allowed to vote. We had by then elected the likes of Washington, Jefferson, Jackson, Lincoln, Wilson and the Roosevelts, but also James Buchanan, Franklin Pierce, and Martin Van Buren. Changes can improve the process, but they cannot guarantee better results.

In the end presidential campaign communication is what we make it. It entails the interplay of campaign organizations, media organizations and citizens all of which are us. It is up to us as individuals to attempt to modify the rules (if we think the electoral college or the laws regulating campaign financing, for example, are bad for the process), to select the best candidates and to encourage the most accurate and helpful campaign reporting. But even more importantly, it is up to us to seek out and to use wisely the information and the choices available to us.

No people living before us have had nearly as many sources of information available to them, but we often respond to the vast array of choices by turning to a handful of familiar sources that provide an unrepresentative and narrow view of the world. It is up to each of us to fulfil our civic responsibilities by staying informed about an array of views that just may be correct even though we prefer not to think so. It is up to us to take responsibility for the political choices we make and the votes we cast, admitting our poor choices and unwise votes and learning from them.

This book has attempted to demystify presidential campaigns by explaining them as the communication process through which American citizens – candidates, media personnel, and citizens – converse about our challenges and who can lead our efforts to face them. Ultimately, how well we conduct those campaigns depends upon the wisdom, the values, the mutual respect, and the commitment that each and every American brings to her or his own presidential campaign communication.

References

ABC News. 2004, September 30. Debate One-Liners, Gaffes of Yesteryear: Memorable Moments from Past Debates. ANCNews.go.com. Retrieved from http://abcnews.go.com/us/vote2004/story?id=96665.

About.com. [2008] Is Barack Obama a Muslim? About.com: Urban Legends. Retrieved 1/18/2009 from http://urbanlegends.about.com/library/bl_barack_obama_muslim.htm.

Allen, Cathy. 2003. How to Ask for Money. In *Winning Elections: Political Campaign Management, Strategy and Tactics*, pp. 248–257. Ed. Ronald A. Faucheux. New York: M. Evans and Co.

Anderson, Benedict. 1983, 1991. *Imagined Communities: Reflections on the Origin and Spread of Nationalism*, Rev. edn. London: Verso.

Antczak, Frederick J. 1989. Teaching Rhetoric and Teaching Morality: Some Problems and Possibilities of Ethical Criticism. *Rhetoric Society Quarterly*, 15–22.

Aristotle. 2004. *Rhetoric*. Trans. W. Rhys Roberts. Retrieved from http://classics.mit.edu/Aristotle/rhetoric.1.i.html.

Auer, J. Jeffrey. 1962. The Counterfeit Debates. In *The Great Debates: Kennedy vs. Nixon*, pp. 142–149. Ed. Sidney Kraus. Bloomington, IN: Indiana University Press.

Barad, Jill. 2003. Inside Political Fundraising: Trade Secrets. In *Winning Elections: Political Campaign Management, Strategy and Tactics*, pp. 258–262. Ed. Ronald A. Faucheux. New York: M. Evans and Co.

Barber, James David. 1985. *The Presidential Character: Predicting Performance in the White House*, 3rd edn. Englewood Cliffs, NJ: Prentice-Hall.

Bellah, Robert N. 1967. Civil Religion in America. *Daedalus*. 40–55. Retrieved 12/15/2008 from http://www.mitpressjournals.org/doi/abs/10.1162/001152605774431464.

Bennett, W. Lance. 2009. *News: The Politics of Illusion*. New York: Pearson Longman.

Benoit, William L. 1999. *Seeing Spots: A Functional Analysis of Presidential Television Advertisements, 1952–1996*. Westport, CT: Greenwood.

——2007. *Communication in Political Campaigns*. Washington, DC: Peter Lang.

Bercovitch, Sacvan. 1975. *The American Jeremiad*. Madison: University of Wisconsin Press.

Bimber, Bruce. 2003. *Information and American Democracy: Technology in the Evolution of Political Power*. New York: Cambridge University Press.

Bimber, Bruce and Richard Davis. 2003. *Campaigning Online: The Internet and U.S. Elections*. New York: Oxford University Press.

Bitzer, Lloyd F. 1980. Functional Communication: A Situational Perspective. In *Rhetoric in Transition: Studies in the Nature and Uses of Rhetoric*, pp. 21–38, ed. Eugene E. White. University Park, PA: Pennsylvania State University Press.

——1968. The Rhetorical Situation. *Philosophy and Rhetoric*, 1–14.

Blue State Digital. 2008. Case Study: My.BarackObama.com. Blue State Digital.com. Retrieved 5/20/9 from http://www.bluestatedigital.com/casestudies/client/obama_for_america_2008.

Blumenthal, Mark. 2007, May 7. Did Nixon Win With Radio Listeners? Pollster.com. Retrieved 3/3/09 from http://www.pollster.com/blogs/debates/2007/05/06-week.

Booker, Christopher. 2004. *The Seven Basic Plots: Why We Tell Stories*. New York: Continuum.

Bormann, Ernest G. 1972. Fantasy and Rhetorical Vision: The Rhetorical Criticism of Social Reality, *Quarterly Journal of Speech*, 396–407.

——1977. Fetching Good Out of Evil: A Rhetorical Use of Calamity, *Quarterly Journal of Speech*, 130–139.

Bormann, Ernest G., John F. Cragan and Donald C. Shields. 2001. Three Decades of Developing, Grounding, and Using Symbolic Convergence Theory (SCT). In *Communication Yearbook 25*, pp. 271–314. Ed. William B. Gudykunst. Lawrence Erlbaum.

Brune, Tom. 2008, April 30. Obama Criticizes, Rejects Pastor in Damage Control. Newsday. com. Retrieved 1/19/09 from http://www.newsday.com/services/newspaper/printedition/wednesday/nation/ny-usobam305668363apr30,0,7201797.story.

Bryant, Donald C. 1953. Rhetoric: Its Functions and Its Scope. *Quarterly Journal of Speech*, 401–424.

Buchanan, Bruce. 1978. *The Presidential Experience: What the Office Does to the Man.* Englewood Cliffs, NJ: Prentice Hall.

Buchanan, Pat. 2008. Pat Buchanan Declares the Existence of a "Culture War" in Amerca, Houston, August 17, 1992. In Ed. Michael A. Cohen. *Live from the Campaign Trail*, pp. 454–461. New York: Walker and Co.

Burke, Kenneth. 1969. *A Rhetoric of Motives.* Berkeley: University of California Press.

Campbell, Joseph. 1949, 1968. *The Hero with a Thousand Faces.* Bollingen Series XVII. Princeton, NJ: Princeton University Press.

Carlin, Diana B. and Mitchel S. McKinney. 1994. *The 1992 Presidential Debates in Focus.* Westport, CT: Praeger.

Carr, David. 2008, November 10. THE MEDIA EQUATION: How Obama Tapped into Social Networks' Power. NYTimes.com. Retrieved 5/19/9 from http://www.nytimes.com/2008/11/10/business/media/10carr.html?_r=1&pagewanted=print.

Catone, Josh. 2008, March 4. How the Barack Obama Campaign Uses Wikis to Organize Volunteers. ReadWriteWeb.com Retrieved 5/19/9 from http://www.readwriteweb.com/archives/barack_obama_campaign_central_desktop.php.

Chadwick, Andrew. 2006. *Internet Politics: States, Citizens, and New Communication Technologies.* New York: Oxford University Press.

Chaffee, Steven. 2000. Book Review: *Televised Presidential Debates and Public Policy. International Journal of Public Opinion Research*, 12 (3), 333–335.

Charland, Maurice. 1987. Constitutive Rhetoric: The Case of the "Peuple Quebecois." *Quarterly Journal of Speech*, 73, 133–150.

CNN. 2008. CNN Election Center 2008. Retrieved from http://www.cnn.com/ELECTION/2008.

Corbett, Peter. 2009, January 5. 2009 Facebook Demographics and Statistics Report: 276 percent Growth in 35–54 Year Old Users. Istrategylabs.com. Retrieved 5/8/2009 from http://www.istrategylabs.com/2009-facebook-demographics-and-statistics-report-276-growth-in-35–54-year-old-users/.

Corcoran, Paul E. 1995. Presidential Endings: Conceding Defeat. In *Presidential Campaign Discourse: Strategic Communication Problems*, pp. 255–292. Ed. Kathleen E. Kendall, Albany, NY: SUNY Press.

Crouse, Timothy. 1972. *The Boys on the Bus.* New York: Ballantine Books.

Daily Howler. 2002, December 3. Inventing Inventing the Internet. The Daily Howler.com. Retrieved 1/22/2009 from http://www.dailyhowler.com/dh120302.shtml.

Devlin, L. Patrick. 1987. *Political Persuasion in Presidential Campaigns.* New Brunswick, NJ: Transaction.

Diamond, Edwin and Stephen Bates. 1984, 1992. *The Spot: The Rise of Political Advertising on Television.* Cambridge, MA: MIT Press.

Diamond, Edwin, Martha McKay and Robert Silverman. 1993. Pop Goes Politics: New Media, Interactive Formats, and the 1992 Presidential Campaign. *American Behavioral Scientist*, 37, 257–261.

Dole, Bob. 1993. A Republican View. *American Behavioral Scientist*, 37, 184–185.

Dukakis, Michael. 1988, July 21. Democratic Nomination Acceptance Address. CNN.com. Retrieved from http://www.cnn.com/ALLPOLITICS/1996/conventions/chicago/facts/famous.speeches/dukakis.88.shtml.

Edelman, Murray. 1964. *The Symbolic Uses of Politics*. Urbana: University of Illinois Press.

Electoral-vote.com.

Entman, Robert M. 1993. Framing: Toward Clarification of a Fractured Paradigm. *Journal of Communication*, 43 (4), 51–58.

Farnsworth, Stephen J. and S. Robert Lichter. 2007. *The Nightly News Nightmare: Television's Coverage of U.S. Presidential Elections, 1988–2004*, 2nd edn. Lanham, MD: Rowman and Littlefield.

Fiorina, Morris, Samuel J. Abrams and Jeremy C. Pope. 2005. *Culture War? The Myth of a Polarized America*, 2nd edn. New York: Longman.

Fisher, Walter R. 1973. Reaffirmation and Subversion of the American Dream. *Quarterly Journal of Speech*, 160–168.

——1987. *Human Communication as Narration: Toward a Philosophy of Reason, Values and Action*. Columbia, SC: University of South Carolina Press.

Fox News. 2008, October 13. America's Election HQ. Obama to Plumber: My Plan Will "Spread the Wealth Around." Retrieved 11/6/2008 from http://elections.foxnews.com/2008/10/13/obama-plumber-plan-spread-wealth.

Friedenberg, Robert V. 2002. *Notable Speeches in Contemporary Presidential Campaigns*. Westport, CT: Praeger/Greenwood.

Fuller, Jack. 1996. *News Values: Ideas for an Information Age*. Chicago: University of Chicago Press.

Gillespie, Martin. 2004, July 27. *John Kerry: Wrong for Catholic–Christian Values*. E-mail posted 7/28/2004 by cpforlife.org. Retrieved 3/8/2008 from http://www.freerepublic.com/focus/f-news/1180523/posts.

Gladwell, Malcolm. 2000. *The Tipping Point: How Little Things Can Make a Big Difference*. New York: Little, Brown.

Goldwater, Barry. 1964, July 16. Speech Accepting the Republican Presidential Nomination. AmericanRhetoric.com. Retrieved from http://www.americanrhetoric.com/speeches/barry-goldwater1964rnc.htm.

Goodnough, Abby. 2007, May 4. Seeking an Edge, Florida Changes Its Primary Date. New York Times.com. Retrieved 12/12/7 from http://www.nytimes.com/2007/05/04/us/politics/04florida.html.

Gore, Al. 1999, March 9. Transcript: Vice President Gore on CNN's "Late Edition." CNN.com. Retrieved from http://www.cnn.com/ALLPOLITICS/stories/1999/03/09/president.2000/transcript.gore/.

Gregg, Hugh. 1997. New Hampshire's First-In-The-Nation Presidential Primary, State of New Hampshire Manual for the General Court (Department of State). No. 55. Retrieved 8/28/2009 from http://www.nh.gov/nhinfo/manual.html.

Gronbeck, Bruce E. 2009, in press. The Web, Campaign 07-08, and Engaged Citizens: Political, Social, and Moral Consequences. In *The 2008 Presidential Campaign: A Communication Perspective*. Ed. Robert E. Denton, Jr. Lanham, MD: Rowman and Littlefield.

Hallman, Tom, Jr. 2009, May. Building Blocks to a Good Story. *Quill*, p. 25. Retrieved from http://web.ebscohost.com.www.lib.ncsu.edu:2048/ehost/pdf?vid=5&hid=101&sid=4bb9ef51-71c8-4a42-88ff-0303f00cee6c%40sessionmgr107.

Halperin, Mark and John F. Harris. 2006. *The Way to Win: Taking the White House in 2008*. New York: Random House.

Hannity, Sean and Alan Colmes. 2008, March 2. Interview Archive: Obama's Pastor: Rev. Jeremiah Wright. FoxNews.com. Retrieved 1/19/09 from http://www.foxnews.com/story/0,2933,256078,00.html.

Harfoush, Rahaf. 2008. Yes We Did.

Hart, Peter. 2008, November/December. Top Troubling Tropes of Campaign '08. Extra!, pp. 10–13.

Hart, Roderick P. and Don Burks. 1972. Rhetorical Sensitivity and Social Interaction, *Communication Monographs*, 75–91.

Hart, Roderick P. and John L. Pauley II, eds. 1977, 2005. *The Political Pulpit Revisited*. West Lafayette, IN: Purdue University Press.

Hart, Roderick P., Robert Carlson and William Eadie. 1980. Attitudes toward Communication and the Assessment of Rhetorical Sensitivity. *Communication Monographs*, 1–22.

Humphrey, Hubert. 1968. The Acceptance Speech of Vice President Hubert H. Humphrey, Democratic National Convention, Chicago, Illinois August 29, 1968. Retrieved 10/25/08 from http://www.4president.org/speeches/hhh1968acceptance.htm.

Ibanga, Imaeyen and Russell Goldman. 2008, November 6. America's Overnight Sensation Joe the Plumber Owes $1,200 in Taxes. *ABC News*. Retrieved 11/6/2008 from http://abcnews. go.com/GMA/Vote2008/Story?id=6047360&page=2.

Jackson, Brooks and Kathleen Hall Jamieson. 2007. *Un-Spun: Finding Facts in a World of [Disinformation]*. New York: Random House Trade Paperbacks.

Jackson, Jesse. 1988. Democratic National Convention Address, 19 July 1988, Atlanta, GA. Retrieved 11/05/07 from www.americanrhetoric.com/speeches/jessejackson1988dnc.htm.

Jacques, Wayne W. and Scott C. Ratzan. 1997. The Internet's World Wide Web and Political Accountability: New Media Coverage of the 1996 Presidential Debates. *American Behavioral Scientist* 40: 1226–1237.

Jamieson, Kathleen Hall. n.d. Prof. Kathleen Hall Jamieson on Tony Schwartz. TonySchwartz. org. Retrieved from http://www.tonyschwartz.org/JamiesonInterview.html.

—— 1984, 1992, 1996. *Packaging the Presidency: A History and Criticism of Presidential Campaign Advertising*. New York: Oxford University Press.

——1992. *Dirty Politics: Deception, Distraction and Democracy*. New York: Oxford University Press.

Jamieson, Kathleen Hall and Paul Waldman. 2003. *The Press Effect: Politicians, Journalists and the Stories that Shape the Political World*. New York: Oxford University Press.

Jarvis, Sharon E. 2005. *The Talk of the Party: Political Labels, Symbolic Capital and American Life*. Lanham, MD: Rowman and Littlefield.

Joel, Mitch. 2008, October 23. Nobody Uses Email Anymore. Twistimage.com. Retrieved from http://www.twistimage.com/blog/archives/nobody-uses-email-anymore.

Kaid, Lynda Lee. 2002. Videostyle and Political Advertising Effects in the 2000 Presidential Campaign. In *The 2000 Presidential Campaign: A Communication Perspective*, pp. 183–197. Ed. Robert E. Denton, Jr., Westport, CT: Praeger.

Kaid, Lynda Lee and Ann Johnson. 2000 *Videostyle in Presidential Campaigns*. Westport, CT: Greenwood Publishing.

Kaid, Lynda Lee and Monica Postelnicu. 2005. Political Advertising in the 2004 Election: Comparison of Traditional Television and Internet Messages. *American Behavioral Scientist* 49: 265–278.

Kaid, Lynda Lee and John C. Tedesco. 1996. Presidential Ads as Nightly News: A Content Analysis of 1988 and 1992 Televised Adwatches. *Journal of Broadcasting and Electronic Media*. Retrieved 2/13/09 from http://web.ebscohost.com.www.lib.ncsu.edu:2048/ehost/detail?vid=12&hid=7&sid=e30ec4f1-5412-4125-91f9-ee6d7fcb0105%40sessionmgr3&bdata=JnNpdGU9ZWhvc3QtbGl2ZSZzY29wZT1zaXRl#db=ufh&AN=9610084588.

Katz, Elihu, Paul F. Lazarsfeld and Elmo Roper. 2006. *Personal Influence: The Part Played by People in Mass Communications*. Piscataway, NJ: Transaction.

Kaus, Mickey. (2008). Hillary Stuns – Four Theories: Bonus 5th Theory just added! *Slate*. Retrieved 1/15/08 from http://www.slate.com/id/2181118.

Keller, Ed and Jon Berry. 2003. *The Influentials*. New York: Free Press.

Kendall, Kathleen E. 2000. *Communication in the Presidential Primaries: Candidates and the Media, 1912–2000*. Westport, CT: Praeger.

Kennedy, John F. 1960, September 12. Address in Houston. Retrieved 9/16/06 from http://www.americanrhetoric.com/speeches/PDFFiles/John%20F.%20Kennedy%20-%20Houston%20Ministerial%20Association%20Address.pdf.

Kern, Montague. 1997. Social Capital and Citizen Interpretation of Political Ads, News, and

Web Site Information in the 1996 Presidential Election. *American Behavioral Scientist*, 40, 1238–1249.

Kernell, Samuel. 1993. *Going Public: New Strategies of Presidential Leadership*, 2nd edn. Washington, DC: CQ Press.

Kerry, John. 2004, July 29. 2004 Democratic National Convention Acceptance Address. AmericanRhetoric.com. Retrieved from http://www.americanrhetoric.com/speeches/convention2004/johnkerry2004dnc.htm.

Kimmel, Lawrence M. 2006, January 16. *Advertising Age*, 77 (3), p. 15. Retrieved 10/31/08 from http://www.lib.ncsu.edu/cgi-bin/proxy.pl?server=http://search.ebscohost.com.www.lib.ncsu.edu:2048/login.aspx?direct=true&db=ufh&AN=19485867&site=ehost-live&scope=site.

Kohut, Andrew. 2005, May 10. Beyond Red vs. Blue: Republicans Divided about Role of Government – Democrats by Social and Personal Values. Pew Research Center for The People and The Press. Retrieved 11/14/2008 from http://people-press.org/reports/pdf/242.pdf.

Kovach, Bill and Tom Rosenstiel. 1999. *Warp Speed: America in the Age of Mixed Media*. New York: Century Foundation Press.

Kull, Steven. 2004, October 21. The Separate Realities of Bush and Kerry Supporters. College Park, MD: Program on International Policy Attitudes/Knowledge Networks.

LA Times Blogs: Top of the Ticket. Unity in Unity, N.H.? Not So Much for Some Hillary Clinton backers. Retrieved 8/4/08 from http://latimesblogs.latimes.com/washington/2008/06/unity-not-so-mu.html.

Lardinois, Frederic. 2008, November 5. Obama's Social Media Advantage. ReadWriteWeb.com. Retrieved 5/19/2009 from http://www.readwriteweb.com/archives/social_media_obama_mccain_comparison.php.

Larson, Charles U. 2001. *Persuasion: Reception and Responsibility*, 9th edn. Belmont, CA: Wadsworth/Thomson Learning.

Lasswell, Harold D. 1948. The Structure and Function of Communication in Society. In *The Communication of Ideas*. Ed. Lyman Bryson. New York, Institute for Religious and Social Studies, distributed by Harper.

Lawson-Borders, Gracie and Rita Kirk. 2005. Blogs in Campaign Communication. *American Behavioral Scientist*, 49, 548–559.

Leighley, Jan E. 2004. *Mass Media and Politics*. Boston: Houghton Mifflin,

Lichtman, Allan J. 2008, June 24. Splintered Conservatives Hurt McCain, Politico.com. Retrieved 8/4/08 from http://www.politico.com/news/stories/0608/11275.html.

Lowi, Theodore J. 1985. *The Personal President: Power Invested Promise Unfulfilled*. Ithaca: Cornell University Press.

Luo, Michael. 2008, February 20. Small Online Contributions Add Up to Huge Fund-Raising Edge for Obama. NYTimes.com. Retrieved 8/28/2009 from http://www.nytimes.com/2008/02/20/us/politics/20obama.html.

Lutz, Monte. 2009. The Social Pulpit: Barack Obama's Social Media Toolkit. Edelman.com. Retrieved 5/20/9 from http://www.edelman.com/image/insights/content/Social%20Pulpit%20-%20Barack%20Obamas%20Social%20Media%20Toolkit%201.09.pdf.

MacDougall, Robert. 2005. Identity, Electronic Ethos, and Blogs: A Technologic Analysis of Symbolic Exchange on the New News Medium. *American Behavioral Scientist*, 49, 575–599.

McCain, John. 2008, February 7. McCain Speaks at CPAC. Human Events.com. Retrieved from http://www.humanevents.com/article.php?id=24891.

——2008, September 4. Republican Party Presidential Nomination Acceptance delivered in Minneapolis-Saint Paul, Minnesota. Retrieved 10/25/08 from http://www.americanrhetoric.com/speeches/convention2008/johnmccain2008rnc.htm.

——1980. The "Ideograph": A Link between Rhetoric and Ideology. *Quarterly Journal of Speech*, 66, 1–16.

McGee, Michael Calvin. 1975. In Search of "The People:" A Rhetorical Alternative, *Quarterly Journal of Speech*, 61, 235–249.

McLuhan, Marshall. 1964. *Understanding Media: The Extensions of Man.* New York: McGraw-Hill.

Media Matters for America. 2007a, January 19. Right-wing Media Figures Claim Clinton Behind Obama/Muslim Smears. MediaMatters.org. Retrieved 1/19/09 from http://mediamatters.org/items/200701200003?f=s_search.

———2007b, January 26. CNN, NBC blame Obama "Opponents" for Smears Advanced by Media. Media Matters for America.com. Retrieved from http://mediamatters.org/research/200701260014

Meyrowitz, Joshua. 1995. The Problem of Getting on the Media Agenda: A Case Study in Competing Logics of Campaign Coverage. In *Presidential Campaign Discourse: Strategic Communication Problems,* pp. 35–68. Ed. Kendall, Kathleen E., Albany, NY: SUNY Press.

Miller, Gerald R. and Michael J. Sunnafrank, 1982. All Is for One but One Is Not for All: A Conceptual Perspective on Interpersonal Communication. In *Human Communication Theory,* pp. 220–242. Ed. Frank E. X. Dance. New York: Harper and Row.

Mindich, David T. Z. 2005. *Tuned Out: Why Americans Under 40 Don't Follow the News.* New York: Oxford University Press.

Montoni, Valeria. 2009, January 20. Obama's Social Media Campaign. Conversation Agent.com. Retrieved 5/19/9 from http://www.conversationagent.com/2009/01/obamas-social-media-campaign.html.

Morain, Dan. 2008, August 17. Obama Fundraising Total: $390 Million. LATimes.com. Retrieved 1/16/2009 from http://articles.latimes.com/2008/aug/17/nation/na-money17.

MSNBC. 2007, February 8. Obama Preserves Public Financing Option. Retrieved 1/16/2009 from http://www.msnbc.msn.com/id/17043002/.

Muir, Janette Kenner. 1994. Video Verite: C-SPAN Covers the Candidates. In *The 1992 Presidential Campaign: A Communication Perspective,* pp. 227–245. Ed. Robert E. Denton, Jr. Westport, CT: Praeger.

Murrow, Edward R. 1958, October 15. *Radio-Television News Directors Association and Foundation Speech.* PBS.org. Retrieved 3/2/09 from http://www.pbs.org/wnet/americanmasters/education/lesson39_organizer1.html.

Muskal, Michael. 2008, June 20. Obama Rejects Public Financing for Campaign; McCain Attacks Decision. LATimes.com. Retrieved 1/16/2009 from http://articles.latimes.com/2008/jun/20/nation/na-campaign20.

My.barackobama.com. 2008. Fight the Smears: The Truth About Barack Obama's Faith. My.barackobama.com. Retrieved from http://my.barackobama.com/page/invite/christian.

Myers, Dee Dee. 1993. New Technology and the 1992 Clinton Presidential Campaign. *American Behavioral Scientist.,* 37, 181–184.

Nader, Ralph. 2002. *Crashing the Party: Taking on the Corporate Government in an Age of Surrender.* New York: St. Martin's Press.

Neustadt, Richard E. 1960, 1990. *Presidential Power and the Modern Presidents: The Politics of Leadership from FDR to Reagan.* New York: Free Press.

Nicholas, Peter and Janet Hook. 2008, June 1. Democrats Debate Seating of Michigan, Florida Delegates. LATimes.com. Retrieved 8/28/2009 from http://articles.latimes.com/2008/jun/01/nation/na-dems1.

Nimmo, Dan. 1994. The Electronic Town Hall in Campaign '92: Interactive Forum or Carnival of Buncombe?. In *The 1992 Presidential Campaign: A Communication Perspective,* pp. 207–226. Ed. Robert E. Denton, Jr. Westport, CT: Praeger.

Nimmo, Dan and James E. Combs. 1983. *Mediated Political Realities.* New York: Longman.

Nixon, Richard M. 1952, September 23. Checkers. AmericanRhetoric.com. Retrieved 2/27/2009 from http://www.americanrhetoric.com/speeches/richardnixoncheckers.html.

———1962. *Six Crises.* New York: Pocket Books.

Noah, Timothy. 2008, January 28. Momentucrats vs. Arithmecrats: Is the Delegate Count Becoming More Important Than the Big Mo? Slate.com. Retrieved from http://www.slate.com/id/2182946/nav/tap3.

Obama, Barack. 2007, February 10. Illinois Sen. Barack Obama's Announcement Speech (as Prepared for Delivery). Associated Press. Washington Post. Retrieved 7/23/08 from http://www.washingtonpost.com/wp-dyn/content/article/2007/02/10/AR2007021000879.html.

——2008a, March 18. A More Perfect Union. Npr.org. Retrieved 1/19/2009 from http://www.npr.org/templates/story/story.php?storyId=88478467.

——2008b, August 28. Democratic National Convention Nomination Acceptance Address. AmericanRhetoric.com. Retrieved from http://www.americanrhetoric.com/speeches/convention2008/barackobama2008dnc.htm.

Owyang, Jeremiah. 2007, April 3. I Only Use Email to Communicate with Old People. Web-strategist.com. Retrieved 5/20/9 from http://www.web-strategist.com/blog/2007/04/03/i-only-use-email-to-communicate-with-old-people/.

——2008, November 3. Snapshot of Presidential Candidate Social Networking Stats: Nov 3, 2008. Web-strategist.com. Retrieved 5/20/9 from http://www.web-strategist.com/blog/2008/11/03/snapshot-of-presidential-candidate-social-networking-stats-nov-2-2008.

Patterson, Thomas E. 1993. *Out of Order*. New York: Alfred A. Knopf.

Patton, George S. 1970. General Patton Addresses the Third Army. *Patton*. AmericanRhetoric.com. Retrieved from http://www.americanrhetoric.com/MovieSpeeches/moviespeech patton3rdarmyaddress.html

Pearce, W. Barnett. 1989. *Communication and the Human Condition*. Carbondale: Southern Illinois University Press.

Perloff, Richard. 1996, September 29. Letter to the editor, *New York Times*.

Pew Project for Excellence in Journalism. 2008, October 22. Winning the Media Campaign. Journalism.org. Retrieved from http://www.journalism.org/node/13307.

——2009. The State of the News Media. Retrieved 4/10/2009 from http://www.stateofthenews-media.com/2009/narrative_localtv_audience.php?cat=1&media=8.

Popkin, Samuel. 1994. *The Reasoning Voter: Persuasion and Communication in Presidential Campaigns*. Chicago: University of Chicago Press.

Quinnipiac University Polling Institute. 2008, October 1. Obama Over 50 Percent In Florida, Ohio, Pennsylvania Quinnipiac University Swing State Poll Finds; Debate, Palin's Fade, Economy Put Democrat On Top. Retrieved 3/7/09 from http://www.quinnipiac.edu/x2882.xml?ReleaseID=1218.

Rheingold, Howard. 2002. *Smart Mobs: The Next Social Revolution*. Cambridge, MA: Basic Books.

Ritter, Kurt W. 1980. American Political Rhetoric and the Jeremiad Tradition: Presidential Nomination Acceptance Addresses, 1960–1976. Central States Speech Journal, 153–171.

Ritter, Kurt and David Henry. 1992. Ronald Reagan: The Great Communicator. Westport, CT: Greenwood.

Rogers, Everett M. 2003. *The Diffusion of Innovations*, 5th edn. New York: Free Press.

Rohter, Larry and Liz Robbins. 2008, October 16. Joe in the Spotlight. The Caucus: New York Times Political Blog. Retrieved 11/6/2008 from http://thecaucus.blogs.nytimes.com/2008/10/16/joe-in-the-spotlight.

Roper Center Public Opinion Archives. 2008. Presidential Approval Ratings. Retrieved 8/4/08 from http://webapps.ropercenter.uconn.edu/CFIDE/roper/presidential.

——2009. Job Performance Ratings for President Carter. Retrieved 3/7/09 from http://webapps.ropercenter.uconn.edu/CFIDE/roper/presidential/webroot/presidential_rating_detail.cfm?allRate=True&presidentName=Carter.

Rutenberg, Jim and Glen Justice. 2004, July 9. THE 2004 CAMPAIGN: POLITICAL MEMO: Some Democrats Urge Kerry to Forgo Public Campaign Financing. NY Times.com. Retrieved 8/28/2009 from http://query.nytimes.com/gst/fullpage.html?res=.

Sabato, Larry J. 2000. *Feeding Frenzy: Attack Journalism and American Politics*. Baltimore: Lanahan Publishers.

Schlussel, Debbie. 2006, December 18. Barack Hussein Obama: Once a Muslim, Always a Muslim. Debbieschlussel.com. Retrieved 1/19/09 from http://www.debbieschlussel.com/archives/2006/12/barack_hussein.html.

Seelye, Katharine Q. 2007, August 22. Behind the Michigan Primary Moves, New York Times. com, retrieved 12/11/7 from http://thecaucus.blogs.nytimes.com/2007/08/22/behind-the-michigan-primary-moves.

Seligman, Lester and Cary Covington. 1989. *The Coalitional Presidency.* Chicago: Dorsey Press.

Shah, Nimesh. 2008a, November 9. Mr. President 2.0: Barack (Social Media) Obama – Part 1. Windchimes – a social media agency. Retrieved 5/19/9 from http://windchimesindia.word press.com/2008/11/09/barackobama1.

——2008b, November 9. Mr. President 2.0: Barack (Social Media) Obama – Part 2. Windchimes – a social media agency. Retrieved 5/19/9 from http://windchimesindia.wordpress. com/2008/11/09/barackobama2.

Shen, Fei. 2008. Staying Alive: The Impact of Media Momentum on Candidacy Attrition in the 1980–2004 Primaries, *International Journal of Press/Politics*, 429–450. Retrieved from http:// hij.sagepub.com/cgi/content/abstract/13/4/429.

Shenkman, Rick. 2008. *Just How Stupid Are We?* New York: Basic Books.

Shirky, Clay. 2008. *Here Comes Everybody: The Power of Organizing without Organizations.* New York: Penguin.

Simons, Herbert W. 1982. Genres, Rules and Collective Rhetorics: Applying the Requirements-Problems-Strategies Approach. *Communication Quarterly*, 181–188.

——1970. Requirements, Problems and Strategies: A Theory of Persuasion for Social Movements. *Quarterly Journal of Speech*, 1–11.

Smith, Ben. 2008, February 14. Obama Spokesman: Public Financing Just an Option. Politico. com. Retrieved 8/28/2009 from http://www.politico.com/blogs/bensmith/0208/Obama_ spokesman_Public_financing_just_an_option.html.

Smith, Craig Allen. 1990. *Political Communication.* San Francisco: Harcourt Brace Jovanovich.

Smith, Craig Allen and Kathy B. Smith. 1994. *The White House Speaks: Presidential Leadership as Persuasion.* Westport, CT: Praeger.

Smith, Craig Allen and Neil Mansharamani. 2002. Challenger and Incumbent Reversal in the 2000 Election. In *The 2000 Presidential Campaign: A Communication Perspective*, pp. 91–116 Ed. Robert E. Denton, Jr. Westport, CT: Praeger.

Smith, Craig R. 1970. Actuality and Potentiality: The Essence of Criticism. *Philosophy and Rhetoric*, 133–140.

Smith, Larry David and Dan Nimmo. 1991. *Cordial Concurrence: Orchestrating National Party Conventions in the Telepolitical Age.* Westport, CT: Praeger.

Snopes.com. 2009, January 9. Who Is Barack Obama?. Snopes.com. Retrieved 8/28/09 from http://www.snopes.com/politics/obama/muslim.asp.

Sosnick, Douglas B., Matthew J. Dowd, and Ron Fournier. 2006. *Applebee's America: How Successful Political, Business, and Religious Leaders Connect with the New American Community.* New York: Simon and Schuster.

Souley, Boubacar and Robert H. Wicks. 2005. Tracking the 2004 Presidential Campaign Web Sites: Similarities and Differences. *American Behavioral Scientist*, 49, 535–547.

Stelzner, Hermann G. 1971. The Quest Story and Nixon's November 3, 1969 Address, *Quarterly, Journal of Speech*, 163–172.

Stewart, Charles J., Craig Allen Smith, and Robert E. Denton, Jr. 2006. *Persuasion and Social Movements*, 5th edn. Prospect Heights, IL: Waveland.

Stewart, Kate, John Russonello, and Rachel Sternfeld. 2006. Understanding the Catholic Vote in 2004. Paper presented at the annual meeting of the American Association for Public Opinion Association, Fontainebleau Resort, Miami Beach, FL. Retrieved from http://www.allacademic. com/meta/p16800_index.html.

Strumpf, Koleman S. (2002). Strategic Competition in Sequential Election Contests. *Public Choice*, 111, 377–397. Retrieved 2/8/7 from http://www.lib.ncsu.edu:2085/content/ 522t4kfv388v3w05/fulltext.pdf.

Stuckey, Mary E. 1991. *The President as Interpreter-in-Chief.* Chatham, NJ: Chatham House.

Survey USA. 2008, November 3. McCain 510 Electoral Votes, Obama 28 . . . How the Map

Looked Exactly 2 Years Ago. Survey USA.com. Retrieved from http://www.surveyusa.com/index. php/2008/11/03/mccain-510-electoral-votes-obama-28-how-the-map-looked-exactly-2-years-ago.

Swanson, David L. 1997. The Political-Media Complex at 50: Putting the 1996 Presidential Campaign in Context. *American Behavioral Scientist*, 40, 1264–1282.

Tedesco, John C. 2000. Network Adwatches: Policing the 1996 Primary and General Election Presidential Ads. *Journal of Broadcasting and Electronic Media*, 541–555.

Trent, Judith S. 1978. Presidential Surfacing: The Ritualistic and Crucial First Act. *Communication Monographs*, 45, 281–292.

Trent, Judith S. and Robert V. Friedenberg. 1983, 1991, 1995, 2004. *Political Campaign Communication*. Westport, CT: Praeger.

Turner, Victor. 1982. *From Ritual to Theatre: The Human Seriousness of Play*. New York: Performing Arts Journal Publications.

TV Basics. 2009. Media Trends Track: TV Households. Retrieved 3/2/09 from http://www.tvb.org/rcentral/mediatrendstrack/tvbasics/02_TVHouseholds.asp.

Vatz, Richard E. 1974. The Myth of the Rhetorical Situation. *Philosophy and Rhetoric*, 6, 154–161.

Waldman, Steven. 2004. By Their Fruits: How to Be a Catholic President in the 21st Century. Slate. Retrieved 3/8/2008 from http://www.slate.com/id/2096910/).

Whillock, Rita Kirk. 1997. Cyber-Politics: The Online Strategies of '96. *American Behavioral Scientist*, 40, 1208–1225.

——1998. Digital Democracy: The '96 Presidential Campaign On-line. In *The 1996 Presidential Campaign: A Communication Perspective*, pp. 179–197. Ed. Robert E. Denton, Jr. Westport, CT: Prager.

Whillock, Rita Kirk and David E. Whillock. 2002. Digital Democracy 2000. In ed., *The 2000 Presidential Campaign: A Communication Perspective*, pp. 167–182. Ed. Robert E. Denton, Jr. Westport, CT: Prager.

Wiener, Jon. 2007, January 15. "24": Torture on TV. *The Notion*. Retrieved from http://www.thenation.com/blogs/notion/157437.

Wiese, Danielle R. and Bruce E. Gronbeck. 2005. Campaign 2004 Developments in Cyberpolitics. In *The 2000 Presidential Campaign: A Communication Perspective*, pp. 217–240. Ed. Robert E. Denton, Jr. Westport, CT: Praeger,

Williams, Andrew Paul and Kaye D. Trammell. 2005. Candidate Campaign E-Mail Messages in the Presidential Election 2004. *American Behavioral Scientist*, 49, 560–574.

Wills, Garry. 2002. *Nixon Agonistes: The Crisis of the Self-Made Man*. Boston: Houghton Mifflin Harcourt.

Windt, Thodore Otto, Jr. 1990. The 1960 Kennedy-Nixon Presidential Debates. In *Rhetorical Studies of National Political Debates*, pp. 1–27. Ed. Robert V. Friedenberg. Westport, CT: Praeger.

Wright, David. 2008, April 29. Obama Rejects Wright, Repudiates "Outrageous" Behavior. ABC News.com. Retrieved 1/19/09 from http://abcnews.go.com/Nightline/Politics/story?id=4751328&page=1.

YouTube. 2008, September 8. Re: Obama Admits Muslim Faith. YouTube.com. Retrieved 1/19/09 from http://www.youtube.com/watch?v=iQqIpdBOg6I.

Zaller, John. 1998, November. The Rule of Product Substitution in Presidential Campaign News. *The Annals of The American Academy of Political and Social Science*, 560 Annals 111. Retrieved 4/7/2009 from http://www.lexisnexis.com.www.lib.ncsu.edu:2048/us/lnacademic/auth/checkbrowser.do?ipcounter=1&cookieState=0&rand=0.36379706742299656&bhcp=1.

Zapor, Patricia. 2007, November 2. Kerry Finds His Voice on Religion, Three Years After the Campaign. Catholic News Service: Washington Letter. Retrieved 3/8/2008 from http://www.catholicnews.com/data/stories/cns/0706270.htm.

Zeleny, Jeff. 2008, June 28. Working Together, Obama and Clinton Try to Show Unity. *New York Times*. Retrieved from http://www.nytimes.com/2008/06/28/us/politics/28unity.html.

Index